CW01649705

The GWR Bristol to Bath Line

COLIN G. MAGGS

AMBERLEY

First published 2012

Amberley Publishing
The Hill, Stroud
Gloucestershire, GL5 4EP

www.amberleybooks.com

Copyright © Colin G. Maggs, 2012

The right of Colin G. Maggs to be identified as the Author
of this work has been asserted in accordance with the
Copyrights, Designs and Patents Act 1988.

All rights reserved. No part of this book may be reprinted
or reproduced or utilised in any form or by any electronic,
mechanical or other means, now known or hereafter invented,
including photocopying and recording, or in any information
storage or retrieval system, without the permission in writing
from the Publishers.

British Library Cataloguing in Publication Data.
A catalogue record for this book is available from the British Library.

ISBN 978 1 4456 0193 9

Typesetting and Origination by Amberley Publishing.
Printed in Great Britain.

Contents

Introduction		5
Acknowledgements		7
1	Planning the Line	9
2	Construction	16
3	Navvies	26
4	Preparations for Opening	30
5	Opening	36
6	Description of the Line	52
7	Development of the Line	115
8	The Line in the Latter Half of the Twentieth Century and to the Present Day	129
9	Passenger Train Services	133
10	Serving Industry	149
11	Locomotives and Locomotive Sheds	163
12	Accidents, Mishaps and Noteworthy Events	196
Appendices		204
Bibliography		220
Index		222

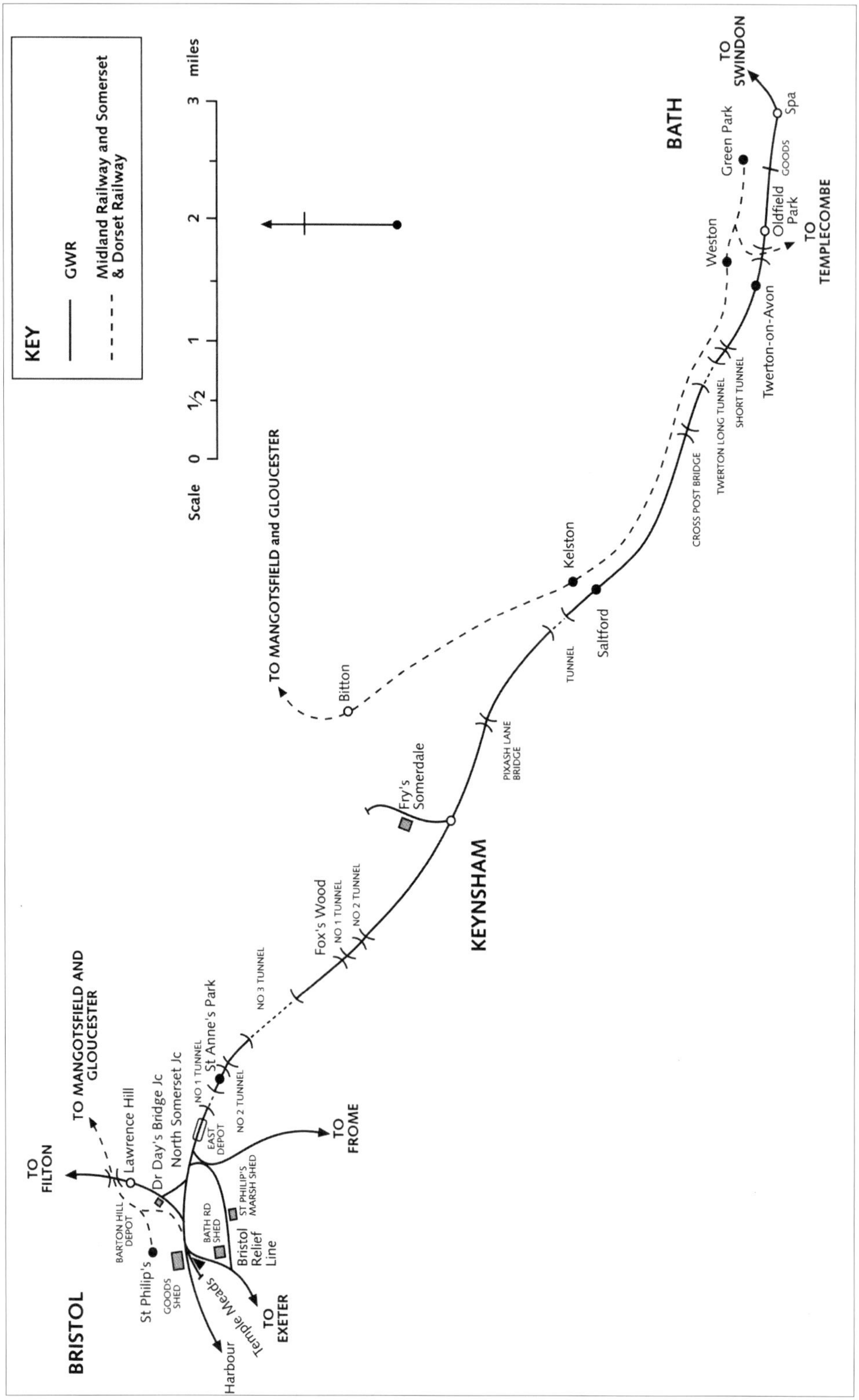

Map of the railway between Bristol and Bath.

Introduction

It was a railway just waiting to be made. The capital, London, was in the east; Bristol, second city in the land, 110 miles to the west or a sea journey of 672 miles. It was true that rivers and the Kennet & Avon Canal provided a shorter waterway, but the effort and time needed to pass the many locks, together with the possibility of hold-ups from flood, drought or ice, made the arrival time or even the day, problematical. By the late 1820s, technology had improved to a state where the very latest form of transport, a steam railway, could make a superior link.

Bristol had developed at the lowest point from which it was possible to bridge the River Avon; indeed, the city's name is derived from 'Brig-Stowe' meaning 'bridge-town'. Ocean-going vessels were able to moor in the city centre, and for centuries Bristolians had traded and manufactured. The city formed the gateway to the West of England from the Midlands and the North.

Some 11 miles to the east of Bristol lay Bath. A place of recreation since Roman times, the city enjoyed a renaissance in the eighteenth century when all who could came to enjoy its social and architectural delights and, if unwell, hoped to be cured by its waters. The Avon is tidal to Hanham Mills, but was unsuitable for navigation upstream early in the eighteenth century and the state of the road between Bristol and Bath left much to be desired; as early as 1619 the mayor and aldermen of Bath had complained that carriage of goods from Bristol was very expensive 'by reason of rockie and mountaynous wayes'.

Several attempts were made to make the Avon navigable to Bath and, in 1724, work started on raising the water level by building six locks. The navigation was fully opened to traffic between Hanham Mills and the City Weir, Bath, on 15 December 1727 when the first bargeload of timber arrived at the Broad Quay. Passengers were carried and even before the navigation was entirely complete, a passenger boat ran regularly between Bristol and Twerton.

Roads had certainly been improved by the turnpike trusts, which had been set up in the eighteenth century, but as time went on something faster and smoother was required so that mail could be sped up and shops supplied more easily and cheaply with a wider variety of goods. If a railway brought raw materials and

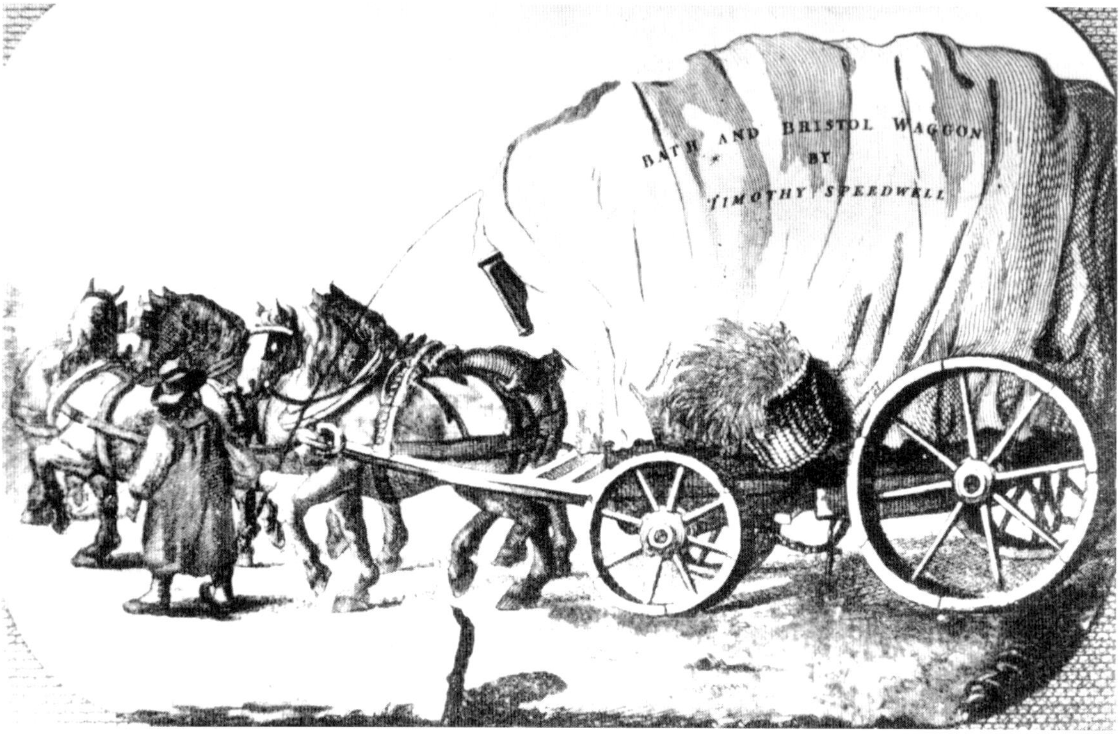

Timothy Speedwell's pre-railway Bath to Bristol wagon. (*Author's Collection*)

carried away the finished product to markets, Bath's economy could benefit from developing its industry.

It proved to be a fascinating line. As the *Railway Magazine* of December 1838 said:

> Every variety of work which can be found on the longest railways (with the exception of crossing a moss) is exhibited in the construction of this short line ... Within the short space of eleven miles and a quarter, we have depots, river, road and occupation bridges, culverts, viaducts, tunnels, covered ways, retaining walls, lofty and extensive embankments and deep cuttings in earth and solid rock ... The Avon valley winds so much and is in some parts so narrow as to render it impracticable for the railway to follow its course for any distance.

From Netham Dam, east of Bristol, almost to Bath station the line runs south of the Avon. Taking water level at Bristol Harbour as datum level, the line commences at Temple Meads at a height of 26 ft and rises to 42½ ft at Bath. No curves are sharper than a mile radius except at stations and on the viaduct east of Temple Meads, where the curve was 30 chains radius. The earthworks almost balanced cuttings.

Acknowledgements

Grateful acknowledgement for assistance is due to: A. Brown, G. Dent, A. H. Dudeney, R. Holmes, Keynsham & Saltford Local History Society, J. King, R. Leitch, Mrs B. Lowe, R. Potter, P. Sims.

It should be noted that times in this book follow the format given in the public timetables. Therefore, times up to June 1963 use the twelve-hour clock, and those after that date, the twenty-four-hour clock.

Chapter One
Planning the Line

The first proposal for a Bristol to London line was the London & Bristol Rail-Road Company promoted by Bristol – not London – merchants in 1824. The scheme was adopted at a meeting held in the London Tavern & Eating House, Rownham Place, Hotwells, Bristol. Among the directors was John Loudon McAdam, road engineer and at that time surveyor to the Bristol Turnpike Trust and many similar bodies. In addition to being a director of the proposed line, McAdam was appointed engineer and in just over two weeks produced plans for a line to London via Mangotsfield, Wootton Bassett, Wantage and Reading. Not surprising in view of his interests, McAdam's scheme provided a turnpike road alongside the railway. Although his plan was adopted by the directors at a meeting at the London Tavern on 2 February 1825, and it was reported that all the shares were taken, no application was made to Parliament for an Act authorising the scheme.

Encouraged by the success of the Stockton & Darlington Railway opened in 1825, Bristolians proposed various schemes to link their city with London, but none came to fruition. On 4 January 1830 a meeting held in the Assembly Rooms, Bath, proposed the Bath & Bristol Railway Company. This locomotive-worked line would have commenced on the north side of Monmouth Street, Bath, just south of Queen Square, and crossed the Avon at Saltford and Brislington to terminate in Bristol at the top of Old Market Street. William Brunton, engineer, who was at one time associated with James Watt, imaginatively proposed that viaducts, instead of embankments, would provide better communication between fields, occupy less land, offer shelter to cattle, and produce and 'exhibit long trains of elegant arches in substantial masonry, which will be useful to the farmer and magnificent to view'. This scheme was swallowed by a Bristol to London plan that moved Bath station to the south of the city where there was room for the line to be extended eastwards.

On 26 February 1831 the Southampton, London & Branch Railway & Dock Company was formed for building a line from Southampton to London, the 'Branch' being a line from Basingstoke to Bath and Bristol. On 11 July 1832, the London & Southampton promoters resolved to put all their efforts into

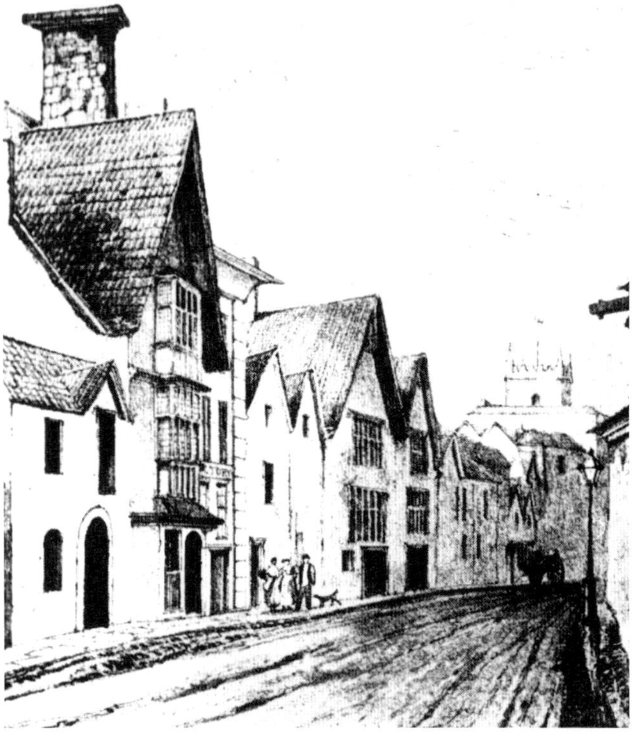

Temple Back, Bristol, where the originators of the Great Western Railway met. (*Author's Collection*)

making a main line before attempting to form the branch. This disappointed the latter's supporters, so in the autumn of 1832 four Bristolians – George Jones, John Harford, Thomas Richard Guppy and William Tothill – met in a small office in Temple Back, a site later covered by Temple Meads goods depot. They formed a committee of fifteen prominent citizens representing five public bodies: Bristol Corporation, the Society of Merchant Venturers, the Bristol Dock Company, the Bristol Chamber of Commerce and the Bristol & Gloucestershire Railway. The latter had opened its horse-worked mineral line from Coalpit Heath to Mangotsfield in July 1832, but was not opened to Bristol itself until 6 August 1835. Thomas Guppy (1797–1882) was an interesting character who had acquired numerous skills. After serving an engineering apprenticeship, he manufactured copper. He then studied architecture and drawing and went on to design better rigging for ships. In 1826, in association with his brother, Thomas ran the Friars Sugar Refinery.

The committee first met on 21 January 1833 with John Cave, ex-mayor, in the chair and representing Bristol Corporation, and William Tothill, Bristol Chamber of Commerce, as secretary. All representatives reported that their organisations looked favourably on the undertaking and would provide funds for a preliminary survey. The post of engineer was advertised and offered to Isambard Kingdom Brunel, then aged twenty-seven and well known in Bristol for having submitted the winning design for the Clifton Suspension Bridge. He was also engineer to

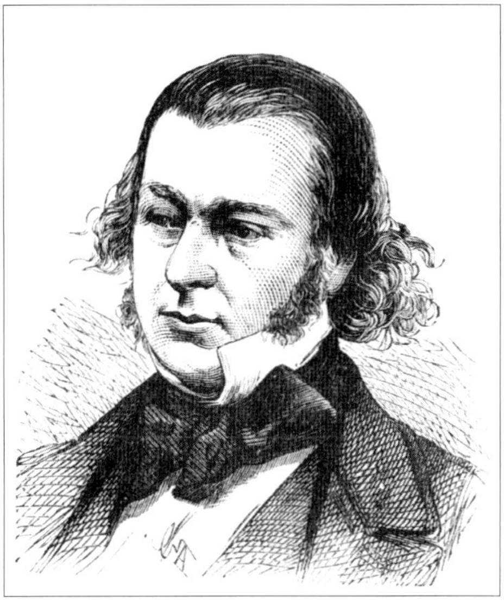

Isambard Kingdom Brunel, 9 April 1806 – 15 September 1859; appointed engineer to the Great Western Railway in 1833. (*Author's Collection*)

the Bristol Dock Co. and responsible for improvements to the Floating Harbour. Following his appointment on 7 March 1833, he set out to make a survey with W. H. Townsend, land surveyor and valuer, who had earlier carried out a similar task for the Bristol & Gloucestershire Railway. East of Bath there were two options to reach Reading: via Bradford-on-Avon and the Vale of Pewsey, or by way of Swindon and the Vale of White Horse. Brunel recommended the latter.

A detailed report was presented to a public meeting at the Guildhall, Bristol, on 30 July 1833 and it was resolved that 'a Company should be formed for the establishment of Railway communication between Bristol and London, and for that purpose a body of Directors for Bristol be appointed, who, in conjunction with a similar body to be appointed in London, shall constitute a General Board of Management for securing subscriptions and obtaining an Act of Parliament for effecting the same object'.

George Gibbs, a member of the Society of Merchant Venturers, persuaded his cousin, George Henry Gibbs, head of a London firm, to set up a London committee whose secretary was Charles Alexander Saunders. The first joint meeting of the two committees was held in Messrs Gibbs' counting house, Lime Street, London, on 19 August 1833 when the title 'Great Western Railway' was adopted. It was preferred to the alternative 'Bristol & London Railroad' because it was believed that as Bristol's trade may have been thought to be declining in favour of Liverpool, having 'Bristol' in the title could raise apprehension among investors.

The cost of the line was estimated at £2,805,330 and the anticipated annual revenue £747,752. Saunders travelled around the country rousing enthusiasm and obtained the opinions of members of the Commons and the Lords. Despite his efforts, by the end of October 1833 applications had been made for only about a quarter of the capital and Parliament required at least a half before

Water Carriage.

The Kennet and Avon Canal affords a direct Communication with London; and Goods are in general conveyed thither in five or six days from the following Warehouses:

A. J. DREWE's (late Betts and Drewe) Fly-Boats, daily, to and from Steel-yard Wharf, Thames street, London; and Darlington Wharf, near Sydney wharf, Bath, in five days regularly.

EUCLID SHAW and Co.'s Fly Boats, from Bull Wharf, Upper Thames street, London; to Sydney Wharf, Bath, in five days; and Bull Wharf, Redcliffe street, Bristol, in six days.

C. and R. PARKER' sFly-Boats, to and from Redcliff Back, Bristol, and Dorchester street, Bath, every day; and deliver goods at each place every morning; and to Marlborough, Bradford, Trowbridge, Devizes, Salisbury, Andover, &c., three times a week.

The *City of Bath*, Steam-Boat, for the conveyance of Passengers and Goods to and from Bristol; leaves the Old Bridge, Bath, every morning, (except Sunday) at 8, and returns the same evening.

An advertisement in the *Bath Directory* 1833, giving details of waterborne passenger and goods services London–Bath–Bristol.

the Bill could be proceeded with. A proportion of the cash received by Bristol merchants for the emancipation of slaves was used by them to invest in the GWR.

The Parliamentary Committee first met on 16 April 1834 and evidence was given of the great benefit a railway would offer to the transport of goods: three hours by rail from Bath to London instead of at least three days, and Bristol to Bath in one hour instead of a whole day. Francis Berry, linen draper of Bath, gave evidence in favour of the line, claiming a depreciation of 20 per cent in goods owing to the change of fashion while they were in course of transit by barge! A Bristol wine merchant complained that beer and spirits carried on the canal were frequently pilfered or adulterated *en route*, a favourite practice being the abstraction of a portion of the contents of a cask and its replacement with water – known colloquially as 'sucking the monkey'. There was plenty of time for this as a barge could take three, or sometimes as many as six, weeks to travel from Bristol to London. Charles Ludlow Walker said that in the winter of 1833/34, for two to three weeks floods on the Avon delayed his goods in transit Bristol to London. Benjamin Collins, a Bath butcher, said that it took over a day to drive sheep from Bristol to Bath and that 'heavy sheep' had to be conveyed in road wagons. Land carriage took at least six hours and water at least ten hours and often more. The charge for goods Bristol to Bath by river was *6d* per cwt for light goods and *5d* for heavy. Thirteen coaches ran daily between Bristol and Bath, i.e. 188 weekly, plus twelve weekly Bristol to Trowbridge, twenty-six weekly Bristol to Portsmouth and six weekly Bristol to Brighton. The fare Bristol to Bath was 4*s* o*d* inside, 2*s* 6*d* outside with a journey time of under two hours, whereas it was anticipated that rail would do it in thirty minutes with a charge of 1*s* 6*d* inside and 1*s* o*d* outside. The *Bath Chronicle* reporter commented:

> Many witnesses from the clothing districts of the West, stated that the railway would be of great benefit to them in the conveyance of wools and cloths, and would enable them to export from Bristol to Ireland and New York. Very interesting evidence was given, as to the advantages which the farmer and landowner would derive from the conveyance of their cattle without fatigue, for the cheap conveyance of manure, and for the opening of new and distant markets for their produce. Country-killed meat brought a higher price by a penny per pound than the meat from Smithfield market. If the railway was established it would be a great boon to the working~man, for the vast quantities of pigs, cattle, poultry, &c, which would flow in at a cheap rate from Ireland. Eggs, butter and cheese are now imported in large quantities from the continent for London consumption, which, it was proved, could, by means of the proposed railway, bring cheaper articles, at a cheaper rate, from our own producers in the west.

The reporter continued: 'The evidence appears to have made a considerable impression on several of the committee, who were believed to be previously sceptical to the immense advantages which would accrue to trade, agriculture and commerce, when the work shall have been completed'. Rather surprisingly, the Kennet & Avon Canal Company (K&ACC) did not oppose the GWR Bill and in June 1835 sold some land at Twerton, formerly owned by the abortive Bath & Bristol Canal Company, to the GWR for £10,000. In due course, the K&ACC and the Avon Navigation passed into GWR hands by GWR Act No. 1 of 30 June 1852, and through traffic Bristol to London by canal had ceased by the 1890s.

The estimated cost of building the line Bristol to Bath was:

Cuttings and embankments, 840,000 cubic yds at 10*d* yd	£35,000
Tunnels	£31,192
Masonry, excluding tunnels	£71,120
Rails, roads etc., 11½ miles at £3,238 6*s* 8*d* per mile	£40,079
Fencing, 10 miles at £352 per mile	£3,520
Stations	£8,000
Locomotives	£18,000
Total	£206,911

The GWR seal.

On the fifty-seventh day of the hearing the committee approved and it passed the Commons with 182 for and 92 against, but the Lords rejected it on 25 July 1834 by 47 to 30, so the scheme, which an opposing Counsel described as neither 'great' nor 'western', or even a 'railway', temporarily fell into abeyance.

The directors slightly modified the plan, effecting one economy by keeping the line on the Somerset bank and thus eliminating two crossings of the Avon at Hanham. The promoters drummed up support all over the West of England and South Wales, Charles Saunders himself visiting such places as Gloucester, Cheltenham, Stroud, Cirencester, Dursley, Wotton-under-Edge and Chippenham. His 'sad harassing work', as he put it in a letter to Thomas Merriman Ward, his assistant, had brought forth dividends, for a capital of £2 million had been raised by the end of February 1835 and another application was made to Parliament. The chief opposition came from the London & Southampton Railway, which was promoting a Basingstoke, Bath & Bristol Railway.

At a meeting at Basingstoke on 16 July 1834 the London & Southampton resolved that 'the Basing & Bath line be forthwith formed ... that Messrs Giles and Brunton be appointed engineers, and that the necessary steps be immediately taken for raising the subscriptions and completing the capital'. Meetings at Bradford-on-Avon, Trowbridge, Devizes, Hungerford and Newbury in July 1834 supported the line as these places were hopeful of being situated on a railway, but a public meeting at the White Hart Inn, Bath, on 12 September 1834 proved less supportive. The GWR secretary, Charles Saunders, alleged that the London

& Southampton planned to end its line at Bath and accused the company of a 'gross perversion of the truth' against the GWR. Enthusiastic cheering followed, along with repeated calls for Brunel who eventually attacked the Basing & Bath line. The meeting declared its support for the GWR rather than the Basing & Bath Railway. On 26 May 1835 the Commons Committee decided in favour of the GWR and on 28 August the GWR Bill passed the Lords on a vote of 49 to 27, the Bill receiving Royal Assent on 31 August 1835. The Bill itself is 250 ft in length, weighs over 9 lb and consists of 130 skins or pieces of parchment double-folded for half an inch at the top and bottom, and sewn together with twine in large stitches. The lines of writing are spaced at half-inch intervals.

Before this Act was passed, the promoters had spent £88,710 – almost half of this on legal expenses. By 1835, the total subscribed for the GWR was £2,034,000, of which the Bristol Committee had subscribed £169,300 compared with the £71,400 of their London counterparts; furthermore, Bristol businessmen persuaded colleagues in other areas to subscribe. The 1835 Act 5 & 6 William IV c107 stipulated that eight directors should be resident within 20 miles of Bristol and eight within a similar distance of London. Because of the company's expansion, this ruling was annulled in 1849.

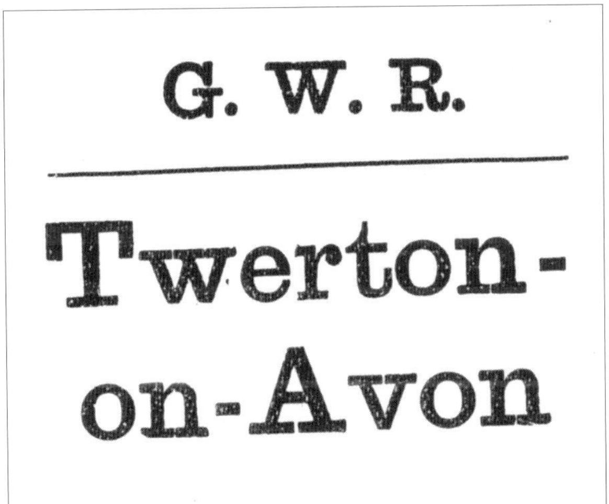

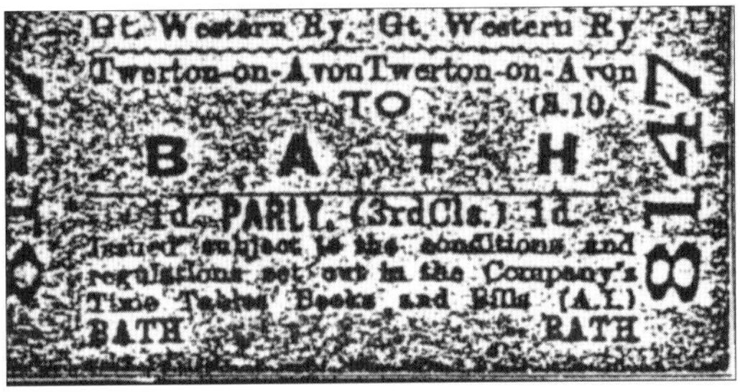

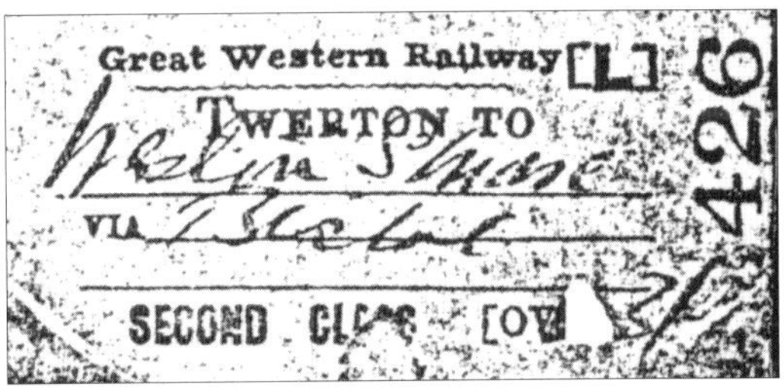

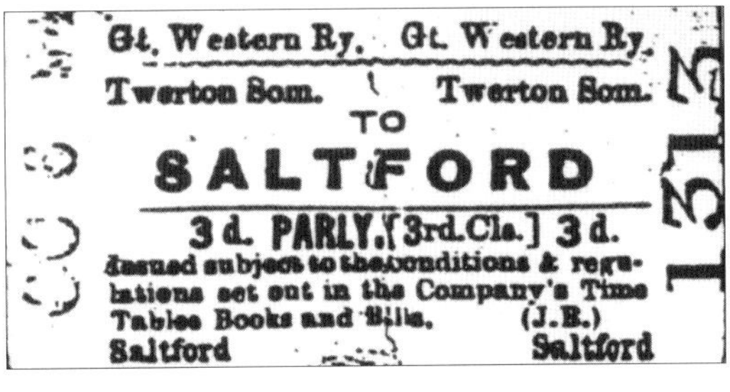

Tickets: Twerton-on-Avon to Bath, issued 1 April 1902. Twerton to Weston-super-Mare. Twerton to Saltford.

Chapter Two

Construction

No time was wasted after the passing of the Act, for on 3 September 1835 Brunel wrote to Osborne & Ward, Bristol solicitors, and to W. H. Townsend, surveyor, asking them to take steps to get the thick underwood at Brislington cleared so that on his arrival the following week he could lay out the exact route, identify locations for the tunnel shafts and ascertain the nature of the ground through which they were to be driven.

G. E. Frere was appointed resident engineer to the Bristol end of the GWR, though Brunel seemed to delegate little responsibility as he continually dashed to and fro between the London and Bristol sections checking for faulty work by the contractors. Frere had a staff of five engineers under him, including Thomas Edward Milles Marsh, resident engineer at Bath. The Bristol Committee had authority to act independently of its London counterpart and permitted a much greater expenditure on station buildings, architectural decorations and ornamental works generally. The environment was respected, the *Bath Chronicle* of 28 May 1840 reporting, 'Trees have been spared wherever practicable, and the masonry of the work has been executed so as to harmonise with neighbouring buildings and other objects.'

During the autumn and winter of 1835, most of the land was either purchased or its price agreed, so in March 1836 the first contract was let to William Ranger. This comprised a length from the Avon Bridge at Bristol, through the three tunnels near Brislington to the east end of Keynsham embankment at Pixash Lane, midway between Keynsham and Saltford. No time was wasted and Ranger started work in April 1836. At Saltford brass mills, though not on a wall accessible today to the visiting public, is a crudely carved stone, probably by one of the mill workers to mark the commencement of the nearby cutting: 'Begun diggin [*sic*] the Rail Road June 11 1836.'

When the British Association met at Bristol in 1836, the GWR directors invited members to view the railway construction and a flotilla of sixty boats set off from Bristol towards Bath. The party landed at Twerton to view work on the two tunnels. In August 1836 the directors reported that all the major structures had been started and that they anticipated the line opening in February 1838.

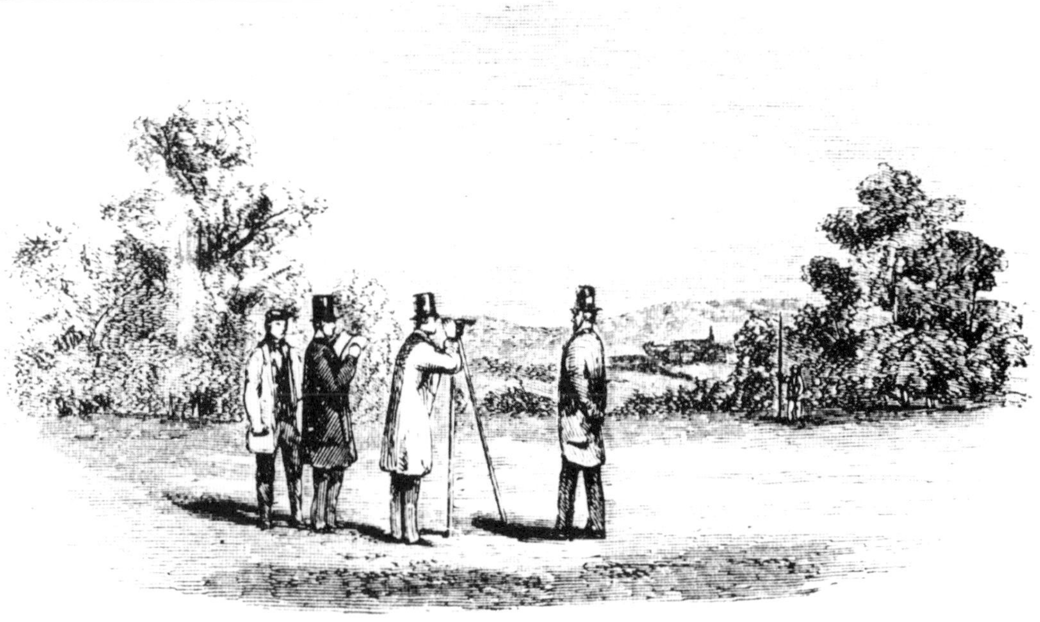

A LEVELLING PARTY.

Surveyors planning the route of a railway. (*F. S. Williams*)

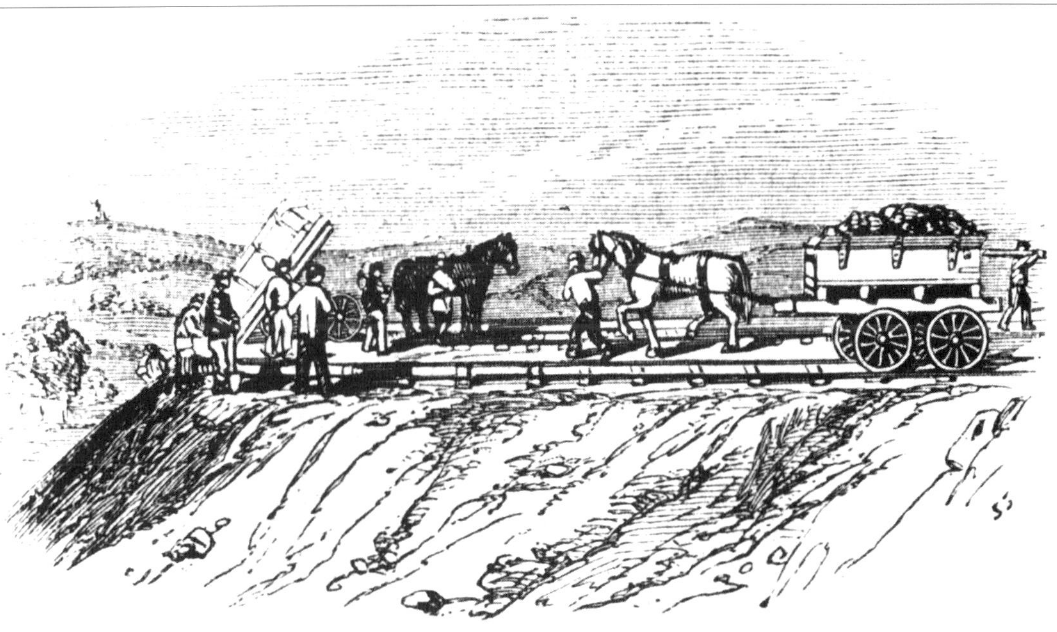

THE "TIP."

A horse drawing a wagon of spoil excavated from a cutting and tipped to form an embankment. (*F. S. Williams*)

A year later they informed shareholders that, after a delay, work on the Avon Bridge, Bristol, was proceeding 'With spirit'; Bristol No. 3 Tunnel was well on its way to completion; Keynsham embankment was finished, while at Saltford the other long and high embankment was progressing. Tunnelling commenced by first making a driftway 7 ft wide and 8 ft high at a cost of £10 10*s* 0*d* per lineal yard.

Difficulties encountered in obtaining possession of land prevented works starting in the Bath area, but these problems were settled in August 1837 and the contractor commenced work. The same month the committee realised that its plans, expressed in February 1837, to have the line open in the spring of 1838 were not to be achieved. Ranger's contract stated that stone for the construction of Avon Bridge and other masonry should come from the tunnels and cuttings east of No. 1 Tunnel, and as soon as the heading through the latter was complete 'and good materials for building the foundations and lower work of the Avon Bridge have been obtained, the bridge must be commenced'. However, Ranger proved to be a man of straw, lacking both capital and energy. The company had already relieved him of part of his contract to enable him to concentrate on the remainder, but this failed to help him so by the late spring of 1838 he was behind with the Avon Bridge and headings through Tunnels No. 1, 2 and 3. The GWR therefore gave him seven days' notice on 30 June 1838, thus exercising the clause in his contract that allowed the company, in the event of his work being unsatisfactory, to seize his plant and complete the work itself. Ranger valued his plant at £70,000, took legal proceedings and in July 1838 filed his bill against the GWR, claiming 'that by fraud of the directors, he had been deceived as to the nature of the soil he should have to cut into … he was induced to believe it was sandstone, whereas in truth, it was Dun Stone, or Pennant, or Hanham Stone, all being much harder, and more difficult to work than sandstone'. He further claimed that the engineer's certificates, which had to be produced before the GWR would issue payment, had been granted late, thus delaying settlement. Eventually, the Vice Chancellor of England by decree dated 13 July 1844 dismissed Ranger's bill with costs. He appealed and on 16 May 1854 the Lord Chancellor reversed the decree. The case ended on 17 June 1854 when Lord Cranworth held that Ranger could not reject the terms of the contract and claim *quantum meruit* – compensation for work done where the amount was not stipulated beforehand.

John Sharp of Durham worked at Keynsham as Ranger's foreman and was in charge of 600 men. His weekly pay was £1 4*s* 0*d*, rising to £2 10*s* 0*d*, which put him on a par with Brunel's young engineers who were paid an annual starting salary of £150. Sharp saw that Ranger was failing and so set up on his own as a subcontractor, subcontractors having no capital commitments, and some no moral commitments either. One, 'Ready-money Tom', hired horses and disappeared in default to their owner of £150, while regarding John Dean, the *Bristol Journal* reported on 19 September 1845, 'From his supposed responsible

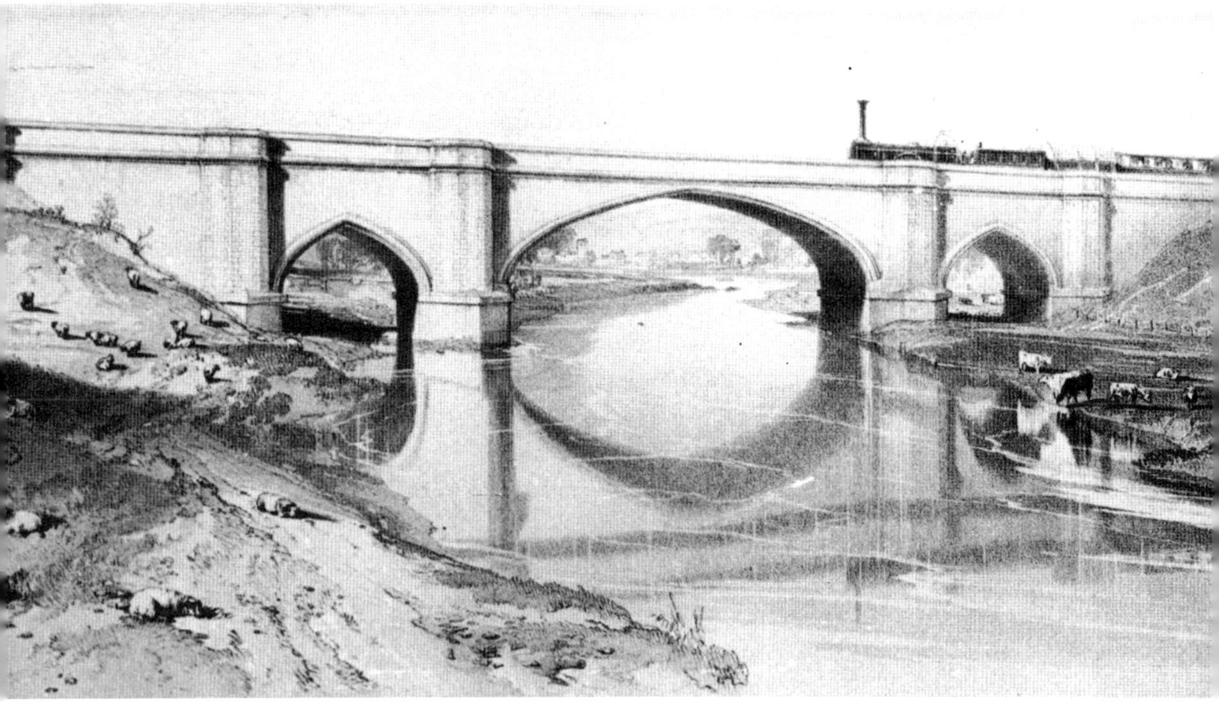

Above: Avon Bridge, Bristol, *c.* 1855, situated just west of the later East Depot; it was later flanked by steel girder bridges carrying additional lines. (*Author's Collection*)

Right: The west portal of Bristol No. 1 Tunnel in 1846 with Fire Fly class *Acheron* emerging. The tunnel, 326 yd in length, was opened out in 1889. (*J. C. Bourne*)

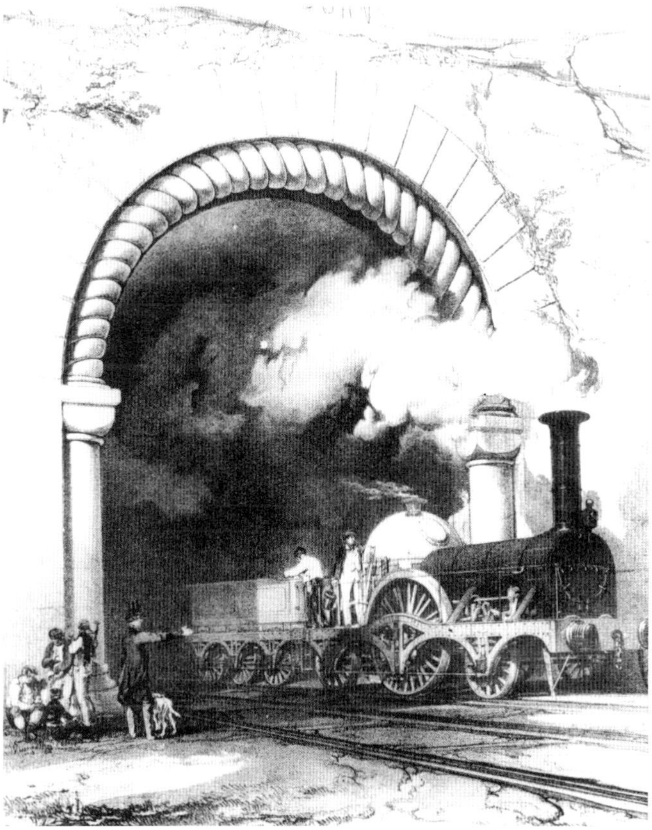

CONTRACTS FOR WORKS.

GREAT WESTERN RAILWAY.

BRISTOL.

NOTICE is hereby Given, that the Directors will receive, at their Office in BRISTOL, on or before FRIDAY, the twentieth day of December next, at twelve o'Clock, TENDERS for the execution of the following Works:

CONTRACT, BATH DEPOT.

The Construction of a Viaduct, Offices, &c., in the Ham Gardens at Bath,

The Drawings and Specifications of the Works will be exhibited at the Company's Office, Claverton Street, Bath; and printed forms of Tender may be had at the same Office on and after Monday, the second of December.

The Directors will not consider themselves bound to accept the lowest Tender, and they expect the several parties to attend at the Office, at one o'Clock on the twentieth of December.

CHARLES A. SAUNDERS, }
THOMAS OSLER, } *Secretaries.*

Corn Street; Bristol, Nov. 27, 1839.

Advertisement in the *Bath & Cheltenham Gazette* of 17 December 1839 for the construction of the GWR at Bath.

situation had no difficulty in borrowing horses from various farmers for railway work, but at the termination of the engagement ... neither Dean nor the horses borrowed could be found'.

Work on the Bristol tunnels in Ranger's contract proceeded under the GWR's engineer and most of the work was sublet in small portions. The remainder of the contract was taken by David McIntosh. At the GWR's half-yearly meeting on 15 August 1838 it was announced that Bristol No. 1 Tunnel was on the point of completion, although 'The time which has been lost on these and other works is irretrievable, and your Directors fear they cannot calculate on completing the line between Bristol and Bath till the autumn of 1839'.

Ranger was not the only contractor to take litigation. In 1847 David McIntosh of 39 Bloomsbury Square, London, who held the contract for building the line from Pixash Lane to Oak Street, west of Bath station, filed a bill against the GWR, secretary C. A. Saunders, and Brunel, claiming over and above the sums paid for his construction works between Bristol and Bath and near Slough. In 1855 the court found in favour of McIntosh, but the GWR appealed on the ground that the items were not specified. The original judgement, that the GWR owed him £200,000 plus 4 per cent per annum interest, was upheld on 28 June 1865 by which date several of the parties of the original suit were dead. The GWR was also required to pay McIntosh's legal costs and this expense sent the company to the verge of bankruptcy and for a period shareholders were paid in shares rather than cash.

Unlike later railways, which favoured lengthy contracts, the Bristol Committee preferred using many contractors, a policy which had the advantage that if a contractor failed, only a small length was involved. On the other hand, however, small contractors were probably backed by less experience and capital, and failure was therefore more likely. Messrs Brown & Son were responsible for Temple Meads passenger station and Thomas Wilcox & Sons for the goods station; James Ridewood for the viaduct approaching Bath station; James Scott for the station itself; and William Chadwick for the bridge over the Avon immediately to the west.

At the GWR annual meeting in August 1839 the directors were able to report good progress and that completion was within sight. Bristol No. 1, Saltford and Twerton Tunnels were complete, No. 2 would be finished in three weeks and No. 3, the longest and most difficult, would be ready in about two months. Regarding the bridges at Bristol, the Floating Harbour Bridge had been delayed first of all by difficulties with the foundations and then by poor work from Ranger, which had to be almost entirely redone. The directors said that its centreings were about to be erected. Work on the Feeder Bridge, so called because it supplied the Floating Harbour with water, was proceeding rapidly, work made easier because of its timber construction. The Avon Bridge had been complete for some time and its centreings lowered. The viaduct and embankment between the Floating Harbour Bridge and the Feeder Bridge were nearly finished.

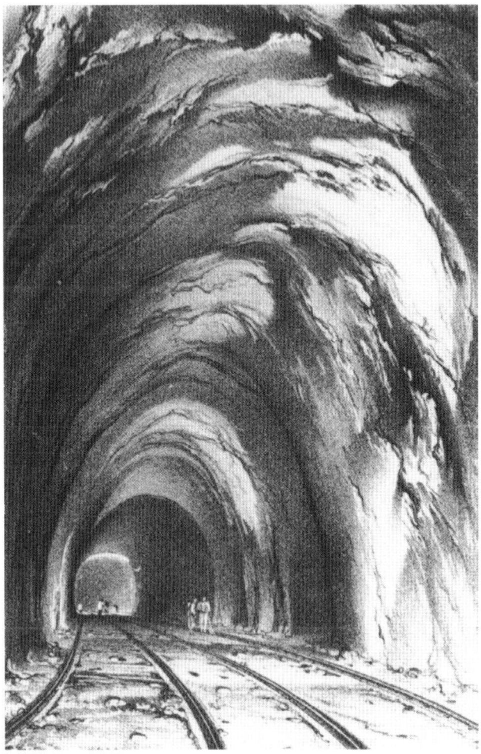

The unlined portion of Bristol No. 3 Tunnel in 1846 with the lined portion beyond. (*J. C. Bourne*)

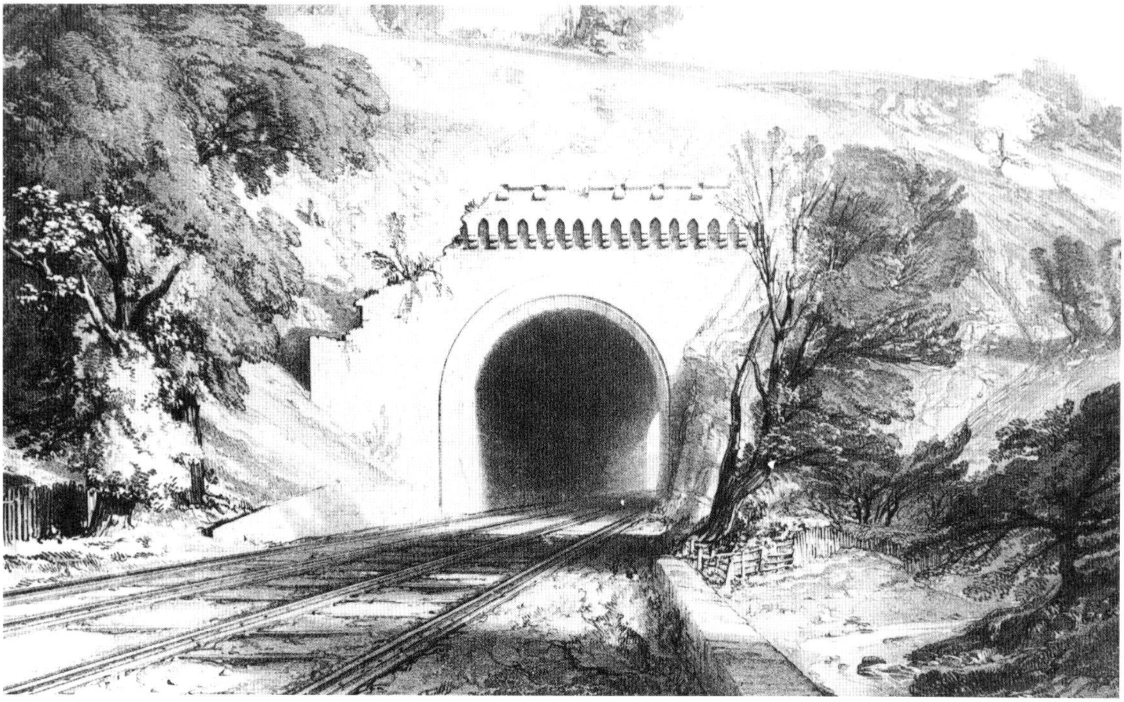

The west portal of the 154-yd-long Bristol No. 2 Tunnel in 1846 showing the 'ruined' appearance. (*J. C. Bourne*)

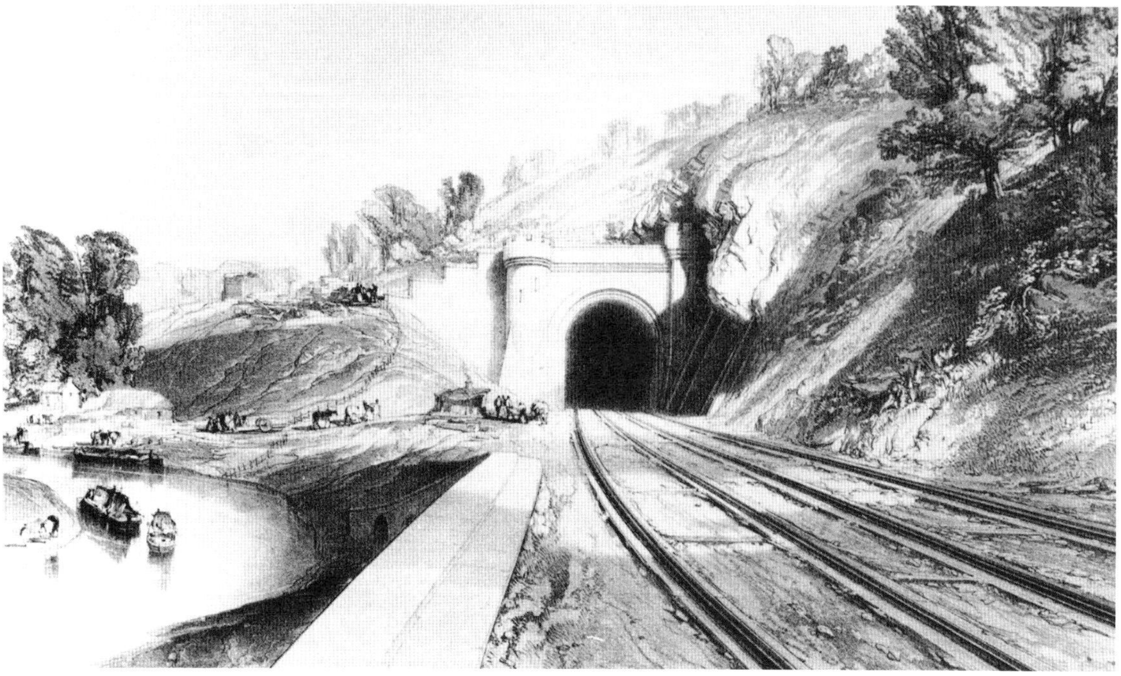

The west portal of the 1,017-yd-long Bristol No. 3 Tunnel, 1846. Notice, lower left, the retaining wall. (*J. C. Bourne*)

Most of the formation between Bristol No. 3 Tunnel and Cross Post Bridge, which carried the turnpike road (now the A4) across the railway at Newton St Loe, was ready to receive the permanent way, which consisted of 62 lb/yd bridge rail on longitudinal timbers of 14 in by 7 in section and about 30 ft in length. These timbers were bolted to cross timbers at 15-ft intervals. The timber used was kyanised, that is, preserved by being saturated in a solution of bichloride of mercury (this method had been discovered by a Dr Kyan). It was about the last length of track to use this process as creosoting was soon found to be superior.

The 1½-mile-long Saltford embankment was built on rather soft ground adjacent to the river. Material for its foundation is believed to have been obtained from the spoil heaps of the nearby Globe Colliery, and certainly it included burnt clay, which formed an excellent binding material. Work on the iron skew Cross Post Bridge had been delayed by difficulties raised by the Bath Road Trustees, but it would be completed within a few weeks. Beyond it, the line to Bath was virtually complete, though work on the bridge over the Avon and the station itself had not begun. Part of the problem was obtaining the land required. On 19 September 1837 an Inquisition was held at the White Lion Hotel, Bath, to assess the claim of Thomas Peacock, who owned property that the GWR required in Claverton Street. Peacock's original claim was for £2,800; he reduced it to £2,400 and the verdict of the jury was £1,150. The GWR had offered him £1,600!

Although in August 1839 the directors believed that the line would open in the spring of 1840, nature decreed otherwise because the unusually wet winter caused a four-month delay. In February 1840 Brunel explained in his report:

> At the Bristol extremity the floods in the Avon have interfered with the supply of building materials; and at Bath and in its immediate neighbourhood the unprecedented continuation of a state of flood in the river for a long period and to within the last few days has rendered it impossible to carry on the works of the Bridges or even of the Station, the site of which has been flooded. Such a complete suspension of the works at some points and such delays at others have resulted from these and other causes indirectly consequent upon them that certainly not less than four months additional time will be required for the completion of some of these works, the whole of which would otherwise have been finished within a month or two of the present time, which must delay the opening to the end of the summer instead of the spring.
>
> The works of the Station at Bristol, including the viaduct and offices, are rapidly advancing; but at Bath the causes I have referred to have prevented till within the last few days anything more than the commencement of the approaches.
>
> Between these two extremities all the principal works - the Tunnelling, Cutting, and Embankments - are so far completed that, had the weather permitted it, the ballasting and permanent way would have been by this time in a very forward state. The excavation of the Tunnels is everywhere opened throughout, and the only work

> remaining to be done to them consists of the formation of the permanent drains and the finishing of detached parts of masonry, which in the general progress of the work had been injured or condemned, and the completion of one of the tunnel fronts. A few weeks will complete everything but the permanent rails, but many parts of the line, long since prepared, have not been in a state to allow of men or horses passing over them without destroying that portion of the forming which the rains had allowed to be completed, so that not more than 2½ miles of ballasting have been actually finished.

The 'tunnel front' mentioned in the penultimate sentence was the west portal of Bristol No. 2. The wet weather continued and caused a landslip, the resulting gradient rendering a retaining wall unnecessary. Brunel imaginatively trained ivy over the pseudo-ruined towers to age the feature. To speed work on No. 3 Tunnel, three shafts were opened, giving six additional working faces and a further six smaller shafts were found essential to remove fumes from the blasting powder, large fans being erected at the tops of the shafts in order to create a draught. Five of the nine shafts were left open when the works were complete.

All tunnels between Bristol and Bath were constructed on the same principle. A bottom heading was driven from end to end before the enlargement was commenced. Enlargement from the bottom heading proved costly and troublesome, more particularly as the excavated material was removed through the heading and severe problems were met in trying to keep the thoroughfare clear. When being excavated, spoil fell on the road and if not immediately removed, delayed the whole of the tunnel work by interrupting the circulation of wagons. Where lining was applied to tunnels, top headings were driven and as soon as the excavation for a length was complete, the lining was commenced.

In May 1840 the parish of Newton St Loe served notice on the GWR as the company had 'caused to be stopped up' the northern end of Mead Lane, which ran from the village to the turnpike road approximately midway between Cross Post overbridge and the Globe Inn. Under the GWR Act, the company was liable to a fine of £20 a day if it stopped a road. Newton St Loe claimed a total of £2,300 for stoppages from 30 January to 22 May 1840. The trouble arose because the GWR needed to divert the turnpike road at the entrance to Mead Lane and to divert it required laying earth 5 ft 6 in to 8 ft 4 in across the lane. This meant that the gradient from Mead Lane up to the turnpike road was so steep that four horses were required to draw a two-horse load, and the junction was so acute and the rerouted turnpike road so narrow that, with four horses, the lead animals did not have room to turn. Consequently, when proceeding from Newton to Bath, an alternative route ¼ mile longer had to be taken.

On 7 February 1840 Mr Sergeant, the Newton waywarden, wrote to the GWR requiring it to remove the obstruction. The result was that the railway 'doubled the number of hands on the work rendering the obstruction worse!' On 5 March Sergeant gave notice to the magistrates of his intention to cut through the obstruction. This he did and the lane remained open until 4 April when the GWR filled the gap and built an 8-ft-high strong wall across it. Resolved not to be beaten, Sergeant applied for another magistrates' order and on 7 April he and his men again cut through to the turnpike road. Next morning the GWR replaced the earth Sergeant's men had moved 'and for some days a large force was employed by both sides, one party in cutting a channel through and the other filling it up. So great was the number of men employed by the GWR that, on 8 April, a waggon got into a cutting, and was half covered up before it could get through' (*Bath Chronicle*, 2 July 1840).

The railway company proved stronger and the obstruction continued. When the case was heard on 25 June, the magistrates were of the opinion that the GWR was liable to a penalty for 118 days and so was required to pay £1,140 and Newton's costs. On 15 July, when the GWR agreed to tail off the embankment in a satisfactory manner, the parish agreed that the injunction against the GWR be dissolved.

EXPEDITIOUS POSTING!

LION HOTEL, BATH.

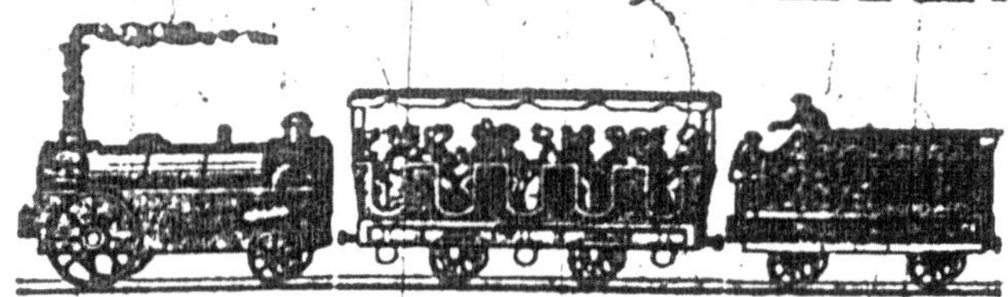

VIA GREAT WESTERN RAILWAY, from the FARRINGDON ROAD STATION.

FIFTY MILES FROM BATH.

ROUTE:

		Miles.
Chippenham	*Angel*	14
Lyneham		10
Swindon	*Goddard Arms*	10
Station		16

Railroad Charge thence to London:

Carriage	£1	16	0
Each Person in the First Class Train	0	14	0
——— Second Class ditto	0	10	0

☞ Every information will be given at the LION HOTEL COACH OFFICE relative to the Hours of departure of Trains from the Farringdon Road Station.

Superior Coaches, six times a-day, in direct communication with the above Railway.

WILLIAM LANE, PROPRIETOR.

Advertisement in the *Bath & Cheltenham Gazette* 1 September 1840 for stagecoach travel from Bath to the railhead at Farringdon Road, opened 20 July 1840, and thence by rail to Paddington.

Chapter Three

Navvies

Navvies earned between 4*s* and 8*s* a day, a very good wage compared with agricultural labourers, who earned only 9*s* to 12*s* a week except during spring when overtime could raise it to 15*s* weekly. The *Bath Chronicle* for 21 November 1839 printed a delightful word-picture of a navvy:

> The navigator appears to belong to no country, he wanders from one public work to another – now alone, then with a party of two or three; as long as he has sixpence in his pocket seems content, but sets so little value on the earnings of his slavish employment as never to be at case unless in squandering them, although well paid for his labour. Go where he will, he finds some of his comrades whom he has met in some part of England before, and makes enquiries as to their mode of living, the wages they were paid since they last met, etc. His attire is peculiar. On his head he wears a kind of white felt hat, the brim of which is turned up all round, and generally a tobacco pipe is stuck in the band, which is of some glaring colour, a velveteen shooting jacket with white buttons, and scarlet plush waistcoat of large dimensions, with little black spots on it, sometimes a bright coloured neckerchief round his neck, and sometimes nothing at all; inexpressibles [trousers] of corduroy retained in their position by a leather strap round the waist, and tied and buttoned at the knee; sometimes white stockings or grey worsted encircling most robust knees and high-laced boots of strong build complete his dress. His 'dicky' or small smock frock, is slung, when he travels, at his back, and by the arms in front; in this he carries what else he has in the world, except the clothes he wears. In some things he makes an attempt at taste – in the dressing of the hair, by wearing one or more ringlets on each side of his face, upon which great value is placed. He knows no other pleasure or domestic comfort than is afforded in a public house or beer-shop, brawling or drinking with his companions after the toils of the day.

Navvies normally enjoyed a rest on Sundays, though a few had to be employed on such work as tunnelling where no cessation was possible without danger. The *Bath Chronicle* for 26 July 1838 said, 'It is contrary to the interest of the contractors that work should be done on a Sunday, as the men who are employed on that day always expect and obtain a higher rate of wages.' Often local people raised a subscription to pay for a chaplain to minister to the needs of navvies, and in the spring of 1840 special Sunday services were held in the railway chapel, Temple Meads, by their chaplain the Revd W. C. Osborn. Those who did not attend services tended to spend their wealth on drink and then end up fighting. On 5 July 1837 Twerton Vestry petitioned the Bath magistrates for thirteen special constables 'in consequence of fighting and drunkenness on the Rail Road'. However, navvies could also have a more creditable side to their character, as was shown on 27 March 1840 when two boys aged four and seven were on the river bank near the Old Bridge, Bath. The younger fell in and was rescued by workmen from the skew bridge, at no small risk to themselves as their heavy shoes and clothes dragged them down into the water.

County rivalry could raise its ugly head, the *Bristol Journal* of 28 April 1838 recording:

> On Monday last [23 April] a number of navigators working on the Great Western Railway, amounting to upwards of 300, principally natives of the County of Gloucester, tumultuously assembled, and made an attack on the workmen employed at tunnel No. 3, Keynsham, who are most of them from Devonshire, and the lower parts of Somerset. The ostensible motive for the attack was a belief that the latter were working under price; to this was added a local or county feud, as the rallying cry of onslaught was 'Gloucester against Devon'. The result was a regular fight with various dangerous weapons ready to hand, such as spades, pickaxes, crowbars, etc. The contest was long and severe, in which several were most dangerously hurt, & one man was obliged to be taken to the Infirmary, but no one was killed. The insubordination continued for several succeeding days, and was not repressed without the aid of the military.
>
> From further enquiries we learn, that a jealousy has long subsisted between the Devon men, & those from other counties, but the immediate cause of the late outbreak arose from the following circumstance. A few weeks ago, the company arranged with the contractor to take the working of the tunnel No. 3 out of his hands, and they then engaged a number of 'gangmen' who were paid a stipulated sum per yard for the work done by their men. It appears that the Devon men have been long accustomed to the use of a ponderous instrument called a 'jumper', for breaking the rock, and that they were thus enabled to execute more work, and accordingly gain higher wages, than the workmen from other neighbourhoods; and the 'Gloucester men' being at least three times more numerous than the Devonians, the former came to a resolution of driving 'the strangers' from the works. The consequence has been that during the past week very few men have been employed on the Western railroad in this neighbourhood. In several affrays there have been many heads broken, but we have heard of only one serious injury, and that was upon a man named Richard Thomas, now in the Infirmary, who it is feared has received a severe injury of the spine.

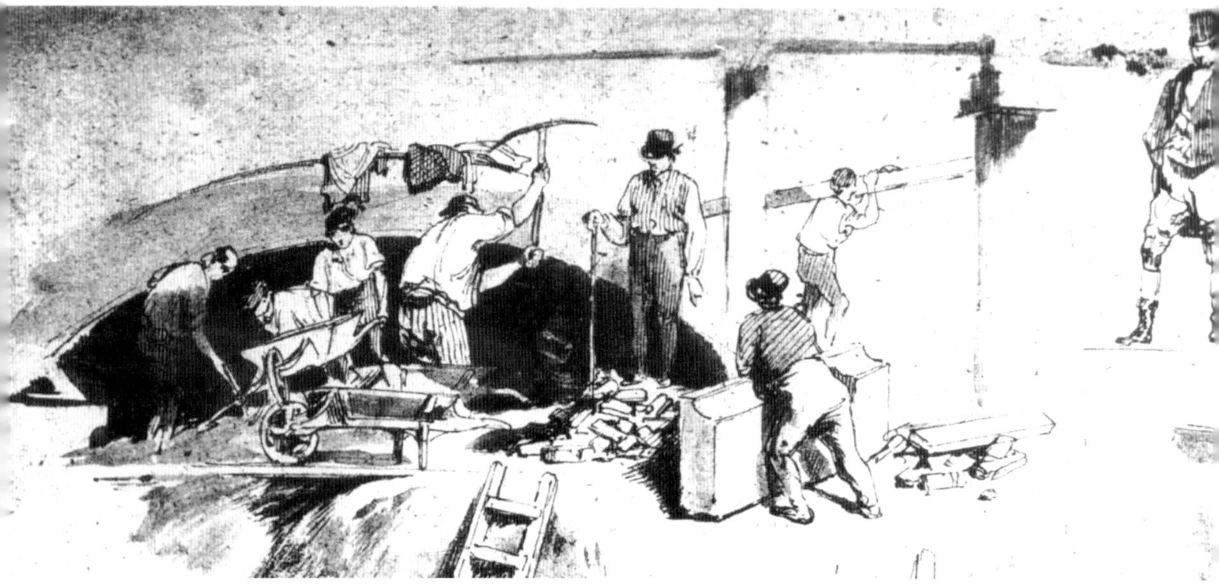

Navvies at work. (*J. C. Bourne*)

That Monday evening some Gloucestershire men entered Bristol and were stopped by the police. To prevent further trouble a detachment of troops quartered at Bath arrived at Bristol on the Wednesday.

Because navvies were not all local men, some had to find a bed to sleep in. This could be in a cottage, house, inn or hut. No. 18 High Street, Saltford, once a large farmhouse, from 1836 was known as the 'Railroad Arms', and navvies slept in its attics. The 'Ship Inn', now a private house, at the foot of Saltford Hill, contained just inside the front door a pigeon-hole window, which was used as a navvies' pay office.

Unlike the section of line between Bath and Chippenham, very few injuries to navvies were recorded in the local papers. On 20 June 1838, when building the arch of Twerton Tunnel, the plank on which four workmen were standing snapped. Henry Hillier received a compound fracture of the knee joint requiring amputation; Peter Holbrook suffered a compound fracture of the leg; William Bunbell had a severe injury to his spine; while Thomas Claverly's scalp was bruised and lacerated. All four were taken to the Bath United Hospital (the prefix 'Royal' was not granted until 23 May 1864). Four days after admission the *Bath & Cheltenham Gazette* reported that 'The unfortunate sufferers are doing well.' In November 1838 a cutting slipped, killing one navvy and seriously injuring three others who were taken to the Bristol Infirmary; then on 7 February 1839 brickwork in No. 3 Tunnel fell, killing three men and, when their colleagues rushed to help, a further fall caused injuries to nine more. On the morning of 12 August 1840, as Edward Greenland was taking down the centreings of Claverton Street Bridge, Bath, one of the massive timbers fell and broke his leg in three places.

What could well have been a fatal accident happened to William Chadwick, contractor for building the skew bridge across the Avon immediately west of Bath station. On 21 August 1840 he was on the bridge inspecting progress and, while standing on one of the highest parts of a rib and engaged in conversation with one of his men, he lost his balance. In trying to regain it, he stepped over the beam and plunged 30 ft towards the river. This would have been bad enough, but in falling he came into contact with a piece of timber and then fell violently onto the coffer dam. Chadwick was rescued, placed in a boat and brought ashore where he regained consciousness – bruised, but with no broken bones.

Termination of employment also caused problems. On 6 January 1841 navvy John Edwards, aged thirty-two, died 'from want of necessities of life' at his lodging in Wood Street, Bath, parallel with the railway viaduct. Unemployed for five weeks, Edwards had been ill for four days and he and his wife were in a state of 'the most deplorable wretchedness'. The inquest at the Bell public house, Lower Bristol Road, found that the cold weather and lack of nourishment caused his death. He had not applied to the relieving officer for help as he had hoped for a change in the weather and a chance of obtaining employment. He had a child about 1½ years old.

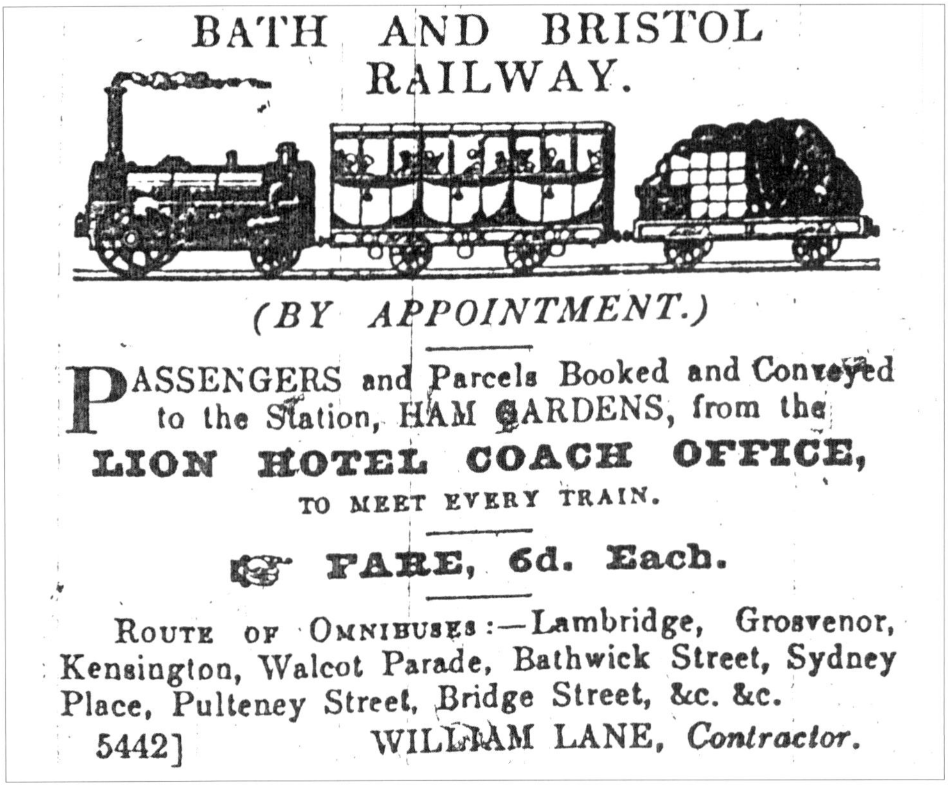

Advertisement in the *Bath & Cheltenham Gazette* 1 September 1840.

Chapter Four
Preparations for Opening

By the autumn of 1839 the work most in arrears was the skew bridge across the Avon immediately west of Bath station. Tenders for the 500 tons of ironwork required had been invited in May 1839, but difficulties arose and, probably with a view to faster completion, Brunel decided to construct it of laminated timber; this proved to be his only bridge of this type. August 1839 saw a mud barge brought to the site to clear the river bottom and deepen the stream where barges passed. Work on the coffer dam for the central pier was completed by the second week in September. The *Bath & Cheltenham Gazette* of 17 September 1839 reported: 'Hundreds of our fellow-citizens of all classes daily visit the locality to witness the interesting and novel operations of the workmen'. The dam was nearly cleared of water when heavy rains caused a great rise in the river level to inundate the works. In December 1839 it was still not clear of water and only on 30 April 1840 did the *Bath Chronicle* report that foundations for the central pier were being made.

J. C. Bourne describes the bridge's details in his *History of the Great Western Railway:*

> The angle at which the Bridge crosses the River is so considerable that, although the space from quay to quay is only 80 feet, the space traversed by the railway is 164 feet. The bridge is of two arches, each of 80-ft span. Each arch is composed of six ribs placed about 5 feet apart and springing from the abutment and a central pier of masonry. Each rib is constructed of five horizontal layers of Memel timber held together by bolts and iron straps. The end or butt of each rib is enclosed in a shoe or socket of cast iron, resting with the intervention of a plate upon the springing stones, the shoes on the middle pier being common to the two ribs. The spandrels of the four external ribs are filled up with an ornamental framework of cast iron supporting the parapets. The interior ribs are connected by cross struts and ties. The cornice and parapet are both of timber; the latter is framed in open work of a lozenge pattern. The abutments are flanked by plain turreted piers, and the tow-path is carried on an iron gallery beneath the western arch.

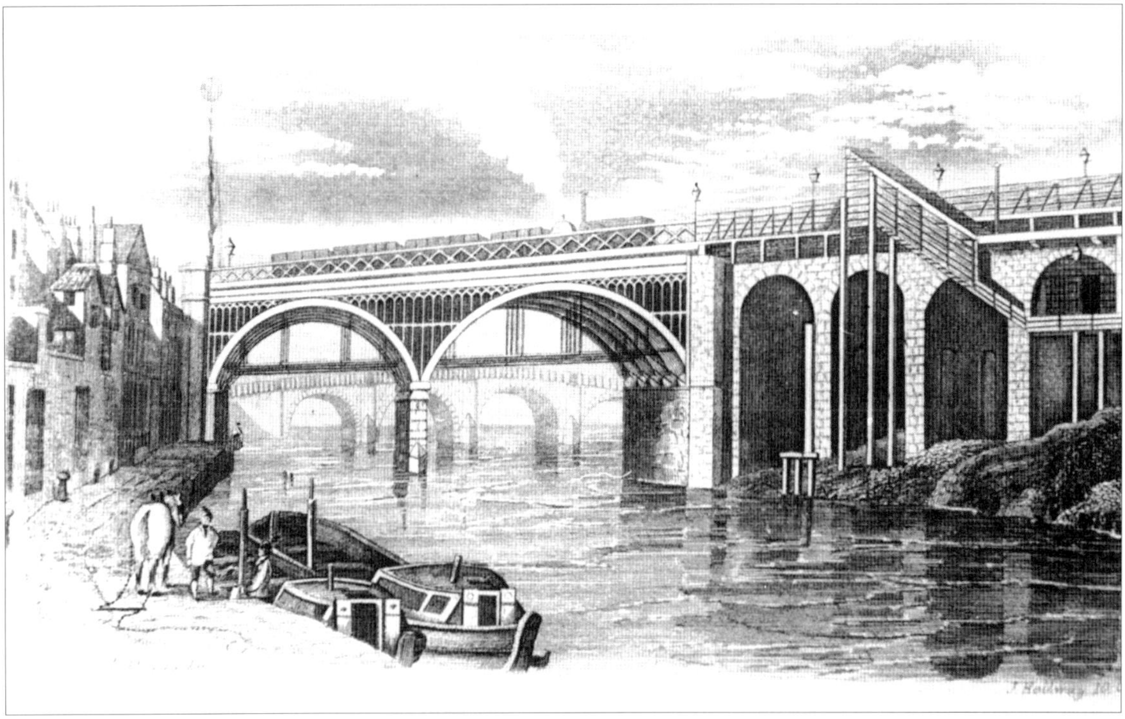

The timber-built skew bridge over the Avon immediately west of Bath station, which is just off the right-hand edge of the picture. A disc and crossbar signal is set to 'Clear'. Barges for water transport down the river to Bristol are moored at the quay. The artist has inaccurately placed the locomotive's smokebox adjacent to the haystack firebox. (*T. Holloway*)

The timber was kyanised before being bolted together. G. A. Sekon in his *History of the Great Western Railway* said it was the most oblique bridge ever built of wood. The timber was steam-bent to the desired curvature and secured by bolts and iron plates. When the scaffolding was removed in January 1841, the *Bath Chronicle* of 7 January waxed enthusiasm:

> The structure now stands forth in all its singular beauty. We question whether the country contains a more curious specimen of bridge architecture on the same scale. Viewed as a whole, it has an elegantly light and airy appearance - so light and airy, indeed, that, at first glance, it seems hardly strong enough to bear the weight of the heavy trains continually passing over it. But when its details are examined, immense strength is found united to grace of outline. The interior of the structure bears some resemblance to the large wooden roofs under which ships of war have of late years been built in the government dockyards.

All laminated timber arches had a life usually limited to twenty-five years because they were too flexible; flexing caused the laminations to separate and the subsequent ingress of water led to decay. This laminated skew bridge's life of thirty-eight years was only exceeded by Valentine's glued laminated bowstring arch carrying the East Anglian Railway over the River Wissey.

December 1839 saw work proceeding on the viaduct immediately west of the river crossing, with the centreings of the Wells Road arch removed and re-erected a few yards east, where the line was to cross Claverton Street. Of the viaduct itself, the *Bath Chronicle* reported: 'The arch and 2 Gothic towers are pronounced to be excellent specimens of workmanship; and the entire viaduct, from the taste evinced in its design, will form, when completed, quite an ornament to the neighbourhood'. This section was built by Messrs Rennie & Co., who had gained a high reputation building the London & Birmingham Railway.

At the GWR half-yearly meeting in February 1840 it was reported that floods had caused problems. At the Bristol end they had interfered with the supply of building material, while at Bath it was impossible to carry on the works of bridges and on the station site, which was flooded: 'Many parts of the line, long since prepared, have not been in a state to allow of men or horses passing over them without destroying that portion of the forming which the rain had allowed to be completed, so that not more than about 2 and a ½ miles of ballasting have actually been completed.' It was estimated that the wet weather was responsible for delaying the opening by at least four months.

Zealous efforts were made during the spring of 1840 to complete the line at an early date. Relays of men allowed work to continue day and night and even, to the disgust of Bath citizens, on Sundays. In May 1840 the *Bath Chronicle* reported that all along the banks of the Avon were piles of timber and rails landed from barges and that the permanent way had been laid near Keynsham where a locomotive was at work assisting with the ballasting. The line was fenced with wooden posts and four rails. The thirty-five bridges comprised five river bridges and thirty road or occupation bridges, and an additional twenty culverts or drains carried brooks under the line.

On 17 July 1840 the foundations of two or three arches at Temple Meads showed signs of weakness due to the substrata being unsound and sank 8–10 ft when several hundred tons of earth were placed on them. Navvies found a fine example of a mammoth's tooth in a bed of new red sandstone below the surface at Bristol between the bridge over the Feeder and that across the Floating Harbour, while a fossil coniferous tree was discovered 100 ft below the surface while cutting No. 3 Tunnel.

The *Bristol Standard* in early August 1840 commented:

> As the period approaches for the completion of the line from this city to Bath, public interest seems to increase, and our generally quiet town-folk, shaking off their old apathy and conquering their well-known aversion to those novelties yclept 'improvements', are stealing out in thousands watching the progress of the works, not a few biting their nails at thought that they have suffered a good investment to pass by unheeded. This line now possesses in a high degree, public confidence

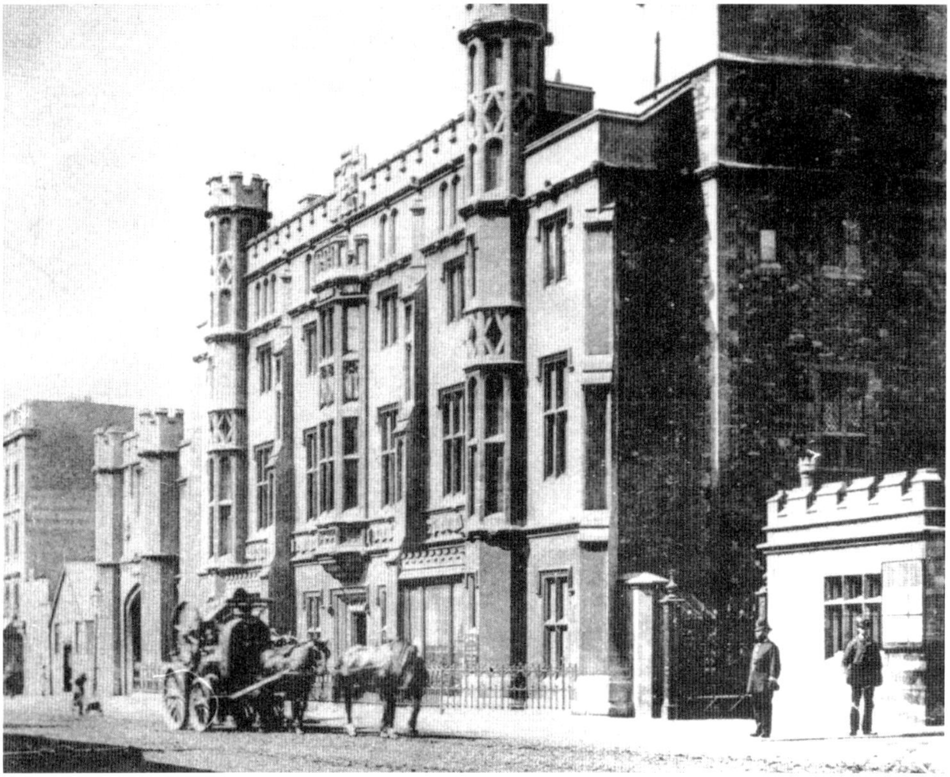

The 'baronial hall' appearance of Temple Meads station. The horse is drawing a steam engine for powering machinery. (*Author's Collection*)

> in Bristol, and when fairly opened to Bath, Bristol will send forth her thousands, whirling along the beautiful banks of the Avon, to visit the sister city. We opine this will prove the most profitable portion of the line yet opened, and we shall very soon be enabled to dispense with the old road and all its cumbrous apparatus, its slow movements and many disappointments, and avail ourselves of the 'new order of things' and 'go a-head' steaming it in about fifteen minutes.

The reporter also inspected *Arrow*, built for the line by Stothert, Slaughter & Co., Bristol. She was placed on the line on 4 August, and 'is expected to attain a speed of 90 to 100 miles per hour'.

The *Bath Chronicle* leader writer 27 August 1840 displayed great enthusiasm:

> The sharp, shrill scream of the steam whistle, and the rapid beatings of the locomotive engine in its experimental and other trips – new sounds to our city – now give daily notice to our fellow citizens that the Railway between Bath and Bristol is on the eve of actually being opened. At our end of the line the artisans have been working – swarms like bees. The achievements which labour and skill can perform have been particularly exemplified at the works at Claverton street. To

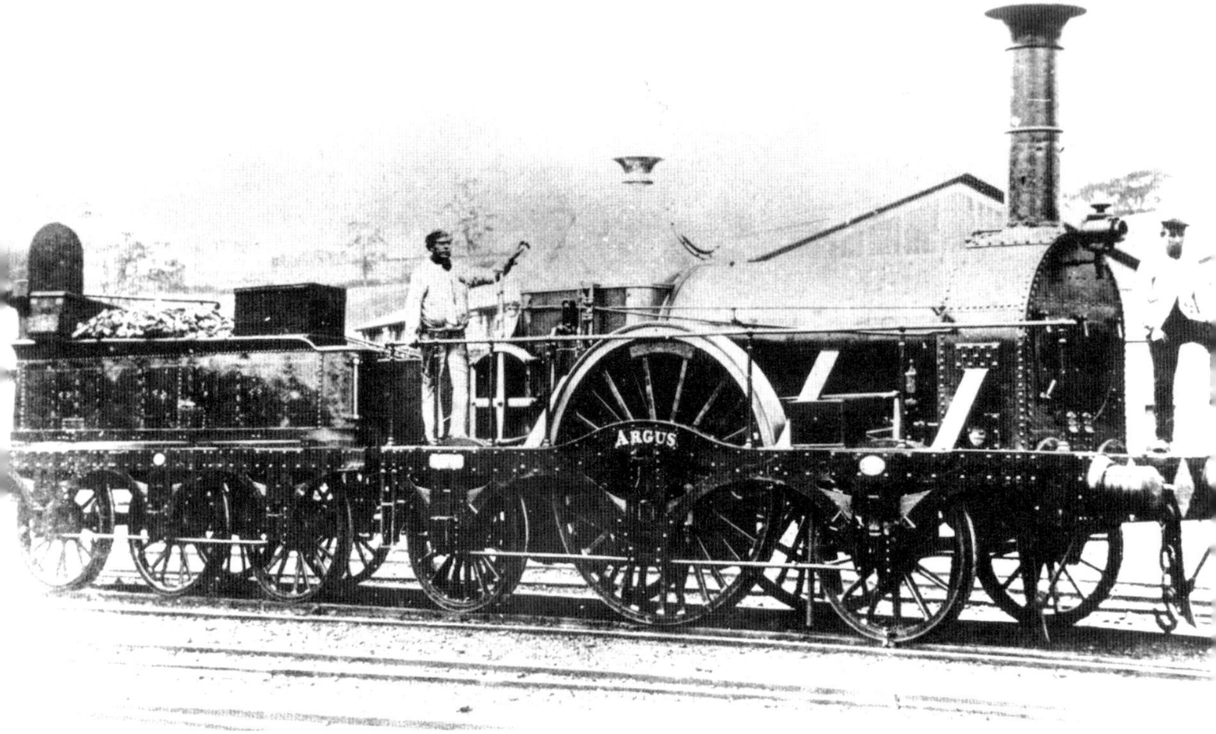

Fire Fly class 2-2-2 *Argus* at Bristol *c.* 1850. (*Author's Collection*)

those who have been in the habit of passing the spot day after day, it has appeared as if piers and arches were rising out of the ground by force of magic. Count the arches as you went by at evening – and lo! in the morning, another arch, bringing the Railway one stride nearer the river's brink. The beautifully-scientific 'skew bridge' is rapidly approaching completion.

From and after Monday next the good folks of Bath and Bristol will be whirled to, and back from each of these cities in the space of about twenty minutes – a revolution in travelling which, to use a frequently-heard form of expression, 'Would make our forefathers stare if they could witness it'. But what is this to the almost miraculous capability of visiting London, remaining there for several hours, and returning to Bath in one day, which will be afforded to us by the Railway at no great distance of time.

Much discussion is naturally excited in our city touching the effect which the Railway, when completed in its extreme length, will have on Bath. There can, we think, be no well-grounded doubt that it will ultimately be productive of the best results to us.

A reporter in the same issue wrote:

> Crowds of spectators are every day attracted to the works at the 'Skew Bridge' over which the Great Western Railway is to cross the Avon. The cast iron standards for the support of the road way, and the longitudinal timbers on which the permanent rails are to be laid, are nearly all in place. The masonry on each side of the water is now already completed. The depot [station] cannot be finished in time for the opening on Monday, but temporary offices are being rapidly constructed.
>
> Relays of men are now employed on the works night and day; not a moment is lost at mealtimes for the instant one man lays down his tools for the purpose of taking refreshment, another supplies his place. At the Bristol terminus, everything proceeds in the most satisfactory manner. Several fresh arrivals of carriages have taken place within the last few days, and, we understand, that there are now about forty on the line; those belonging to the first class being fitted up in the most splendid manner.

The *Bristol Standard* was equally enthusiastic: 'During the past week many splendid runs have been made on the line by the powerful engines already here. On Friday last [21 August] we saw a locomotive, which had a large party of gentlemen, including Mr Brunel and some of the Directors, at the rate of 60 miles per hour from Bristol to Bath and on their return the distance was done in 16½ minutes, exclusive of stoppage. "Lynx" was placed on the line 18 August.' Describing the engines, the same reporter said: 'They move with noiseless rapidity, and no sound is heard by the "breathing", as it may be termed, of the monster who rushes past at a pace double that of the fleetest horse.'

The excitement and novelty of completing the railway was well expressed in the 3 September 1840 issue of the *Bath Chronicle:*

> Stones and timbers seemed to be literally moving together. At night the works presented a most singular and imposing appearance. The workmen carried on their operations by the light of numerous huge fires, which not only illuminated the immediate neighbourhood, but threw into the sky a red and lurid reflection which could be seen several miles off. Thousands of our fellow citizens visited the works, for the purpose of looking on the novel and striking spectacle which they furnished. And it was well worth an inspection. The glare of the fires, brightly mirrored in the bosom of the river - the columns of smoke continually rising into the air - the busy figures moving about in all directions, as they took, each to his part in the business of the night - and the dense crowds assembled to witness the various operations, afforded altogether a fine field for the studies of a painter, and furnished abundant food for the most interesting reflection.

Chapter Five

Opening

Six of Daniel Gooch's new Fire Fly class 2-2-2 engines arrived in early August 1840: *Arrow* and *Dart* had been built locally by Stothert, Slaughter & Co. at Bristol, while *Fire Ball* and *Spit Fire* had been made by Jones, Turner & Evans at Newton-le-Willows (they arrived at Bristol on board the *SS Brigand*). *Lynx* had been built by Sharp, Roberts & Co., Manchester and *Meridian* by R. & W. Hawthorn, Newcastle-upon-Tyne. Regarding *Arrow*, the *Bristol Gazette* of 13 August 1840 said that following completion at St Philip's works it 'excited great curiosity as it proceeded up Old Market, the sun shining upon the bright brass and ironwork producing a dazzling effect. We hear that it is the first specimen of the kind manufactured in the West of England, and that the beauty and excellence of the workmanship are highly creditable to the firm.'

The editorial of the *Bath & Cheltenham Gazette*, 1 September 1840, said: 'Under the magic influence of the Railway, Bath and Bristol, the respective abodes of Fashion and Commerce, will, as it were, be placed side by side. Bath will become a second Clifton to Bristol; indeed will be reached in far less time than a pedestrian starting from St Mary Redcliffe can gain St Vincent's Rocks.'

Until 21 August the longest moving thing that most people would have seen would have been a horse drawing a cart, but that day they saw a locomotive hauling a train of twenty-four wagons loaded with gravel for ballasting the permanent way. On the same day the first passengers were carried between Bristol and Bath, the *Bristol Journal* reporting:

> The first railway journey between the cities of Bristol and Bath was made on Friday last the 21st August, 1840, and in case this notice of it should go down to future times, when perhaps still speedier means of locomotion may be in fashion, we think it worth while to give some particulars of the trip. The party consisted of five of the Directors: Messrs R. Bright, W. Tothill, T. R. Guppy, C. B. Fripp and R. Scott, attended by Mr Brunel, Mr Clarke, the Superintendent and some other officers of the Company. In consequence of the rails not being quite finished at the station in Temple Meads, it was not easy to get a carriage upon the line at the Engine-house, and the party were therefore content 'to take their places' on the engine and tender.

The engine selected for the first part of the journey was the 'Arrow', the first Bristol made locomotive and a very creditable specimen it is.

The start was made from a point nearly opposite to the Engine-house at 20 minutes after 4 o'clock, and after threading the darksome passage of Tunnels Nos 1, 2 and 3, and skimming over the new embankment at Fox's Wood, the engine was stopped at the Keynsham Station at 4h. 30m. Here the Directors alighted and after a delay of 8 minutes they started again, on the other line of rails, with the 'Meridian'. As the engine flew onwards, the party was greeted with hearty cheers from bands of workmen and spectators at different points, and after making a short stoppage near the Cross Post Bridge to take up the assistant engineer, Mr Frere (who we regret to hear has lately met with a serious accident from a fall), the Directors completed their trip to Bath, arriving at the Oak Street Viaduct at 4h. 53m.

After staying some time to inspect the bridge over the Avon the party again took their places on the engine and the start was made at 32 minutes after 5. A short stoppage was again made at the Cross Post Bridge and then the Keynsham Station was reached at 5.45. Here the Directors again 'took flight' by the 'Arrow', which landed them safely at the Engine-house in St Philip's in 10½ minutes. In consequence of the numerous workmen still at work on the line it was not thought prudent to make any trial of speed, but our readers will see that the trip was performed to Bath in 33 minutes including two stoppages, one of these 8 minutes. Such a run as this must be quite sufficient to secure an abundant traffic as soon as the line is opened to the public.

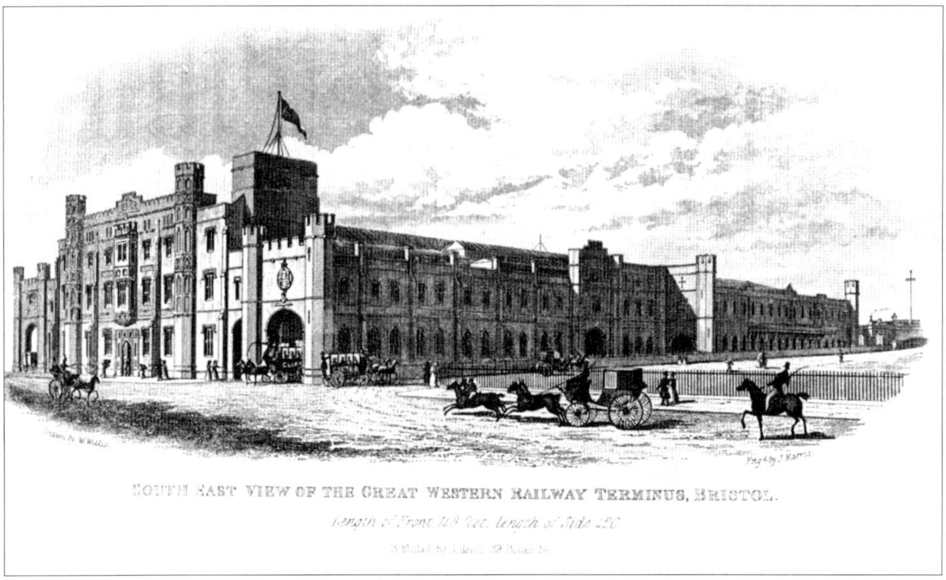

Temple Meads street frontage *c.* 1842. The departure side is through the left-hand arch and the arrival side on the right. The tower surmounted by a flagstaff is a water tank for the hydraulic lifts. Platforms are in the upper storey of the building beyond the arrival archway. Notice the disc and crossbar signal on the far right. (*J. Harris*)

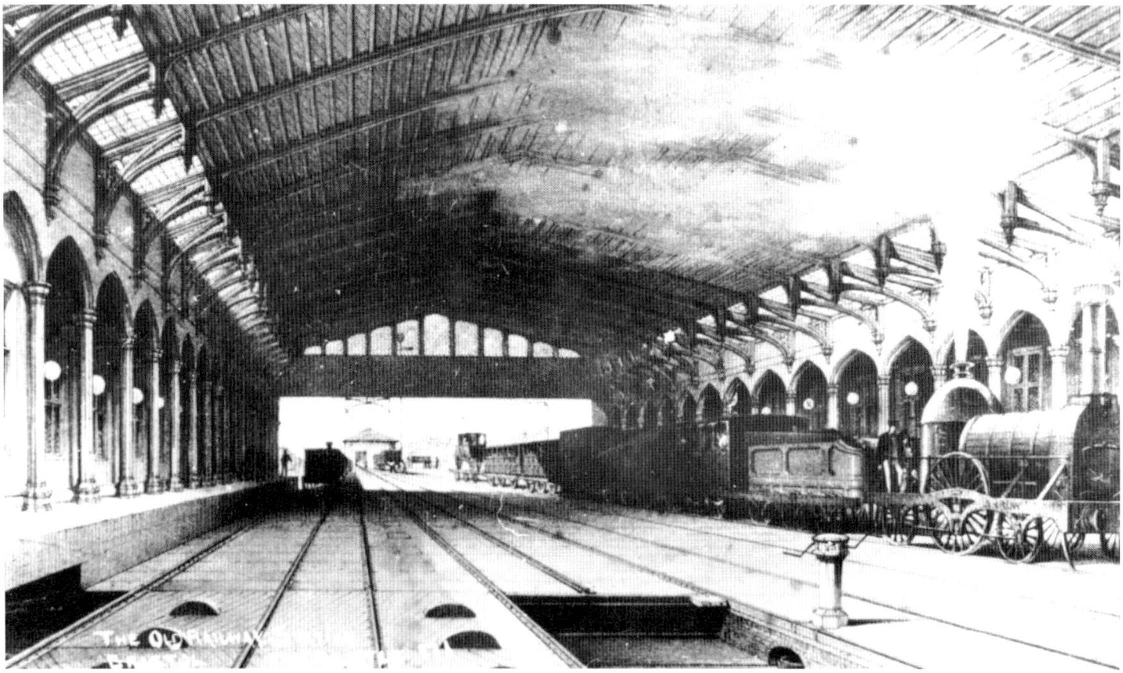

Fire Fly class 2-2-2 *Arrow* arrives at Temple Meads *c.* 1840. Notice the carriage on the rear wagon. In the foreground is a hand-operated traverser for moving rolling stock from one road to another. (*F. Little*)

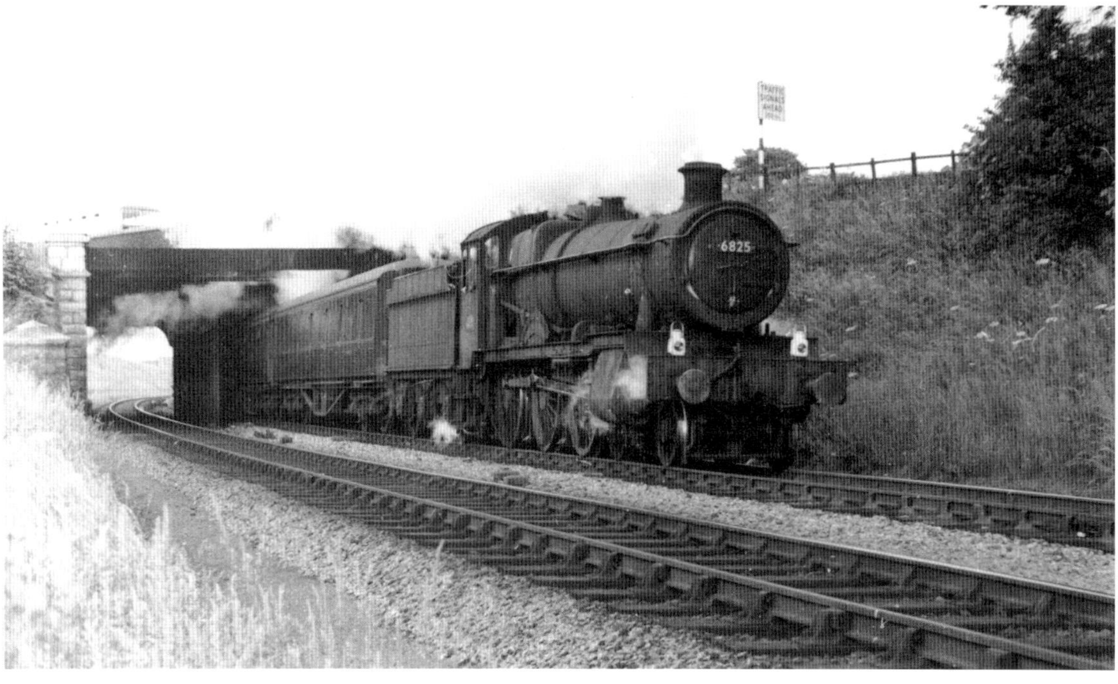

A Down express hauled by 4-6-0 No. 6825 *Llanvair Grange* passes beneath Cross Post Bridge *c.* 1962. (*Dr T. R. N. Edwards*)

As it had been announced that the line between Bristol and Bath was to open on 31 August 1840 great efforts were made to keep to this scheduled date. Since the permanent offices at Temple Meads could not be finished in time, during the last two weeks of August, temporary offices were erected. A thousand men were at work either on or near the river bridge immediately west of Bath station. At Bristol the last rail into Temple Meads was laid only half an hour before the first train left.

It was planned that *Meridian*, driven by Cuthbert Davison who had experience of locomotive operation at Newcastle, would drive the first timetabled train between Bristol and Bath, but in the event *Fire Ball* was ready earlier and the honour fell to her. Davison drove the second train and said later that he never forgot the thousands of cheering people he saw along the route and the immense crowds assembled at Bath.

The *Bath & Cheltenham Gazette* of 1 September 1840 commented:

> Others feared, from the rapidity with which the bridge at this end of the line was constructed, that the works were in so incomplete a state, that the most fearful accidents would be likely to ensue. But on visiting the Station yesterday morning we perceived that the calculations of the contractors had been too nicely made, and that although the works presented an unfinished appearance, the massive and solid masonry which supports the sleepers and permanent rails was sufficient to afford all the security which is obtained on that part of the road which is finished with greater nicety.
>
> For the last three weeks nothing could exceed the exertions made to open the line by the day fixed upon. The contractors appeared to have put an embargo upon all the disposable labour of the city and its suburbs. Men and boys – masons, carpenters, and labourers – carts, waggons, and machinery – horses from all parts of the vicinage – seemed to have been 'pressed into the service' and the bustle caused by the continued arrival of immense loads of freestone, soil [*sic*] for ballasting the line, and other materials, was quite unprecedented in this usually non-commercial neighbourhood. That such activity and excitement on public works were never before witnessed by our citizens was attested by the crowds which were always assembled at the scene of operation; to many of whom the neighbourhood of the line had become quite the place whither each brought his quota of gossip; and carried away that collected by his (or rather *her)* neighbour. No sooner had one gazer satisfied his curiosity than his place was occupied by a companion, who in his turn gave place to a third; and this was the case not only throughout the day but for a great part of the twenty-four hours. In consequence of the urgency of the case, workmen were kept on the line during the whole of the night, and during the hours usually devoted to slumber – in which, it has been said, both peasant and prince forget their joys and sorrows, and are placed on an equality – the neighbourhood resounded with the vociferations of the operative, and the stroke of his hammer. On Saturday night, especially, the scene was most extraordinary. Throughout the

> whole extent of the Company's extensive premises in the Ham Gardens, on the skew bridge, along the Railway itself, from the Old Bridge to the terminus, and even on the turnpike road which runs at the foot of the viaduct, once forming part of Claverton street, large heaps of blazing coal and pitch (aided by numberless lanterns) diffused a powerful but lurid light, by which the workmen followed their avocations with great diligence and spirit. Immense crowds intent on watching the progress of the works and speculating on the probability of their completion by Monday, were collecting near the Old Bridge and in Philip street, who seemed disposed to protract their vigils until a late (or early) hour. From the Old Bridge to the bottom of Southgate street the effect of these nocturnal operations was perfectly unique, as, in consequence of the number of lights along the skew bridge and the portion of the Railway on each side of it, the direction and exact situation of the line was distinctly visible, notwithstanding the darkness.

The *Bristol Standard* reported:

> Precisely at half past seven the hoarding which had closed up the passenger entrance at the northern gate fell inwards, and formed a platform leading to a gravelled path over which we were the first of the public who walked towards the booking office.
>
> Having paid our money, we proceeded up a flight of stairs which led us to the passengers' starting platform. The railway guards dressed in handsome liveries, were in attendance and with the utmost promptitude, passengers were shown into the carriages.

A Bath Chronicle reporter who went to Bristol to travel on the first train wrote:

> As the time of departure drew nigh, passengers began to arrive in rapid succession, and in a few minutes the train, consisting of three elegant first class, and five second class carriages, was nearly filled. The arrangements of the Company were admirable; not the slightest confusion occurred, and all was ready for the start at eight o'clock, when the bell was rung, and 'The Fireball' engine was attached to the train, At ten minutes past eight it was in motion, and glided beautifully off with gradual quickening of speed until it was lost to the sight of the spectators who had assembled at and around the Depot. As the train proceeded towards Keynsham, the scene became extremely animated. Thousands of gazers of all classes had gathered together at the various places affording good views of the line, and enthusiastically evinced their admiration and delight. The Keynsham Station was reached in 14 minutes. Here there was a stoppage of three minutes for the purpose of taking up and setting down passengers, after which the well-filled train proceeded rapidly towards Bath, the countryside on each side of the line displaying countless groups of spectators anxious to get a glimpse of the new and surprising mode of travelling.

> The train reached this city in exactly 30 minutes, exclusive of stoppages, from the time of leaving the Bristol Depot. For the sake of safety on this, the first day of actually travelling in the ordinary sense, the great speed which will generally be attained on the railway was very properly avoided. At the Bath end of the line a large multitude of spectators had congregated to witness the opening. Stall street, the Bristol road, Claverton street were densely thronged and all the thoroughfares from which a view of the line could be obtained, and most of the elevated positions around the city, were crowded with curious gazers. Merry peals from the Abbey bells, and occasional discharges of firearms, marked the day as one of especial rejoicing. The crowds which gathered to witness the arrival and departure of the first trains did not diminish during the day. The GWR directors attended 'a splendid breakfast' at the White Hart Inn, Bath.

The *Bristol Standard* account was written from a slightly different perspective:

> The train soon arrived at the tunnels, which form the only unpleasant part of the ride, as in two of them the passengers were for a short time in complete darkness ... The passage across the Avon over the extraordinary timber bridge near the entrance into Bath was made with the greatest caution. Confident assertions had been made that it would not be in a fit state to permit the passage of the train by the day fixed for the opening of the line; but the unremitting exertions of Mr. Brunel and those immediately under him so hastened the work that it was completed in time, though we understand that the last rail was not laid until seven o'clock on Monday morning.

W. Tyte in his *History of Lyncombe & Widcombe* wrote:

> There were then no houses below Beechen Cliff Wood. An unfenced meadow extended from Lyncombe Hill on the east, to Holloway on the west. Hundreds of people thronged this field on the memorable August morning, sunny as it was, to witness the arrival of the first train, and join in the cheer of welcome when the locomotive came in sight, soon to disappear in the station. The most conspicuous feature about the engine was a large dome-shaped boiler, [*sic* firebox] which gleamed brightly in the sunshine ... The year 1840 may, indeed, be generally considered as the dividing line between the old order of things and the new – between the age of the stage coach and the age of the iron horse.

The station used at Bath was a temporary affair to the west of the permanent station and on the site of the later goods depot, and it was not until 1 October 1840 that the *Bath Chronicle* reported that T. Lewis, the contractor responsible for erecting the station, was 'advancing with great rapidity' and already joists had been laid for the first floor.

The first Down train left Bath soon after 9.30 a.m. drawn by *Arrow*, and more than half an hour late because of a defective wheel on a second-class coach.

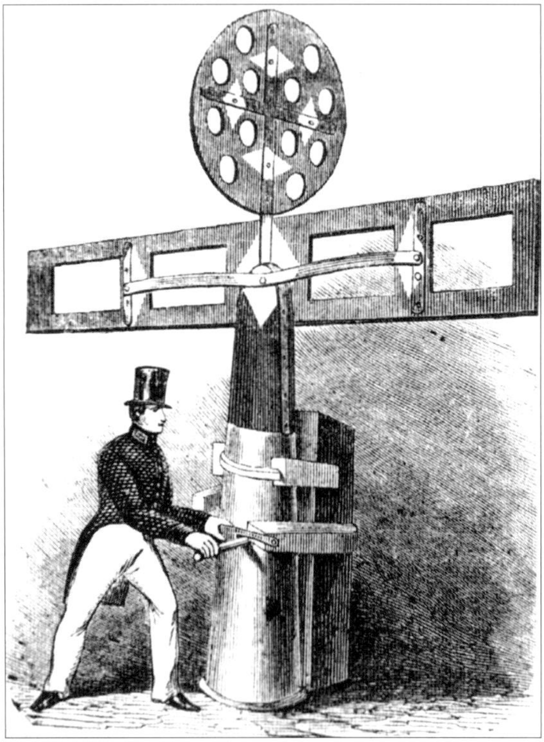

The first junction signal on the GWR was at Bristol between the passenger station and the goods depot. (*Author's Collection*)

After the train had finally set off, the alarm was raised that one of its coaches was on fire. A stop was made at Twerton to examine the train and it was found that a wheel grating on the under part of the carriage was generating sparks. This was a design fault and occurred on several trains during the day. This delay to the first Down train meant that the second Up train arrived at Bath before the first Down had arrived at Bristol and led the reporter of the *Bristol Journal* to conjecture that the second Up train carried fewer passengers than the first 'because nervous Bristolians waited to make sure their friends were safe before making the journey'.

The *Bath & Cheltenham Gazette* recorded the arrival of the first train at Bath:

> At about 20 minutes to 9 the sounding of the bell announced the approach of the 'monster' with his screaming note and tribe of vehicles. The *Fire Ball* was decorated with small flags, and as it passed along the line was greeted with the most enthusiastic cheering of the spectators and workmen, the passengers responding by a waving of hats and handkerchiefs from the window of the train. On reaching its destination the shouting was prodigiously increased. Each of the six carriages was filled by most respectable parties, who were quickly *disembogued* and the engine replenished with water. The belfry of the Abbey church contributed its quota to the hilarity of the day, and a few of the principal shops were partially closed. The

> first trip was performed in the space of 30 minutes; a period perhaps longer than some might have anticipated, but easily to be accounted for, on the ground of the full power of the engines not being tested, in consequence of the recent erection of a great portion of the works, and the fear of their being shaken by too great a speed.
>
> If, in the morning, Bristol sent forth its thousands to witness the opening of the line from Bristol to Bath, in the evening it sent forth its tens of thousands. The scene up the Bath road, on Pile hill, and every spot along both sides of the line, as far as we could catch a glimpse, up to the entrance of No. 1 tunnel, was nearly one mass of human beings, who 'one and all' expressed their hearty satisfaction by continued cheering and waving of handkerchiefs as the different trains passed, demonstrations which were enthusiastically responded to by the passengers; and all seemed gratified at the opening of a means of conveyance that has brought two of the principal cities in the country within a few minutes' ride of each other.

The *Bristol Standard* reporter was enthusiastic: 'We have travelled in some parts of this district at a rate exceeding 60 miles per hour, and with a steadiness which prevented any uncomfortable sensation from passing over the ground at this extraordinary speed.' It was acknowledged that *Arrow*, a Bristol-built engine, was the fastest and on one trip drew a train from Bath to Bristol in thirteen minutes and the steam was 'shut off' at the entrance to No. 2 tunnel, the train afterwards coming up to the terminus, a distance of 1¾ miles, by its own momentum.

> We think it not amiss to say, at the time when the Public attention is painfully excited by dreadful casualties on *other lines*, that, though nearly two millions of passengers have passed over that part of the Great Western line already open to the Public [Paddington–Faringdon Road], not one individual has lost his life, or any serious accident occurred. This is in a great measure to be attributed to the width of the gauge, which renders it an but impossible for the carriages to run off the rails, and which, whilst it is productive of a vast superiority in *speed*, ensures also a superiority on a point of infinitely more importance, that of *safety.*

Throughout the opening day people crowded into trains for the novelty of the ride, 'with none of the bumpiness of some other lines'. Trains were scheduled to take twenty-five minutes between the cities including the stop at Keynsham. Up trains left Bristol on the hour at 8, 9, 10, 11 a.m., noon and 2, 4, 5, 7 and 8 p.m. The first-class single fare was 2*s* 6*d*, and 5,880 passengers were carried on the first day with £476 taken in fares, which compared favourably with only £226 when the GWR opened between Paddington and Maidenhead. Takings comprised: Bristol: £223 17*s* 1½*d*; Keynsham: £21 14*s* 0*d*; and Bath: £230 19*s* 0*d*. On Tuesday a total of 3,364 passengers were carried, respective receipts being £131 11*s* 11½*d*; £9 19*s* 4½*d*; and £122 10*s* 6*d*. Total receipts taken from

19,618 passengers travelling over this stretch of line from Monday 31 August to Sunday 6 September inclusive was £1,570 10*s* 10*d*, of which £4 13*s* 6*d* was for parcels.

Several minor teething troubles were experienced. On 10 September, the 5.00 p.m. Bath to Bristol was an hour late leaving because a coach was derailed on the crossover between the Up and Down lines. The *Bath Chronicle* for 17 September 1840 reported:

> A large body of the Company's servants immediately rendered every assistance, but it was nearly six o'clock before the carriage was replaced on the line. About half past five the train from Bristol came in sight, but in consequence of the admirably arranged signals, the steam was let off, and the engine stopped before it arrived at the obstruction.

There were the makings of a serious accident on 13 September. The 8.00 p.m. train, consisting of 'nine crowded coaches', left Temple Meads a few minutes late drawn by *Lynx*, a Fire Fly class 2-2-2 running tender-first. Half a mile from Temple Meads, at the junction (later to become South Wales Junction) with the line to the locomotive shed, following the departure of *Lynx* to the station to pick up its train, the switchman failed to set the points for the main line, so at 12–15 mph the train took the turnout to the shed. The driver shut off steam and the guards applied their brakes. The *Bath Chronicle* for 17 September wrote: 'The harsh grating sound occasioned by the sudden application of the breaks [*sic*], gave the first intimation to the passengers that something was wrong. As alarm soon spread from carriage to carriage, and the inquiry had scarcely been made "What's the matter?" when the tender of the "Lynx" engine came into contact with the "Arrow".'

The *Bath & Cheltenham Gazette*, 15 September, continues the story:

> The concussion was such as to bring the parties sitting opposite each other so closely in contact, that several of them sustained violent blows. As might be imagined, the fears of the travellers got the better of their judgments, and most gave their lungs full play, in which harmonic exercise the fair sex by no means played 'second fiddle'. Besides injuries done to the ladies' bonnets and other articles of their dress of similar fragile texture, a very few pounds will put it all right. The 'switch man' deemed it prudent to 'make himself scarce' at the Station, yesterday morning.

The train finally left about 9.00 p.m.

The public took some time to grow aware of the danger of railways. In the afternoon of 23 September, a cowman, Robert Ruddell, aged eighty, crossed the line at Gravel-pits, Keynsham, while carrying out his duties. The *Bath Chronicle* of 24 September 1840 recorded:

> He was induced, at the request of one of the [railway] police, who knew that he was deaf and feeble through his great age, to sit down on a post until after the five o'clock up-train from Bristol to this city, should have passed. He, however, unfortunately left his seat too soon and got between the rails just as the train came in sight, and, notwithstanding the whistle of the engine and other signals used to warn him out of the way, he did not move, and the whole train passed over him causing his instant death and terrible mutilation.

It also took some time for passengers to adapt themselves to obeying railway bye-laws, one of which barred smoking on GWR premises. A directors' minute of 14 October 1840 reads:

> The circumstances attending the case of two first class passengers having on the 9th instant smoked cigars at the Bath station, where they were remonstrated with by the police sergeant, who showed them the Bye-laws of the Company, and one of whom afterwards resumed smoking in the carriage between Bath and Keynsham, was reported to the Committee, by the Secretary, who had been directed to take steps for the infliction of the penalty, having presented a letter from the offending parties strongly expressive of their contrition, it was ordered that further proceedings should be stayed on their paying the amount of the fine incurred – Forty shillings – to be appropriated in donations of £1 each, to the Bristol Infirmary and to the General Hospital, with an announcement of the same to the public in each of the Bristol newspapers.

However, the message does not seem to have got through to smokers, for on 11 March 1845 Joseph Smith was fined *2s 6d* and costs for smoking a cigar in a second-class carriage between Saltford and Bath.

Apparently, the behaviour of railway servants was not above criticism either, for on 7 January 1841 a railway police inspector travelling on the 6.00 p.m. Bristol to Bath discovered the policeman in No. 3 Tunnel asleep beside a fire he had made, having placed his signal lantern to be seen by passing trains. For this serious neglect of duty he was taken next morning to the magistrates at Keynsham and committed to Shepton Mallet gaol for a month's hard labour.

In its issue of 13 October 1840, the *Bath & Cheltenham Gazette* bore a bouquet for other GWR officials:

> Travelling by Railway to Bristol a day or two back, I put my head out of the carriage window to catch a sight of a train to Bath, which had passed in a twinkling before: away went my hat to the no small, but good-natured merriment of my fellow-travellers. This happened about Saltford. When the train stopped at Keynsham, I apprized an officer of my loss. He said I should have my hat again; and directed me to give a certain notice at the office in Bristol. On my return thither in the evening, my hat was obligingly restored to me. The exceeding civility I experienced from the

> Company's servants has led me to wish to indulge grateful pleasure, in thus publicly recording a circumstances, as also that others might profit by my want of caution.

The rolling stock was carefully described in the *Bath Chronicle* 3 September:

> The carriages are of splendid construction: those of the first class being fitted up with an attention to luxurious comfort which we are told, coach-builders are not in the general habit of putting even into gentlemen's carriages. The second class carriages also afford very excellent accommodation. There is a total absence of the unpleasant jerkings and 'bumpings' which are felt by passengers on other lines and which, indeed, were experienced on the Great Western between Maidenhead and Paddington, until removed by an alteration in the principle of laying down the rails.

The six-wheel first-class coaches had four compartments, each subdivided by a central partition into two smaller sections that could each contain four passengers. The length of a coach body was 24 ft and the whole weighed 7 tons 16 cwt. Second-class coaches were similar, roofed, but open at the sides above waist level, so the wise did not select a seat by the door if it was raining. Each of the six compartments accommodated twelve passengers. The seats were only 15 in back to front. Each coach weighed 6 tons 13 cwt. When partially concealed by a doorway, the 'splashers' of the 4-ft diameter wheels protruding above the coach floors of both classes could cause an unwary passenger to make an undignified and possibly painful exit, especially if he happened to collide with a pillar close to the platform edge such as was found at Bath or Bristol. For many years, luggage was carried on coach roofs, wheeled steps used for loading and a slanting board for unloading.

Third-class coaches were open trucks with seats and were in fact referred to as 'open trucks' in official correspondence. They made one concession to comfort – drainage holes were provided in the floor so that passengers did not have to paddle in wet weather. The holes were a mixed blessing, however, as they caused a certain amount of draught.

Many bets were placed on when the line would open between Bristol and Bath as indispensable works were incomplete and remained so until the opening day. Although trains did run on the promised opening day, some losers objected to paying on the grounds that many of their bets were guarded by the proviso that the railway should not only be opened to passengers, but also to general traffic. To settle these disputes, a case was brought to the Bath Court of Requests on 23 September. The Chief Commissioner decided that as some goods were carried and this was advertised in the bills, the railway was indeed open to general traffic.

At both Bath and Bristol, in an attempt to offset stagecoach losses, omnibuses and coaches acted as feeders to the railway and Moses Pickwick, a Bath coach operator, ran coaches on behalf of the GWR between Bath and the London end of the line – variously Faringdon Road, Hay Lane (west of Swindon), and Chippenham, until rail communication was completed throughout on 30 June 1841. Dickens, who at one time lived in Bath, took the coach owner's name for a character in his *Pickwick Papers*. These feeder buses, perhaps driven by ex-stagecoach drivers, came up for criticism in the *Bath Chronicle* on 31 July 1841: 'Our attention has been drawn to the furious rate at which the Omnibuses drive through Orange Grove, the Walks and Pierrepont-street, on their way to the Railway Station. by which much danger arises to persons who may happen at the time to be crossing the road.'

The *Bath & Cheltenham Gazette* for 8 September 1840 attempted to compare the number of people travelling between Bath and Bristol by road and rail:

38	average number of coaches Bath to Bristol
10	average number of passengers when coaches fully laden
380	one day's maximum number of passengers carried by coaches
2280	six day's maximum number of passengers carried by coach to Bristol
2280	six day's maximum number of passengers carried by coach from Bristol
4560	
380	probable number of Sunday passengers by coach
4940	
19618	passengers carried by railway in first week
4940	maximum number of coach passengers
14678	difference of number of passengers in favour of railway in first week

This table gives the maximum number of coach passengers, as it proved impractical to ascertain the actual number carried.

To counteract railway competition of an approximate hourly train service, coach proprietors ran a road service every half hour, but all to no avail as most were taken off the road, though until October 1843 one continued to carry passengers from Bristol to London at a rate of a penny a mile. One optimistic coachman commented that it would be a long time before the last of his profession would be seen on the Bath Road as 'Many persons prefer glorifying in the beauty of a set of bays, to being whirled along by a pot of boiling water'. In 1849 a coach resumed running between Bristol and Bath until its withdrawal in 1858. Intriguingly, the railway's opening even affected what crops were grown; because of the decrease in the number of horses required for road work, some Mendip farmers began to plant potatoes instead of oats.

Saltford and Twerton stations opened on 16 December 1840. Third-class passenger traffic and goods were not carried between Bristol and Bath until the opening of the line to London on 30 June 1841. The GWR wished to keep the three classes separate, and at principal stations second-class passengers were prohibited from coming into contact with those travelling first. In June 1842

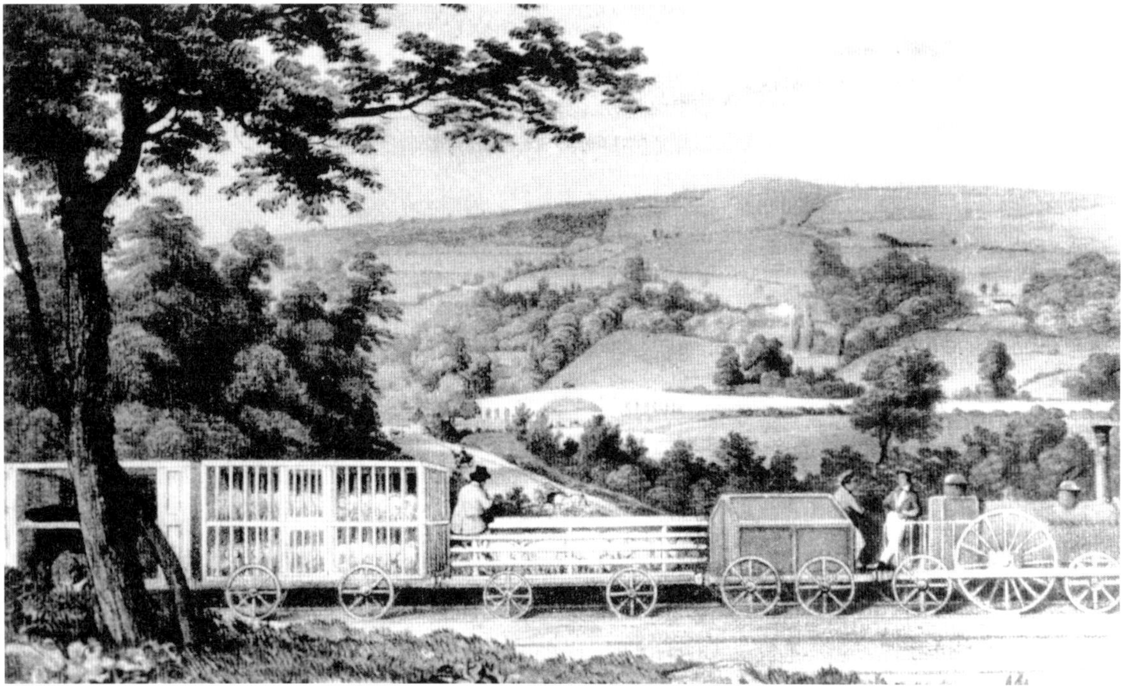

Goods traffic on the railway between Bristol and Bath began on 30 June 1841. In this engraving, *c.* 1841, an Up train has almost reached Twerton Viaduct. The wheels being outside the body gave broad-gauge vehicles great stability. Notice the shepherd travelling with his flock in the first wagon, also the double-deck pig truck. The locomotive crew appear relaxed. The New Bridge is in the background. (*Author's Collection*)

pens were provided for first- and second-class passengers on the Up platform at Bath and the former had the use of a waiting room adjoining their pen. Even separate exits were provided from the platform.

Third-class passengers were treated hardly better than cattle, and were carried only by goods train. In 1841 this led to Sir Frederick Smith reporting to the Board of Trade:

> The third class carriages have seats 18 inches high, but the sides and ends are only two feet above the floor, so that a person standing up, either when the train is unexpectedly put in motion or stopped, is, if near the side or end, in great danger of being thrown out of the carriage, and those sitting near the sides are also in danger of falling; besides which, the exposure to the cutting winds of the winter must be very injurious to the traveller, who, if proceeding from London to Bristol, often remains exposed for ten or twelve hours a great part of which is in the night-time.

This state of affairs led to the passing of Gladstone's Regulation of Railways Act on 9 August 1844, which required all companies operating passenger services to run daily at least one train each way calling at all stations and at a fare not exceeding a penny a mile. The minimum overall speed, including stops, was required to be 12 mph and seated accommodation protected from the weather. The receipts from these Parliamentary trains were not subject to passenger duty, which was a tax on passengers introduced to compensate for the alleged loss of revenue caused by the railway's abstraction of road coach traffic, which was also taxed. The Parliamentary fare distinction disappeared with the passing of the Cheap Trains Act in 1883, when all third-class fares were reduced to a penny a mile and most third-class fares made exempt from tax. The Finance Act of 1929 removed duty from all fares.

Although the Regulations of Railways Act implemented on the GWR on 1 November 1844 required at least one covered passenger vehicle on a third-class train, the open variety still continued to be used to provide extra seating, or for those fond of fresh air. Although in the twenty-first century the idea of open coaches seems somewhat harsh, it must be remembered that they were comparable to travelling outside on a stagecoach. Some passengers travelling in open third-class coaches wore goggles of fine gauze to protect their eyes from cinders.

Being exposed to the weather certainly had its dangers. On Friday 14 March 1845 John Jonathan, a wire worker aged about fifty, travelled to Bath on the 10.10 a.m. third-class train from Temple Meads. On arrival at Bath, Porter John Fennell found that Mr Jonathan was unable to leave his open coach unaided, and so assisted him to the platform where he expressed a wish for a pint of ale. After the train had left, Fennell carried him down the stairs to street level and asked one of the urchins who frequented the station to take him to William Knee's Railway Station Tavern at 6 Newark Street, 150 yd or so distant. Before crossing Dorchester Street, John Jonathan collapsed and so was carried to Bright's the chemist at 24–25 Southgate Street while medical aid was sought from Dr John Lloyd of 31 Claverton Street. Unfortunately, the efforts of those concerned were in vain and Jonathan died.

An inquest was held the following day at the Full Moon, Southgate Street, during which the jury viewed the very emaciated body. Mrs Jonathan revealed that her husband had suffered illnesses for fifteen years and had been affected with a severe cough on 1 March. As their finances were insufficient to allow both to travel by train, she saw him to Temple Meads. In an effort to keep warm he wore two pairs of trousers, two waistcoats, two body coats and a woollen scarf. Mrs Jonathan then walked to Bath, arriving about 3.00 p.m., and found him deceased.

The jury brought in a verdict 'That the deceased died by the visitation of God, but that his death was accelerated by the inclemency of the weather to which he was exposed in a third class carriage of the Great Western Railway Company, the weather being unusually severe for March'. Ironically, a closed third-class carriage was included in the rake of coaches, but Jonathan's son said that his father (presumably ignorant of Gladstone's Act of the previous August)

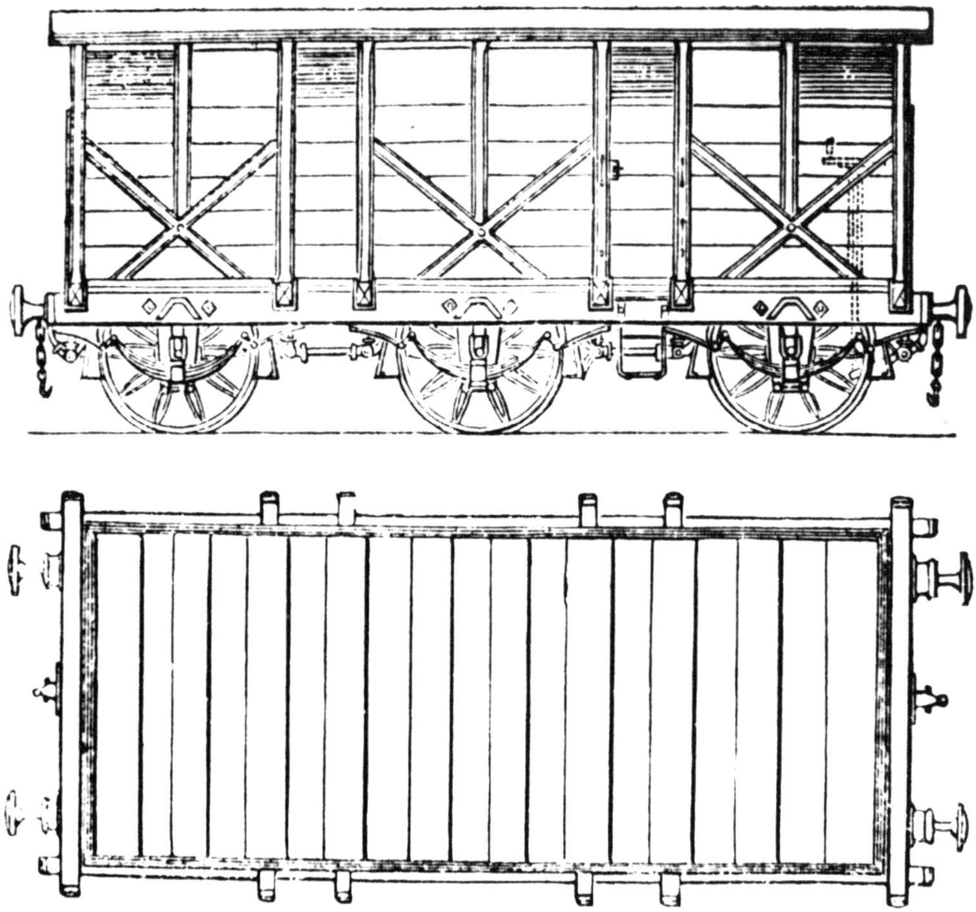

A GWR third-class coach. Seated passengers had no view, no illlumination and only one door each side. (*Pictorial Times*, 1845)

was unaware of any coach for third-class passengers other than the open one. The jury recommended that the GWR provide more closed accommodation for second- and third-class passengers, asking the directors that the promise given at their last half-yearly meeting to close those carriages be quickly carried out.

In deference to public wishes, from 6 June 1842 the GWR discontinued the practice of locking coach doors on the platform side, though it continued to lock them on the off side. Leaving doors unlocked led to wooden barriers being erected at stations to enable tickets to be checked at the termination, instead of the commencement, of a journey. This system meant that the GWR had to ban friends meeting or seeing passengers off, since tricksters, if asked for their tickets, could reply, 'Oh, we're not passengers, we've come here to meet some friends'. With the new system, non-travellers wishing to enter a platform had to be at the station well before the arrival or departure of a train in order to collect a pass written out and stamped by the clerk and then sent to the superintendent, who might be on duty some distance from the booking office.

The *Bath & Cheltenham Gazette*, 30 June 1842 commented:

> Then when you arrived at the top of the stairs at Bath, you found there was no liberty of walking up and down the spacious platform as before, but waiting passengers were railed off in a small enclosure somewhat like a sheep-pen at a country market, the occupants of which were subject to draughts of air from various quarters, without having it in their power to escape colds and coughs by the exercise of walking up and down. We had not been there two minutes before there was an influx into the enclosure of a recruiting corporal and nine recruits, who, being greatly elated with beer, were in what is commonly called 'high feather', and commenced entertaining each other with all kinds of obscenities and blasphemings, in the attempt to avoid the hearing of which, the ladies who were present had to huddle themselves up into the furthest corner of the small enclosure, which however, was by no means sufficiently remote to prevent their ears from being still polluted with the blackguardisms and shocking impieties of the persons to whom we have alluded.

At Bath the GWR had its own fire engine and on 18 June 1841, when a fire broke out at Messrs Williams' brewery on Broad Quay, while the Sun Fire Insurance engine kept on the premises was immediately brought into operation, the GWR machine quickly arrived too, manned by GWR employees, and the flames were soon extinguished.

From June 1844 until 1861 when the GWR took over, Messrs Brotherhood, Chippenham, held the maintenance contract for the section of line Bristol to Reading. He grazed sheep and cattle on embankments and made hay.

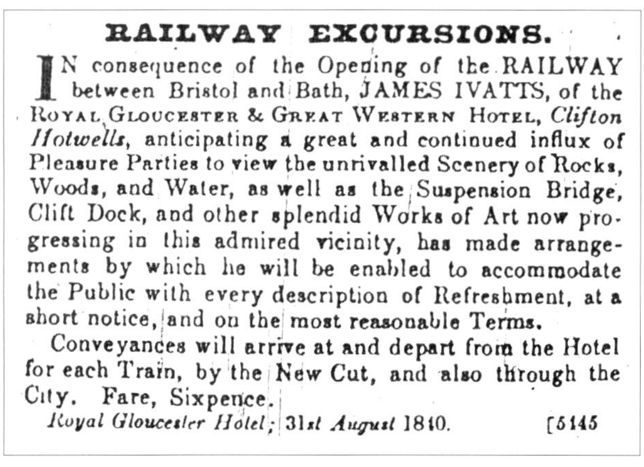

RAILWAY EXCURSIONS.

IN consequence of the Opening of the RAILWAY between Bristol and Bath, JAMES IVATTS, of the ROYAL GLOUCESTER & GREAT WESTERN HOTEL, *Clifton Hotwells*, anticipating a great and continued influx of Pleasure Parties to view the unrivalled Scenery of Rocks, Woods, and Water, as well as the Suspension Bridge, Clift Dock, and other splendid Works of Art now progressing in this admired vicinity, has made arrangements by which he will be enabled to accommodate the Public with every description of Refreshment, at a short notice, and on the most reasonable Terms.

Conveyances will arrive at and depart from the Hotel for each Train, by the New Cut, and also through the City. Fare, Sixpence.

Royal Gloucester Hotel; 31*st August* 1840. [6145

Advertisement in the *Bath & Cheltenham Gazette* 1 September 1840.

Chapter Six

Description of the Line

Temple Meads station had to be constructed 15 ft above ground level to give clearance to waterborne traffic passing under the Floating Harbour Bridge immediately east of the station. The site was only about half a mile from the heart of the city and to have taken the railway any closer would have been expensive as the land was already built up with houses and commercial premises, and influential landowners may have been alienated. Temple Meads in the 1830s consisted of open fields, a cattle market and cholera burial ground, and the fact that the 19 acres of meadows were owned by Bristol Corporation facilitated the purchase. William Brunton's 1830 Bath & Bristol Railway envisaged a terminus near Old Market, while the Basingstoke & Bath favoured Redcliffe Wharf for goods and the nearby Somerset Square for passengers. Brunel took a subcommittee of three directors to the base of St Mary Redcliffe Church spire to survey the options and Temple Meads was the only one with space for development.

The fact that trains at Temple Meads used a first-storey level allowed Brunel to design the station like a Tudor mansion, thus giving a grand finale to the style that characterised many of the bridges, tunnels and stations westwards from Bath. Behind the splendid Bath stone Tudor façade facing Temple Gate were GWR offices. Above the centre oriel were the arms of the cities of Bristol and London, adopted by the GWR for its own arms. Flanking the façade were two gateways, the one on the left giving access to the departure side and having a clock, while that on the right led from the arrival side and no timepiece was deemed necessary. The latter gateway was probably removed when the covered tramway terminus, formerly a stable for 208 tramway horses, adjacent to the train shed was electrified on 13 July 1899. The tramway was most convenient, obviating, as it did, a walk with heavy luggage to or from Temple Gate, not to mention useful for those on a circular tour from South Wales to Temple Meads by train, then tram to Hotwells and Campbell's steamer back across the Channel. The tram rails, though not the tram station, still remain, seventy years after the system's closure.

On the ground floor of the departure side of Brunel's building were the booking offices. Passengers used stairs to gain the platforms, but luggage was taken up by

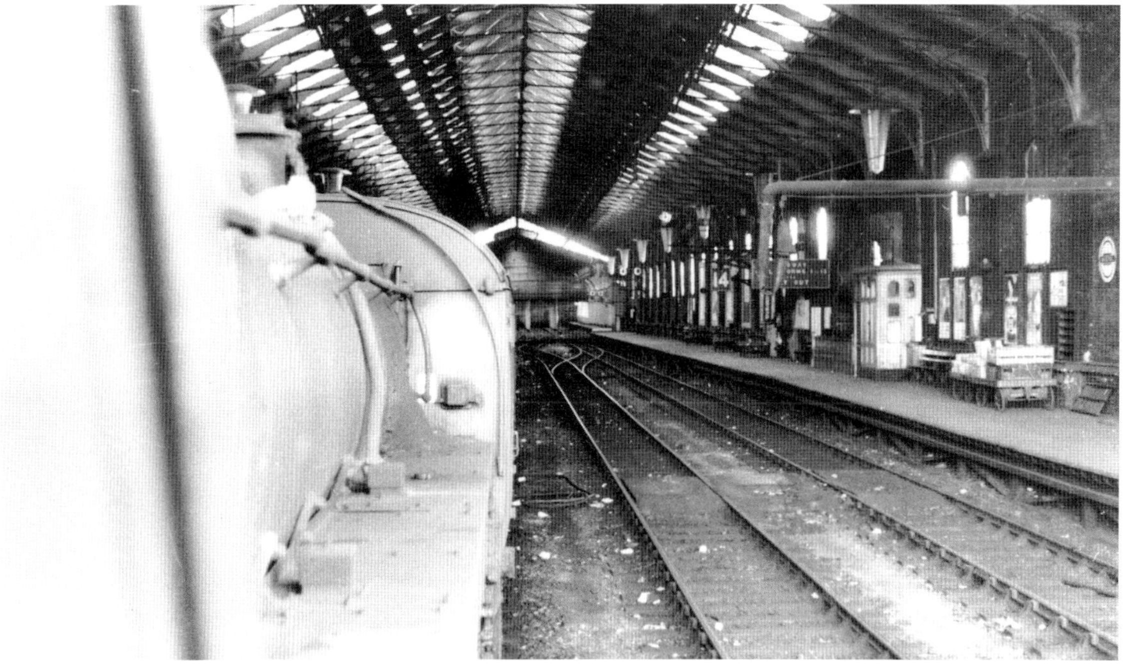

The terminal train shed, Temple Meads, October 1963, viewed from a locomotive footplate. Notice on the right the unusually long arm of a water crane. (*W. F. Grainger*)

hydraulic lift. The train shed was truly impressive. Its timber cantilever roof had a span of 72 ft unsupported by any cross tie or abutment. Each principal beam met its counterpart in the centre of the roof, the weight carried on octagonal columns and the tail ends held down by the side walls and, because the beams did not press against each other, there was no outward thrust. From a practical point of view, the octagonal piers were rather close to the platform edge and offered little clearance when coach doors were opened, but matters were improved when the broad gauge was abolished and platforms could be widened. Beyond the terminal end of the platforms was the low, flat-ceilinged sector table area, the office block above being supported on plain iron columns. It was not unknown for steam from the engines to seep up through the floorboards.

When the Bristol & Exeter Railway opened to Bridgwater on 25 May 1841, it first used the GWR's terminus at Bristol, which proved not entirely satisfactory as it involved the time-wasting procedure of backing trains into or out of the station. The Bristol & Gloucester Railway, opened on 8 July 1844, also used Temple Meads. The station then became rather overcrowded, but matters were eased the following year when the Bristol & Exeter Railway opened its own terminus at right angles to that of the GWR. A double-track curve linked the throats of the two stations and, as an 'express platform' was provided by the B&ER on the Up curve, through trains no longer needed to reverse. This platform was used by trains in both directions.

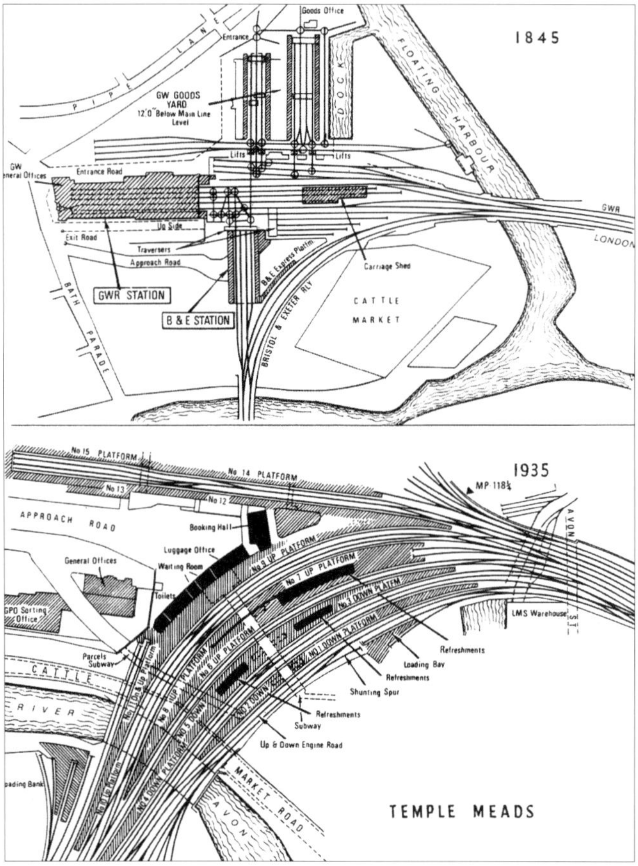

Plans of Bristol Temple Meads and its environs.

In 1863 the two platforms at Temple Meads had to cater for GWR trains running to and from London and the West of England, the Westbury and New Passage Pier branches, and the Midland Railway's Birmingham services. Two years previously, the GWR had promoted a plan for extending the three railways to a new central station in Queen Square. When this suggestion was rejected by a narrow majority of the city council, the three companies decided to build a new joint station at Temple Meads instead, and on 19 June 1865 they obtained an Act for carrying out this work. New capital was restricted to a total of £150,000 in shares and £50,000 in loans, taken up jointly by the three companies. However, because of disputes regarding the proportionate division of its cost, another six years passed before work began and, during the interim, the branch to Portishead opened. In 1871 new roads, Victoria Street and Temple Street, were opened to create a better link between Temple Meads and the city centre.

Sir Matthew Digby Wyatt, a friend who had assisted Brunel with the 1854 Paddington station, was architect for the Temple Meads enlargement and carried out the work most skilfully, blending the old and new superbly. The unpretentious wooden B&ER terminus was demolished and a great curved train shed with a span of 125 ft was built on the site of the former B&ER express platform, creating a station V-shape in plan. Vernon & Evans of the Central Iron Works, Cheltenham, were appointed contractors for the metalwork. Brunel's original terminal train shed was lengthened in similar style to the initial building, but with metal roof supports and thin ties.

A wide, gently rising carriageway approached the architecturally pleasing main entrance on the Up side, with offices and a 100-ft-high clock tower of Draycot stone approximately on the site of the former B&ER terminus. The approach road to the Down side curved around the B&ER office block and passed below the line. Francis Fox of the B&ER shared in the design, the green and gold exterior canopy virtually identical with that which he designed for Weston-super-Mare.

Each company had its own booking hall within the Great Hall, passengers entering by separate doors: the MR on the left, the B&ER centre and the GWR right, a scroll above each bearing the appropriate initials. Inside the entrance doors were porters' booths built of pine, but the imposing pine entrance doors had to be left open in winter and caused the hall to be cold and draughty. They have been replaced with glass swing doors.

A new Down through platform, the first section of the new station, was brought into use on Monday 6 July 1874 and the whole completed on 1 January 1878. It now had seven platforms. No. 1, the Down main, was 804 ft in length, and Nos 2 and 3 each of 429 ft. No. 2, an island platform, was used mainly by terminating Down MR trains, and passengers could walk straight across the platform to a Down GWR train to continue their journey. No. 3 was the GWR Up main; No. 4 the MR departure platform, also taking in the former engine shed roads; and No. 5 the lengthened southern platform of the original terminus and used for New Passage, or later for South Wales trains. Platform 7 was for the arrival and departure of Clifton Down and Avonmouth trains. The main refreshment rooms were in the apex between the old and new stations, though small refreshment rooms were provided on the main Down platform. Temple Meads had two carriage sheds, one on the Up side at the west end and the other on the Down side at the east end. The former was accessed by turntable and a tight curve, while the latter shed could only be reached via a turntable. Both sheds closed by about 1920.

Despite the enlargement, traffic grew to such an extent that congestion still occurred. A report made in 1876, two years before its official completion, stated that 'The station is clearly much less than adequate for the amount of traffic to be handled'. One improvement brought into use on 2 October 1892 was a widened bridge over the New Cut so that the No. 1 platform could be lengthened and a Down bay provided. The abolition of broad gauge in 1892 offered more space within Wyatt's train shed and an additional island platform opened north of the existing one on 15 January 1899. In 1902 a timber footbridge was built in Brunel's train shed, ruining the end-to-end vista, but this was replaced by a subway in the 1930s.

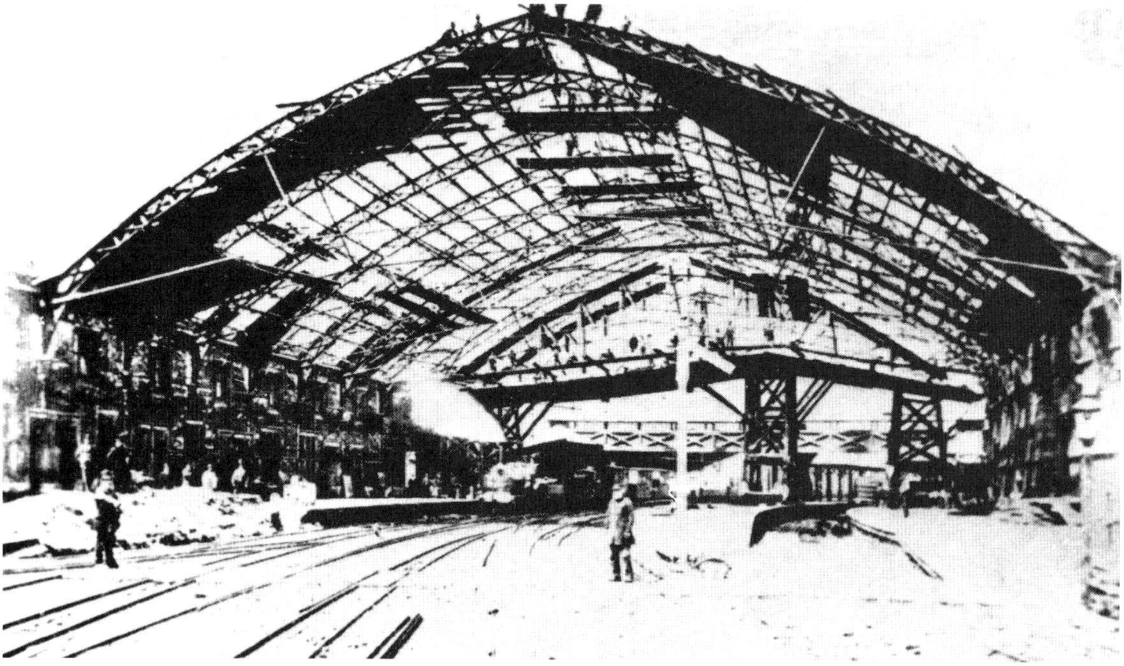

View north to Sir Matthew Digby Wyatt's train shed under construction, August 1876. (*Author's Collection*)

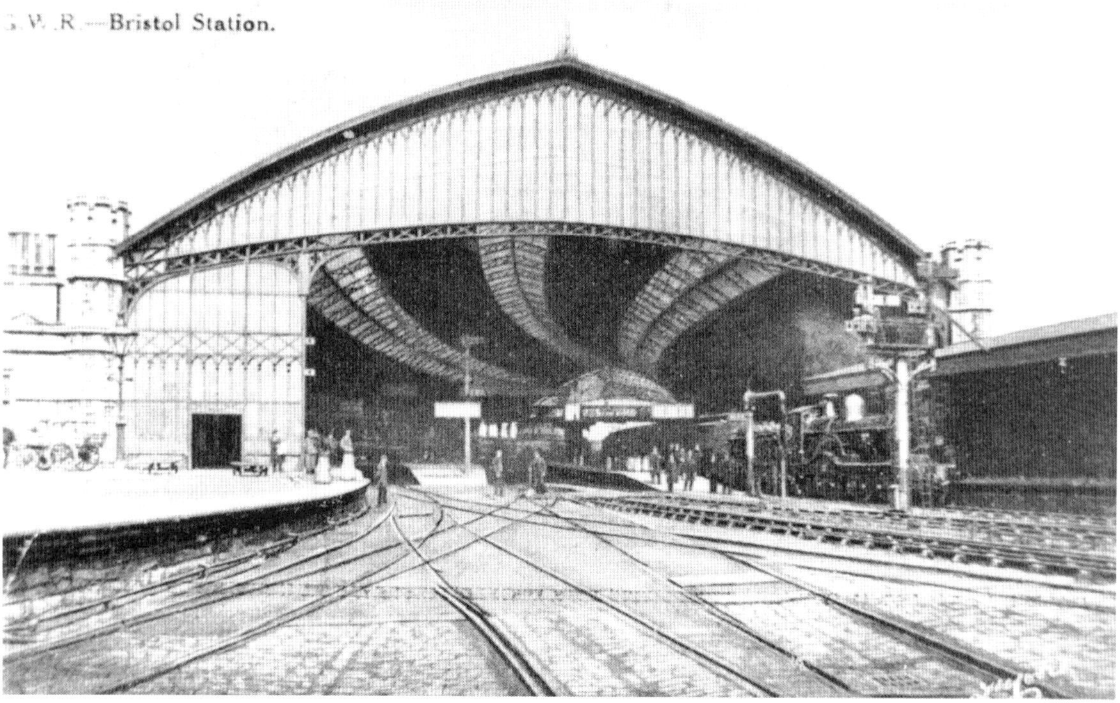

View north to Wyatt's train shed *c.* 1900. Notice the paved area in the foreground to facilitate shunting with horses. A 4-2-2 heads a Down train. (*Author's Collection*)

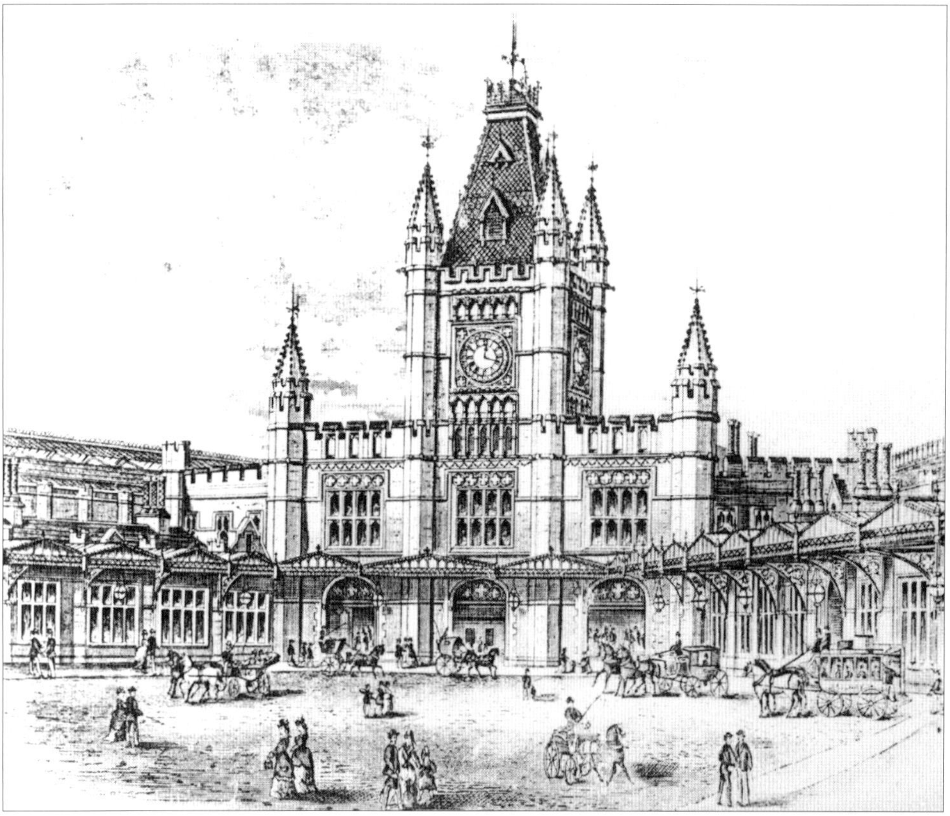

Above: The entrance to Temple Meads *c.* 1879 following Wyatt's extension. Notice the horse bus, right. (*Author's Collection*)

Right: The ecclesiastical-looking window in the entrance hall, Temple Meads, 4 September 1986. (*Author*)

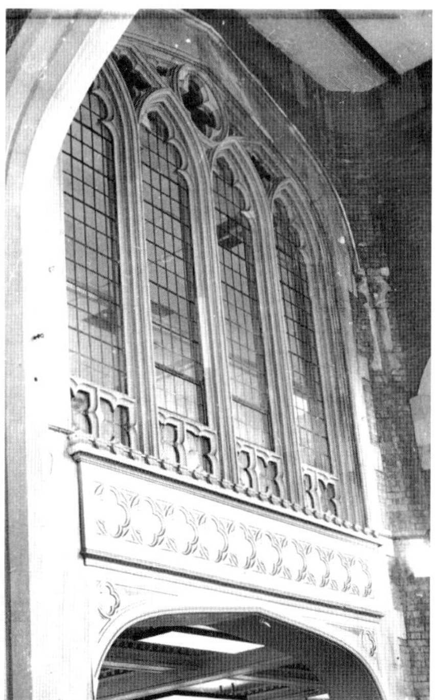

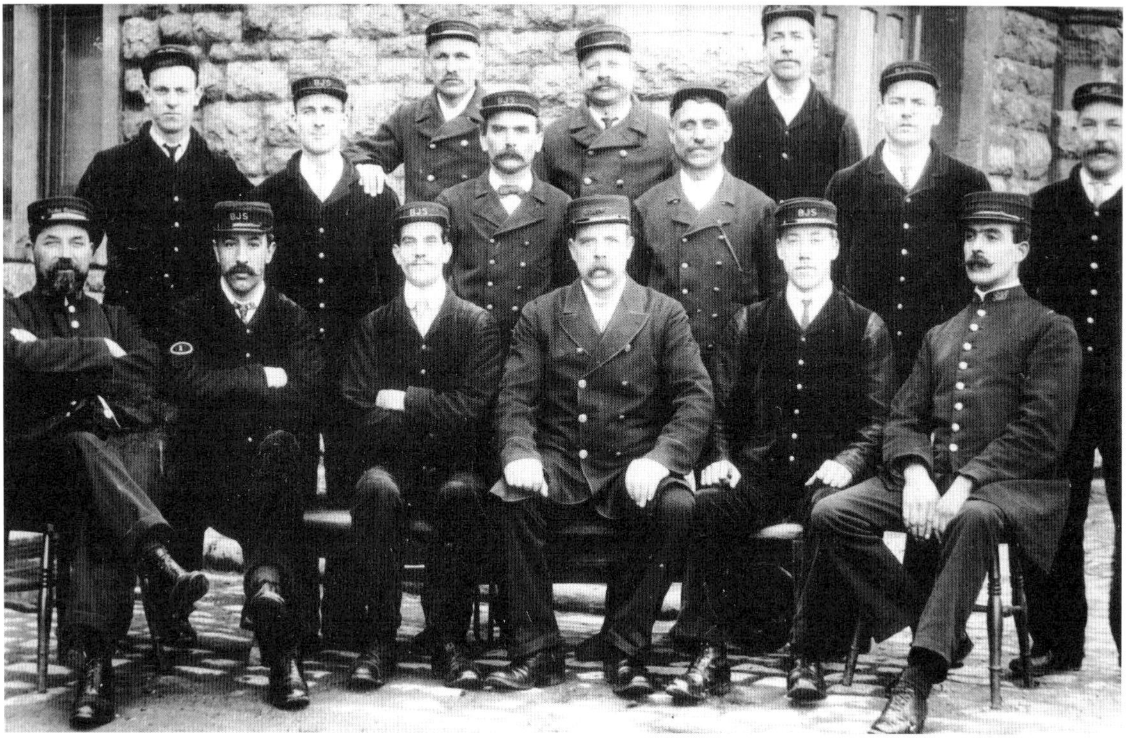

Temple Meads Joint station staff with 'BJS' on their caps. The Inspector is seated in the centre of the front row, while at both ends is a Ticket Examiner. (*M. J. Tozer Collection*)

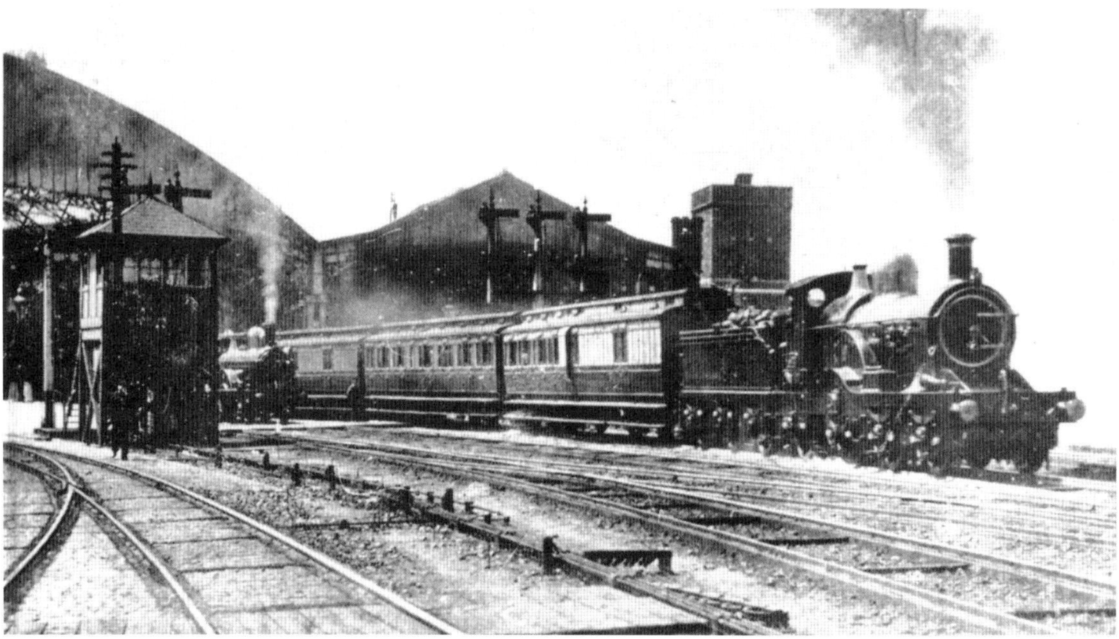

The Up Cornishman leaves Temple Meads *c.* 1895 behind a 4-2-2 locomotive. 'G' signal box is on the left, opened 1878 and closed *c.* 1898. (*Author's Collection*)

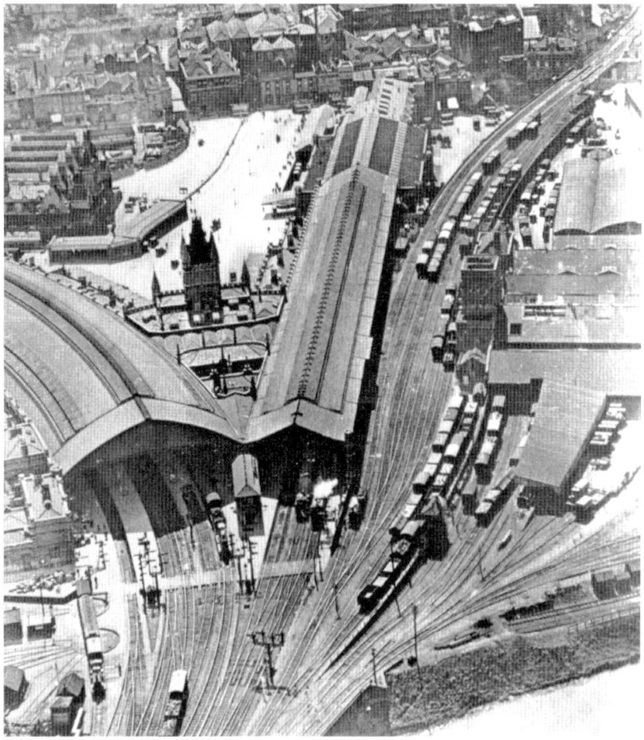

Temple Meads from the air *c.* 1925. The terminal platforms are in the centre, Wyatt's train shed on the left and the goods depot on the right. (*Author's Collection*)

Because of complaints of congestion, on 11 August 1906 Temple Meads was the subject of a report. Although Platform 1 had a length of 963 ft ramp-to-ramp, only 574 ft could be used without blocking the entrance to the engine shed and the rail exit from No. 2 platform. Other platform lengths were: No. 2 – 510 ft; bay platform – 370 ft; No. 3 – 428 ft; No. 4 – 564 ft; in Brunel's train shed No. 5 – 614 ft; No. 6 – 350 ft; and Nos 7 and 8 – 1,025 ft. The report stated that MR trains used No. 2 and, especially during the summer, they overlapped the platform at its eastern end by three to four coaches; furthermore, to exchange vehicles with the GWR, the train was required to draw forward and thus foul No. 1 platform. Frequently, a string of engines occupied No. 3 platform road and stood there until they could be disposed. At times congestion was so severe that on one side of Temple Meads trains stood block-to-block from Bath to Bristol and on the other side from Yatton to Bristol.

In 1914 the GWR decided to extend the station and install labour-saving signalling, but these plans were scuppered by the outbreak of the First World War. By the 1920s, when improvements had been made to the standard of living, traffic had grown to such an extent that on Bank Holidays the service was horrendous. Trains could be held in block from Highbridge waiting for a platform at Temple Meads and often had to stand outside the station for an hour. On summer Saturdays between 1920 and 1930 it was not unknown for local trains to take two hours to travel the last mile to reach a platform and on at least

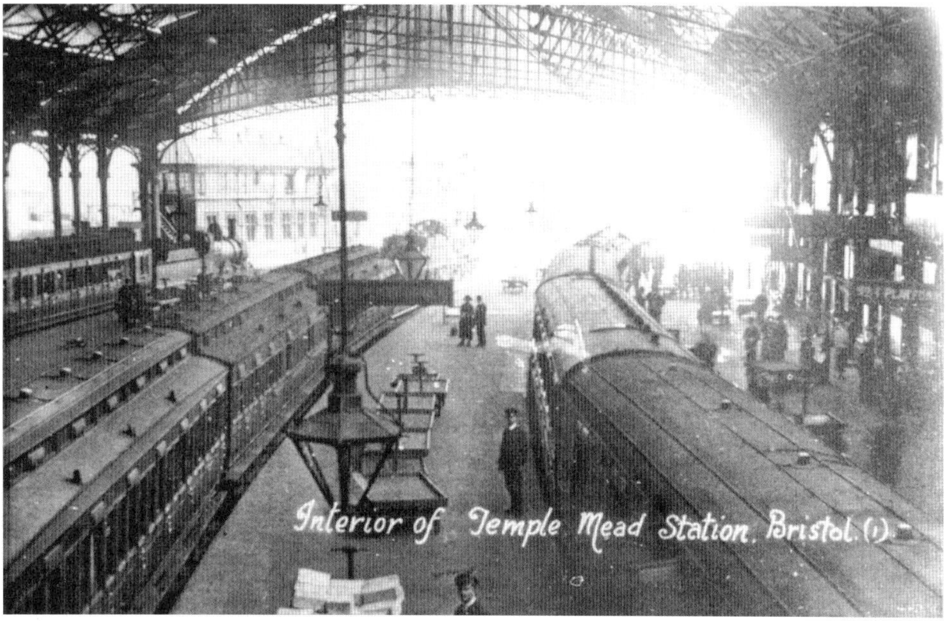

View east from the footbridge inside Wyatt's train shed. (*Author's Collection*)

one occasion, the time was three hours twenty minutes. The Joint companies could not be blamed for this state of affairs, as there was no room for expansion except over the cattle market sited on the inside of the curve and this was owned by Bristol Corporation, which was not anxious to sell.

When the Labour Government took power following the General Election of 1929, unemployment stood at over one rmillion. J. H. Thomas, a former railwayman and Lord Privy Seal, was responsible for drafting the Loans & Guarantees (1929) Act whereby the government would guarantee and pay the interest for two, three or four years on the capital expended on a scheme of development. The GWR was one of the first railway companies to seize advantage of the scheme and by the late autumn of 1929 had proposed a capital expenditure of £4½ million, offering direct employment for 200,000 man-months. Bristol was part of this scheme, the work including the enlargement of Temple Meads passenger station; quadrupling the line between Temple Meads and Portishead Junction; reconstruction and enlargement of Bath Road locomotive depot; and the provision of additional sidings.

P. E. Culverhouse was the architect, and the main contractors, Shanks & McEwan, Glasgow, commenced work in 1930. Temple Meads was more than doubled in size, the number of platforms increased from nine to fifteen, and now took in much of the cattle market. Some of the platforms had scissors crossovers midway so that they could be used either by one long train, or by two shorter ones. The longest platform, the combined Nos 9 and 10 at 1,366 ft, was the tenth longest in the country, and a great improvement on 920 ft, previously the longest at Temple Meads. The collective length of the platforms at the enlarged station totalled 2 miles.

All the principal platforms were provided with refreshment and waiting rooms. Passengers reached their platform via a 300-ft-long, 30-ft-wide subway, which also provided access to hairdressing salons and baths. Parcels were carried on electric trolleys along a dedicated subway. In 1935 well over four million parcels were handled at the station every year, the outgoing number being 40 per cent in excess of the inflow.

The new buildings were faced with white or brown Carrara glazed bricks, imitating marble and set on a grey concrete plinth, the platforms' roofs being of the 'umbrella' type. The two rather narrow island platforms under Wyatt's train shed were removed to allow the old Up and Down through platforms to be widened, and while this work took place, all Up and Down traffic used the new platforms, Nos 1 to 5, built on the site of the former carriageway to the Down side. These new platforms came into use on 26 February 1934, the day all platforms were renumbered. The platforms within Wyatt's train shed were reopened on 25 March 1935; this almost completed the work of extending the station, which now had five Up and five Down through platforms, a bay for Portishead trains, and four platforms in the old terminus. The booking office, set back to offer a spacious circulating area, was provided with a modern cast-iron and bronze front. Rather surprisingly, especially in view of the fact that Temple Meads had Brush arc lighting for a short period circa 1880, gas lighting was used for the new platforms; during this period this type of lighting was more likely to be taken out and replaced with electric lighting but here it remained until 1960 when fluorescent tubes were installed.

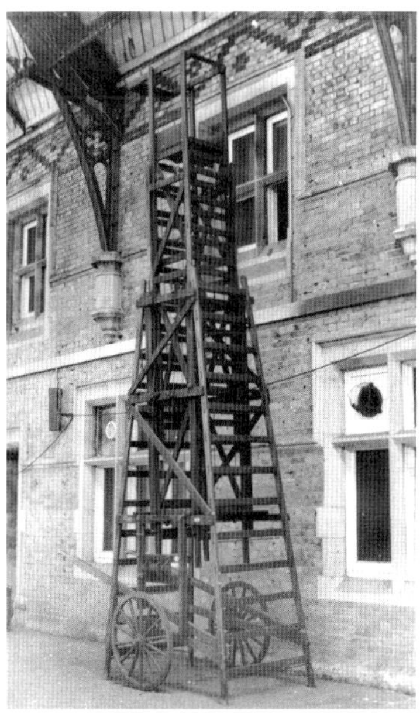

Temple Meads' tower wagon, 8 May 1987. (*Author*)

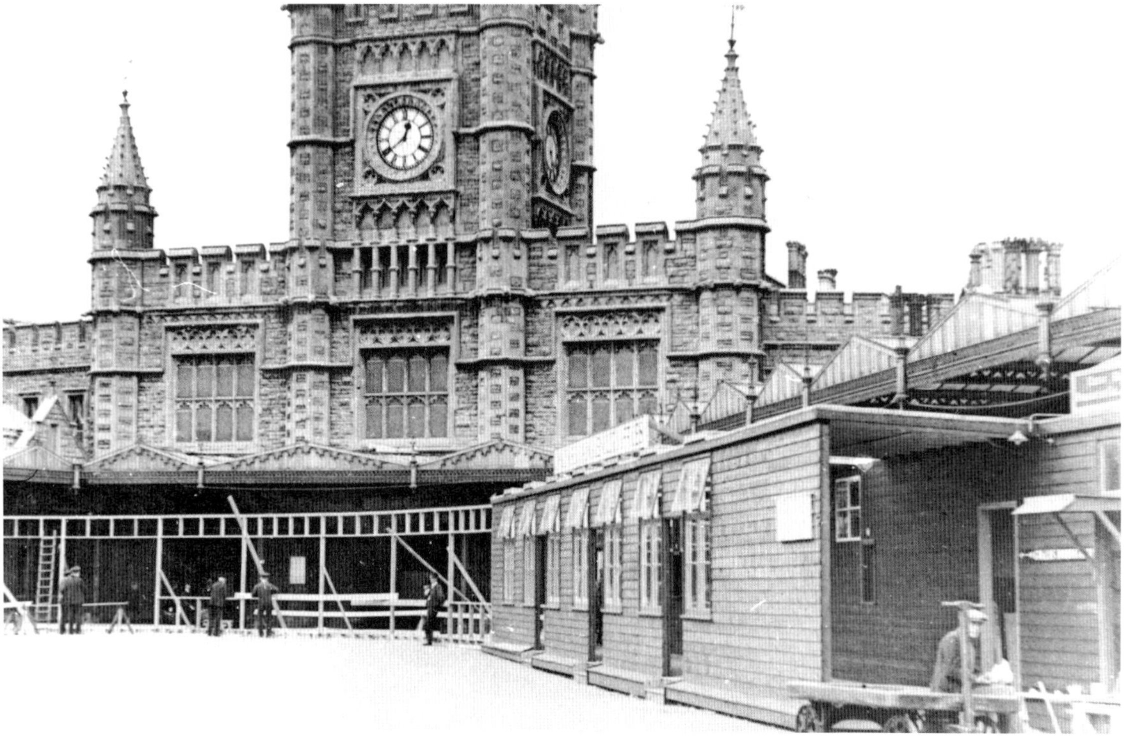

Temporary office accommodation provided *c.* 1933 during the reconstruction of Temple Meads. (*Author's Collection*)

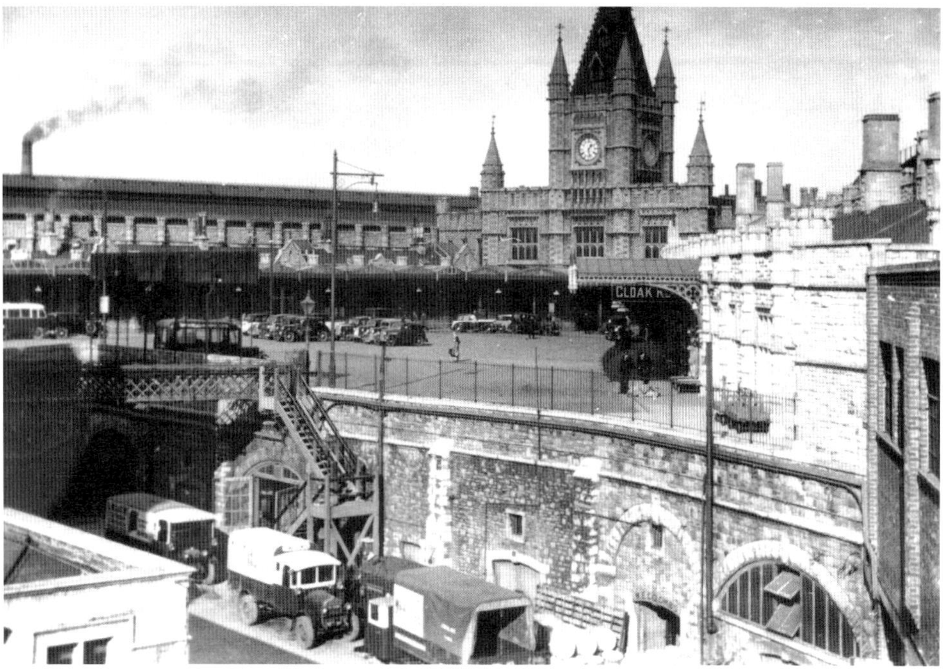

Temple Meads, 1937. Notice the parcel delivery vans at the lower level. (*Author's Collection*)

With the abolition of many stopping trains in the 1960s, the platforms in Brunel's train shed became surplus to requirements and on 12 September 1965 the shed was closed to rail traffic and became a car park the following year. Now one of the oldest surviving terminal stations in the country, it is a Grade I listed building. Pigeons and starlings found Wyatt's train shed an ideal roost. As the droppings from these unpaying guests were objectionable, from 1969 nets were hung from the 75-ft-high roof apex to just above rolling stock roof level, thus keeping out most of the birds. When in 1991 the train shed was repainted, details were highlighted in different colours to bring out the features. At the same time the subway was retiled to offer a more modern appearance.

Between 1998 and 2001 the Grade I listed building had its external façades and clock tower restored and the station was generally refurbished. Ticket barriers were installed and it reverted to being a 'closed' station again in September 2002. The final night of mail operations was on 12 May 2000, and by 2004 the station closed from about 01.30 until 04.30

Unlike most stations, Temple Meads had a superintendent rather than a stationmaster, the difference being that the former was responsible only for railway operation and the fabric of the building; other duties normally undertaken by a stationmaster were covered by separate posts such a goods superintendent, guards' inspector, parcel agent and passenger manager. As Temple Meads was a joint station, the post of superintendent was filled alternately by a man from the GWR and LMS. All porters were appointed by the GWR and received an average of about £1 daily in tips; they were not at all anxious to achieve the higher grade post of shunter because when learning that new job, they were still paid porters' wages and received no tips to supplement it. Hence the station was always short of shunters.

In 1876 Temple Meads was controlled by two signal boxes: 'B', an overhead box on the east bank of the Floating Harbour, and 'C' at the fork of Brunel's and Wyatt's train sheds. In 1878 'G' at the east end of the platform replaced 'C' box, and 'F' box opened at the south end of the station. By 1909 the layout was controlled by four boxes, two of which each contained 105 levers. The 1930s extension demanded replacement signalling so coloured lights were introduced. Temple Meads East box, the largest on the GWR, had 368 levers, twenty-three of these spare as the LMS refused to contribute towards the cost of transferring the frame from the Old Station box in Brunel's train shed and so this was retained and continued to use manual signalling. The East box was continuously manned by three special-class signalmen and a booking boy. There were no fewer than twenty-three block bells, each of sufficiently different tone to enable a trained ear to identify it. The box had three storeys, while the West and Loco boxes at the other end of the station had but two. Built in red brick with Flemish bond relieved by white stone lintels, the architecture of the three boxes still looked modern when replaced thirty-five years later by an MAS (Multiple Aspect Signalling) box situated, perhaps rather insensitively, at the mouth of Brunel's

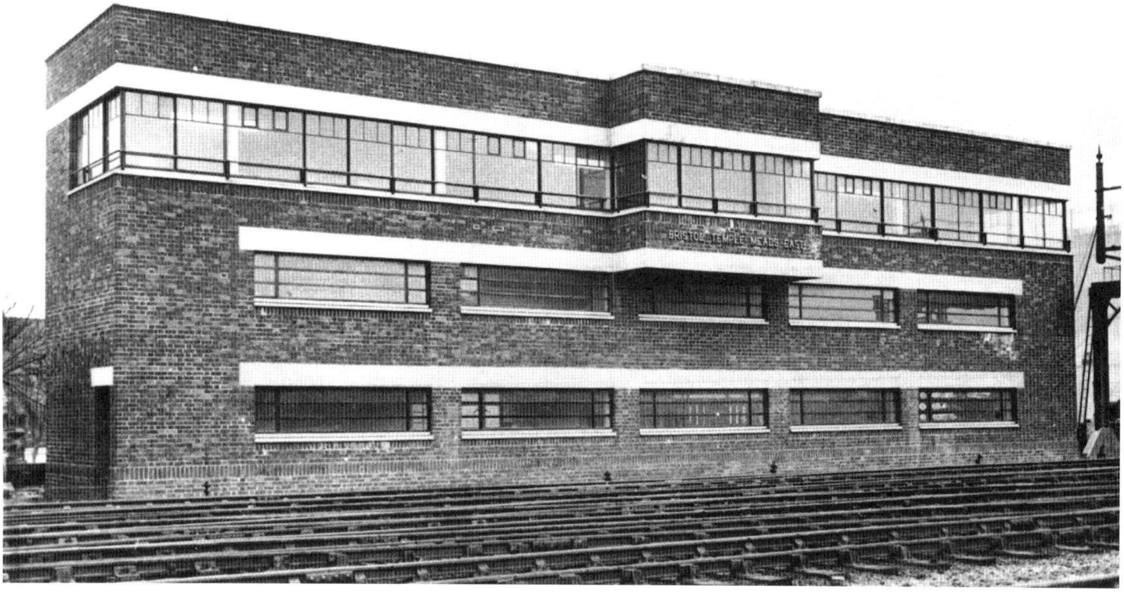

The well-designed exterior of Bristol East signal box, 26 March 1935. (*Author's Collection*)

train shed. Temple Meads West box had 328 levers, twenty bells and was also manned by three men and a lad.

Immediately east of Temple Meads the line crossed the Floating Harbour and on the far bank passed over the extreme end of the MR Avonside goods depot. Not far beyond the shunting neck of Temple Meads goods depot, the MR's Gloucester line branched off and immediately beyond was South Wales Junction, originally serving the line to New Passage Pier and the ferry to Portskewett and later giving access to the Severn Tunnel and the line to Wootton Bassett via Badminton. South Wales Junction is the western apex of a triangular junction, the northern being Dr Day's Bridge Junction and currently named Bristol Loop Junction. Between the MR and South Wales lines were three buildings later to become part of the EWS Barton Hill depot. At the base of the triangle was the broad to standard-gauge transfer shed and Kingsland Road sidings. Once a major yard with twenty-three roads, it dealt with a variety of traffic including sixty wagons of coal unloaded by grab daily for the nearby gasworks. Bristol Loop Junction is sited on the bridge over The Feeder and immediately beyond was North Somerset Junction signal box where, until its closure on 14 July 1968, the line to Radstock and Frome curved southwards. It also gave access to the Bristol Avoiding Line, opened 10 April 1892, which allowed nonstop traffic to evade Temple Meads. It was particularly useful on summer Saturdays when trains ran through from the Midlands to the West and many of these specials were headed by mixed traffic engines from St Philip's Marsh shed adjacent to this relief line.

A glue factory sited near North Somerset Junction box emitted such an appalling smell that some signalmen smoked pipes to make the atmosphere more pleasant. East Depot Junction was where goods trains coming off the North Somerset line could run direct into the East Depot. This curve was taken out of use on 20 July 1970. Immediately beyond were three parallel bridges across the Avon: north to south was the Up Viaduct at 186 yd; the Main River Viaduct was 108 yd; and the Main Down Viaduct 141 yd. The latter fell out of use following the closure on 7 August 1967 of Bristol East Depot described on p. 129.

Bristol No. 1 Tunnel, 326 yd in length through red sandstone, had its sides 'neatly trimmed and dressed; any hollow, formed of careless working, filled up with rubble masonry, well-bonded into the natural rock'. Its west portal was in Norman style with massive cable-twist moulding. The tunnel was 30 ft wide and 35 ft high at its entrances, with a general height of 30 ft above rail level and its greatest depth below the surface of the ground was 76 ft. The four ventilation shafts for carrying off the fumes of the blasting powder were all filled when the tunnel was completed. Its east portal was similar to that of No. 2 Tunnel, but without the tower. The necessity to create shunting necks on the Up side to serve the East Depot demanded demolition of the tunnel and the widening of the resulting cutting. This work, taking a year, was finished on Sunday 31 March 1889 and had been completed without interrupting traffic. East Depot signal box looked very precarious supported on four girders let into the vertical side of the cutting, and its access stairway was roofed to protect users from falling rocks.

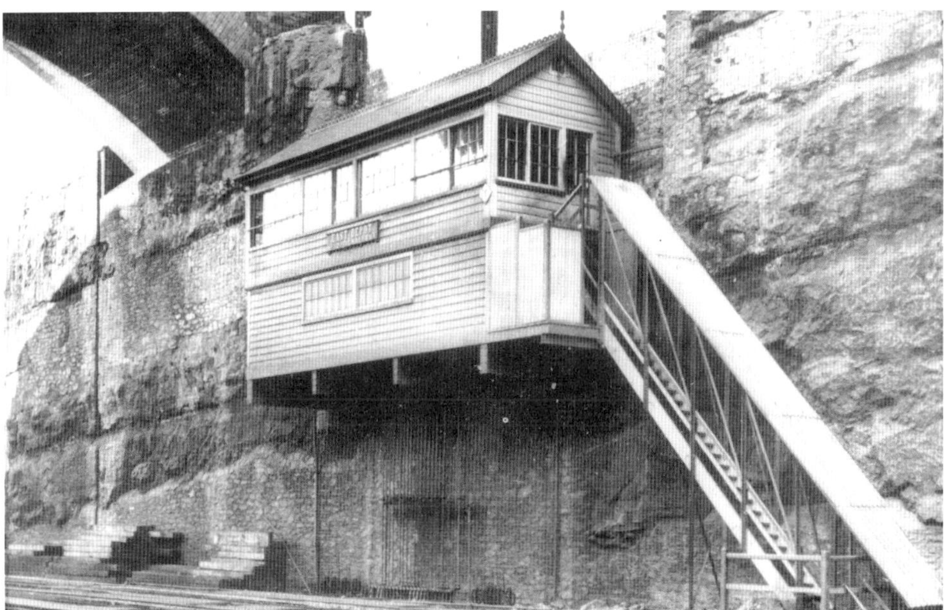

Bristol East Depot signal box, supported on four girders let into the vertically-sided cutting. The stairway is protected against falling rock. (*Author's Collection*)

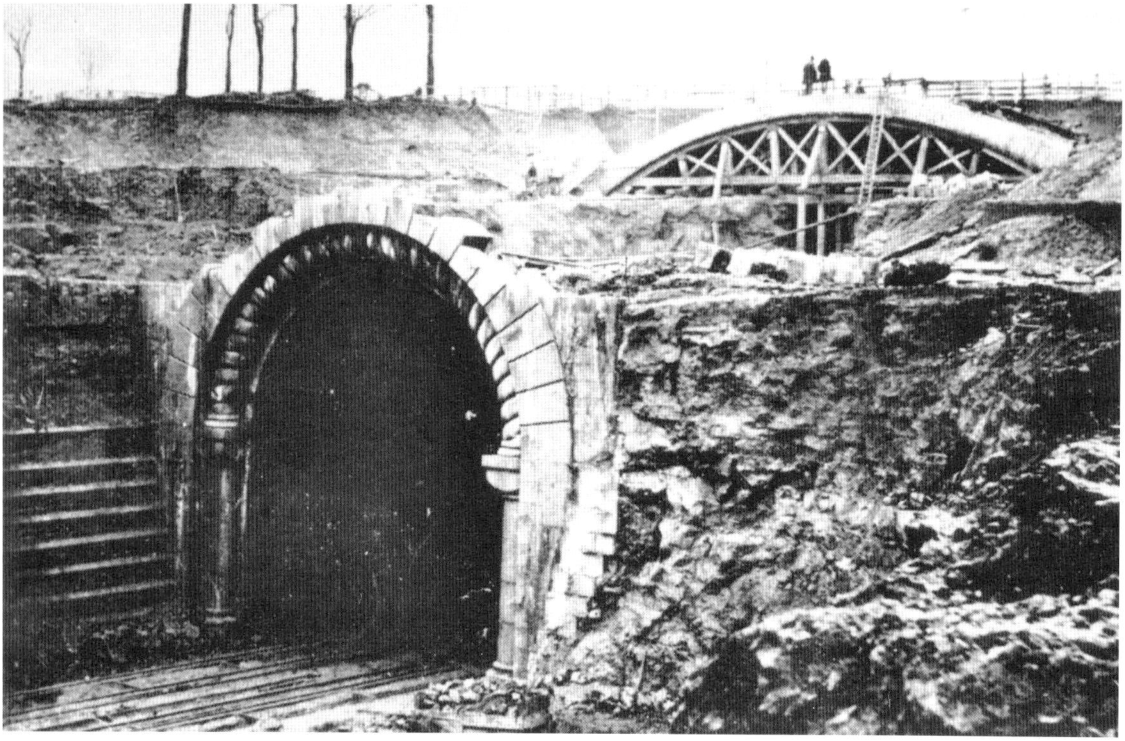

Bristol No. 1 Tunnel being demolished and Langdon Road Bridge (beyond) under construction to span the resultant cutting. (*Author's Collection*)

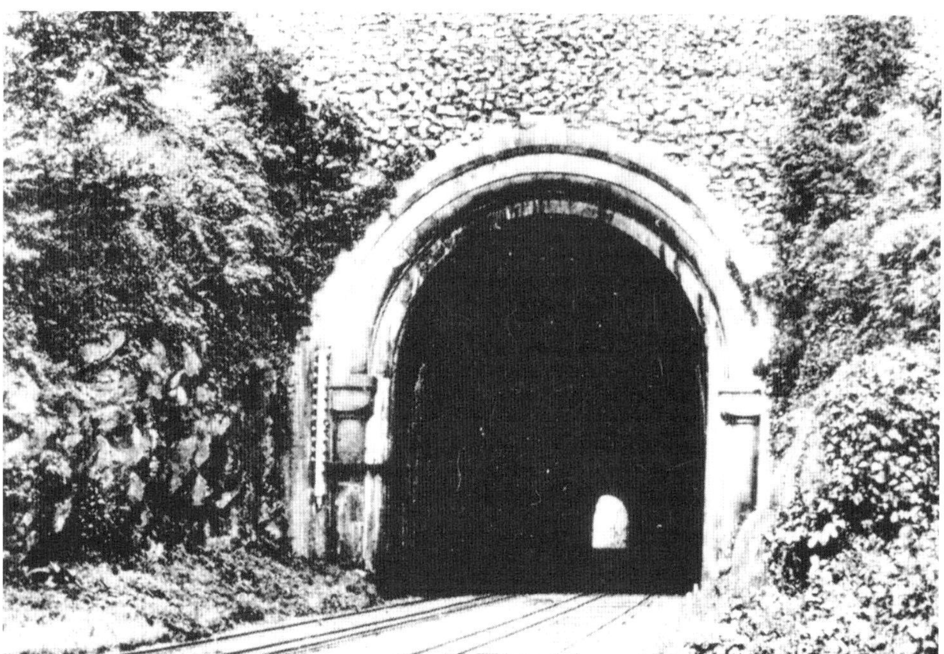

The east portal of Bristol No. 1 Tunnel *c.* 1887. Notice the mixed gauge track. (*Author's Collection*)

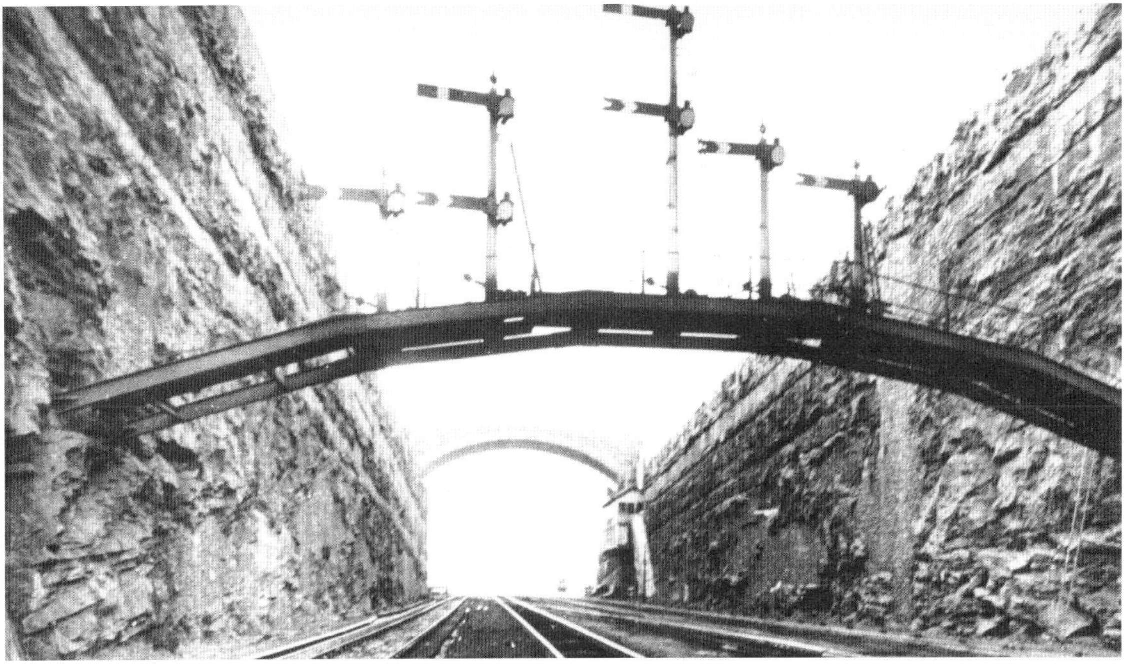

View from St Anne's Park through the cutting, formerly Bristol No. 1 Tunnel, towards Bristol East Depot. (*Author's Collection*)

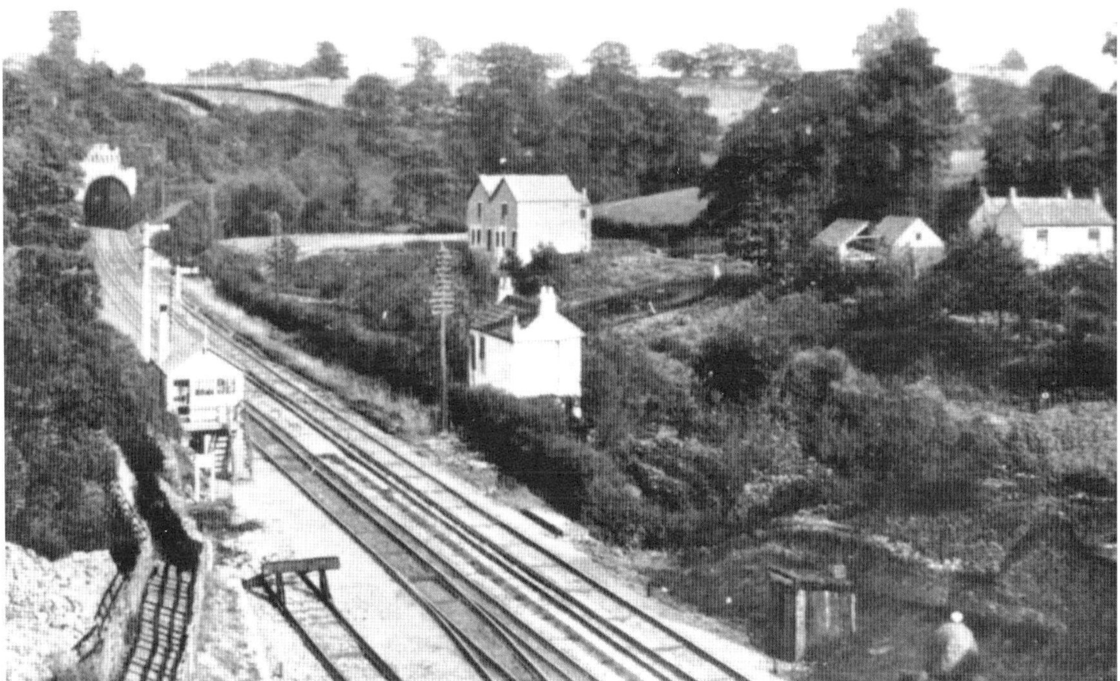

The site of St Anne's Park station *c.* 1890. Bristol No. 2 Tunnel is in the distance. The 'apple and pear' can be seen in the lower right-hand corner. (*Author's Collection*)

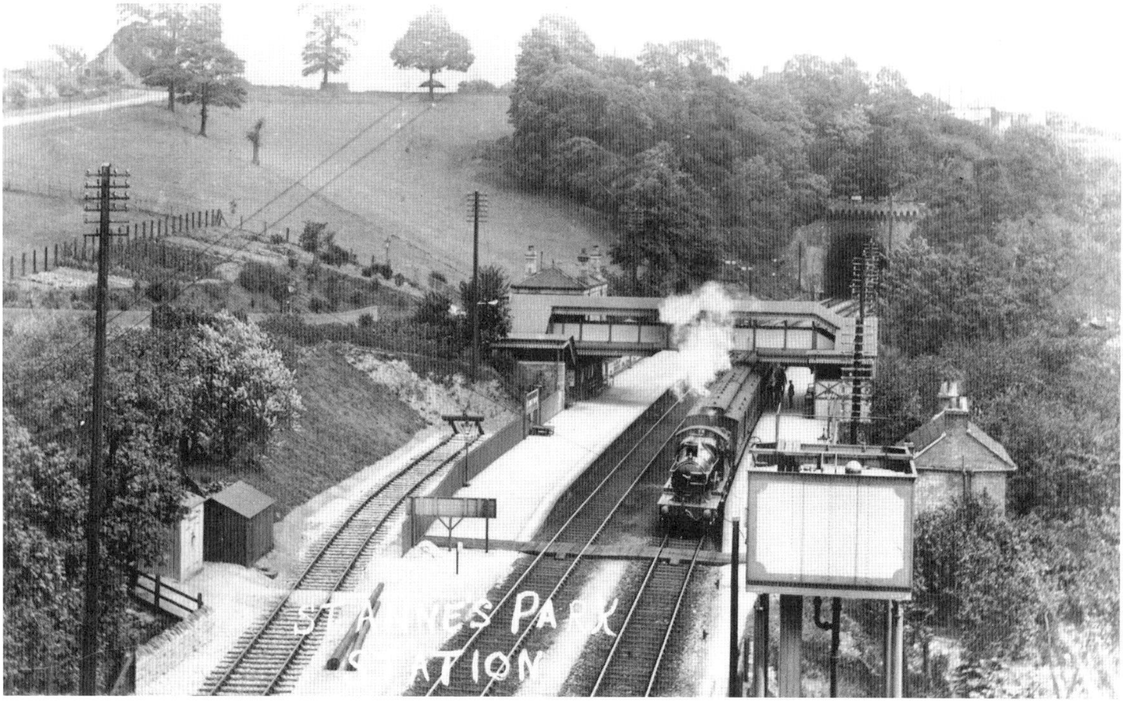

A Down stopping train hauled by a City class 4-4-0 calls at St Anne's Park *c.* 1907. The west portal of Bristol No. 2 Tunnel is beyond the platforms. (*Author's Collection*)

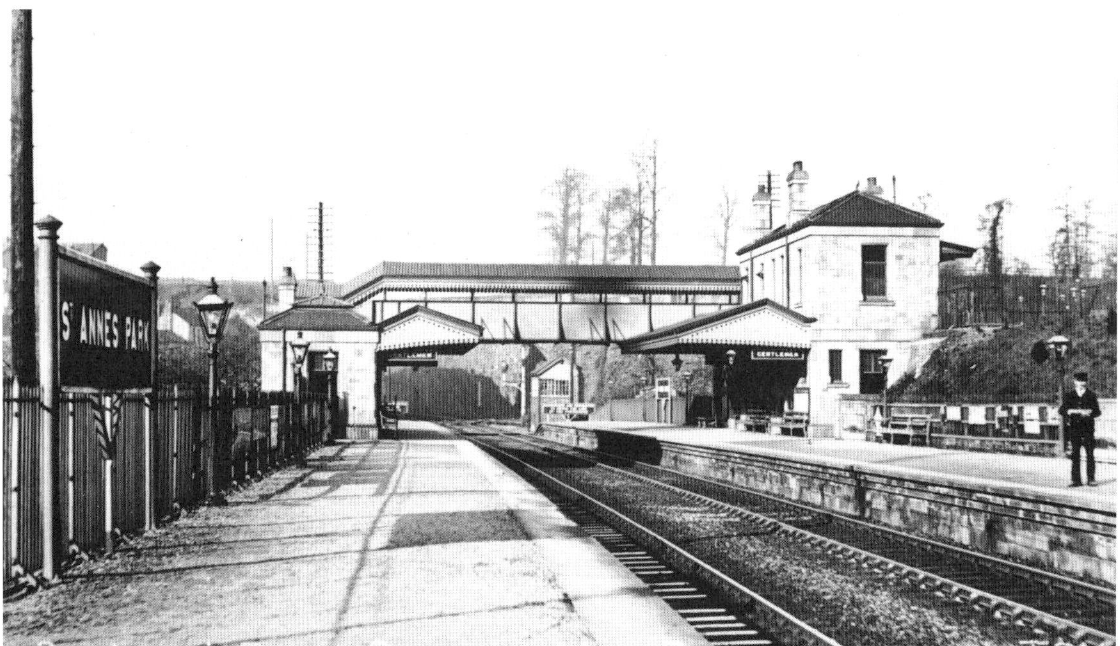

St Anne's Park, view Down *c.* 1908. The signal box closed 4 February 1909. (*M. J. Tozer Collection*)

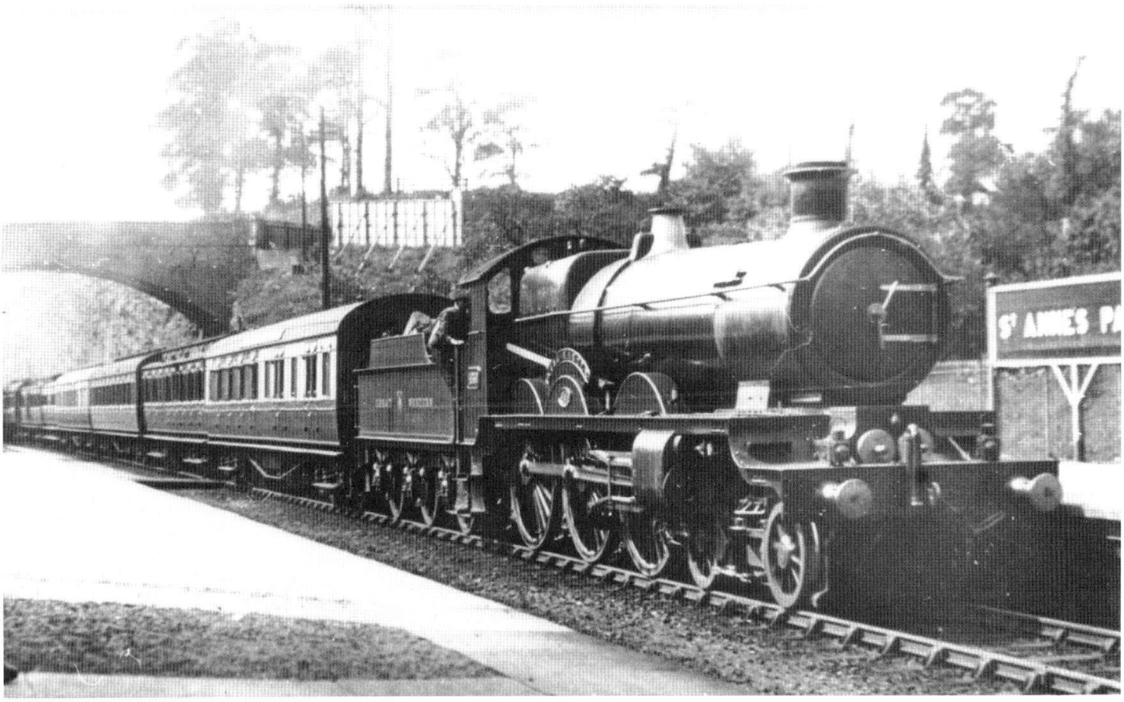

Above: Star class 4-6-0 No. 4030 *King Harold* passes through St Anne's Park with an Up express composed of a great variety of coaches. (*Author's Collection*)

Right: View east *c.* 1880 from the site of St Anne's Park station to the west portal of Bristol No. 2 tunnel. The track is mixed gauge. (*Author's Collection*)

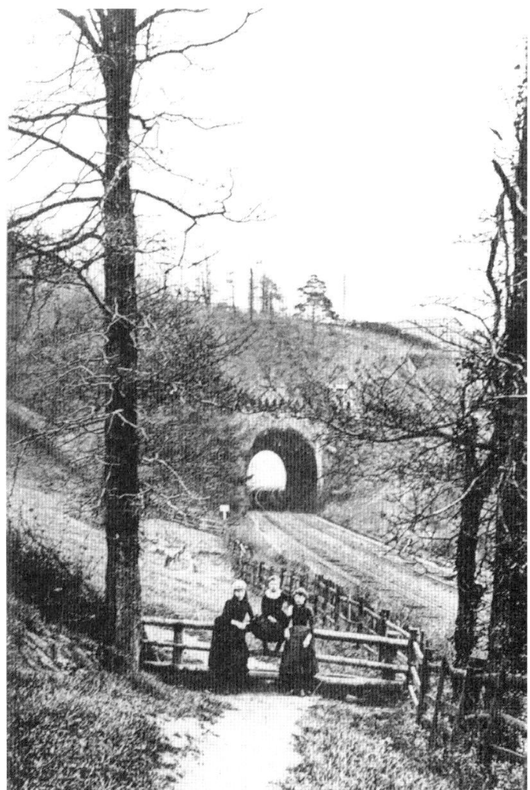

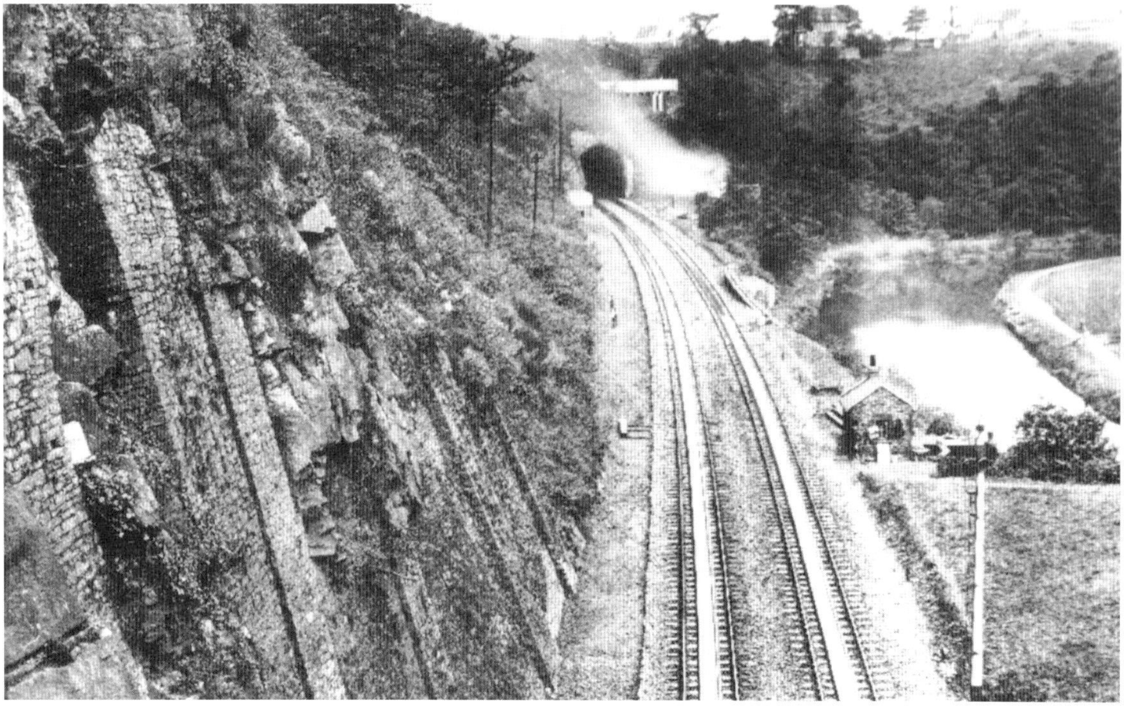

The position of Fox's Wood water troughs from 27 June 1896 to 30 October 1898, view Down. This image was taken in 1899. Notice the position of the water tank above the eastern mouth of Bristol No. 2 Tunnel. (*Author's Collection*)

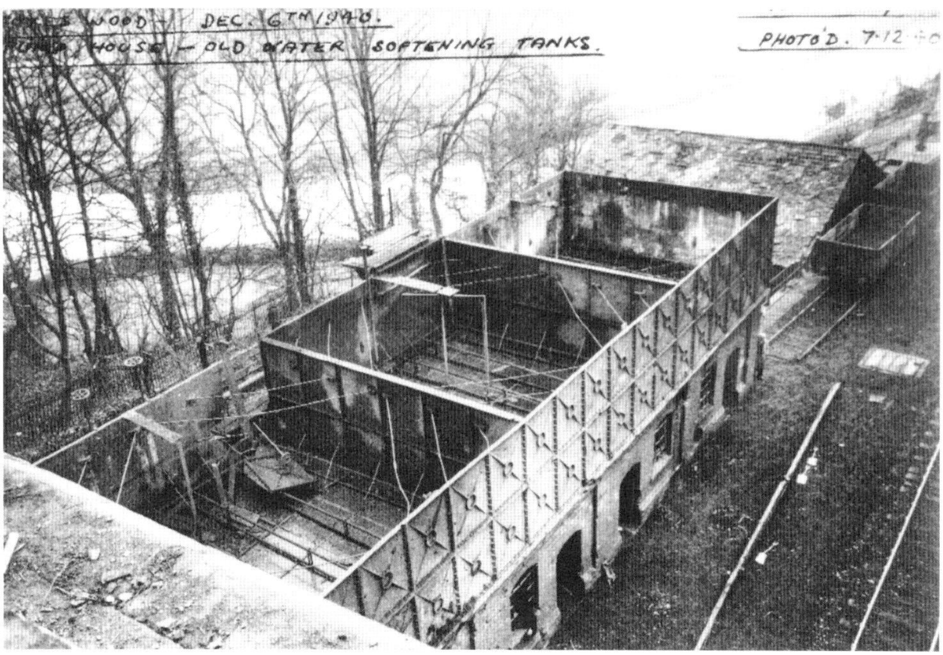

Fox's Wood water-softening plant and pump house following bomb damage, 6 December 1940. (*Author's Collection*)

Today, from the heights of Langton Road Bridge, particularly in the morning, a splendid view is afforded of the East Depot site and the City of Bristol. When No. 1 Tunnel was originally bored, two nodules nicknamed 'the apple and the pear' were discovered in the sandstone and Brunel set them up near its east portal, though they have since been removed.

St Anne's Park station opened on 23 May 1898 to serve a developing suburb and took over from Keynsham the task of ticket collection, Temple Meads being an 'open' station until 1935. It is rumoured that St Anne's Park station was built from the stones of a former prison situated between No. 1 and No. 2 Tunnels. The station, unstaffed from 6 March 1967, closed on 5 January 1970. It dealt with parcels traffic but had no freight facilities. Its signal box, opened in around 1889, closed on 4 February 1909 when it amalgamated with East Depot Main Line box, thus saving the wages of two signalmen at £1 5*s* 0*d* per week each and a £5 annual bonus each.

Beyond the station is Bristol No. 2 (or St Anne's Park) Tunnel, 154 yd in length and with the same cross-section as No. 1, but slightly curved. Its greatest depth below the surface is 99½ ft. During construction a landslip rendered a retaining wall unnecessary and Brunel artistically left its Grade II west portal unfinished so that it resembled a ruined gateway, even going so far as to plant ivy to increase its aged appearance. E. Churton, in *The Rail Road Book of England*, published in 1851, remarked that it was 'so pleasing an object that it has long been considered one of the principal attractions of the neighbourhood'. The use of 'long' is curious as it had only been in existence for about a dozen years. The eastern portal is of coursed stone with arch rings of blue brick.

Close to the east mouth was St Anne's pumping station, which supplied river water to St Philip's Marsh and Bath Road locomotive sheds, and also for carriage washing and cleaning cattle pens. As the pump was steam-powered, a short siding was provided off the Up line to bring in coal. This siding was brought into use on 31 October 1901 and taken out of use on 18 May 1969. Latterly, an electric pump was used. The points were operated from a ground frame electrically interlocked with East Depot Main Line signal box. A 'Wrong Line Order' was issued by the signalman so that when work at the siding was completed, the train could return down the Up line. On the return journey, the shunter appointed by the East Depot yard master was required to ride on the leading vehicle, keep a sharp lookout and give a hand signal to the driver if necessary. Although the river water was generally of reasonable quality, at spring tides a slight salt contamination would cause priming. On 6 December 1940 a bomb destroyed the filter and so water was pumped direct, resulting in an eel spending three years in the water tank of a 0-6-0PT.

Close by were Fox's Wood Troughs, built at a cost of £2,600, including the Archbutt & Deeley water treatment plant. They were first used on 27 June 1896 when Achilles class 4-2-2 No. 3042 *Frederick Saunders* was able to run a nonstop special carrying the Prince of Wales from Cardiff to Paddington. The

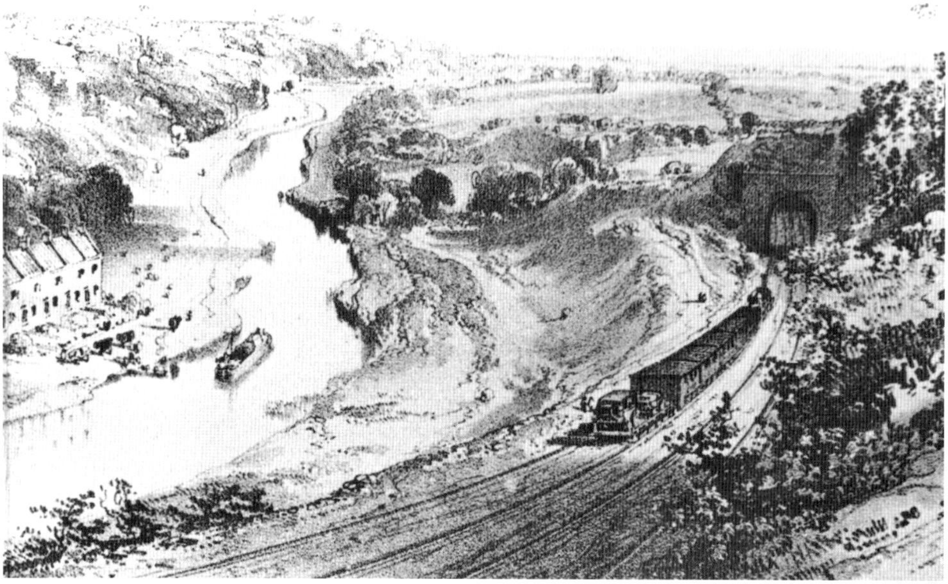

An Up train about to enter Fox's Wood No. 1 Tunnel, 1846. It was opened out by 1894. A carriage truck is at the rear of the train. (*J. C. Bourne*)

name 'Fox' was not derived from the animal, but from a Quaker doctor, Edward Long Fox, who built Brislington House as a private asylum. He practised much more humane treatment for the insane than was usual at the time and arranged for suitable entertainments such as brass bands to play on the lawns. The troughs were taken out of use on 30 October 1898, their short life perhaps being attributable to the fact that they were situated partly over a masonry viaduct and its decaying arches were attributed to splashing from the troughs. Remedial work required the removal of each track in turn. As reinstatement of the troughs would have renewed the problem, they were resited nearer Keynsham.

Between Bristol No. 2 and No. 3 Tunnels, the railway runs on a shelf very close to the Avon. No. 3, or Fox's Wood Tunnel, is 1,017 yd in length, the same cross-section as the other two and is Grade II listed. In its construction, three main shafts were cut in addition to six smaller ones to disperse fumes from the blasting powder. Shaft No. 3 was the deepest at 116½ ft. In the process of sinking some of the shafts, workmen came across old coal workings, which caused slight interruptions to the job. On completion, five shafts were retained for ventilation. The tunnel's west portal resembles a castle gateway and Brunel left the east mouth, 40 ft in height and rough-hewn to look like a cave, but later an arch of engineer's blue brick was added. As the tunnel was cut through hard rock, no lining was required.

East of the tunnel the Avon had to be diverted for a short distance to the extent of half its breadth in order to form a shelf to carry the railway. At the east end of the shelf were sidings on both sides of the line serving Fox's Wood Quarry. The

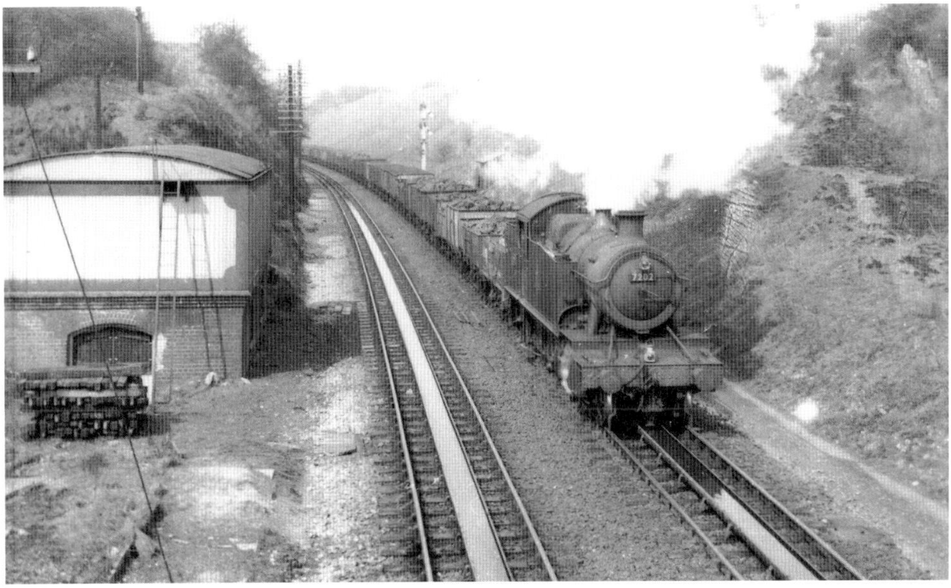

72XX class 2-8-2T No. 7202 passes Keynsham trough's water tank, 3 April 1956. (*R. E. Toop*)

signal box (its water cans were collected by the No. 15 Transfer train East Depot to Keynsham and refilled at Keynsham station) closed on 20 November 1960, by which date all the sidings had been removed. Originally the quarry had been situated on the north side only, between railway and river, but by 1894 the 53-yd-long Fox's Wood No. 1 Tunnel and the 37-yd No. 2 Tunnel had been opened out as the quarry developed. Stone from this quarry was used for various buildings, one being the carriage shop at Swindon works. For safety, before carrying out blasting. regulations required the foreman to go to the signal box and be given a token of authority and while he held it the signalman gave the 'Obstruction Danger' signal to the boxes on either side and pegged his telegraph to 'Train on Line'.

At the east end of the quarry the 620-yd-long water troughs stretched towards Keynsham. Opened on 30 June 1899 to replace those further west that had been closed the previous year, they were fed from Fox's Wood pumping station. The troughs were of galvanised steel plate in 10 ft lengths, 18 in wide and 6 in deep; the normal height of the water was 5 in. To ensure gentle entry and exit of a water scoop, the track and troughs sloped at each end at 1 in 360. These slopes were 60 yd in length and dry for about 30 ft from each extremity, the water gradually deepening. A sensitive float-operated valve controlled the flow of water to the troughs, which could be filled in approximately three minutes. The length ganger was responsible for breaking and clearing any frozen ice, or if the thickness exceeded an eight of an inch, to close them. These troughs were taken out of use in May 1961 and removed that August. Latterly, they had been used only by Cardiff to Portsmouth trains and following the closure of the troughs, engines took water at Bath.

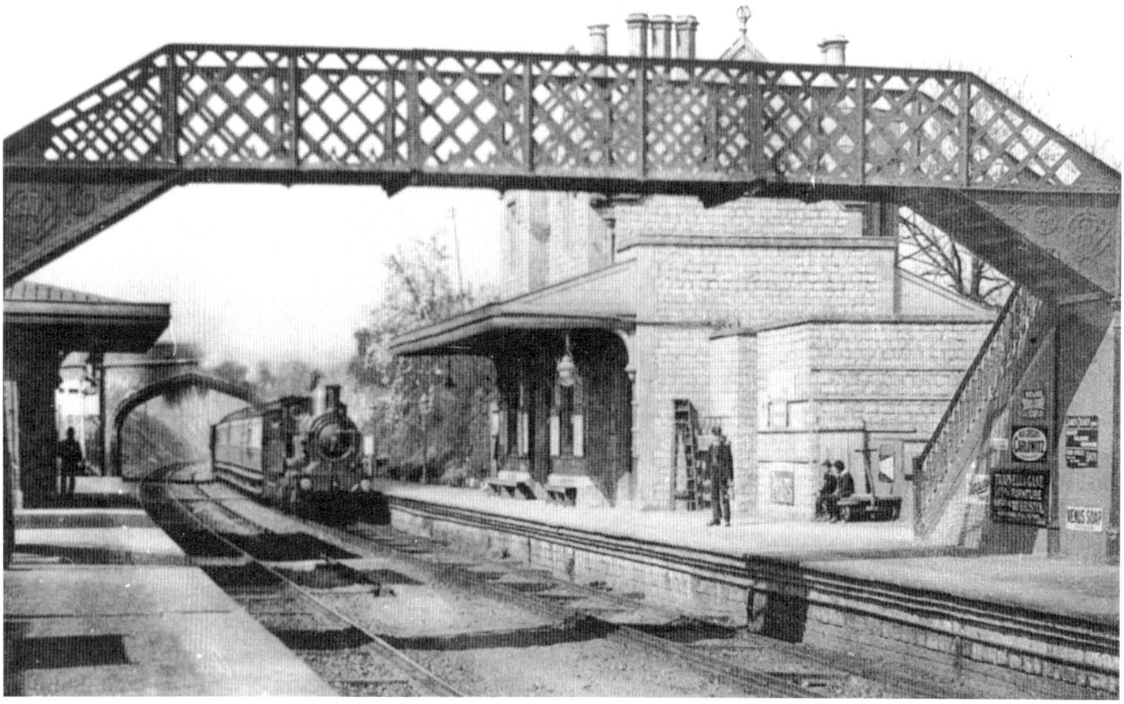

An Up passenger train at Keynsham, 1898. The rail is on longitudinal sleepers. (*Author's Collection*)

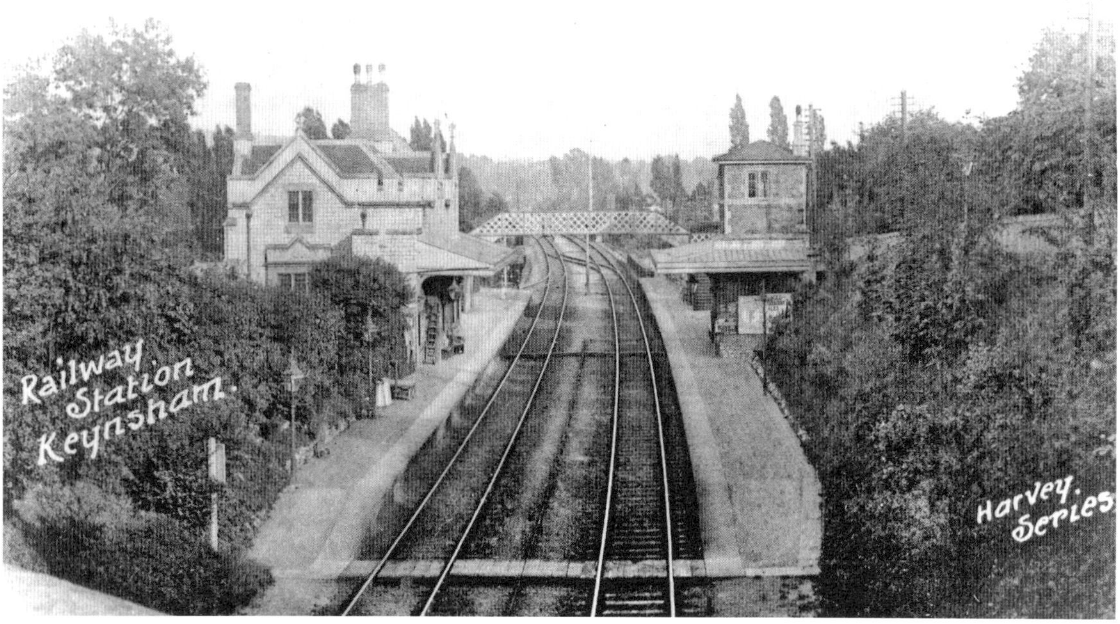

Keynsham station, view Up. (*Author's Collection*)

The line crosses Keynsham Hams on an embankment about 30 ft high. Following the opening of Fry's chocolate works on its north side, the factory's name, 'Somerdale', was announced in large white concrete block capital letters on the slope facing the A4 road. The lettering necessarily had to be camouflaged during the Second World War to prevent it acting as a location aid for hostile aircraft.

At Keynsham the two-storey Tudor-style stone building set on the Up platform was the oldest intermediate station between Bristol and Bath. George Measom, in his *Official Guide to the Great Western Railway*, published in 1861, said that the station was 'constructed of hammer dressed lias, with Bath stone quoins and dressings'. The stationmaster of that period lived on its upper floor. Until 1851 the building contained the tessellated pavement removed from the Roman villa discovered when a cutting was made in the parish of Newton St Loe [see p. 82]. In 1884 the directors authorised the expenditure for widening the Down platform, providing a new waiting room and erecting a footbridge. In 1907 major improvements were carried out to the station:

a) a stone building was erected on the Down platform containing a booking office, stationmaster's office, waiting room and toilets
b) the platforms were extended 80 ft
c) the open footbridge linking the platforms was roofed.

Station Road overbridge was replaced on 22 November 1931 by a steel structure. The original bridge was in the Tudor arch style used for most of the over- and under-bridges and built of blue has from Fox's Wood Quarry. It was built with lime set so hard that a pneumatic drill could scarcely penetrate. The new bridge with its greater span allowed the platforms to be almost doubled in length to cope with Fry's workers' trains and also excursion trains carrying visitors to the model factory. Initially, two of the Down workers' trains stood head-to-tail at the Down platform, but the installation of a crossover at the station's west end on 24 July 1933 permitted one Down train to leave from the Up platform, though this was rarely practised.

Following the opening of Fry's factory, from 1 February 1925 the station was renamed Keynsham & Somerdale, but reverted to Keynsham on 6 May 1974. Unstaffed from 23 May 1966, the platforms were shortened and the original buildings demolished in June 1970 and replaced with bus stop-type shelters until December 1985 when the station was upgraded and the car park extended. The cost of over £100,000 was jointly funded by Avon County Council and British Rail. The footbridge was replaced, the original being removed to Buckfastleigh on the South Devon Railway. In 1999 about 550 passengers were using Keynsham station daily. In 2010, in preparation for regular HST stops, the west end of the platforms was refurbished and brought back into use.

The initial goods facilities were minimal. From the short loading dock siding at the east end of the Up platform, a wagon turntable gave access to

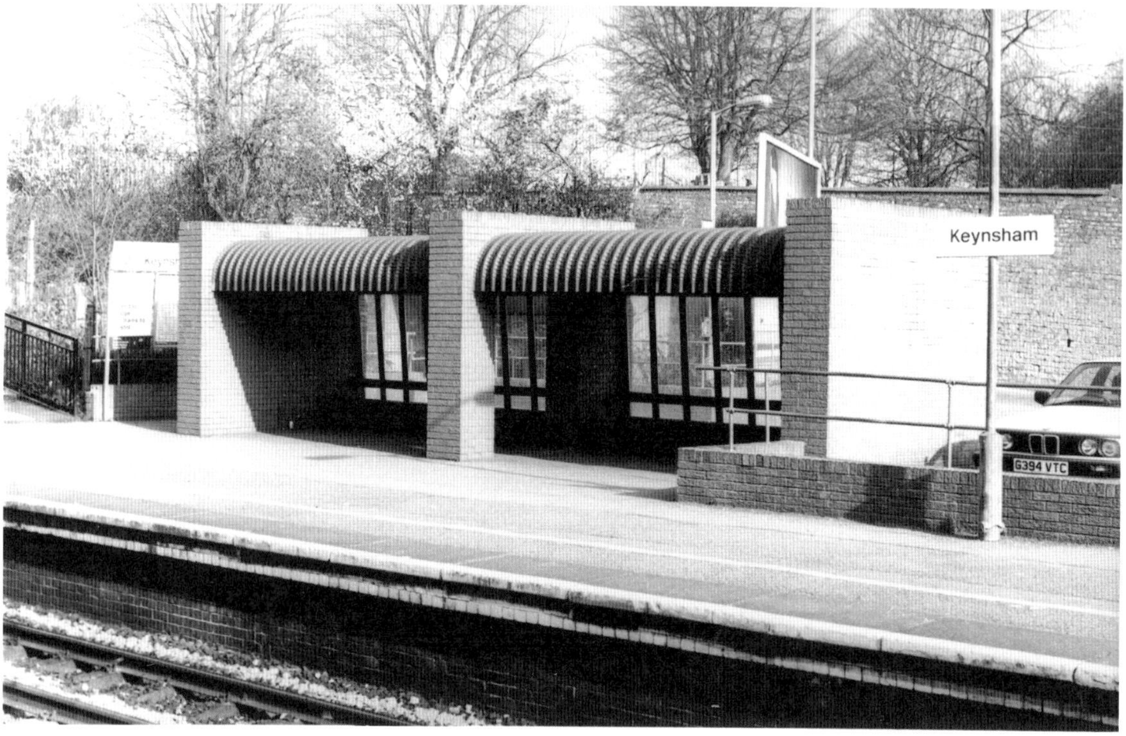

The unattractive waiting shelter on Keynsham Up platform, 17 March 1990. (*Author*)

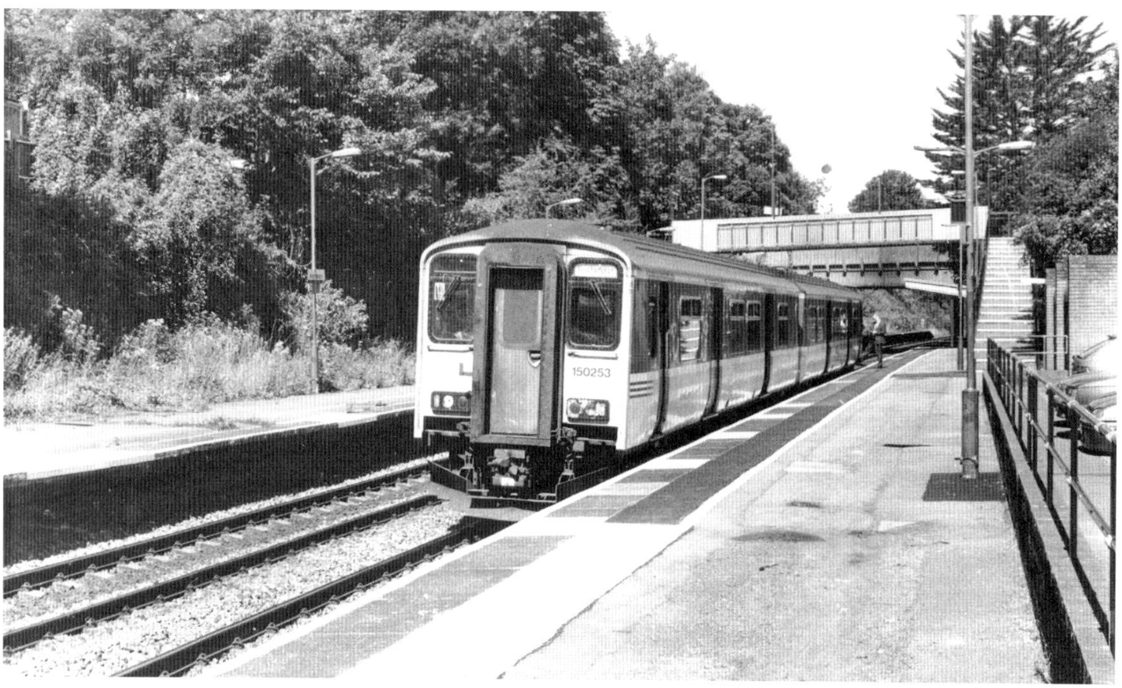

150 253 calls at Keynsham with the 10.33 Temple Meads to Southampton, 23 July 1999. (*Author*)

two sidings on the site of part of the present car park. In January 1854, to no avail, Keynsham folk appealed for a proper goods depot, necessary because freight movements had increased. On 16 January 1911 a goods yard and standard GWR red-brick goods shed, cattle dock and 6-ton crane were opened ¼ mile east of the passenger station. A new signal box, Keynsham East, had been opened on 29 September 1909 at the same time as a Down goods loop, while two Up goods loops of sixty-three wagon capacity were added in July 1932. Keynsham East box, destroyed by fire on 16 May 1956, was replaced by another a month later. To cater for the exit from the Down goods loop, Keynsham station signal box was replaced in 1909 by Keynsham West box, sited closer to the loop. This box had quite a brief life and was replaced by a new Keynsham West box closer to the east end of the Down platform and opened on 24 July 1933. This new box was built by the local firm Edward Wiggins & Son for £542. The goods depot closed on 29 November 1965.

During the nineteenth century, bargees regularly travelled to and from the station. It was usual for a barge to be moored at Hanham Mills from Saturday to Monday and for the men to return home by train, reaching the station by trespassing along the side of the line. On 18 July 1891 one bargeman and his son did just this. As they approached, a Down goods drowned the sound of the 5.15 p.m. Up express, which killed the lad.

On some Saturdays around 1910, crowds arrived on a train from Bristol to carry out illegal rabbit coursing. Some passengers carried boxes of rabbits while others had dogs. The rabbits were released and the dogs killed them. The sport usually ended before the police arrived.

The bridge over Broadmead Lane is interesting. Initially, it was a typical stone-built, Tudor-style affair then, in 1909, in order to carry the Down Goods Loop, it was widened on the south side in engineer's brick. In 1932 it was widened on its north side in the same material for the two Up loops. At a casual glance it appears to have a round-topped section all the way through, but closer inspection reveals that its central part has a stone Tudor arch.

East of Keynsham, in an adjoining field belonging to the GWR, a deposit of gravel was found suitable for ballasting the line. Saltford Tunnel, the least pretentious on the Bristol to Bath length, has plain Tudor-Gothic portals, both ends identical. But for a landslip when it was being bored, the tunnel would have been longer than the present 176 yd; its other dimensions are 30 ft width and 32½ ft height. The tunnel is drained by a conduit below High Street and emerging into the Avon over a quarter of a mile distant. For its initial length the drain is a perfect 2-ft-square brick-built channel, but it then becomes just a roughly hewn gully supported by pit props. Tunnel House, a Grade II structure set directly above the tunnel, is the oldest inhabited house in Somerset and one of the oldest in England. Although its frontage is seventeenth-century, the interior is Norman.

Saltford station opened on 16 December 1840. The original timber office block went up in flames on 3 August 1873, having been set alight by a spark or coal from a locomotive. The station was still usable, but inconvenienced regatta goers the following day. The main building on the Down platform was replaced by a stone structure, though tenders were not advertised until November 1874. In the spring of 1951 the timber extensions added in June 1909 to the east end of both platforms were replaced by brick and pre-cast concrete slabs. No goods yard was provided until 8 November 1909. The single siding, with 3-ton yard crane, mainly dealing with coal, agricultural supplies and supplies for Earl Temple's estate at Newton Park, was taken out of use on 20 November 1960 when track circuit block signalling, together with automatic signals, was installed between Keynsham & Somerdale East box and Bath Goods.

The first Bath Regatta was held at Saltford in July 1849 and was served by a special train. In later years, during the regatta, several additional trains stopped at Saltford and on at least one occasion a steam railmotor carried Monkton Combe School crew and supporters from Monkton Combe to Saltford. Some spectators for the Bath Races held on Lansdown travelled by rail to Saltford, crossed the river and walked to the course, 2½ miles distance and involving a climb of 700 ft. On race days the ferryman borrowed a larger boat and strung a rope across the river to make his task easier. Members of the Avon Rowing Club, which had a boathouse at Saltford, had the privilege of cheap return tickets to the station. One Temple Meads signalman, Bob Potter, lived at Stanton Prior, 3½ miles from Saltford station. In around 1938 the GWR arranged for the 5.15 a.m. Bath to Temple Meads to be stopped specially at Saltford to pick him up. On dark mornings he was required to light the gas lamps on the footbridge to help show the driver the location of the platform.

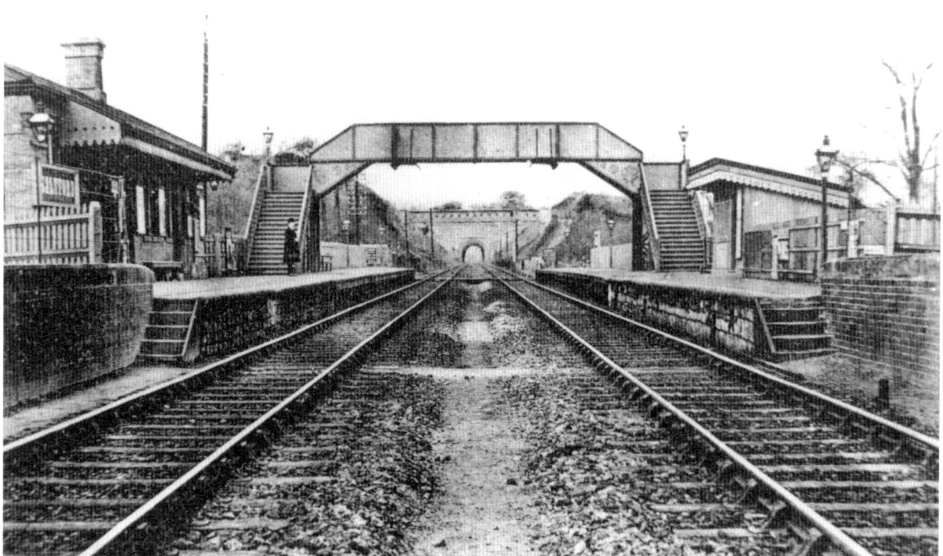

Saltford, view Down before the platforms were extended and the goods yard laid in 1909. (*M. J. Tozer Collection*)

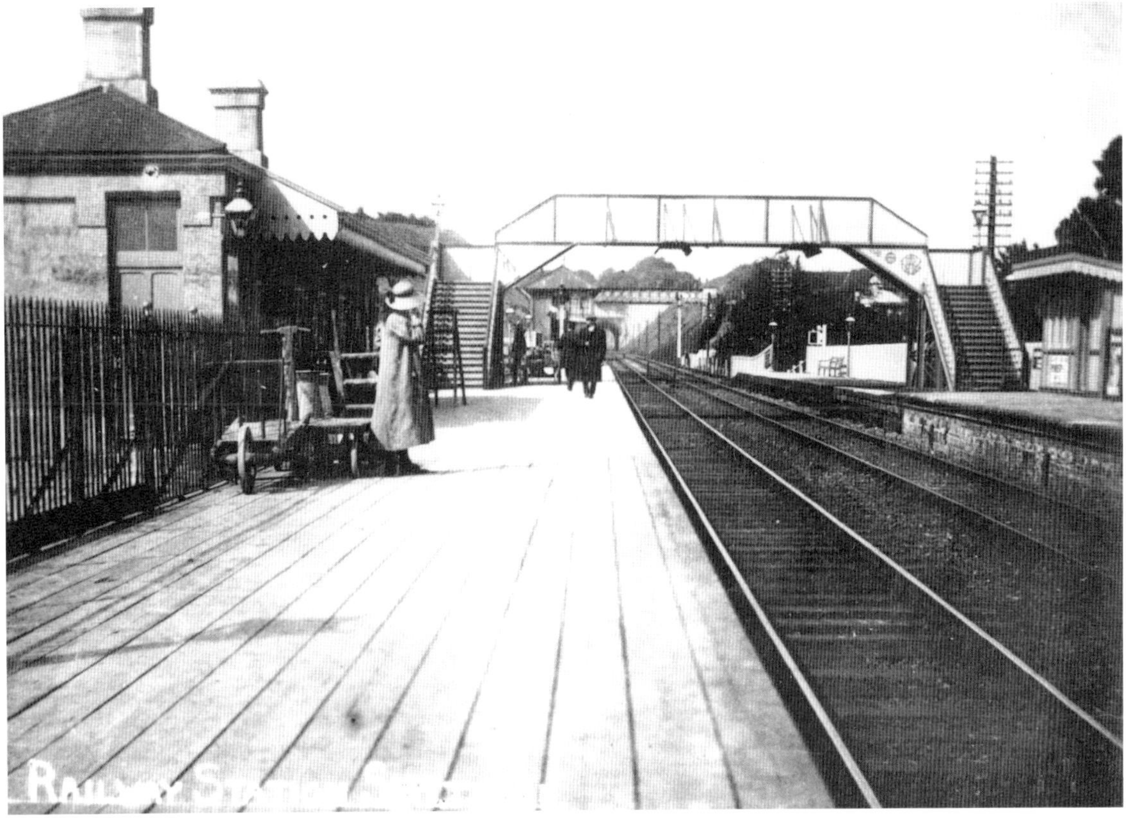

Saltford, view Down *c.* 1910. The platform in the foreground has been extended in timber. (*M. J. Tozer Collection*)

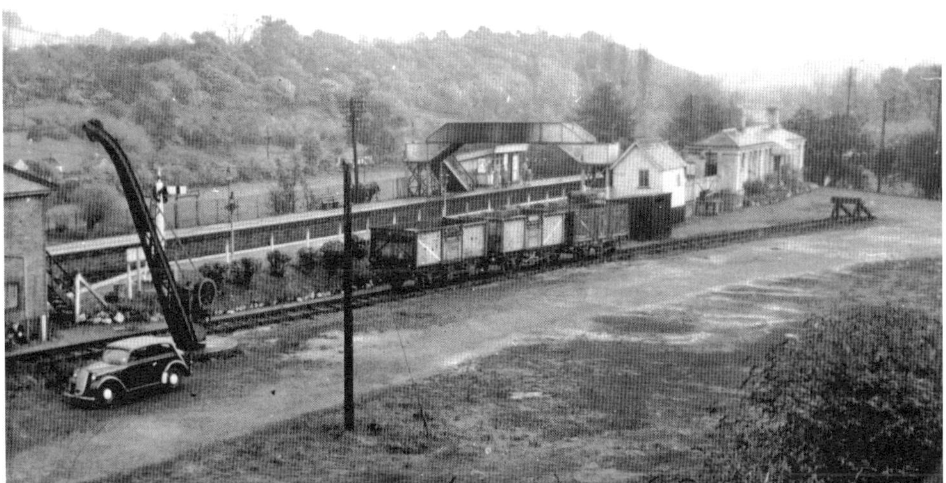

Coal wagons stand in the solitary siding in Saltford goods yard, 10 November 1956. (*Russell Leitch*)

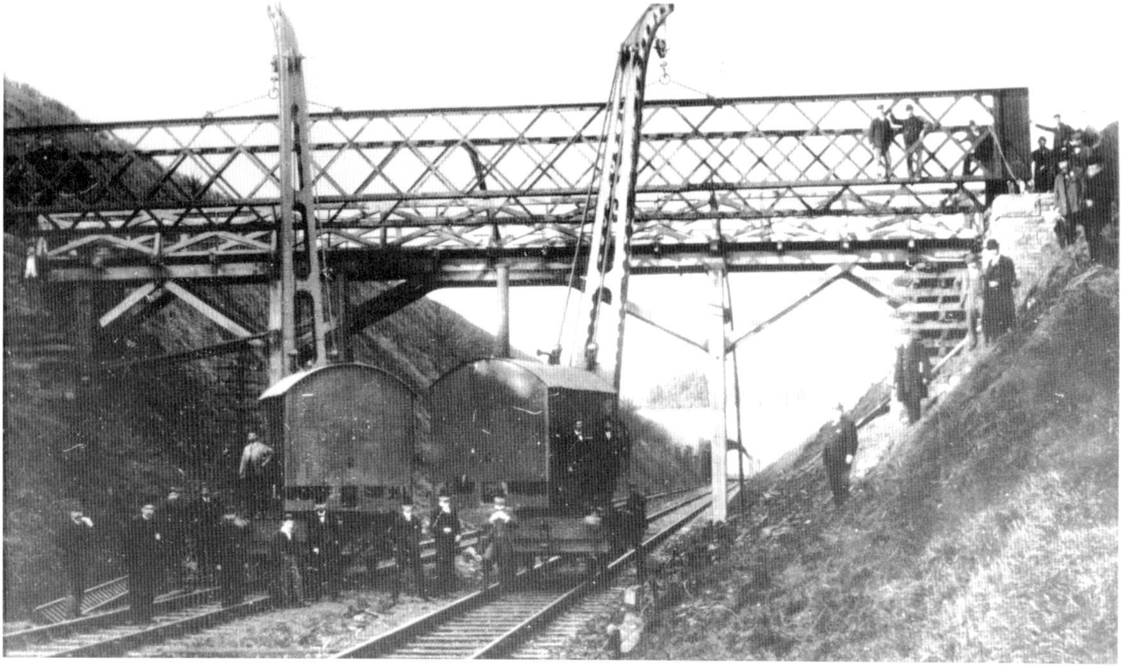

Saltford, view Down in 1898 with cranes replacing the timber footbridge with one of lattice girder pattern. (*Author's Collection*)

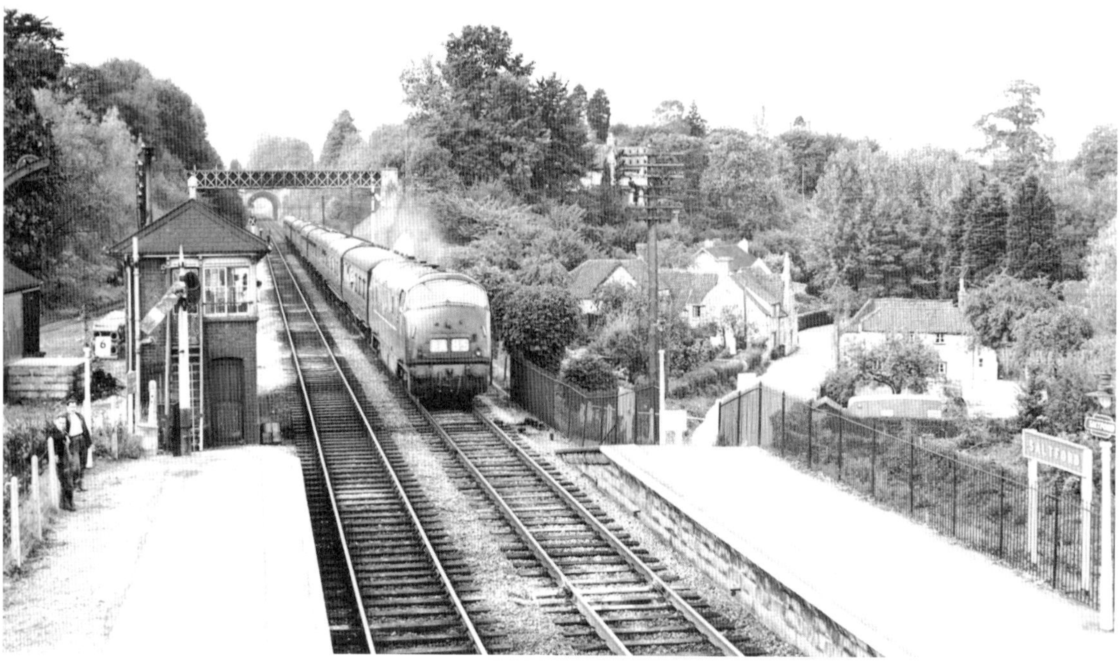

On 4 October 1960 an Up express hauled by a Warship class diesel-hydraulic passes Saltford signal box. Opened 11 May 1909, it closed 20 November 1960. (*Author's Collection*)

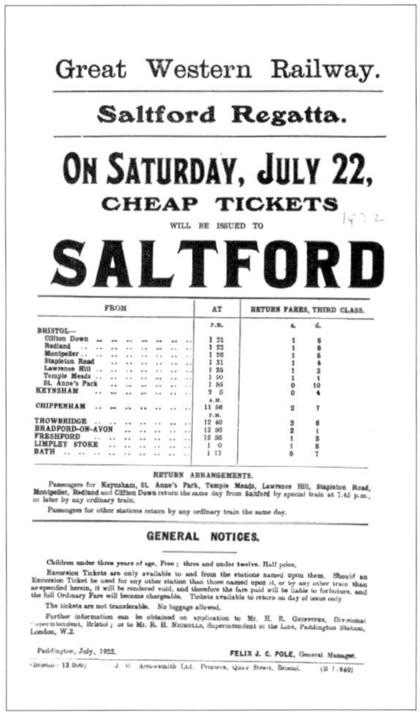

Great Western Railway.

Saltford Regatta.

ON SATURDAY, JULY 22,

CHEAP TICKETS

WILL BE ISSUED TO

SALTFORD

FROM	AT	RETURN FARES, THIRD CLASS. s.	d.
	P.M.		
BRISTOL—			
Clifton Down	1 21	1	6
Redland	1 23	1	6
Montpelier	1 26	1	5
Stapleton Road	1 31	1	4
Lawrence Hill	1 35	1	2
Temple Meads	1 50	1	1
St. Anne's Park	1 56	0	10
KEYNSHAM	2 5	0	4
	A.M.		
CHIPPENHAM	11 56	2	7
	P.M.		
TROWBRIDGE	12 40	2	6
BRADFORD-ON-AVON	12 50	2	1
FRESHFORD	12 56	1	3
LIMPLEY STOKE	1 0	1	3
BATH	1 17	0	7

RETURN ARRANGEMENTS.

Passengers for Keynsham, St. Anne's Park, Temple Meads, Lawrence Hill, Stapleton Road, Montpelier, Redland and Clifton Down return the same day from Saltford by special train at 7.45 p.m., or later by any ordinary train.

Passengers for other stations return by any ordinary train the same day.

GENERAL NOTICES.

Children under three years of age, Free; three and under twelve, Half price.

Excursion Tickets are only available to and from the stations named upon them. Should an Excursion Ticket be used for any other station than those named upon it, or by any other train than as specified herein, it will be rendered void, and therefore the fare paid will be liable to forfeiture, and the full Ordinary Fare will become chargeable. Tickets available to return on day of issue only.

The tickets are not transferable. No luggage allowed.

Further information can be obtained on application to Mr. H. R. Griffiths, Divisional Superintendent, Bristol; or to Mr. R. H. Nicholls, Superintendent of the Line, Paddington Station, London, W.2.

Paddington, July, 1922. FELIX J. C. POLE, General Manager.

(Bristol—13,000) J. W. Arrowsmith Ltd., Printers, Quay Street, Bristol. (B 7/849)

Handbill advertising cheap tickets to Saltford Regatta, 22 July 1922.

Between 1 December 1869 and 1 January 1949, Kelston station on the MR's Mangotsfield to Bath branch was open to passenger traffic and siphoned off a few passengers from the GWR as it was nearer the lower end of Saltford village than the GWR station – in fact, the MR station was ¾ mile over fields from Kelston and much closer to Saltford.

Saltford station marked the western end of an embankment almost 1½ miles in length, stretching to Cross Post Bridge (which carries the present A4 road over the railway). Running beside the Avon, the GWR paralleled the MR line on the other bank, and racing between trains of the rival companies would occasionally take place on this stretch. Opposite Kelston Park, the GWR embankment came so close to the river that it had to be strengthened with stone pitching and the river bank supported with stone, but the flood prevention scheme of the mid-1960s diverted the Avon at this point and it is now further from the railway. The soft ground gave problems in December 1992 when the embankment slipped.

A correspondent to the *Bath & Cheltenham Gazette* of 1 September 1840 said of the embankment:

> It is wonderful to see the many contrivances adopted on the railway for overcoming apparent impossibilities. On one extensive tract of country is alluvium, of course unfit as a foundation. No stone is at hand: what do they do? They dig up the earth and clay, mix it in large heaps with small coal, set fire to it. It burns slowly for a long time, till the coal is expended. When the mass is separated, it is found converted into brick, in pieces the size of one's fist or smaller; this is then spread, and is good as natural stone for the purposes of foundation. Miles have been burnt.

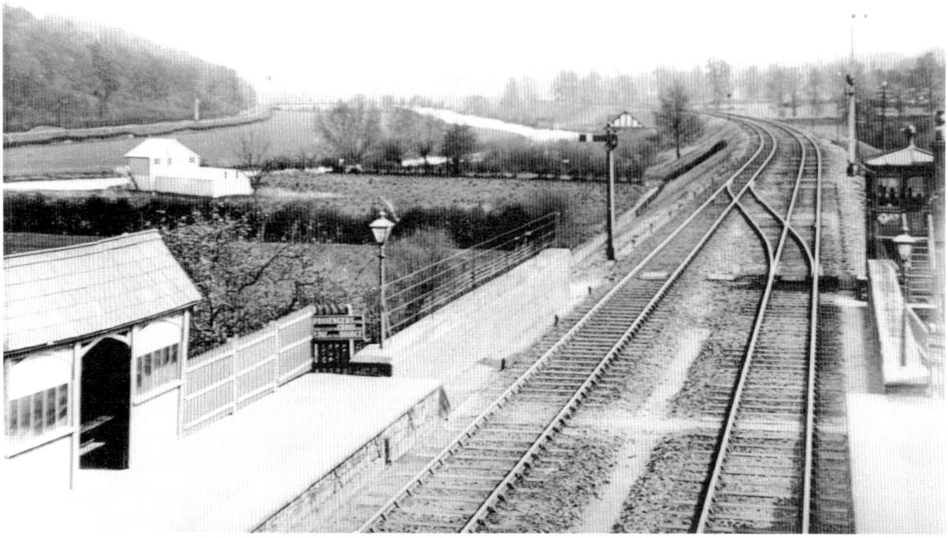

Saltford, view Up *c.* 1905. A lineman sign is on the original signal box which closed 11 May 1909. (*Author's Collection*)

Coal was available from several small pits at Newton St Loe.

In 1947 the route of a connecting line was pegged out across Newton Meadows, the plan being to obviate the reversal of through LMS passenger trains at Bath and avoid the 1:50 climb on the Somerset & Dorset Railway out of Bath. LMS trains would have run over the GWR to a new joint passenger station near the Westmoreland Yard goods depot. Bournemouth trains would then have been routed via the Bradford-on-Avon line and the Camerton branch to join the S&D at Midford. This intention was never carried out.

Cross Post Bridge, built by David McIntosh, is set at an angle of 64 degrees and requires a length of 80 ft to span a distance of 30 ft. Because of this, bearing walls are 171 ft in length and linked by cast-iron girders 34 ft 9 in long, supplied to the contractor by the GWR. The parapet walls each side of the roadway were supported on girders. In 1932 the bridge was strengthened by the introduction of a longitudinal girder placed along the centre line and supported at the ends on columns.

Immediately beyond the bridge the line enters Newton cutting, and at its western end navvies discovered the remains of a large Roman villa measuring 125 ft by 55 ft and proved to be the first important discovery made due to railway construction. It was fortunate that the young civil engineer Thomas Edward Milles Marsh (1818–1907), trained by G. E. Frere, resident engineer of the GWR's Bristol Division, appreciated the value of his findings. Entries in his notebook indicate that site clearance began on 29 October 1837 and continued intermittently until 24 December 1837. He made a full-sized colour tracing of the Orpheus mosaic, which had been carefully covered with flagstones as though its

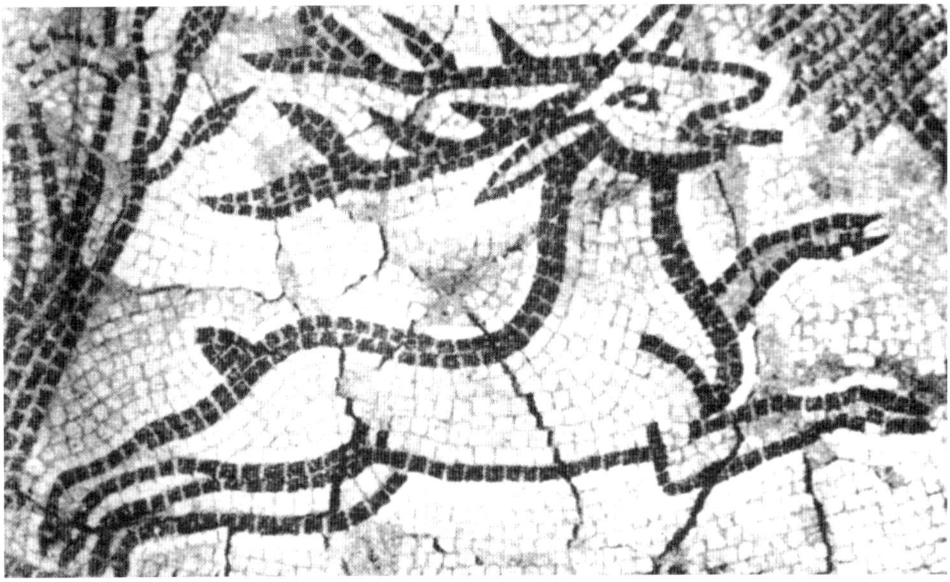

The Roman pavement discovered while excavating Newton Cutting. (*Author's Collection*)

departing owners had wished to preserve it. Marsh made over thirty other plans and drawings, which are now kept in Bristol City Museum. Marsh safely lifted the Orpheus pavement and a geometric mosaic 'in frames and plaster of Paris filling to hold up the Tesserai while undercutting the Bed'. Both mosaics were displayed in Keynsham station, the Orpheus pavement relaid and the mosaic left in its framed panels. Here they remained until 1851, when they were removed. Part of the geometric mosaic was preserved in the Royal Literary & Scientific Institution, Bath, but its collections have since been dispersed and the mosaic's whereabouts has not yet been established. The Orpheus pavement and the rest of the mosaic were moved to the Bristol Institution, the precursor of Bristol City Museum. Some of the gravel in the cutting contained the remains of elephants.

In about 1880 Up and Down refuge sidings, about 750 ft and 860 ft in length respectively, were added near the west portal of Twerton Tunnel. On 24 November 1925 the original small timber-built signal box was replaced by a new structure with a brick lower storey. Latterly, the Up refuge siding was used for storing coaches. Both sidings were taken out of use on 12 November 1950 and the box closed on 20 November 1960 when track circuit block signalling was introduced.

Beyond are the two Twerton Tunnels, both with extremely attractive Tudor-Gothic arches with flanking towers like a castle portico. All four portals are Grade II listed. The topography caused the eastern portal of the 264-yd tunnel to be asymmetrical. Beyond a walled cutting is the 45-yd-long cut-and-cover tunnel, unusual in that it is pointed throughout and has a remarkably flat arch.

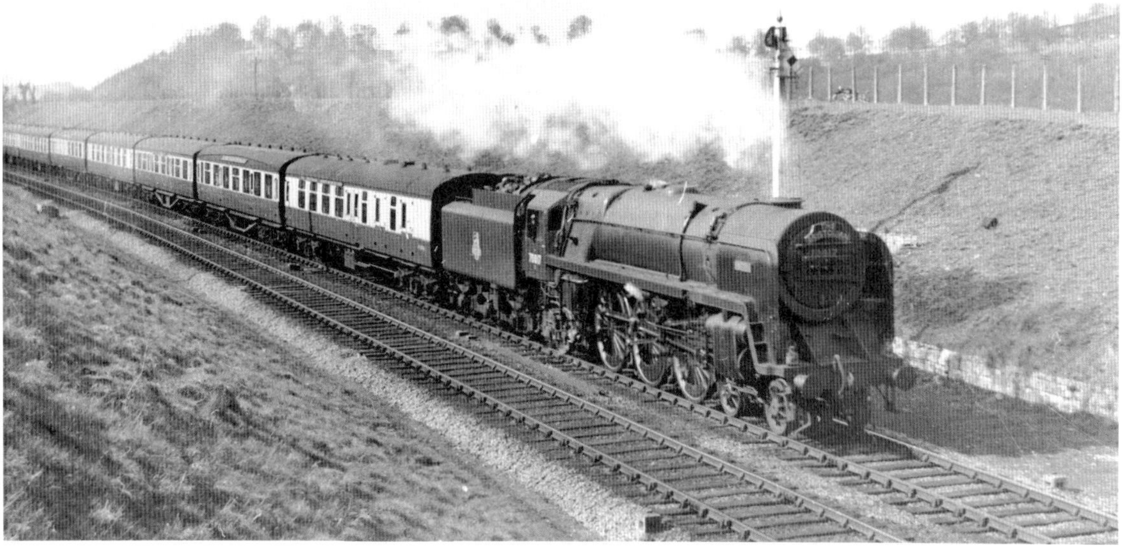

Britannia class Pacific No. 70017 *Arrow* heads the Up *Bristolian* in Newton cutting, 22 March 1952. (*R. E. Toop*)

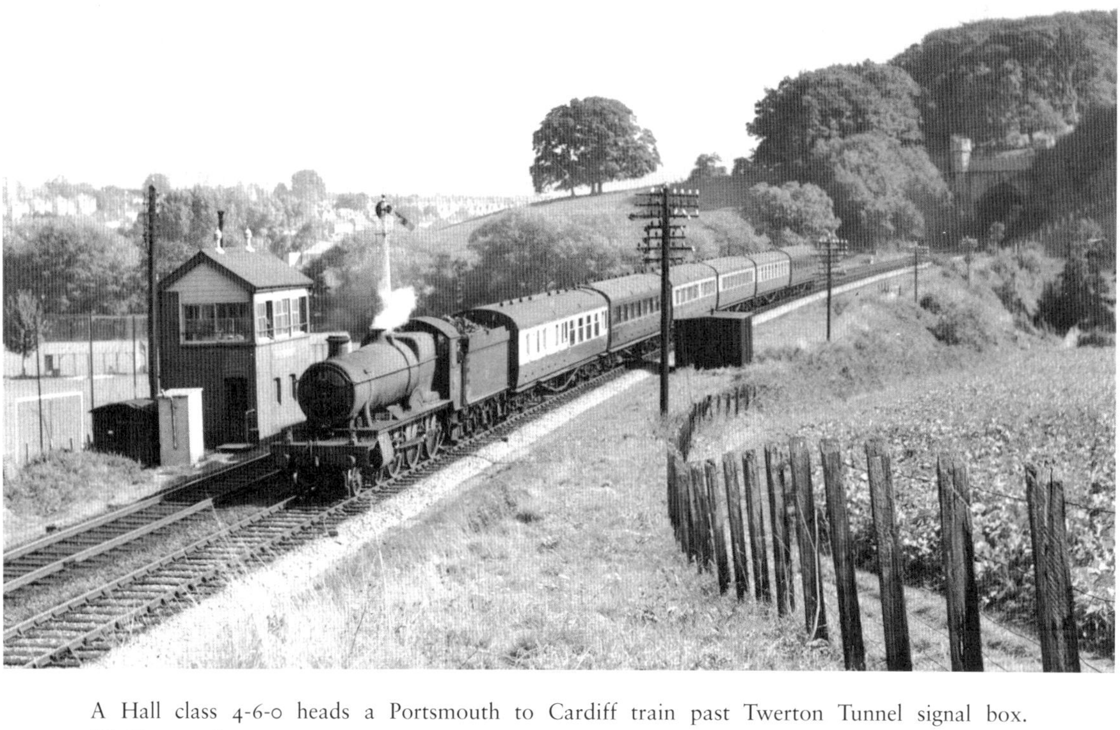

A Hall class 4-6-0 heads a Portsmouth to Cardiff train past Twerton Tunnel signal box. (*K. Hampton*)

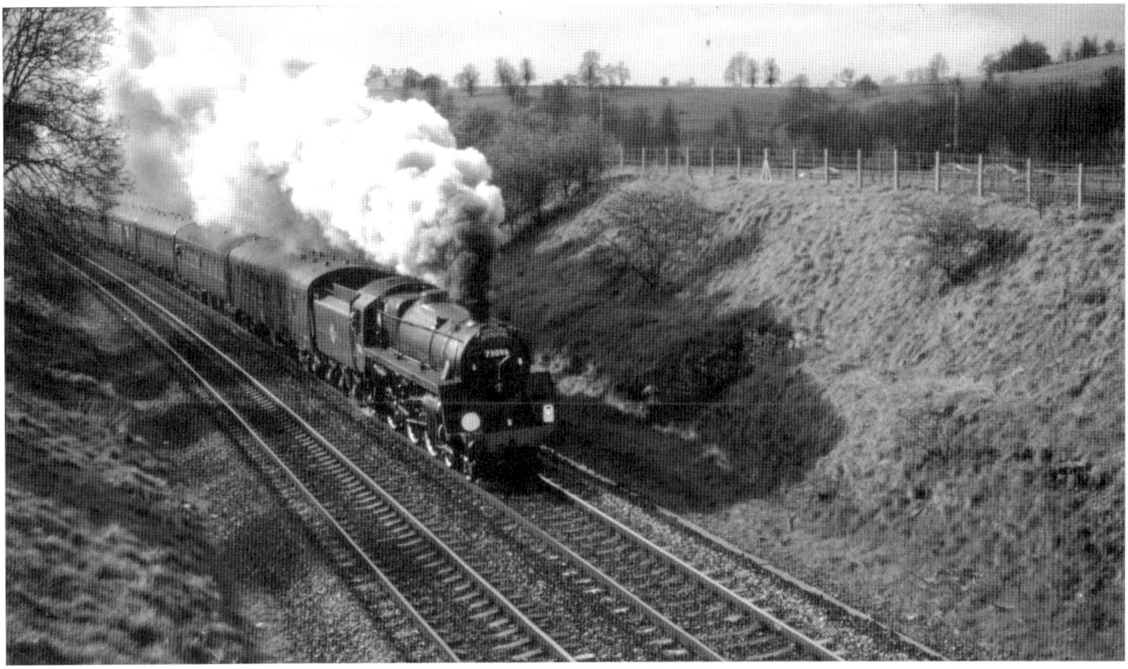

BR Standard class 5 4-6-0 No. 73096 west of Twerton Tunnel with a Bristol to Alton steam special, 4 April 1998. (*Author*)

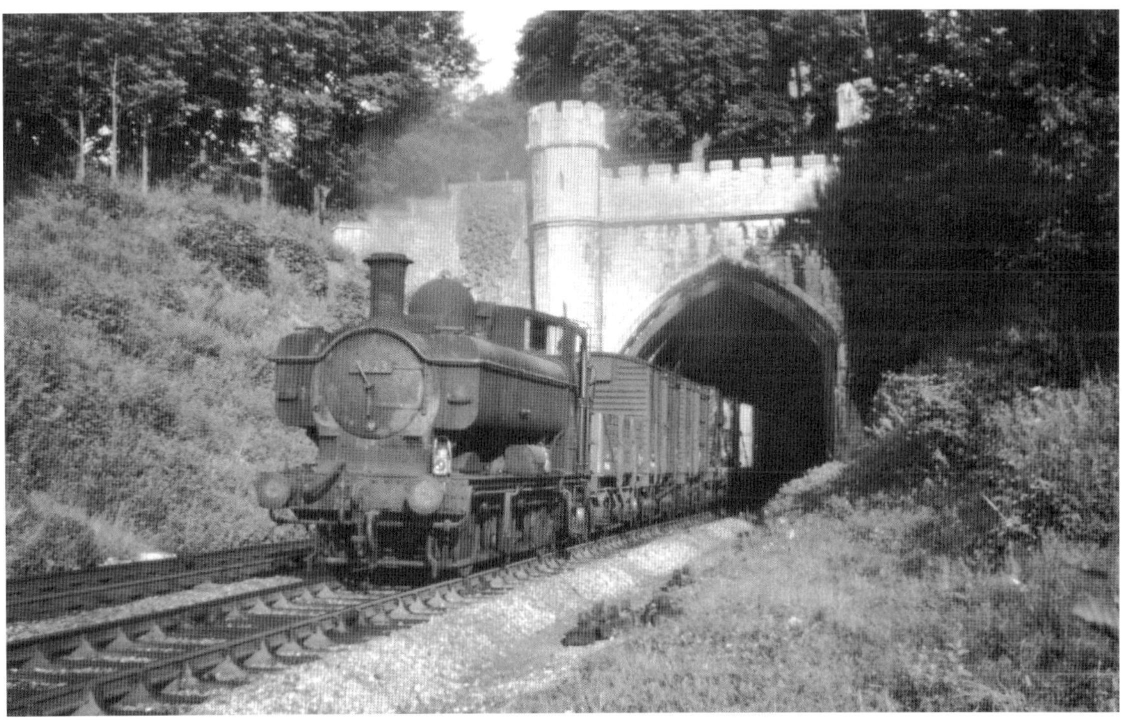

57XX class 0-6-0PT No. 9623 emerges from Twerton Tunnel into the evening sunshine, 30 July 1963. (*Author*)

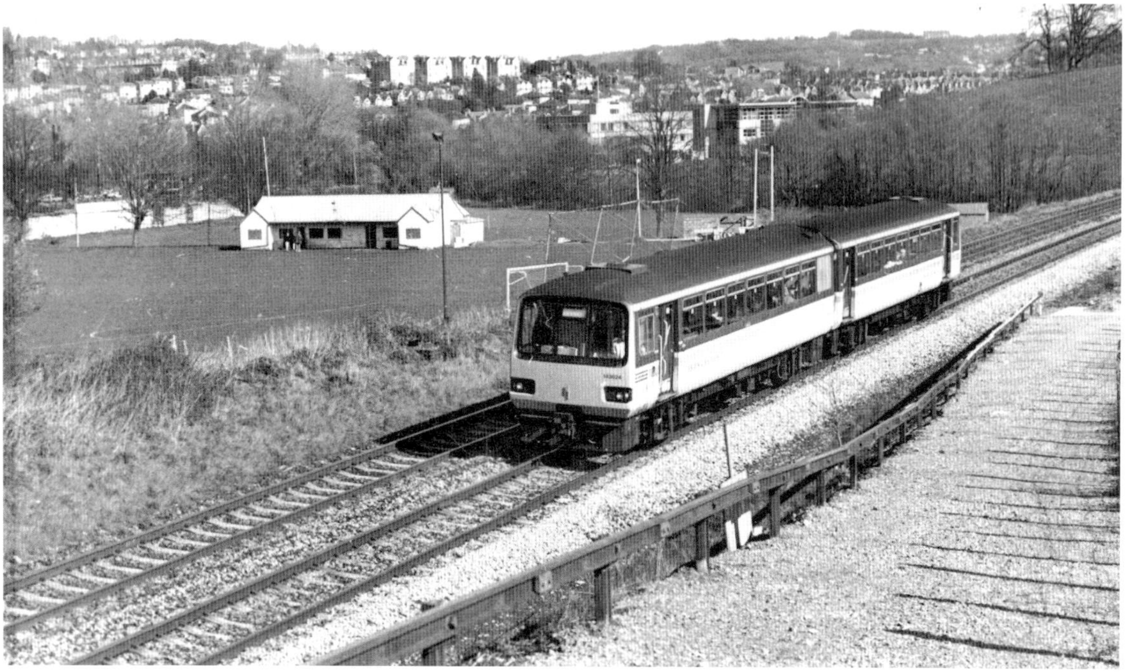

Regional Railways DMU 143 624 working the 13.39 Westbury to Temple Meads passes the site of Twerton Tunnel signal box, 26 March 1994. The ramp on the right leads to the site of a proposed Newton Parkway station. (*Author*)

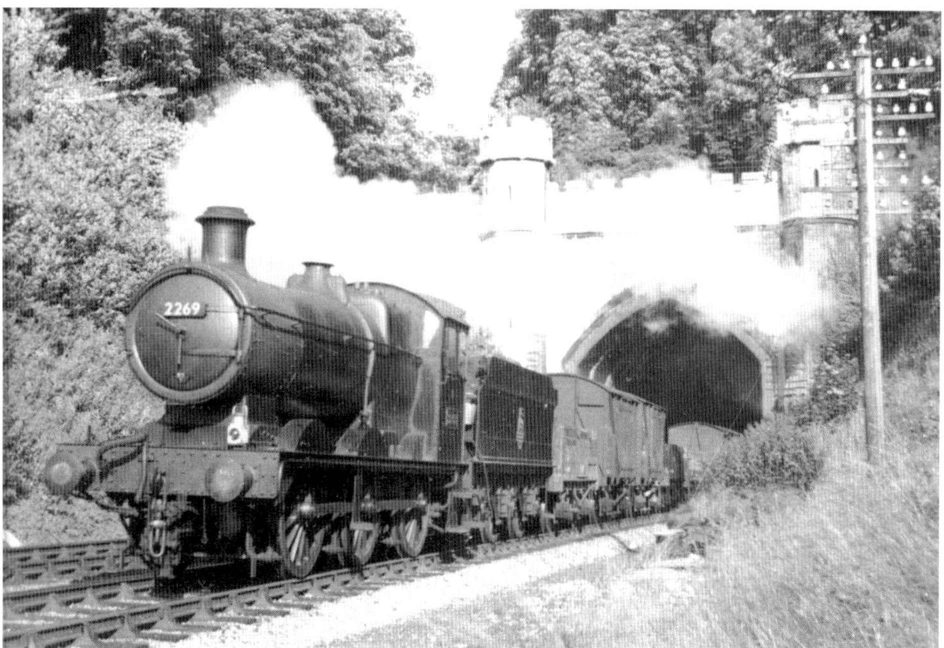

2251 class 0-6-0 No. 2269 at Twerton Tunnel heads a Down freight into the evening sunlight, 23 June 1952. (*R. E. Toop*)

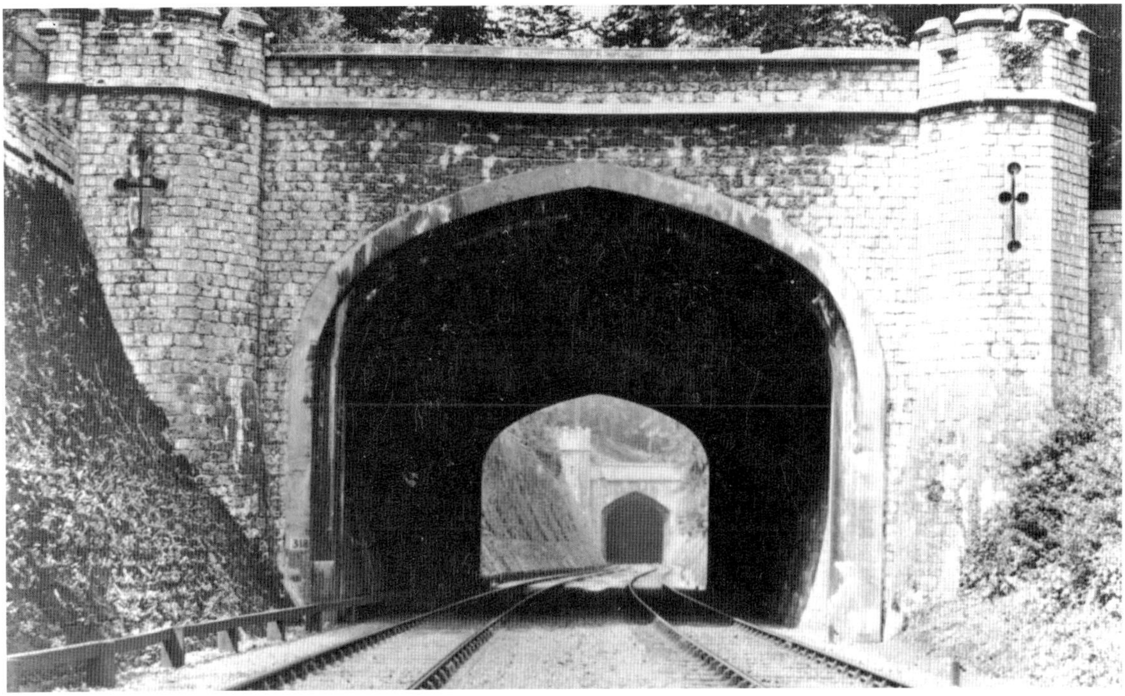

The eastern portals of Twerton Tunnels *c.* 1900. (*Author's Collection*)

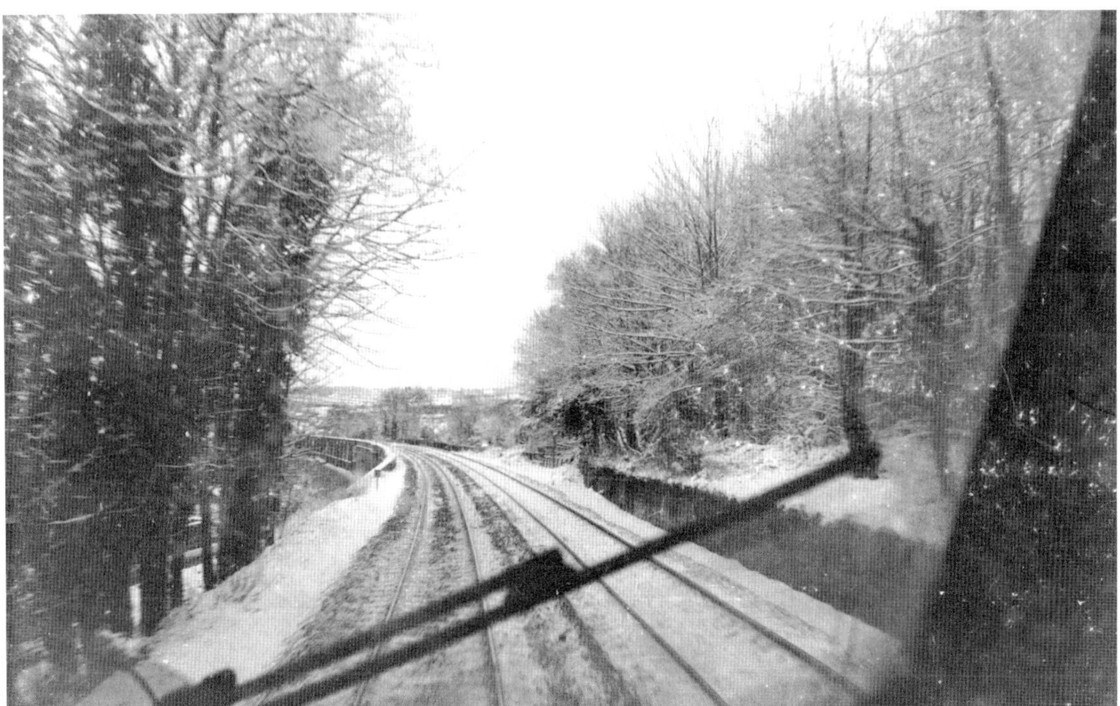

View from an HST cab when emerging from the short Twerton Tunnel with an Up express. (*John Stamp*)

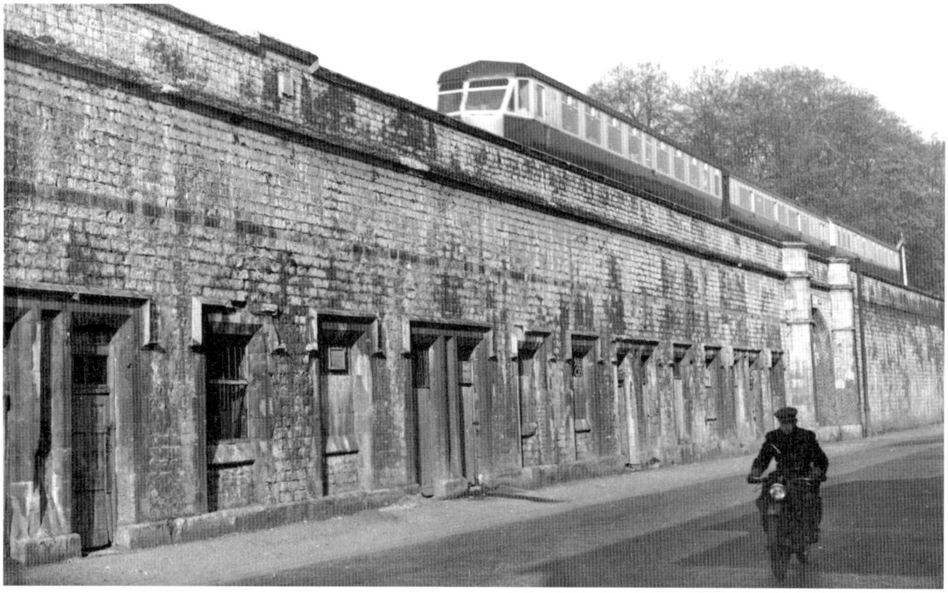

Two ex-GWR diesel railcars and intermediate trailer work the 8.05 a.m. Bristol to Weymouth, 20 April 1954. This section of Twerton Viaduct was built as dwellings. (*Author*)

Beyond is Twerton Viaduct, 638 yd in length. As the line of the railway required the demolition of some cottages belonging to local landowner Charles Wilkins, he was paid £1,000 to demolish and rebuild them as an integral part of the viaduct. Each of the twelve dwellings had two rooms, each with a fireplace. The flue ran horizontally to a chimney designed as a buttress to the outside southern wall of the viaduct. The front room facing the road had a window, but the back room was without. The houses fell out of use as a dwelling, probably in the latter half of the nineteenth century. It is not known why, as vibration and dampness were not a problem. As the cottages on the opposite side of the road were without a garden for drying washing, the cottages beneath the railway were rented by them for a nominal sum and a coal merchant used two for storing coal. Today they are still in use as industrial storage units or workshops.

Because the railway used some of the turnpike land, the GWR built a new level main road immediately on the north side of the viaduct, the inclined Twerton High Street becoming a minor road. In 1967 rotten stones in the viaduct were replaced by concrete blocks. Writing about the viaduct in the *Bath Chronicle* for 16 January 1931, Henry Smethan said: 'My impression was an instant aversion – which I have never conquered – that arose in my childish mind at the sight of the hideous GWR viaduct. It makes a foul blot upon the ancient village. Why Brunel did not design a lower retaining wall with a sloping bank passes understanding. There it stands in stark unrelieved ugliness from the station to Cook's factory.' Certainly, it is the only structure on the line between Bristol and Bath that perhaps may justly be criticised. As well as Twerton having to suffer this eyesore, the building of the line and the construction of the new turnpike road caused about fifty dwellings to be demolished.

The railway was forced through the Twerton vicarage garden because of the position of the cloth mills. The patron, Oriel College, Oxford, received £3,150 in compensation, this sum being used to build a new vicarage nearer the church where George Earle Buckle, later an editor of *The Times*, was born on 10 June 1854. Unfortunately, before the incumbent, the Revd Spencer Malin, and his family had moved into the replacement house, navvies cut through the drains, thereby causing an outbreak of typhoid that resulted in the death of the vicar's son.

Towards the eastern end of the viaduct was Twerton station (Grade II listed), opened on 16 December 1840. Built on the site of a GWR office used during construction work, it is a three-storey building in Tudor style and, like the viaduct, is Grade II listed. Its layout comprised: on ground floor level two kitchens below track level, a sitting room at track level, and an attic above. The station's timber platforms were supported on cast-iron brackets bolted to the face of the skew bridge and viaduct. A wooden waiting shelter was provided on the Down side and a stone-built gentlemen's toilet on the Up side. As there was no access to the Down platform except a foot crossing over the line, a footbridge was added at some date, but was moved to Shrivenham in 1923. By 1884 a signal box controlling four signals was on the Up platform immediately beyond the footbridge. In 1906 these signals were removed in order to save maintenance and oil. It is curious that no goods provision was made for this industrial village. As in longhand the station's name was easily confused with 'Tiverton', it was renamed 'Twerton-on-Avon' in August 1899. The station lost much of its traffic when Bath Electric Tramways opened on 2 January 1904.

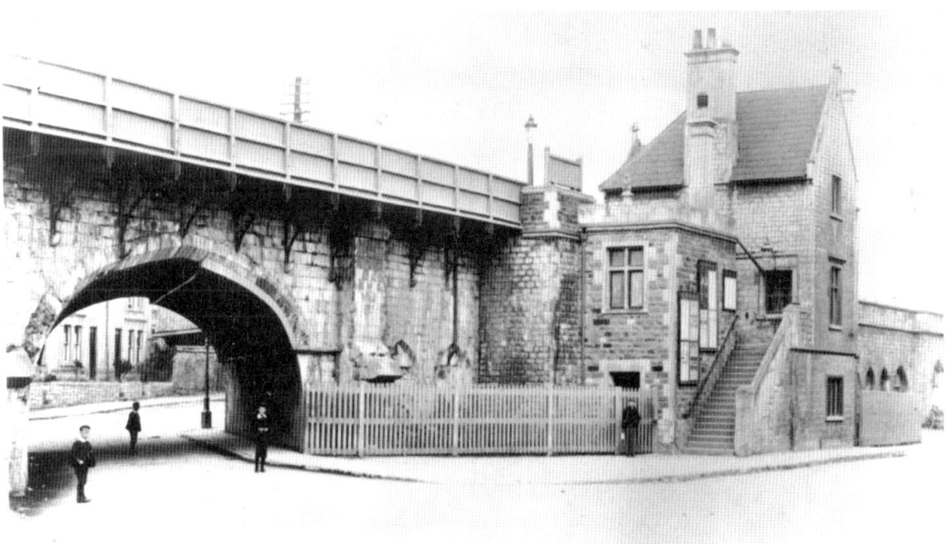

A passenger's approach to Twerton-on-Avon station *c.* 1908. (*Author's Collection*)

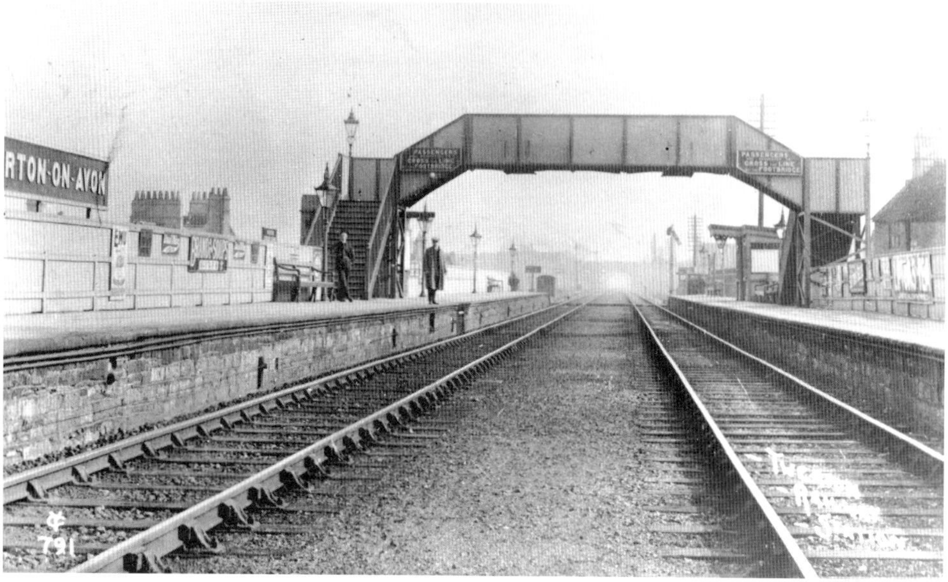

Twerton-on-Avon, view Up *c.* 1900. (*Author's Collection*)

Twerton station came in for criticism in 1875 when the Board of Trade inspector checking the mixed gauge which had recently been laid remarked that wider platforms were required and a proper shelter. 'At present the space between the edge of the platform and the apology for a shelter which is now there, is not three feet.'

In 1905 Twerton stationmaster W. T. Tummy encountered a personal cash flow problem after standing surety for someone and then, when they defaulted, having to place himself in the hands of money lenders. His financial difficulties were compounded by the fact that his wife, eight daughters and a son were constantly ill and requiring medical attention. On 5 July 1905 Tummy was suspended for cash irregularities as £17 8*s* 5*d* received by him on 31 May was not paid to the cashier's office, Bristol, until 1 June. Additionally, in June and July he had under-remitted on some days and over-remitted on others. In addition to the £2 to £3 he received daily for passenger tickets and parcels, he also paid in receipts from the GWR-owned Weston Lock just across the river. The reason for the family's sickness may have been revealed two years later. The track was on, or just below, the level of the bedroom and water seeped from the track into the house wall. Tummy, then reinstated, complained about the condition of his dwelling and the GWR upheld his complaint, the building henceforward only being let for business use. The station closed on 2 April 1917 as a wartime economy measure and never reopened.

Immediately to the east of the station house is a skew bridge of ashlar masonry, built on the mechanically correct principle of spiral tapering courses, the bed joints in every part of the arch being at right angles to the lines of

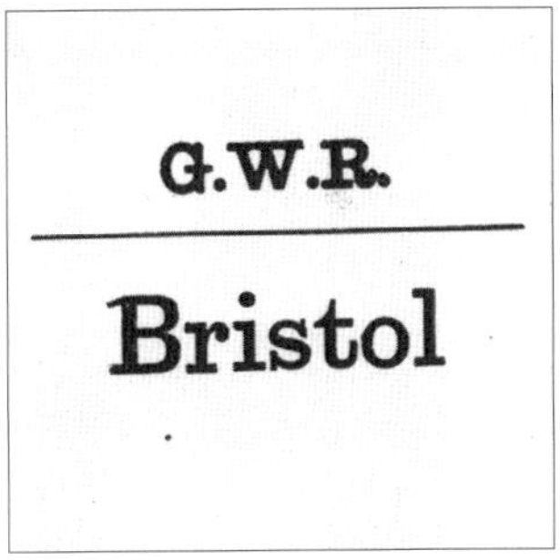

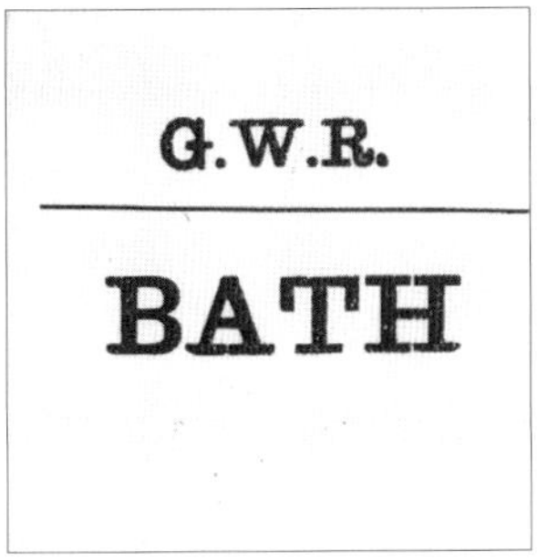

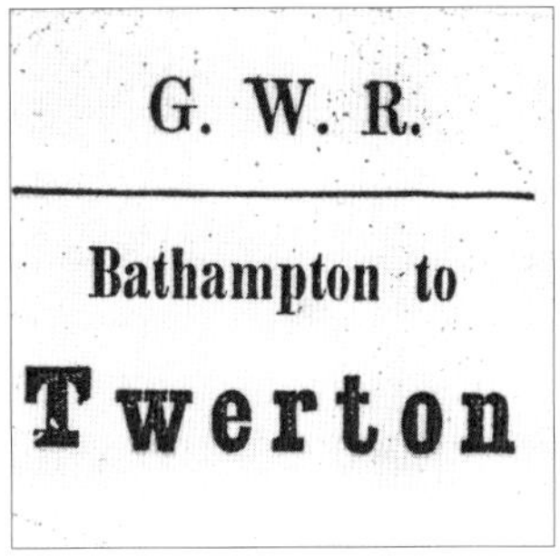

A selection of luggage labels.

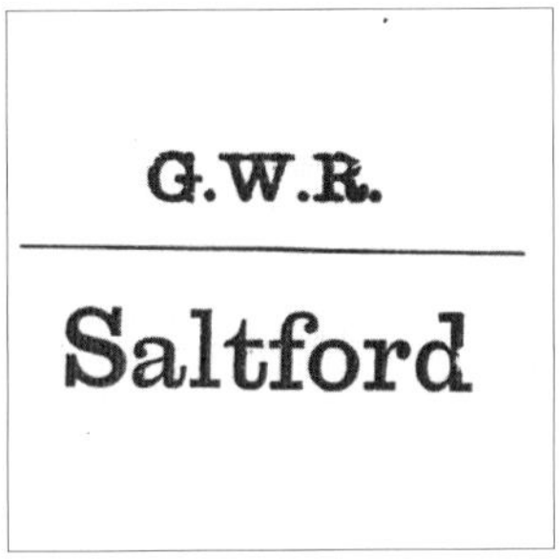

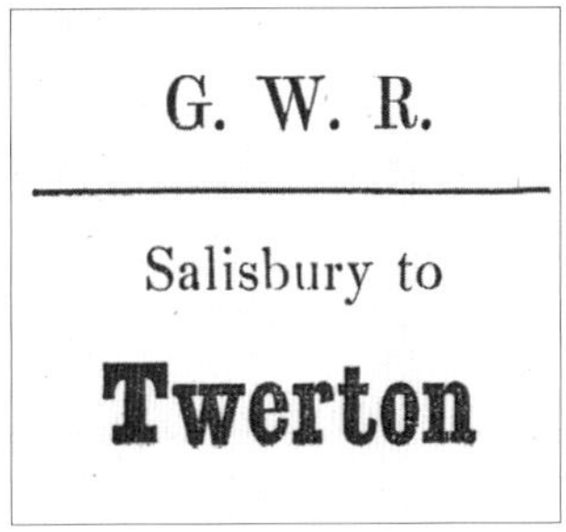

pressure. By using this method, Brunel ensured that the arch did not depend for its stability on the friction and cohesion of the materials, as in many other skew bridges built in the usual way with spiral parallel courses. About 50 yd west of Bellott's Road overbridge was a foot level crossing where boys placed pins on the rails in order to get them flattened. Drivers, knowing the danger to which the lads exposed themselves, threw lumps of coal in the hope of deterring them. From 1874 a brick-built bridge, parallel with the road bridge, carried the Somerset & Dorset Railway's Bath to Evercreech Junction line on a gradient of 1:50.

In 1920 Bath City Council suggested that a station be opened at Brook Road, Oldfield Park, its site being some distance from an electric tram route. In due course Oldfield Park Platform – this use of 'platform' meaning a manned halt and simpler than a fully appointed station – opened on 18 February 1929 to serve a suburb that had developed since the coming of the railway. Its service was good, as all except one stoppping passenger train called. It was open for two shifts, each staffed by a porter. The fare to Bath was 2½*d* single and 3*d* return, compared with 1½*d* single by electric tram. A wooden ticket office was at the head of the steps to the Down platform and both platforms had two corrugated iron arc-roofed shelters. During the 1970s the station was unmanned and had its shelters replaced by those of bus stop type. In 1994 it was refurbished and made accessible to the disabled and since 1992, a ticket booth has been manned Monday to Friday, 6.30 to 10.30 a.m. Indicative of the most popular direction of travel is that two shelters are provided on the Down platform and only one on the Up. The station is useful for those in the area travelling to Bristol, as the bus service to Bristol runs on the other side of the river. In 1986 an average of 120 passengers used Oldfield Park daily, but this figure rose to 260 in 1987, 300 in 1989 and 440 in 1999. In June 1988 Friends of Oldfield Park station was set up when it had a service of nine Down and ten Up trains daily. The group dropped leaflets through letterboxes and pressed for improved services. The group maintains attractive flower beds. Today the station enjoys twenty-four trains each way daily.

East of the station was Westmoreland Road goods depot, opened in 1877 to replace the very cramped goods facilities immediately west of Bath passenger station. At Westmoreland Road a substantial stone-built goods shed still stands and is now in use as offices. Four sidings were on the Up side of the line while almost opposite, but slightly further west, was Bath West with a Down goods loop and four terminal sidings, two of which served a cattle dock. The GWR did not always provide competitive rates, for at the company's half-yearly meeting on 10 August 1893 a shareholder, Colonel Vaughton, revealed that a friend at Bath sent produce to northern counties and paid the GWR approximately £200 a month. When the company raised carriage from 15*s* 10*d* to 16*s* 8*d* a ton, he made enquiries of the Midland Railway, which offered transport at 14*s* 2*d* a ton and secured his custom.

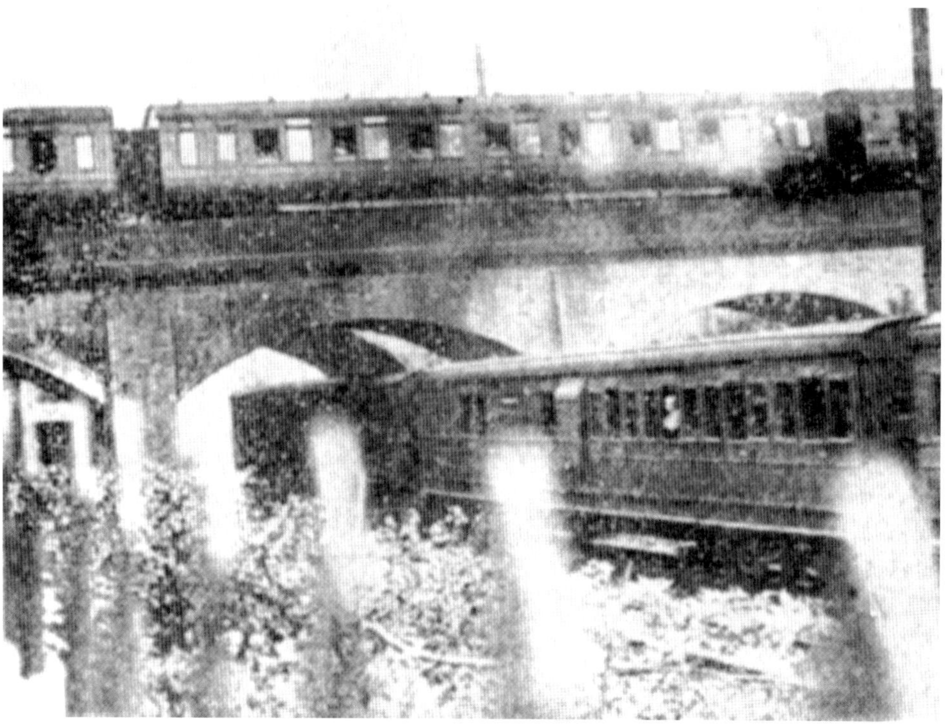

The Somerset & Dorset Railway crosses the GWR east of Twerton station. In 1933 the S&D train is composed of LMS coaches, while that on the GWR is of SR coaches on a Portsmouth to Bristol working. (*Author's Collection*)

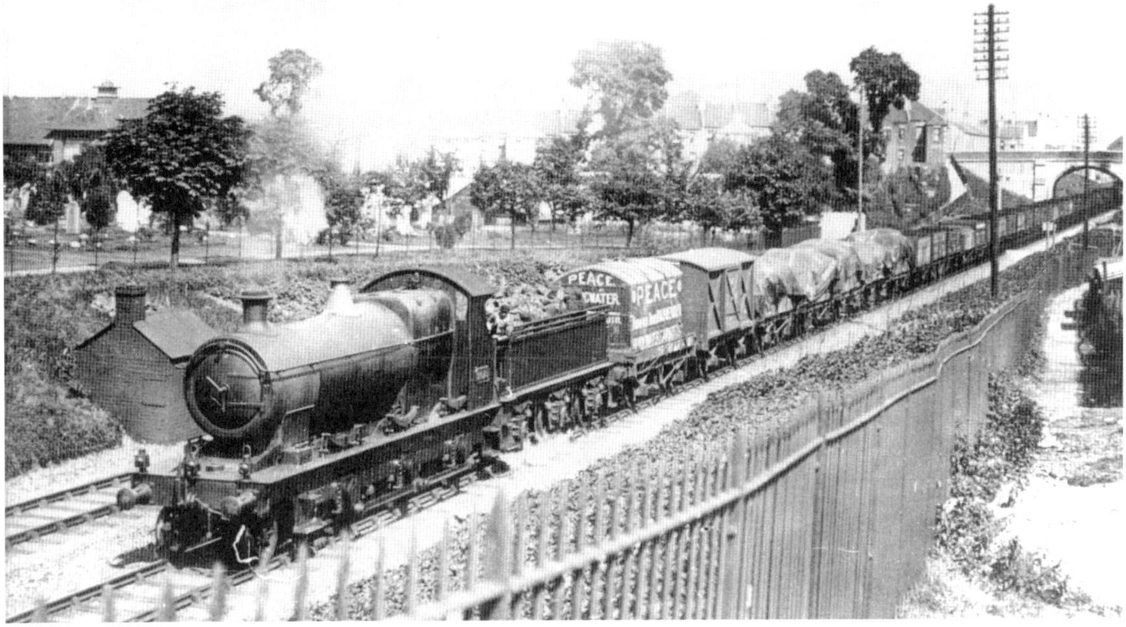

Aberdare class 2-6-0 No. 2673 east of Twerton station with a Down goods *c.* 1905. The headcode displays three lamps, but First World War economies reduced it to two. The container belongs to Alfred Peace, Bridgwater. (*Author's Collection*)

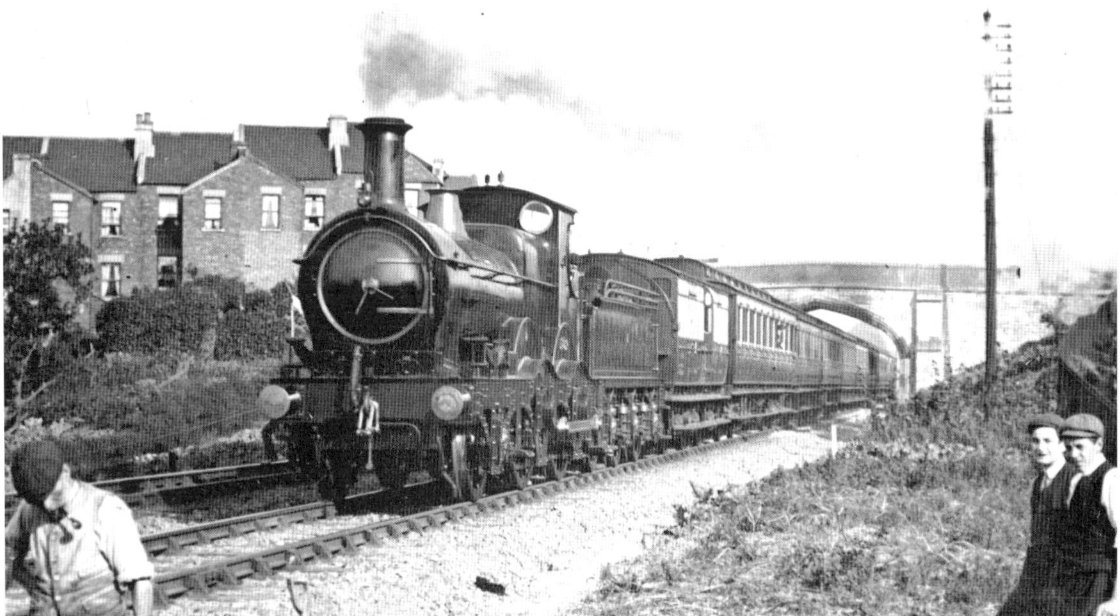

Permanent way workers east of Twerton step aside to allow a Down express headed by Barnum class 2-4-0 No. 3222 to pass. (*Author's Collection*)

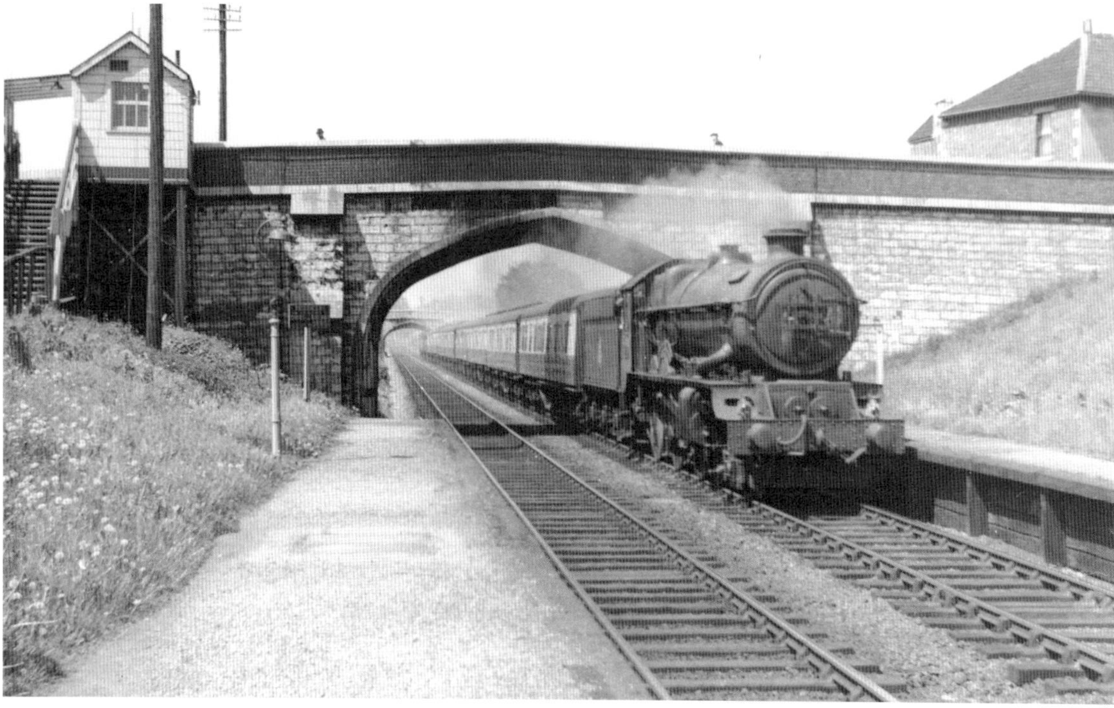

4-6-0 No. 6013 *King Henry VIII* passes Oldfield Park with a Temple Meads to Paddington express, 17 May 1952. (*R. E. Toop*)

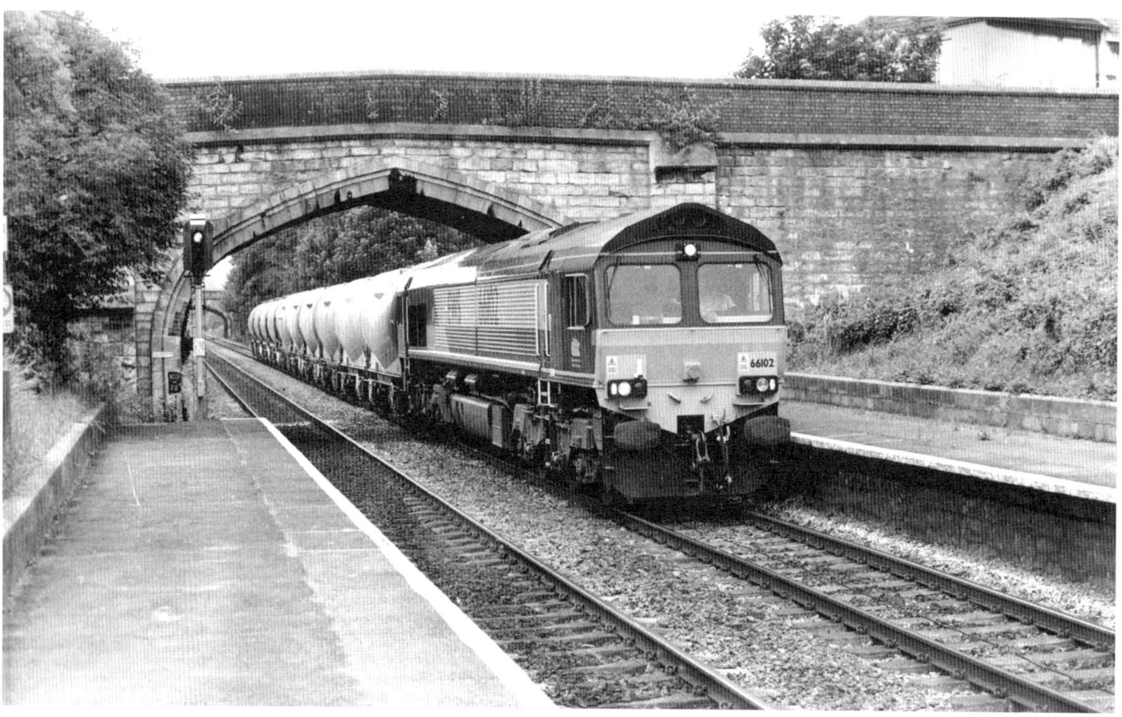

General Motors No. 66102 passes Oldfield Park with a train of Up tankers, 8 July 1999. (*Author*)

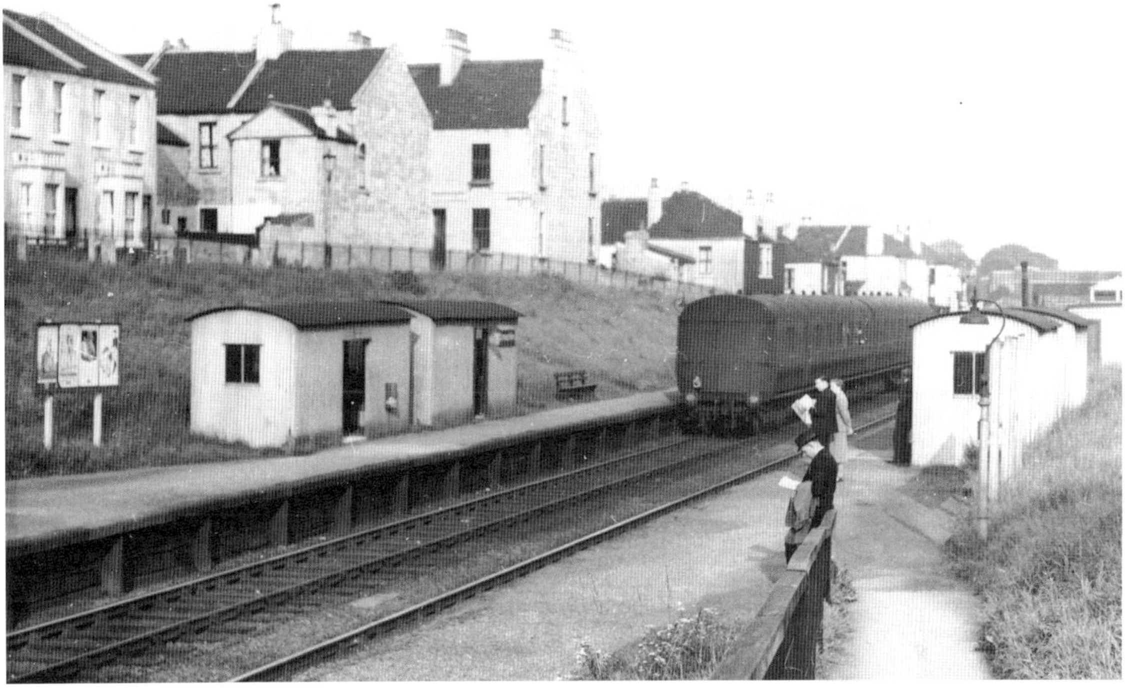

An Up stopping train has just left Oldfield Park and its rather unsightly corrugated-iron waiting shelters, 26 August 1954. (*Author*)

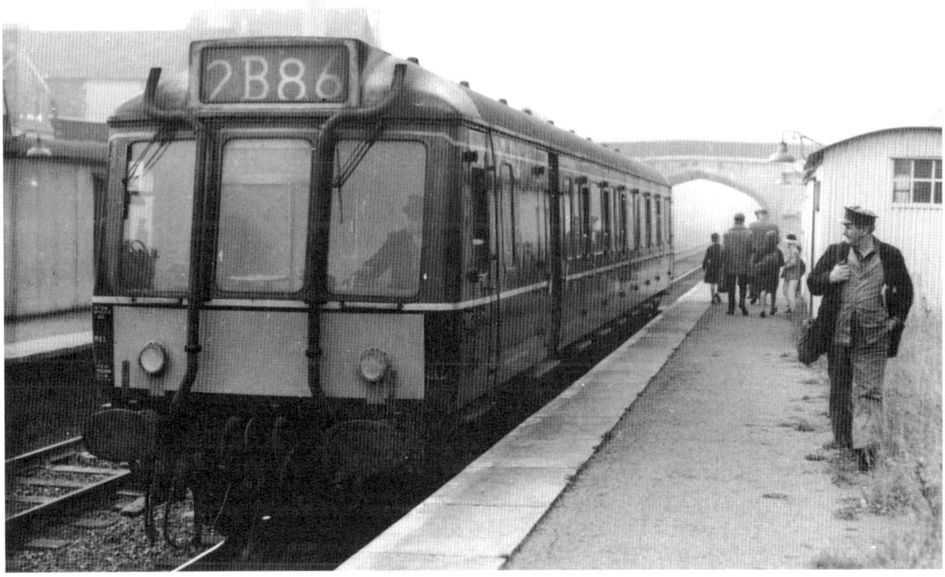

Pressed Steel motor brake second W55032, working the 14.37 Temple Meads to Chippenham, calls at Oldfield Park, 23 October 1965. On the right, Driver Ron Copp is making his way homeward after a spell of duty. (*Author*)

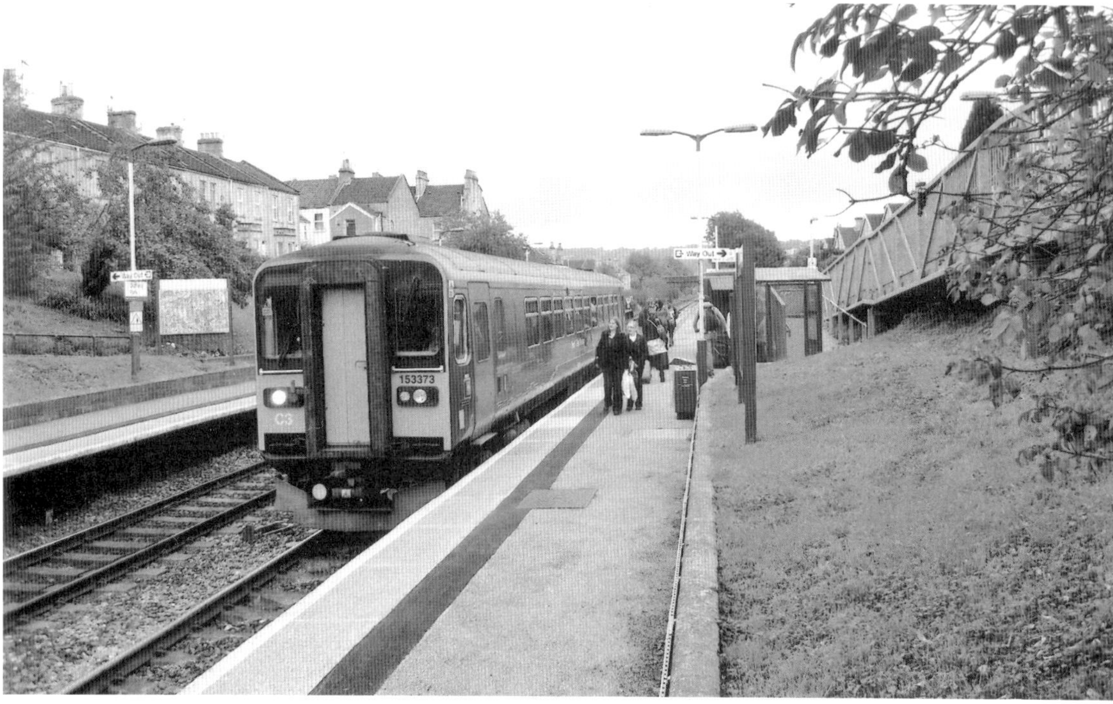

Super Sprinter 153 373 calls at Oldfield Park, 20 September 2011, working the 12.27 Southampton to Temple Meads. (*Author*)

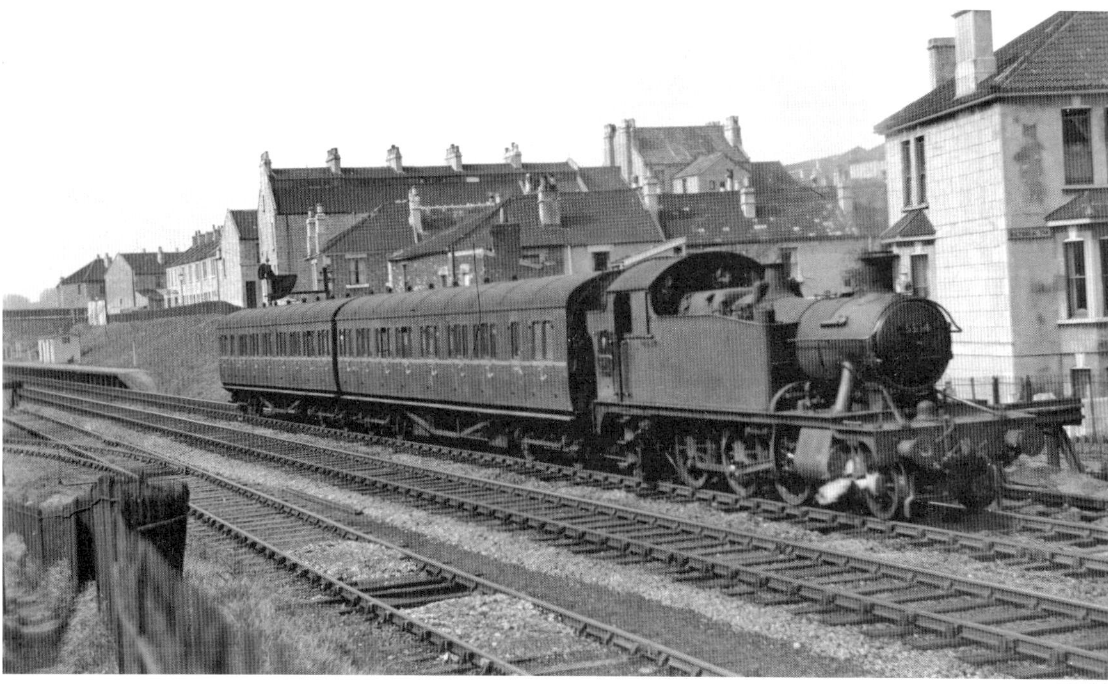

4575 class 2-6-2T No. 5554 leaves Oldfield Park with a Temple Meads to Chippenham train, 9 April 1952. (*R. E. Toop*)

Westmoreland Road and Bath West were both equipped with a 12-ton crane. Among other traffic leaving were crane parts from Stothert & Pitt's works situated on the other side of the road. One unusual event in 1903 was the arrival of Buffalo Bill & His Wild West Show in a special train of twenty-one wagons. Occasionally, particularly heavy traffic arose, such as when the Bath & West Show was held in its home city and animals and implements were brought by rail and had to be transferred to and from the showground. In May 1912, 700 tons were carted to the showground and livestock arrived in 237 cattle trucks, while an additional seventy horse boxes arrived for Bath races. In May 1927 the GWR employed open cattle floats drawn by GWR Fordson tractors to transport livestock to and from the showground. Near the goods shed were small sheds used by various firms for storing supplies. Among the businesses using them were Lyons, Brooke Bond, BP and Shell. The goods depot closed in May 1967 but remained open for full load traffic until 31 December 1980. The site on the Down side was developed as a refuse terminal by Avon County Council at a cost of £350,000. Mondays to Fridays, a train was loaded with eight containers to be taken to a landfill site at Calvert, Buckinghamshire; the first train commenced on 18 November 1985. The service finished in 2009.

An economy was made when Bath Goods signal box opened on 30 April 1911 to replace Westmoreland East and Westmoreland West boxes, the timber superstructure for the latter being returned to the signal depot at Reading, while its brick base was transformed into a permanent way hut.

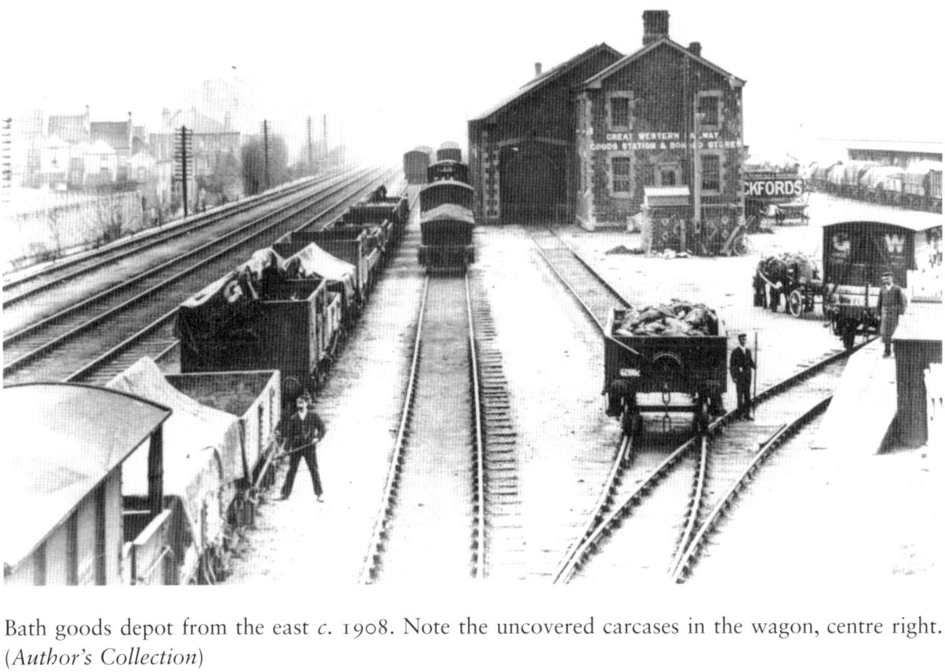

Bath goods depot from the east *c.* 1908. Note the uncovered carcases in the wagon, centre right. (*Author's Collection*)

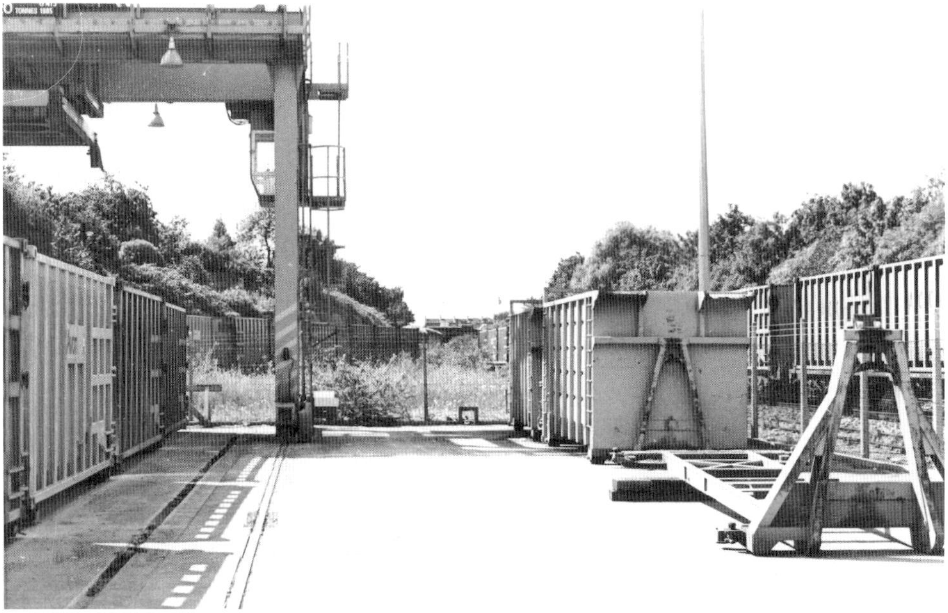

Rubbish transfer station, Westmoreland Road, Bath, 8 August 1991. (*Author*)

At the east end of the yard is St James's Viaduct, 600 yd long, consisting of fifty-five segmental arches, each of 20-ft span. Originally of poor quality Bath stone, parts soon had to be patched with brick and the untidy appearance led to a letter in the *Bath Chronicle* on 7 April 1870. The writer did not infer that the viaduct was insecure, but said that unless constantly repaired 'another decade will severely test it. And I am sure that the directors would act both wisely and prudently by having the whole structure cased with the well-vitrified blue bricks of Staffordshire, set in hydraulic lime, with under arches of the same materials. It will render unnecessary the tinkering and patching which do not add either to its strength or beauty.' The railway heeded his advice.

The land nearby is low-lying and was subject to floods. In November 1882 some inhabitants of Oak Street were rescued by being passed over roof tops to the GWR viaduct. Temporary accommodation was made for them in the waiting rooms at Bath station and children from poor homes fed with food supplied by Bath grocer E. B. Titley and his friends.

In 1902 Bath Corporation converted one of the arches at its eastern end into a mortuary and placed a carved inscription on a stone scroll above the entrance. It was employed in this role until 1948. The adjoining arch housed a bakery. The section of viaduct viewed from the busy Southgate Street was much more decorative, and is now Grade II listed. Castellated, it was flanked by two bridges, one carrying the railway over the Wells Road and the other over Claverton Street. Originally of Tudor-Gothic arch design, unfortunately from an architectural aspect they were reconstructed with steel girders in 1911–12 in order to carry heavier locomotives. When the Wells Road arch was being replaced, for safety, tram passengers were not allowed to remain on the top deck. The railway line was temporarily interlaced across the bridge to avoid the necessity of facing points, and the Up and Down sides replaced separately. In order to meet the residents' wishes that the general appearance of the viaduct be retained as far as possible, the castellated and ornamental stone parapet that extended over the old arches on the side facing the city was carefully removed and rebuilt on the steel girders. Between the two bridges, what appears to be a reproduction of a late medieval rose window is probably a locomotive wheel! Directly below, and beneath the tracks, was a police station, which closed in April 1923, the premises being taken over by a greengrocer's. Below the Wells Road arch a tea and coffee stall was set up. Opening from 5.00 a.m. onwards, it offered a drink to early morning workers.

The original plan was for the railway to run above Claverton Street for 140 ft, thus turning the road into a tunnel. Lyncombe parishioners successfully opposed this plan, agreeing that the viaduct could be built on the site of the road but that a new highway should be constructed immediately to the south. No conveyance of the old road was made, or intended to be made, to the railway company, which was required to build a wall 'so as to prevent the arches being used for any noisy or offensive trade, or any vehicle passing over the footway into them'. In about 1845, the GWR, having let some of the arches, attempted to cut through the boundary wall next to the public footway, but magistrates upheld the parish's claim and fined the GWR 40*s* and costs. On 29 June 1854 the GWR again made an opening. The magistrates declared that the ground belonged to the parish and that the company had no authority to let it.

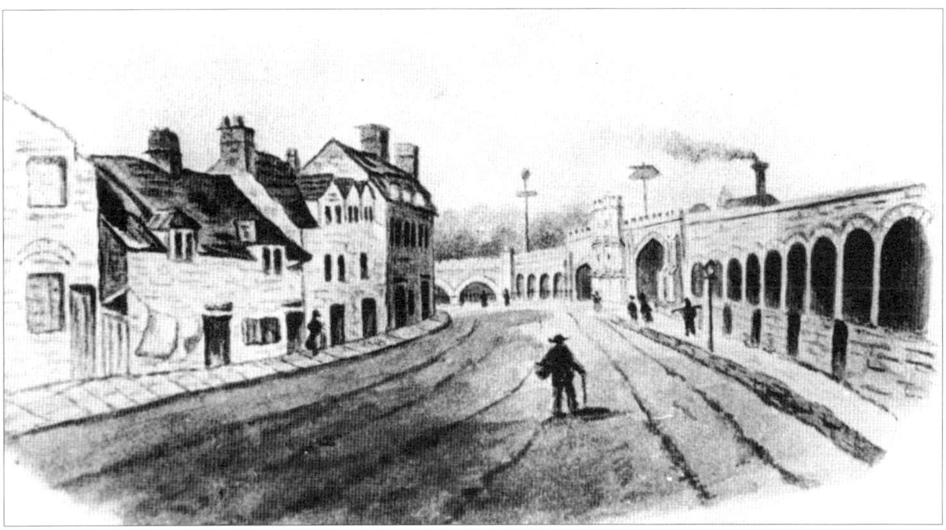

View along the Lower Bristol Road towards the GWR station at Bath, April 1854. (*Author's Collection*)

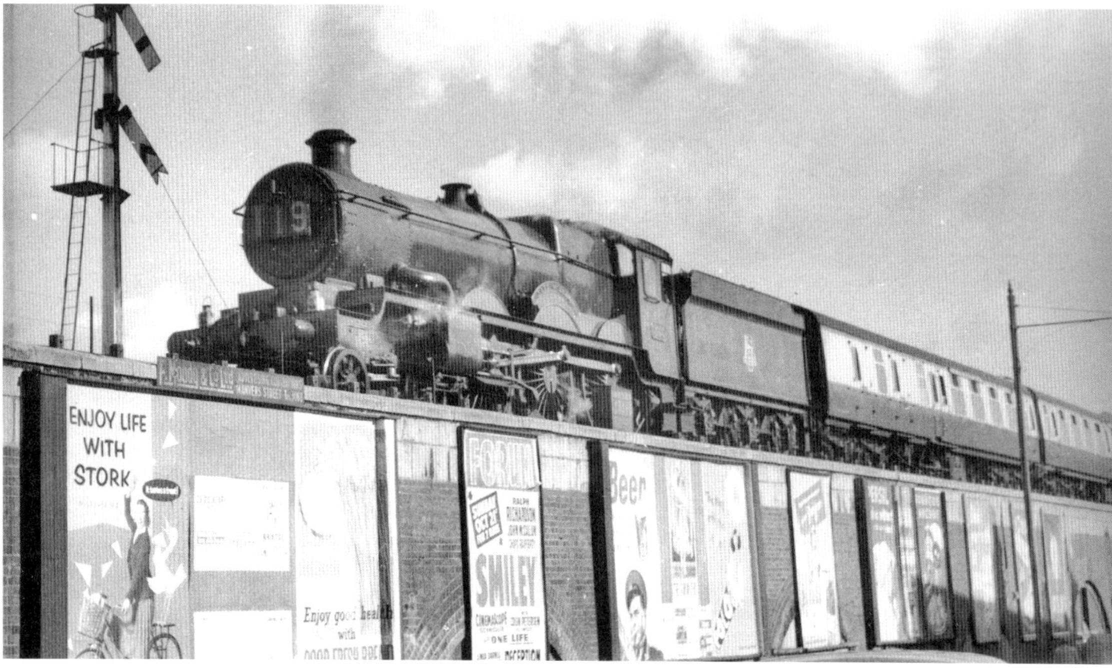

Castle class 4-6-0 No. 5055 *Earl of Eldon* crosses St James' Viaduct with a Down express, 26 October 1956. (*R. E. Toop*)

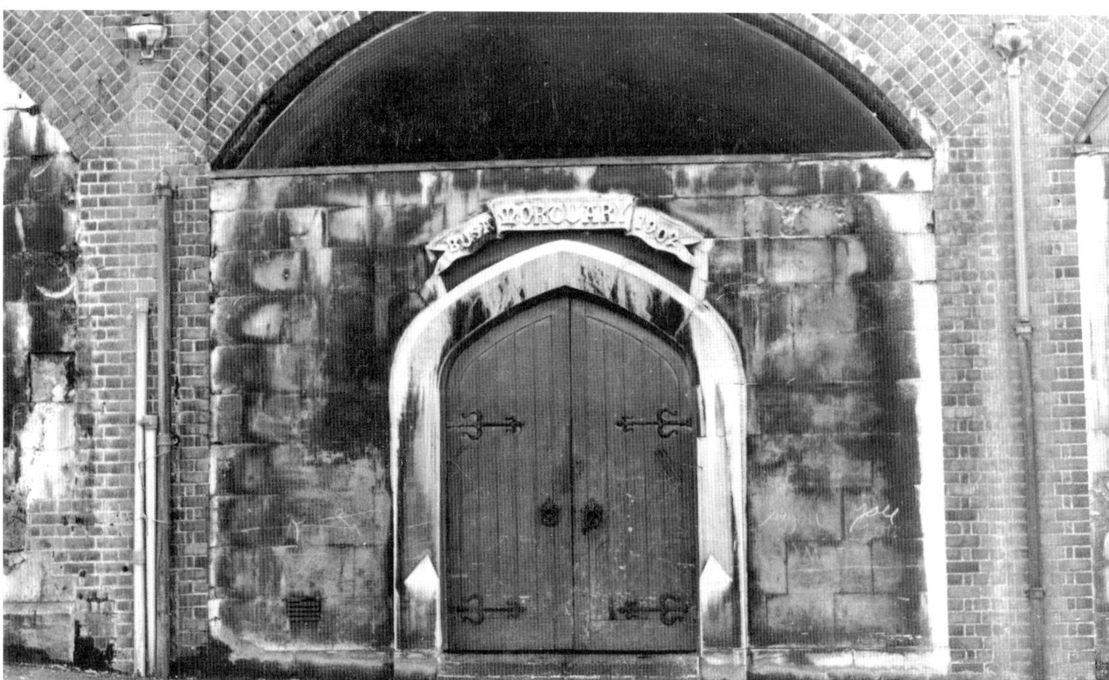

The 'BUSA [Bath Urban Sanitary Authority] Mortuary 1902' in St James' Viaduct, 12 October 1963. (*Author*)

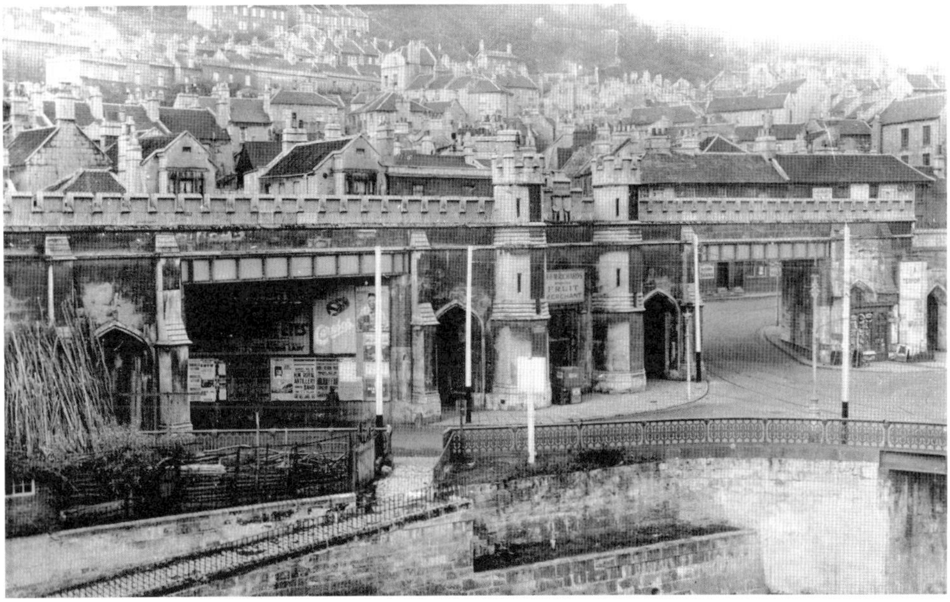

The attractive viaduct west of Bath station, with the Wells Road Bridge, right, and Claverton Street, left, August 1929. The archway between the two towers is leased to N. H. M. Richards, wholesale fruit merchants. The Beau Nash cinema advertises *Through Different Eyes*. (*Author's Collection*)

The skew bridge spanning the Avon immediately west of Bath station was originally intended to be of iron, and indeed tenders were sought in May 1839, but because of delays, it had to be constructed of laminated timber. In 1878 Wakefield Simpson, district engineer, replaced this unique bridge with one of iron girders resting on the same foundation and piers. It was widened in the autumn of 1959 to allow the Up platform to be lengthened.

Bath passenger station, Grade II listed, is placed in a cramped situation between two river bridges set only 700 ft apart, and into this space, in addition to passenger facilities, was originally squeezed an engine shed and goods depot, the latter set at right angles to the main line, access being by wagon turntable. The GWR was required to construct roads to its station: half of Dorchester Street was already there, but Manvers Street had to be built and kept in repair by the company until two-thirds had been lined with buildings, after which the responsibility lay with the landowner, Lord Manvers, from whom the land required for the station was leased on 30 December 1837. The agreement was amended on 25 July 1854 so that the GWR would maintain the road until the buildings on the west side were fit for habitation, when Lord Manvers would take over. When the station site was flooded in March 1840, James Scott was unable to begin work on its construction, with the result that when the line was ready for opening, the station was far from complete, temporary offices having to be erected. On 10 June 1841, the *Bath Chronicle* reported: 'This noble structure is rapidly progressing – the recent fine clear weather has greatly facilitated the works. The building will form a very striking object when finished, and will not only be a great ornament in the locality in which it is situated, but it will also be worthy of the stupendous undertaking with which it is connected.' The station was 'practically finished' for the opening of the extension to Chippenharn on 30 June 1841.

The station's architectural style is debased Elizabethan with Gothic windows and Romanesque ornamentation. The north front, facing the city, is of asymmetrical design with three Jacobean-style gables and a central oriel window. The building was flanked by curved wing walls forming a carriage sweep. In 1845 an eastern wing was built containing, among other things, a first-class waiting room. A canopy above the entrance allowed carriage passengers to alight in the dry. Attractive radial fan lights are set above the doorways.

The building adjacent to the Down platform is much plainer in style but it, too, had an exterior canopy to shelter carriage passengers. Until 1897 the two platforms and the four roads between were covered by a train shed. Of 40-ft span, it was supported at the sides by twenty-six large iron columns placed only 3 ft 2 in from the platform edge and allowing little room for movement when coach doors were open. As the trains are at first-floor level, in order to avoid an outward thrust on the walls built on arches, Brunel designed the roof timbers like long arms of cranes which met in the centre, short arms being held down by the side walls at the rear of the platforms.

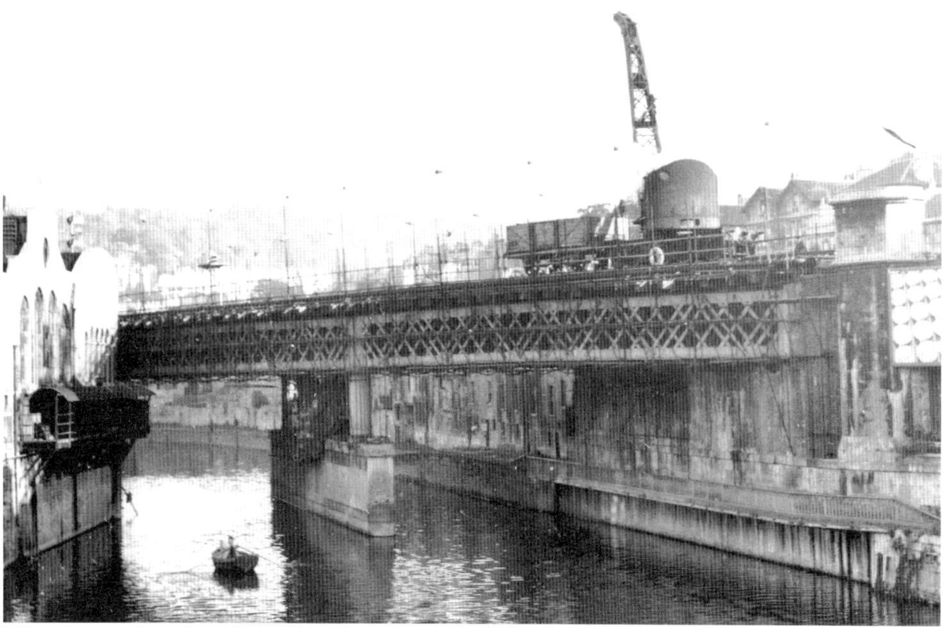

The bridge west of Bath station being widened on 25 October 1959 to allow the Up platform to be lengthened over it. Notice the safety precautions – lifebelt and boat. A steam crane is in use. (*Author*)

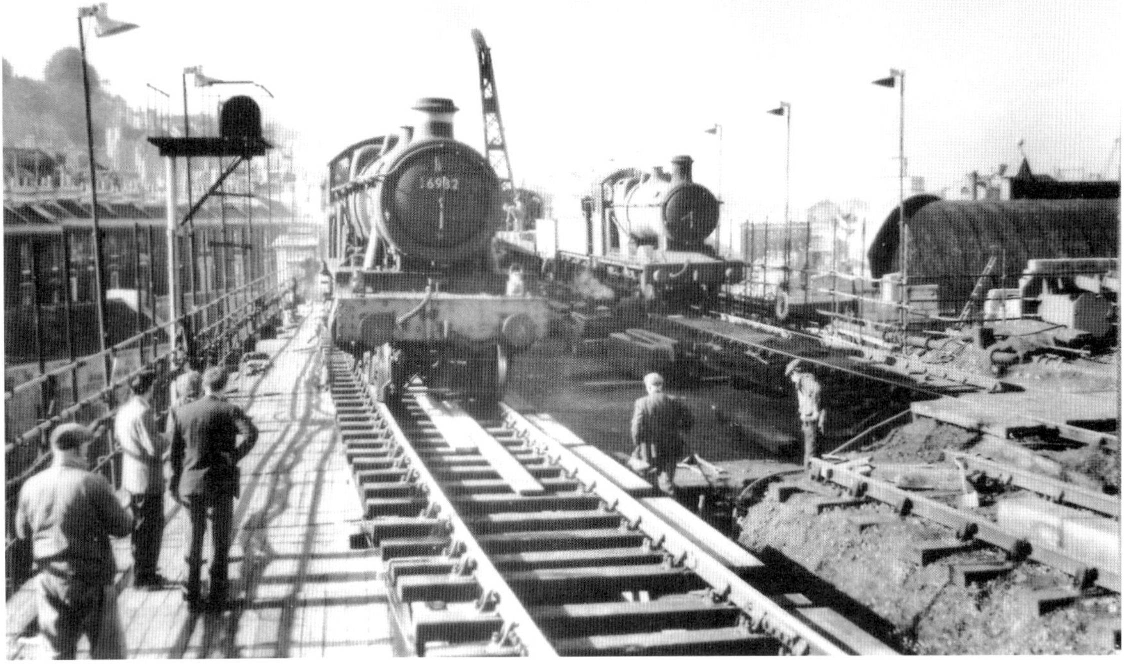

Due to these bridge works, No. 6932 *Burwarton Hall*, heading the 10.10 a.m. Cardiff to Portsmouth on 25 October 1959, has to work 'wrong line'. A 2251 class 0-6-0 stands on the right with a steam crane. (*Author's Collection*)

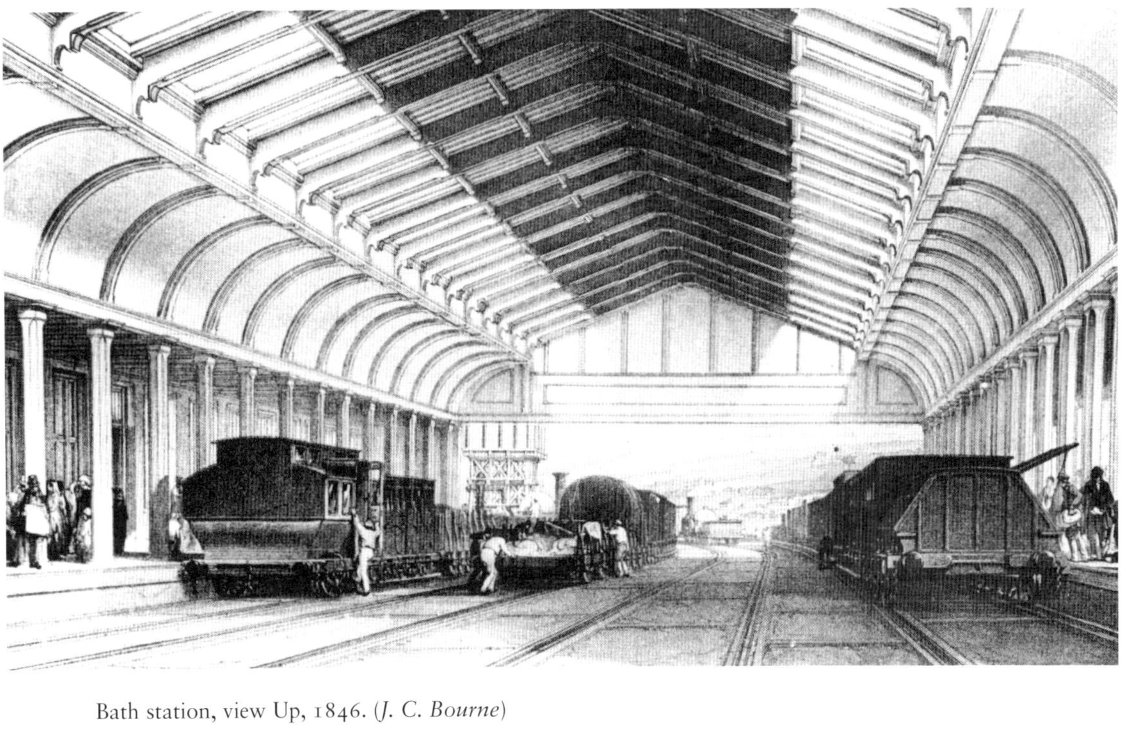

Bath station, view Up, 1846. (*J. C. Bourne*)

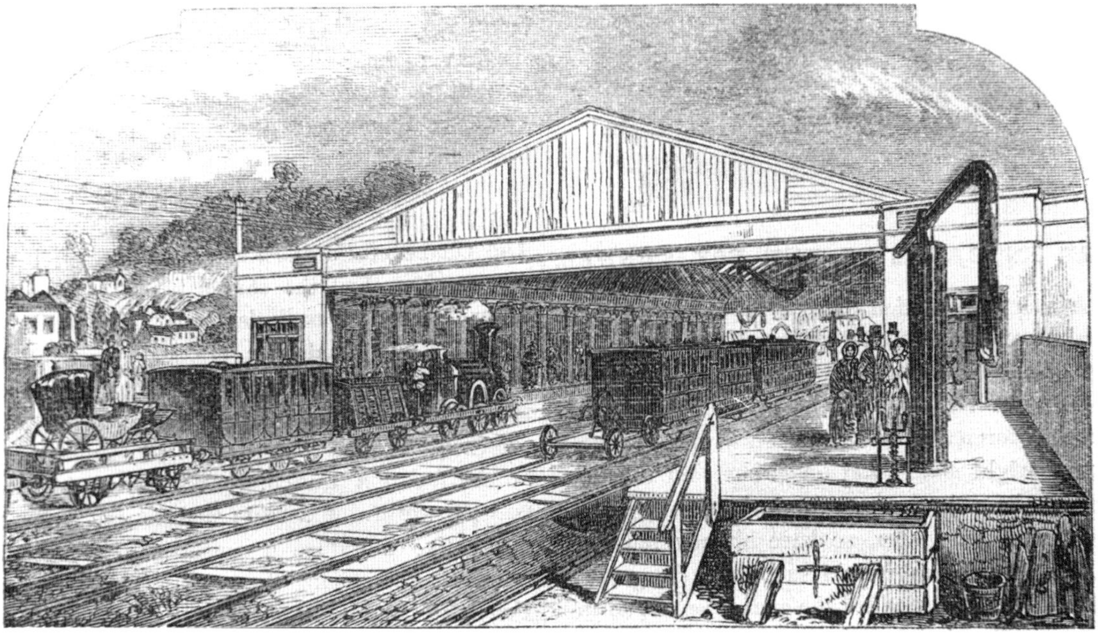

A Down train enters Bath *c.* 1850. Notice the carriage on a wagon. A spare rake of coaches stands on a central siding. The water crane is prominent on the right. (*George Measom*)

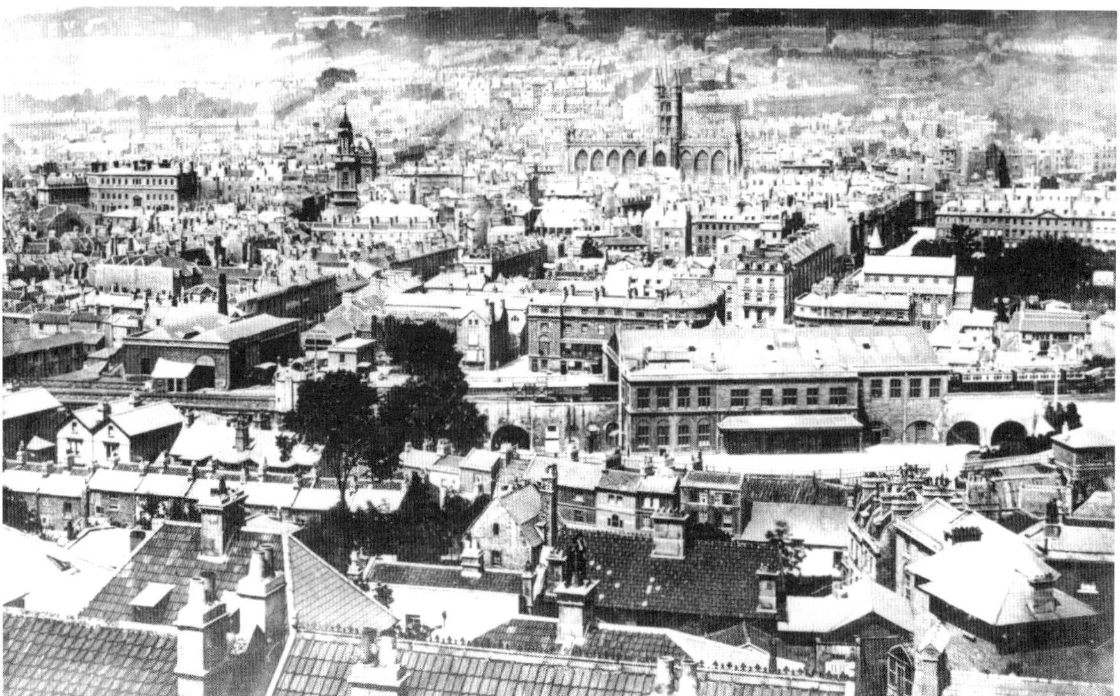

Bath from Beechen Cliff *c.* 1890. The train shed can be seen centre right, and the goods station centre left. (*Author's Collection*)

Towards the end of the nineteenth century many complaints were received about the state of the station and when Princess Helen made a visit on 13 June 1889, instead of her using the dilapidated structure, on arrival at Bath her train was drawn back on the Up line for ½ mile to Sydney Gardens, where a special temporary platform in a beautiful situation awaited. On 2 April 1889 the town clerk had submitted a memorial to the directors signed by 1,100 citizens. It pointed out that except for lengthening the Down platform to 400 ft, and the Up to 270 ft in about 1880, the station was as originally built; the presence of pillars near the platform edge was dangerous; a carriage approach to platform level was required; the staircase was narrow and exceedingly steep – objectionable anywhere, but intolerable at Bath, a resort for invalids. Finally, it was pointed out that the GWR station compared unfavourably with that of the MR.

However, no improvements were made, so on 23 June 1891 the City Council unanimously resolved 'that in consequence of the long delay of the Directors of the Great Western Railway in rectifying the very serious inconvenience of the Bath Station, a Deputation of the Council be appointed to wait upon the Board of Directors to urge speedy action'. Highly skilled in psychology, the GWR arranged for the deputation to travel in a saloon attached to the 9.35 a.m. Up express from Temple Meads on 22 July. The *Bath Chronicle* reported: 'On arriving at Paddington, the Deputation was received by the station master, Mr Hart, formerly associated with the Bath station, and were shown to the official quarters of the magnates of the Company.'

At the meeting:

> The Mayor suggested that the staircases should be abolished, and the booking offices placed on a level with the platform, the gradients to be made as easy as possible, if the present site should be retained; more space and better arrangements for the removal of luggage; better lavatories; a light, and roomy subway; refreshment room; and a new approach from Widcombe. In conclusion His Worship again adverted to the delay in making the alterations, the urgency of which he enforced by referring to the accidents which had occurred from the steepness of the staircases and the humiliation he experienced on Tuesday, when he had to escort the Prince and Princess of Saxe-Weimer down these gloomy descents.

The GWR directors still took no action, so at the company's half-yearly meeting on 11 August 1892, Colonel Vaughton, a shareholder, said that for some years the GWR had been earning £60,000 to £80,000 from the city yet 'Since Bath station had been built by Brunel it had, he believed, never been thoroughly painted'. At the half-yearly meeting on 10 August 1893 John Stone, another shareholder and town clerk at Bath, revealed 'This morning, when leaving Bath I had to mount a staircase, the egress at the top of which was only the width of my walking stick. There is a broad easy staircase, but this is kept shut. There should be a light kept burning in the dark narrow staircase.' Colonel Rich, shareholder and former

Board of Trade Inspector of Railways, corroborated, saying that the station was 'most unfit and dangerous'. The chairman, E. G. Saunders, replied: 'I'm afraid the expenditure at Bath station wouldn't be remunerative. It would improve the accommodation for traffic, but it wouldn't bring us in a shilling directly.'

The meeting stirred the directors into sending a letter, dated 22 August 1893, to the City Council informing it that they would open the wide staircase to the Up platform and provide additional lighting. The city still had to wait almost eighteen months, until 14 February 1895, when the shareholders agreed that a sum of £15,000 be spent on station improvements which were 'in hand'. The work actually began on 23 March 1895 when platelayers slewed the Up line 6 ft towards the Down, allowing carpenters to lay 3,600 ft of planking to widen the platform to give 8–9 ft, instead of 3 ft 2 in, between the platform edge and the obstructive columns. A few weeks later the Down side was similarly treated. The station was electrically lit – it must have been one of the first in the country to have this form of illumination – while skylights made the new booking hall lighter than the old. At first the GWR generated its own power at Bath, but in 1902 the company purchased it from Bath Corporation at 1½*d* a unit, a price the railway considered low enough to abolish its own installation. In 1897 the overall roof of the station was removed despite a letter to the *Bath Chronicle* pleading for the retention of the 'fine train shed'. An Up bay platform holding four coaches was added, the main platforms widened and lengthened as far as possible without blocking access to the stub sidings at the end of both platforms. Wagons were placed on these sidings by a shunting horse, a wagon turntable directing them to the desired line.

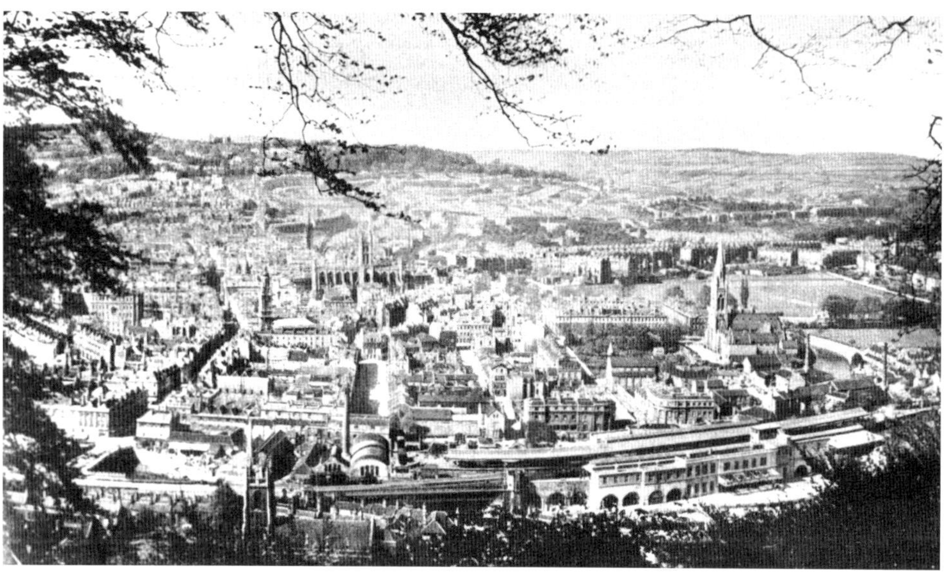

Bath from Beechen Cliff *c.* 1910. The roof of the train shed has been removed, the passenger station extended at both ends and the goods shed removed. (*Author's Collection*)

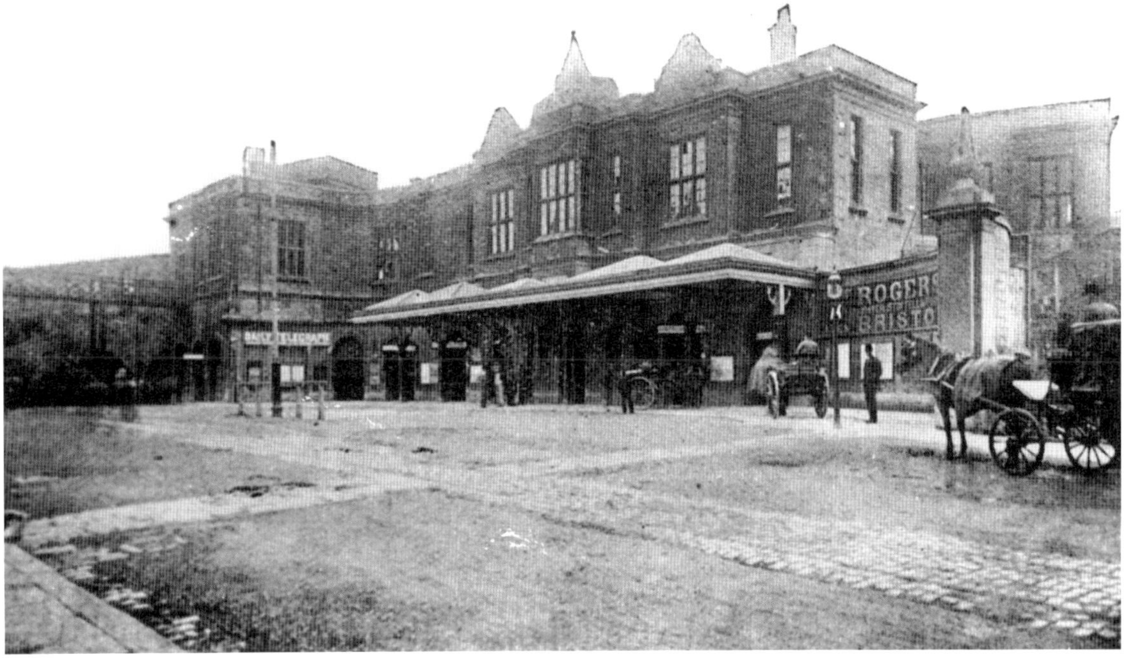

The frontage of Bath station *c.* 1886, showing the old canopy. Horse tram track is in the foreground. (*Author's Collection*)

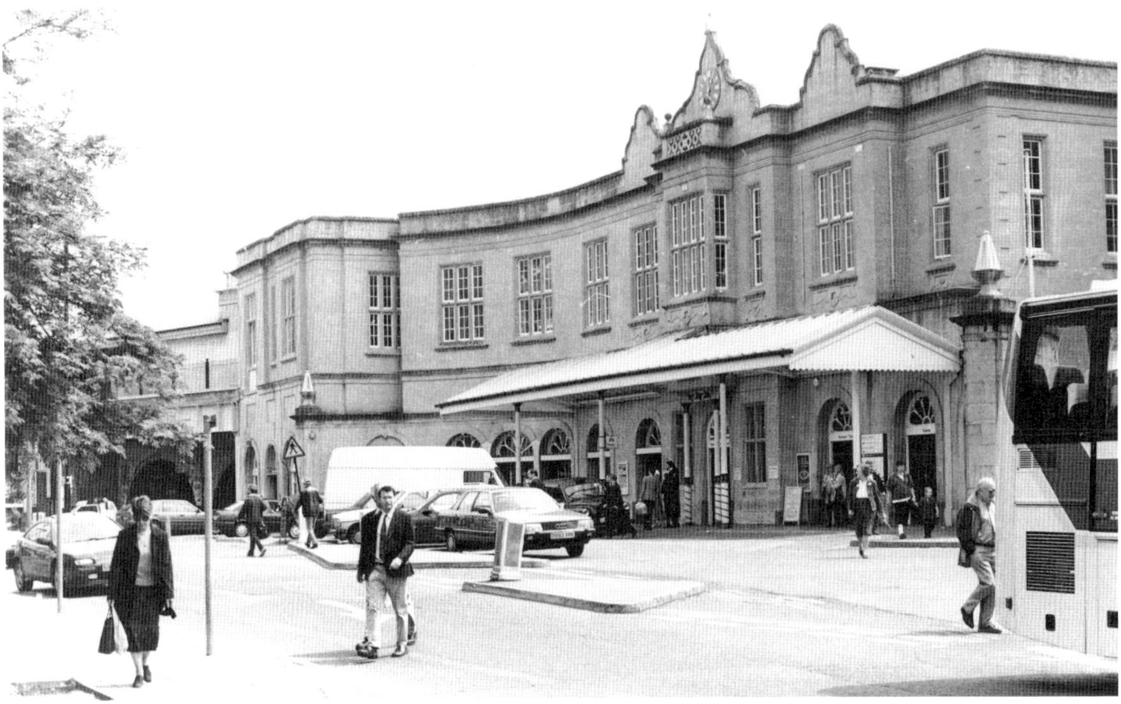

The station from a similar viewpoint, 14 May 1999. (*Author*)

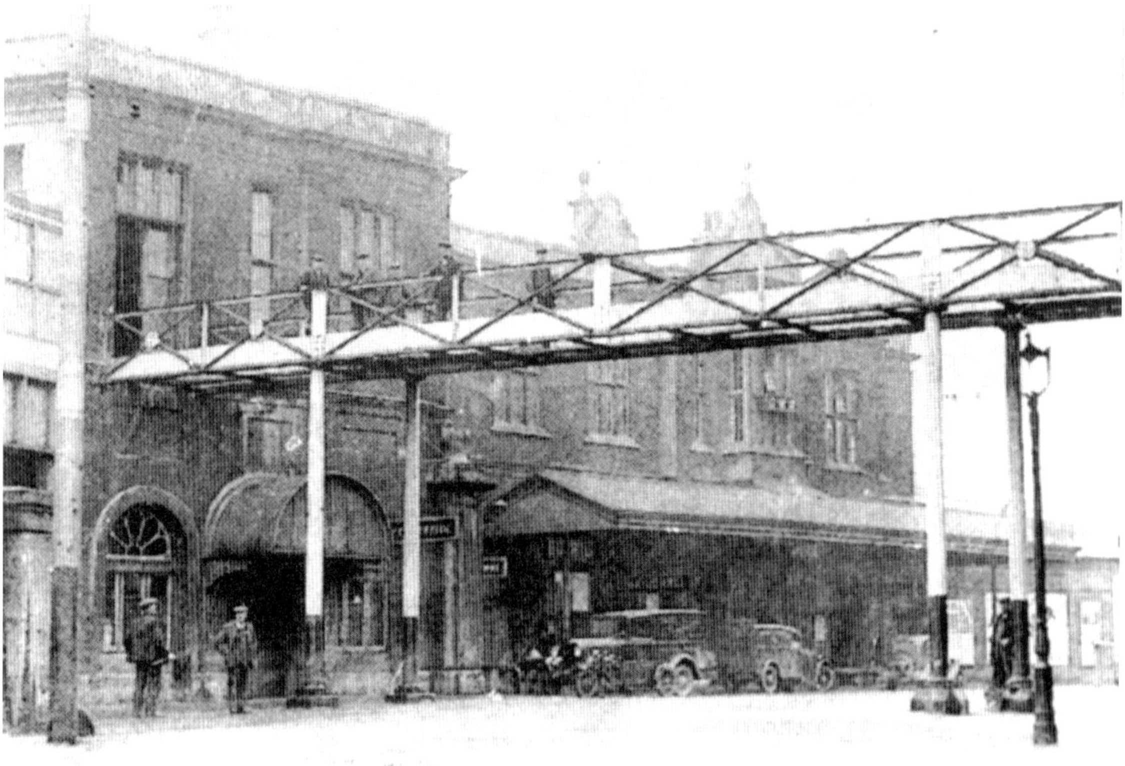

The footbridge spanning the road between the Up platform and the Royal Hotel. In 1936 the dismantling team is ready to start work. (*Author's Collection*)

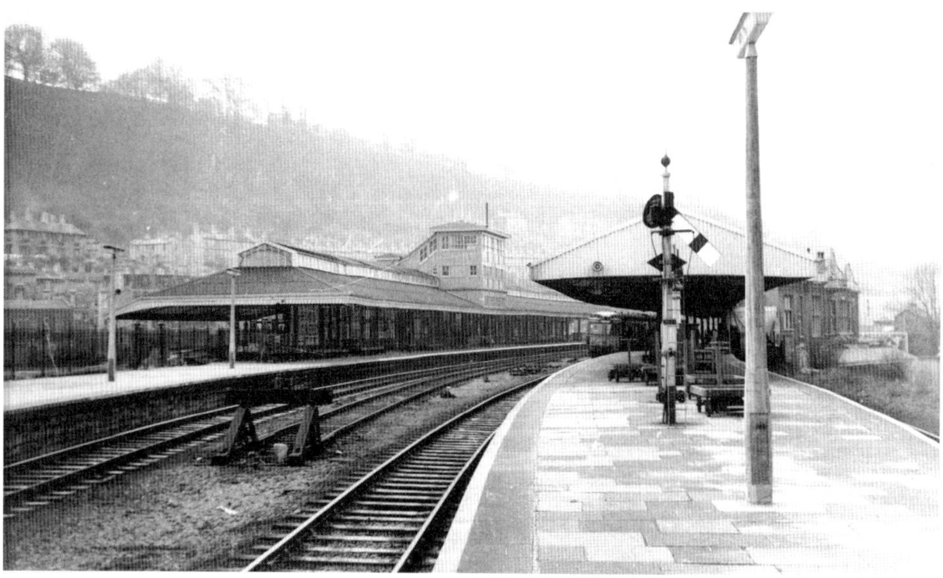

Bath Spa, view Down *c.* 1967. A Swindon cross-country DMU stands at the Up platform. The bay platform is on the right. Notice the signal box, which closed 21 January 1968, above the Down platform canopy. The central loops have become a siding. (*Derrick Payne*)

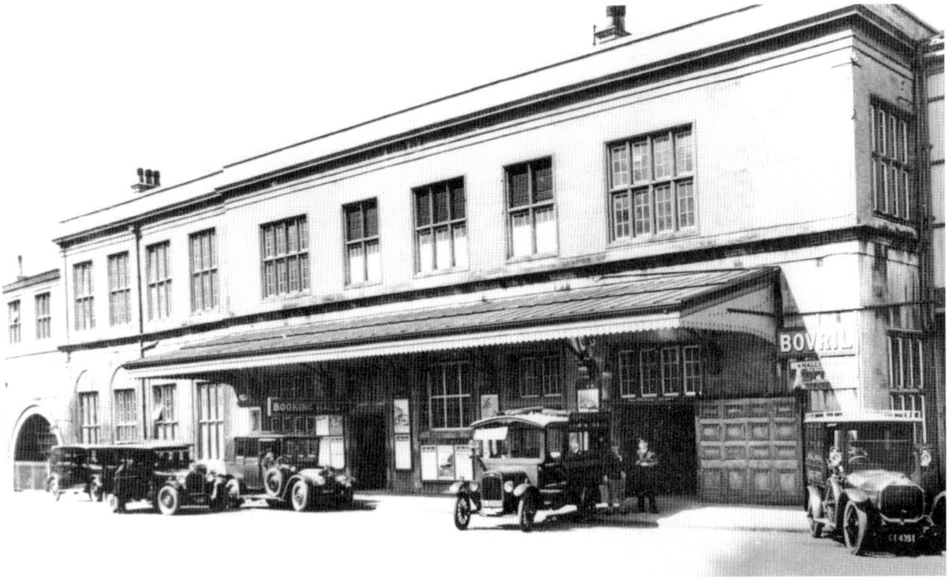

The exterior of Bath station on the Down side, seen about 1925. The second vehicle from the right is a hotel bus. (*Author's Collection*)

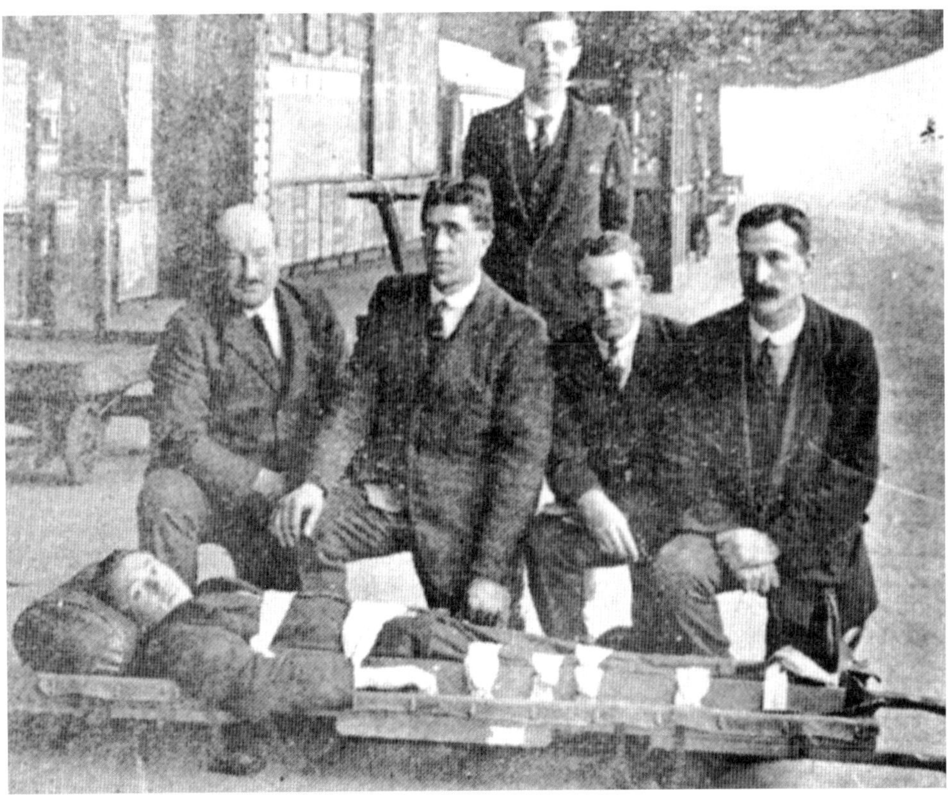

The GWR first aid team at Bath station, 1 March 1925. A 'patient' is strapped securely to the stretcher. Behind the standing gentleman is a coach in the bay platform. (*Author's Collection*)

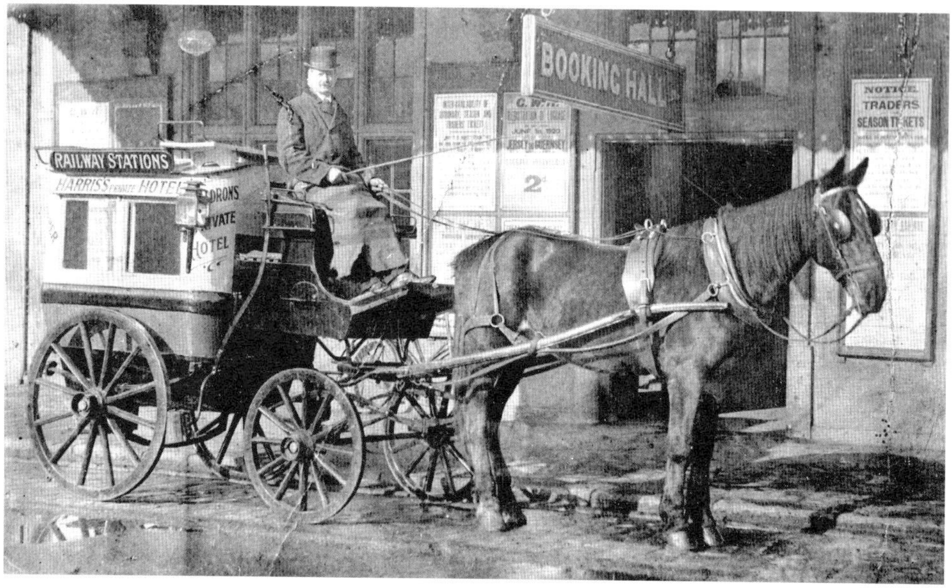

A horse-drawn hotel bus outside Bath station, June 1920. (*Author's Collection*)

The horse was also used to attach four-wheeled vacuum brake-fitted vehicles to the rear of Up trains. It was hooked to the side of a preloaded van, gave a hefty pull and then stepped out of the way, the impetus fly-shunting the van to buffer up to the train standing at the platform. To ease the work of the horse, it was customary for its keeper to use a pinch bar behind a wheel to help set it in motion. One day the horse fell over a low wall onto the roof of a building below track level, the animal landing with its hoofs in the air. Fortunately, the fire brigade was able to retrieve it unharmed. From the opening of the adjacent municipal electricity works in about 1895 until April 1953, coal for the works arriving by rail was drawn to the coal shoots by shunting horse. Prince, the last shunting horse at the station, retired in 1959.

The stub sidings were removed in January 1960, which allowed the platforms to be lengthened, the Down from eight to ten coaches, and the Up from nine to fifteen. It was ironic that soon after the platforms were extended, trains became shorter and the full length of the Up platform is rarely used today. An economy introduced in 1962 was that instead of manned barriers at both the Up and the Down platforms, the barrier was moved to near the booking hall so that at quiet periods one collector could control both platforms. This move introduced the retrograde step of having to close the Widcombe entrance. At the same time a Westinghouse-Garrard mechanical ticket machine was installed to print tickets, about 400,000 being issued annually.

Recent work at Bath included the installation of a new GWR-style canopy on the exterior of the south side of the station and new lifts, while a contentious proposal is the removal of the carriage ramp to the Up platform.

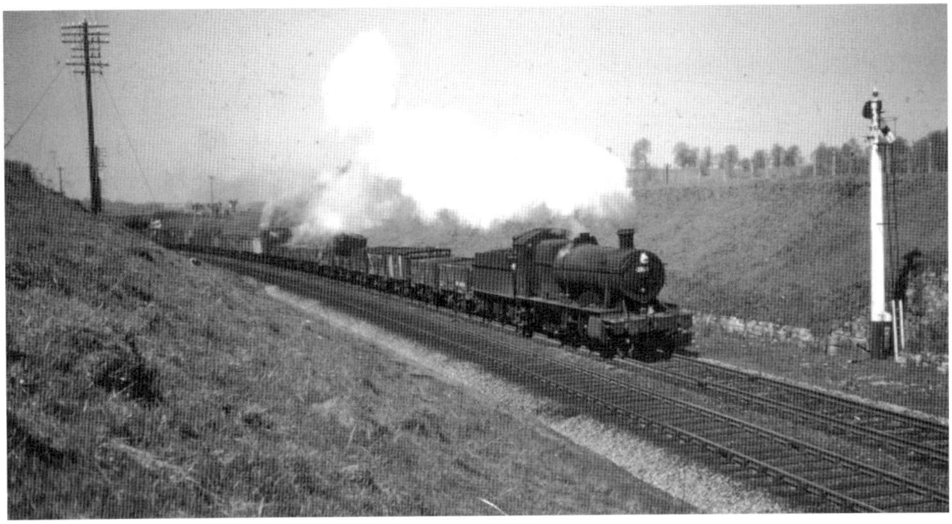

28XX class 2-8-0 No. 2828 heads an Up freight near Twerton Tunnel signal box *c.* 1957. The Down track is bullhead rail, but the Up has been relaid with flat-bottomed rail. The site of the Up refuge siding, lifted 12 November 1950, can be seen on the far side of the train. When this line was constructed, a Roman villa was discovered at the far end of the cutting and was the first important archaeogical discovery made in railway building. (*J. A. Reid*)

The GWR opened its very first cloakroom for passengers' left luggage at Bath on 13 July 1846 and, for a fee of 2*d*, items were kept separately and locked up, a printed receipt given to the passenger. Surprisingly, although the *Bath Chronicle* reported it as a great success and well patronised, after only a week's use the GWR directors ordered the scheme to be abandoned. Another early trial at Bath was the issue of 1*d* platform tickets from 6 February 1913. Supplied by two automatic machines costing £40 each, the first day's takings were 15*s* 9*d*. No fewer than 12,019 tickets were sold during March, bringing an income of £50 1*s* 7*d*.

Each platform was served by two hydraulic lifts: one for passengers and the other for luggage. The passenger lift could accommodate twenty people in wheelchairs. Sumptuously appointed with beech and pine panels held in place by wooden nails, it was thoroughly cleaned daily. The lift serving the Down platform has recently been restored and exhibited as a fixed feature. An employee on the platform who wanted to raise the luggage lift called as a warning 'Below!' before pulling the operating handle. The header tank was situated at the east end of the Down platform, below the tank supplying locomotive water cranes. As an economy measure, the passenger lifts were closed to general passengers, although retained for the disabled, on 30 March 1925, thereby releasing three collectors for other duties. In 1965/66 the four hydraulic lifts were removed and the pump station near the Up end of the Down side demolished, as were the cottages occupied by the permanent way inspector and the bridge inspector who also dealt with the Severn Tunnel. The luggage subway and rear luggage entrance were closed.

The booking office had a window for Up line tickets and another for Down trains, though on Thursdays the Down window was used for employees to collect their pay and therefore closed for passengers. A third window was opened on Mondays for issuing season tickets. One regular weekly passenger required a 19*s* 1*d* return to Parkstone. He always tendered a £1 note plus 1*d* and a cigarette, and received 1*s* change. Wages for Bath railwaymen were sent from Bristol by rail, someone ringing through to say which train they were on and so alerting the chief clerk and an assistant to be on the platform to pick up the cash. Booking clerks made up the wages of the station staff, station signalmen, Westmoreland Goods Yard staff, Oldfield Park Platform staff, permanent way staff and bridge inspector's staff. The money was placed in numbered tins that were small and designed for sovereigns, so it was difficult squeezing in £1 notes and pushing the lids on. An innovation on 14 March 1910 was a lady booking clerk, though lady clerks had already been introduced in the goods and telegraph departments at Bristol. At the end of a duty, each clerk placed the cash he received from ticket sales into a 'drop safe' fixed in the booking office for which only the chief clerk held the key. He cashed up every afternoon and forwarded the takings to Temple Meads in a travelling safe.

During and after the Second World War, on Thursday evenings, two booking clerks regularly travelled by taxi to RAF Colerne with tickets for travel from Bristol Temple Meads, Gloucester, Salisbury and Swindon stations, road transport taking them from the air base to these stations. On a fine summer Sunday in the 1950s, a clerk might book 500 adult cheap day returns to Weston-super-Mare together with 100 child's tickets, and perhaps fifty adults to Weymouth and twenty-five children. A spare train for Weston was stabled on the centre road at Bath for use if required, while another for Weymouth was ready at Temple Meads. Stothert & Pitt's Social Club had tickets on a sale or return basis and made an annual trip to such places as Paignton and London using scheduled trains, but having reserved seats.

A letter in the *Bath Chronicle* on 8 March 1877 revealed one or two interesting fare anomalies:

> If your journey is from Bristol to Exeter you may save more than 4*s* by travelling 12 miles in the opposite direction to Bath the lowest fares being - Bristol to Bath 11½*d* Bath to Exeter 7*s* 3*d* and Bristol to Exeter 12*s* 6*d*. Should you be travelling from Bath to Exeter, and wish to find out what your fare is before asking for your ticket, don't be angry when you discover that in the table of fares hung up at Bath station, there is a blank opposite the word 'Exeter'. This is an infringement of the law of the land, but the Great Western is a very important Company, and rises superior to such paltry regulations as private individuals are amenable to.
>
> Again, check any tendency to wrath if you are charged 9*s* 5*d* as a minimum fare from Bath to Bridgwater, 45 miles, while a friend travelling in the same train to Exeter, 87 miles, pays 7*s* 3*d*.

The Up platform had two refreshment rooms – one for first-class passengers and the other for all classes – but on the Down side only one refreshment room was provided. They were staffed by a manageress, about six girls, a cellar lad and a page boy. The cellar lad's uniform was blue and the page boy's brown. The page boy always sold refreshments, whereas the cellar lad only helped out selling to busy trains. If the beer pipes developed a fault, a man came from Swindon to repair them. In the 1920s the girls lived in a hostel at 47 Lower Bristol Road. The two boys each had a trolley and called 'Teas, light refreshments and minerals'. The refreshment rooms made up lunch baskets – perhaps as many as twenty for a football excursion – and it was a sore point with the staff that the manageress always delivered these herself and so received the tip, yet had done none of the work. The lads were provided with a free lunch daily and a bottle of ginger ale. The lunches were good, but one boy grew tired of ginger ale and asked for, and received, tea instead. Railway staff who used the refreshment room said 'OCS' (On Company's Service) and were allowed 1*d* off their bill. Early in 1922 the GWR purchased for £890 No. 8 Lyncombe Hill to be used as the stationmaster's house.

Recycling is no new notion. In 1867 a box to collect newspapers, books and magazines discarded by passengers was fixed to each of the platforms so that the literature could be used by patients of the Royal United and Mineral Water Hospitals. John Menzies' bookstall closed on 27 March 1976, but BR Travel Fare, which provided catering, took over selling magazines and newspapers.

Because the station is situated on a curve, the driver of a long Down train was unable to see his guard giving the 'Right Away'. To overcome this problem, in February 1947 two illuminated indicators were provided on the Down side, one 20 yd and the other 172 yd in advance of the Down starting signal. Having received an intimation from the platform inspector that the train could proceed, the guard operated one of the two push buttons located in boxes on the 4th and 9th platform verandah pillars counting from the London end. This action illuminated the letters 'RA' (Right Away). The indicator situated 20 yd in advance of the Down starter showed only in the Bristol direction, but the indicator 172 yd in advance showed in both directions, so was visible to a driver whether his engine was in advance of, or to the rear of, the indicator. The indicator was automatically cancelled when the track circuit to the rear of the Down advanced starting signal became clear. The apparatus was dismantled in July 1964.

From 1845 until 26 January 1936 an open girder footbridge offered a direct connection between the Up platform and the Royal Hotel, built by Chadwick, the railway contractor, on the opposite side of the street. Giuseppe Garibaldi, Italian patriot and hero, planned to address Bath citizens from this bridge, but the crowd of dignitaries greeting his train prevented him from leaving the coach.

Initially, signalling was by disc and crossbar with a fantail signal indicating Caution. With this time interval system, after the passing of a train, signals

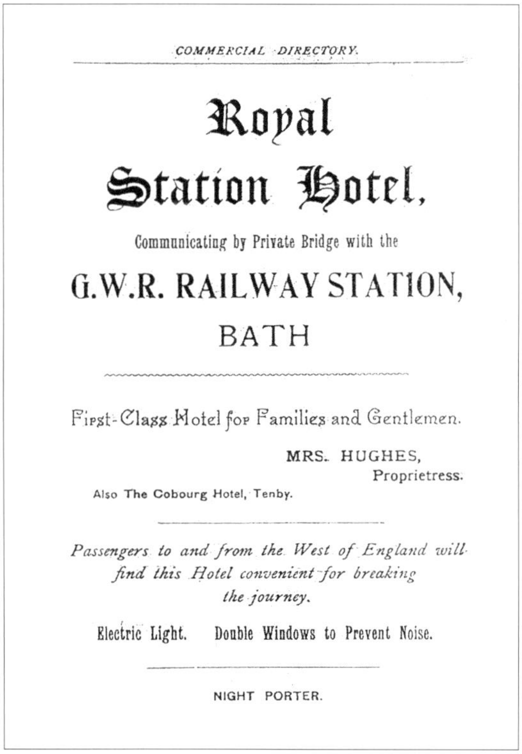

Advertisement for the Royal Hotel, Bath, in the *Post Office Directory*, 1902.

remained at Danger for three minutes, Caution for another seven minutes, and then Clear. In 1852 the system was modified to: after a passenger train, five minutes at Danger and five at Caution; and after a goods, eight minutes at Danger and seven at Caution. Bath and Bristol stations were examples of the few places where the normal position was Danger and a signal only cleared to admit a train. The time interval system lasted until 1877 when it was replaced by the block. In around 1874 signal boxes were brought into use between Paddington and Bristol, working a mixture of disc and crossbar and semaphore signals. Stone-built signal boxes were opened at Bath: No. 1 at the east end and No. 2 at the west end. They were in Elizabethan style to complement the rest of the station. They were superseded by one box above the Down platform canopy when the station was altered in 1897. The box was reached via a spiral staircase and enjoyed a marvellous view over the city, even better than from the east end of the platform, which today is one of the finest from any urban station in the country. The box had no outside balcony and, rather than lean out to clean the windows, some signalmen preferred to remove the beading and lift the whole window pane out. Because of the platform canopy obscuring his view, a signalman was unable to check the tail lamp of a Down train until it was well beyond the platform, so a porter was deputed to check on his behalf and shout up the stairs 'Tail lamp' so that the signalman could 'Clear back'. The box closed on 21 January 1968, when it was abolished under the Bristol Multiple Aspect Signalling (MAS).

Chapter Seven

Development of the Line

The opening of the Severn Tunnel in 1886 brought additional traffic to the Bristol to Bath line because, in addition to catering for all West of England trains, it now had to carry those from South Wales, including Irish traffic, to Southampton and London. Ideally, the line should have been quadrupled, but the many tunnels, viaducts, embankments and cuttings would have rendered the cost prohibitive, so the cheaper expedient was adopted of laying refuge sidings or goods loops at Keynsham, Twerton Tunnel and Westmoreland Road goods depot. Matters were eased by the opening of the South Wales direct line via Badminton in 1903 and the Castle Cary to Cogload Junction cut-off in 1906, which took away much of the West of England traffic.

Bristol to Bathampton had standard-gauge rail added to the broad gauge in June 1874, together with the narrowing of the hitherto broad-gauge lines to Salisbury and Weymouth. The first standard-gauge train ran from Swindon to Bristol, via Trowbridge, as the main line Thingley Junction to Bathampton was still broad gauge, on Sunday afternoon 21 June 1874, when nine long trains of empty carriages were worked. The last public broad-gauge train from Bristol was the Up mail, which departed at 12.45 a.m. on 21 May 1892, hauled by 4-2-2 *Bulkeley.* Thirteen special trains taking broad-gauge rolling stock from Devon and Cornwall passed over the line later that night *en route* for Swindon, while some broad-gauge coaches were placed in sidings at Exeter to be hauled to Swindon later, as the broad rail of the mixed gauge east of Exeter was not immediately lifted.

The opening of Bristol's electric tramway system in 1895 offered no competition to the Bristol to Bath line. In fact, the opening of a tramway station alongside Brunel's terminus encouraged the use of the railway. An Act of 1904 gave the Bristol Tramways & Carriage Co. Ltd powers to extend its Brislington route to Keynsham, which would have competed with the Great Western, but the scheme proved abortive. Bath Electric Tramways opened in 1904 and only competed with the GWR between Twerton and Bath. In 1906 a Light Railway Order was granted for extending its Newton route to Saltford, but lower receipts and the poor state of the money market meant that these powers were never utilised.

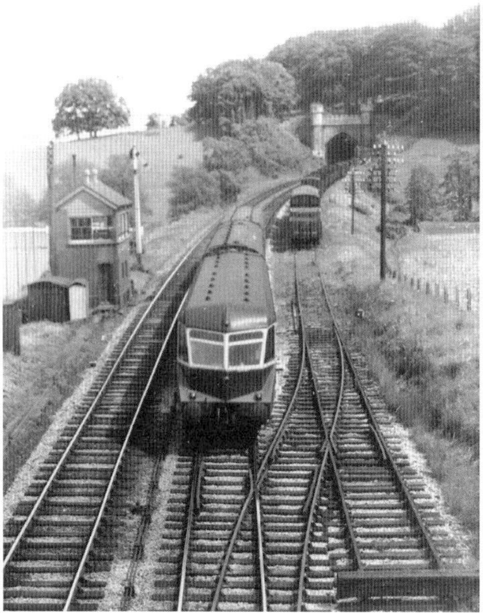

Twin GWR diesel railcars and intermediate trailer pass Twerton Tunnel signal box *c.* 1947. The Down refuge siding is on the right, the Up refuge siding being behind the photographer. (*Dr T. R. N. Edwards*)

On 5 February 1906 the Bristol Tramways & Carriage Co. inaugurated a motor bus service from the tram terminus at Brislington to Saltford and this caused a decrease in GWR receipts of £48 in March and £49 in May. On 20 August 1906 the bus service was extended to link Brislington with the Bath Electric Tramways terminus at the Globe Inn, Newton St Loe, with through tickets available from the centre of Bristol to the centre of Bath. The GWR retaliated and in June 1907 reduced the third-class fare Saltford to Bath from 9*d* to 6*d* and the 1*s* 2*d* return fare to Bristol to 1*s*. This proved a profitable move as receipts from Saltford to the two destinations improved from £180 10*s* 3*d* in July 1906 to £227 5*s* 9*d* in July 1907, an increase of £46 15*s* 6*d*. The inception in February 1925 of a Bristol to London coach service by Greyhound Motors Ltd marked a threat to longer-distance services. By 1929 the Bristol Tramways & Carriage Co. Ltd ran a bus service throughout from the Tramways Centre, Bristol, to Queen's Parade, Bath. Bath was never served regularly by GWR buses, but in 1928 a GWR 'Land Cruise' began at Bath, with many passengers arriving by rail, and visiting the Cheddar Valley, Exmoor, Torquay, Dartmoor and Hardy's Wessex, before returning to Bath six days later.

The First World War had its effect on the line, with trains commandeered for troops and war supplies. The *Bath & Wilts Chronicle* reported as early as 2 September 1914 that a special GWR Red Cross train conveying about 169 wounded men *en route* from Southampton to the Bristol Royal Infirmary had passed through Bath and, as it went by, some of the soldiers threw unstamped letters and postcards on the platform. They were picked up, stamped and posted. During the First World War, about 6,000 ambulance trains passed over the GWR, of which 395 used Temple Meads. There was also a dramatic change in the number of wagons exchanged between the GWR and MR at Bristol: 101,456 in 1913 and 171,203 in 1917.

During the Second World War, as happened in 1914, the Railway Executive Committee took over the responsibility of running the railways in wartime Britain. The outbreak of war brought trains of evacuees to the area to escape the expected bombing of the South East. From 1 to 4 September 1939 about 800 children arrived at Bath on each of approximately a dozen special trains, and of each 800, 280 were billeted within the city. Many regular trains were cancelled and on Monday 25 September a war timetable began, with all West of England trains running via Bristol and calling at Bath and Temple Meads. Restaurant and sleeping cars were withdrawn and the maximum start-to-stop speed of an express limited to 45 mph, with an overall limit of 60 mph. Expresses were often sixteen coaches in length as, for example, the 10.30 a.m. Cornish Riviera Express from Paddington had to carry passengers who would normally have used the 10.00 a.m. Bristolian or the 11.15 a.m. to Temple Meads and Weston-super-Mare. From 16 October the Railway Executive allowed the restoration of some restaurant cars and on 30 October the Cornish Riviera resumed its normal route via the Westbury cut-off.

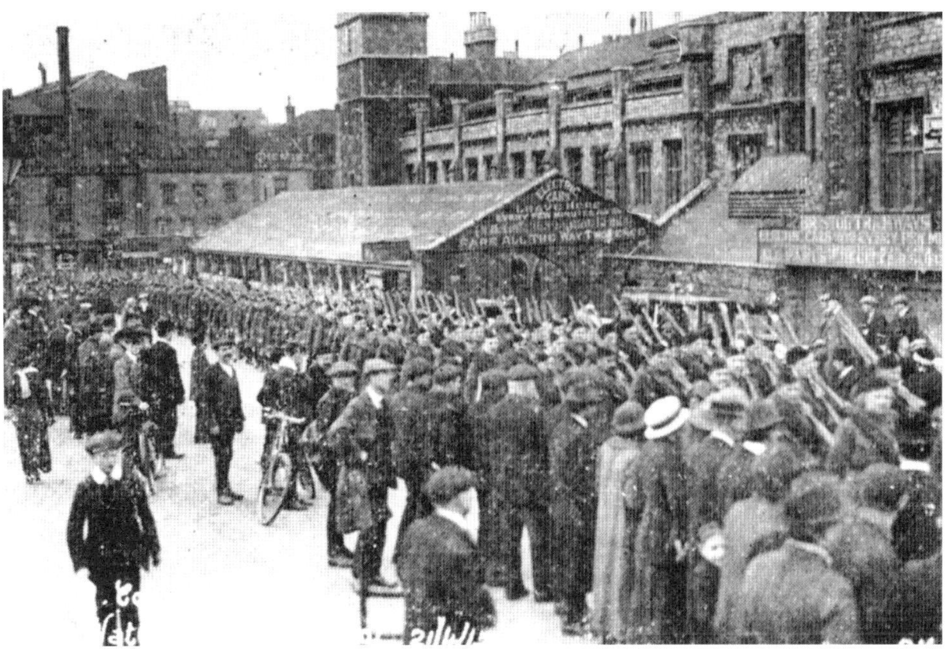

The Black Watch Regiment marches up the Temple Meads approach road to entrain, 21 January 1915. The roof of the electric tram station can be seen in the centre of the picture. (*Author's Collection*)

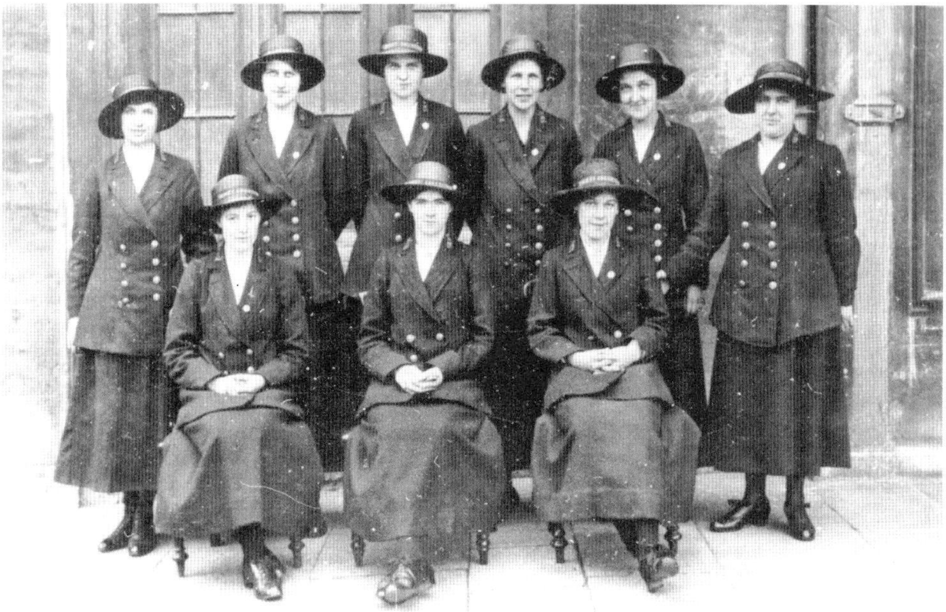

Female staff at Bath station *c.* 1916. (*Author's Collection*)

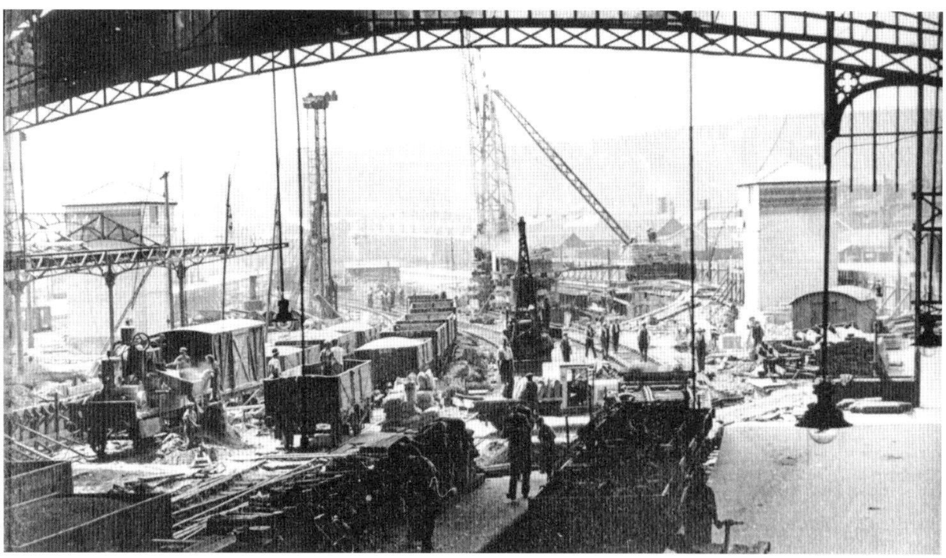

Above: Temple Meads during reconstruction *c.* 1932. The centre platforms in Wyatt's train shed are being removed. The towers, left and right, contain lift shafts. (*Peter Davey Collection*)

Opposite top: The centre platforms being removed from Wyatt's train shed *c.* 1932. Roads Reconstruction Co.'s wagons stand on the left. (*Author's Collection*)

Opposite middle: View of the 1930s platforms showing the Carrara glazed bricks and the grey concrete plinth. Notice glass in the canopy lighting the platform. (*Author*)

Opposite bottom: Temple Meads, view Down during construction. (*Author's Collection*)

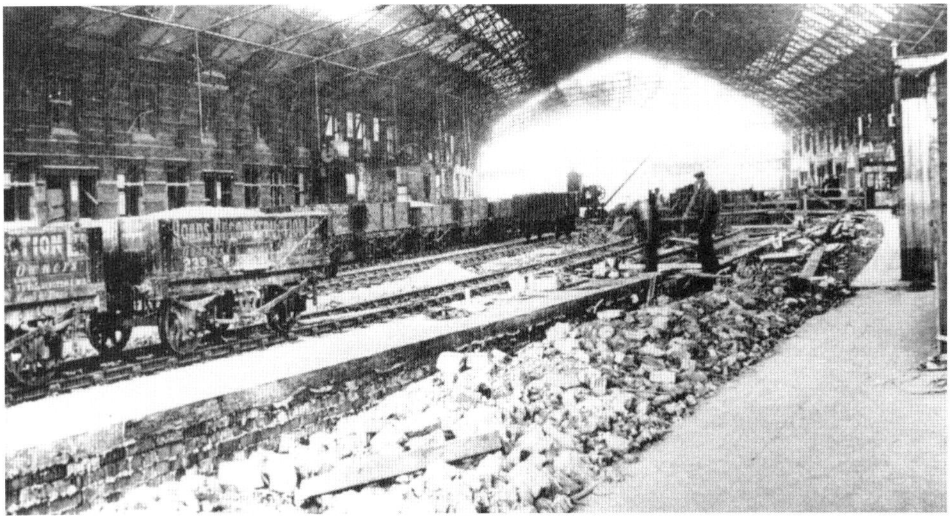

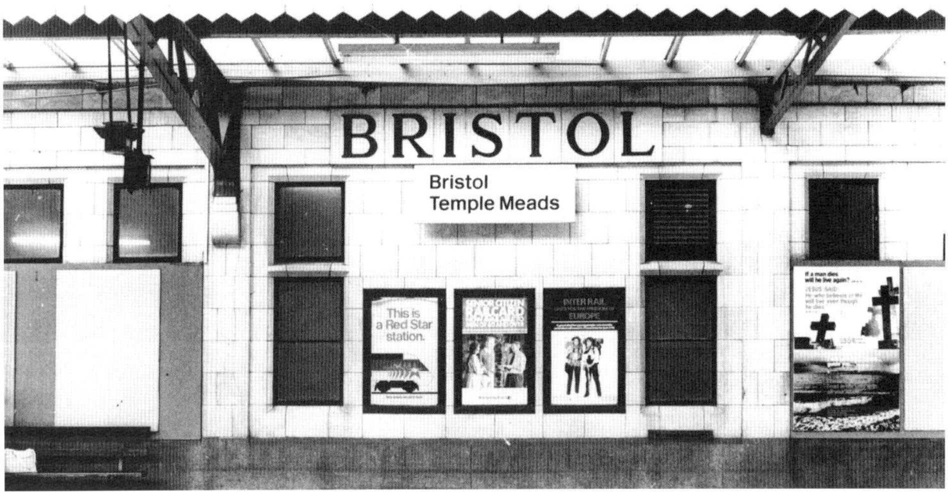
BRISTOL
Bristol
Temple Meads
This is
a Red Star
station.
INTER RAIL
EUROPE
If a man dies
will he live again?

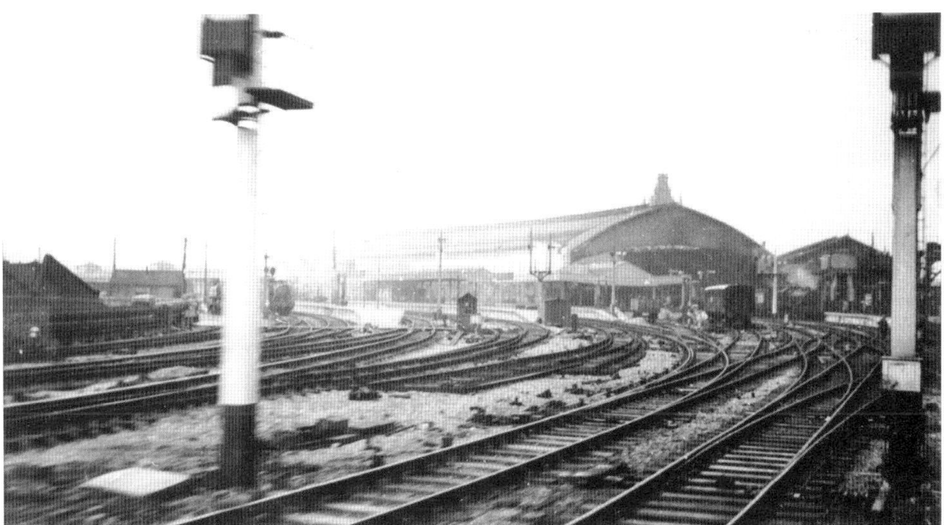

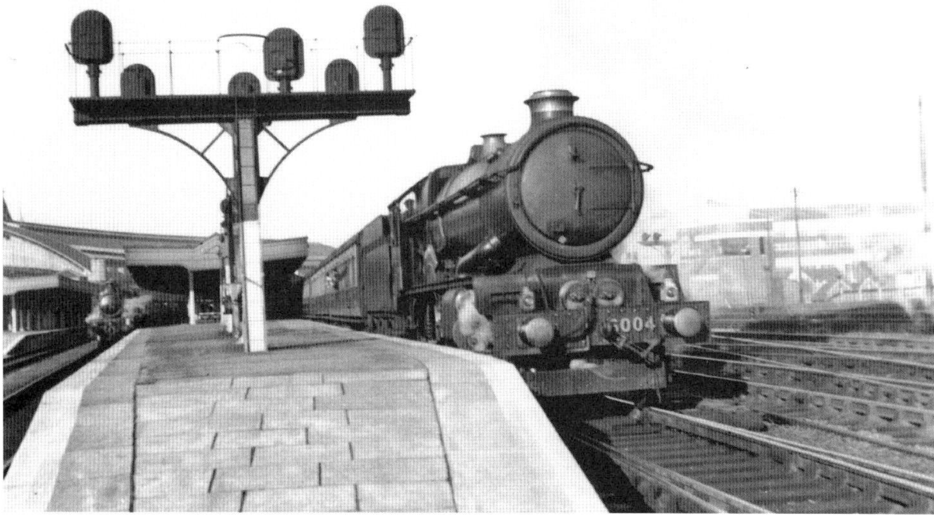

No. 6004 *King George III* at Temple Meads with the 10.30 a.m. Paddington to Plymouth wartime emergency service, September 1939. On the left a 51XX class 2-6-2T heads a train to Weston-super-Mare. (*E. J. M. Hayward*)

The wartime blackout made life difficult for railwaymen and passengers alike. Goods yards had subdued lighting, which made potentially risky shunting operations even more hazardous. Stations were dimly lit; window blinds had to be pulled down and, to avoid any chinks of light escaping, a broad band of black paint was brushed on the glass adjacent to the framing. Locomotives with side window cabs had these plated over and all engines were supplied with tarpaulins that could be fixed between cab roof and tender to conceal light from open firebox doors. It was difficult to black out the light completely from a locomotive smokebox and Bristolians were concerned that the emissions from the many engines in the city would be seen by enemy raiders. One night the RAF flew over Bristol to establish the severity of the danger. It reported: 'Intensive observation from the air did not reveal any lighting due to railway operations'. The truth was that only very large lights were visible to aircraft and locomotive fireboxes did not enter this category. As it was essential that signalmen could see trains, it was impossible to black out signal boxes, but they were lit by reflected light from a lamp that shone up to the ceiling. Temple Meads and Bath stations both had basement arches adapted as air-raid shelters.

As many railwaymen went off to join the services, their jobs were replaced by females. An advertisement for women porters at Temple Meads received 250 applicants.

In addition to their normal jobs, railwaymen had the additional task of being on a fire-watching rota so that, in the event of incendiary bombs falling, they could either remove the danger with a shovel, douse the flames with a stirrup

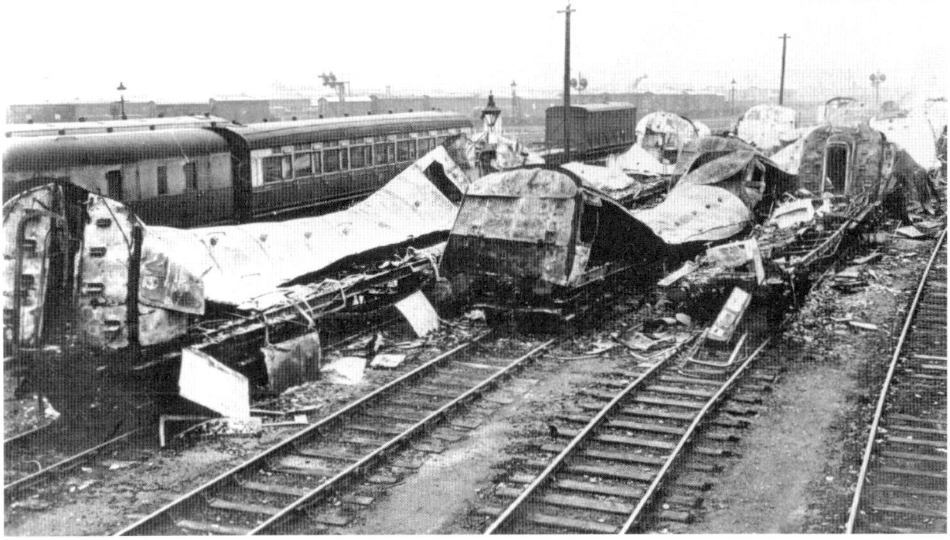

Coaches in Dr Day's sidings damaged in the 24 November 1940 raid. Wagons stand in the Kingsland Road sidings. (*Author's Collection*)

pump, or, if the fire had too great a hold, summon the fire service. Other railwaymen during their 'spare time' joined the Local Defence Volunteers (later to become the Home Guard), and were on duty patrolling strategic goods yards, bridges and tunnels in the Bristol and Bath area against attack by German saboteurs or paratroops. When not working, fire-watching or on Home Guard duty, the men were most likely to be found working on a lineside allotment growing food to eke out the food ration. Some of these allotments, begun in 1941, were situated between the rear of Bath station and the river, but they had fallen out of use by the 1950s. Soon after the evacuation of Dunkirk in June 1940, station nameboards were removed – as were road signposts – in order to make it more difficult for invading forces to identify where they were.

Temple Meads did not escape the war unscathed, as being a vital railway centre it was a prime German target. It experienced its first raid on 25 June 1940: of the fifteen bombs, several failed to explode but six passenger coaches received severe damage and an ambulance train was hit. On 24 November 1940 Temple Meads received three direct hits, blocking several lines and the adjacent platforms and the train shed. Tracks at East Depot were damaged in the same raid. On 2 December 1940 the station was bombed and some lines put out of action for several hours. Four days later, the 7.10 p.m. to Salisbury, leaving Platform 6, received a direct hit killing fifteen passengers and seriously injuring twenty-three; on the footplate, the driver of 2-6-0 No. 4358 was among those killed, while his fireman was seriously injured. A train of empty coaching stock caught fire, wrecking three beyond repair. Incendiary bombs damaged the train shed, luggage lift and telegraph office, and parcels and letters were destroyed.

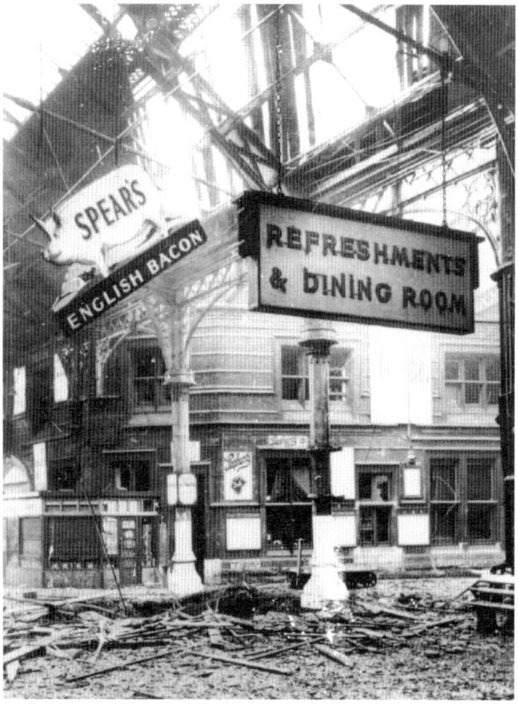

Platform 9 at Temple Meads following the raid of 24 November 1940. (*Author's Collection*)

On 3 January 1941 incendiary bombs fell on Temple Meads. It was believed that they were all extinguished, but one, lodged behind the tower clock, started a fire which burned out the booking offices. Army huts were hastily erected in the station approach and utilised as temporary premises. The telegraph office and main refreshment room also suffered from the fire. Arches below the station were set up as an emergency centre for key railway personnel. The huge goods shed almost entirely escaped injury, only one corner being slightly damaged. On 16/17 March 1941 the refreshment room on Platform 4 was damaged. One raid put Bristol East signal box out of action so a GWR signalman, together with four soldiers and a sergeant from the Royal Engineers, worked all trains in and out of the east end of the station until repairs were effected.

Places outside Bristol did not escape either. When Bristol was bombed on 25 June 1940, one German plane, presumably unable to penetrate the anti-aircraft defences, dropped a bomb that fell on Cross Post Bridge carrying the A4 over the railway west of Twerton Tunnel. Both road and railway were blocked until repairs could be made, when three of the transverse girders were replaced by steel girders of similar proportions. On 6 December 1940 a bomb fell close to the east portal of Bristol No. 2 Tunnel and damaged a coach of a Portsmouth Harbour to Cardiff express. On 9 October 1941 Saltford was the scene of a disaster when a Westland Whirlwind fighter aircraft crashed in the goods yard, embedding itself in the weighbridge pit and killing Pilot Ormonde Hoskins. A rabbit's foot found in the cockpit had failed to bring him luck.

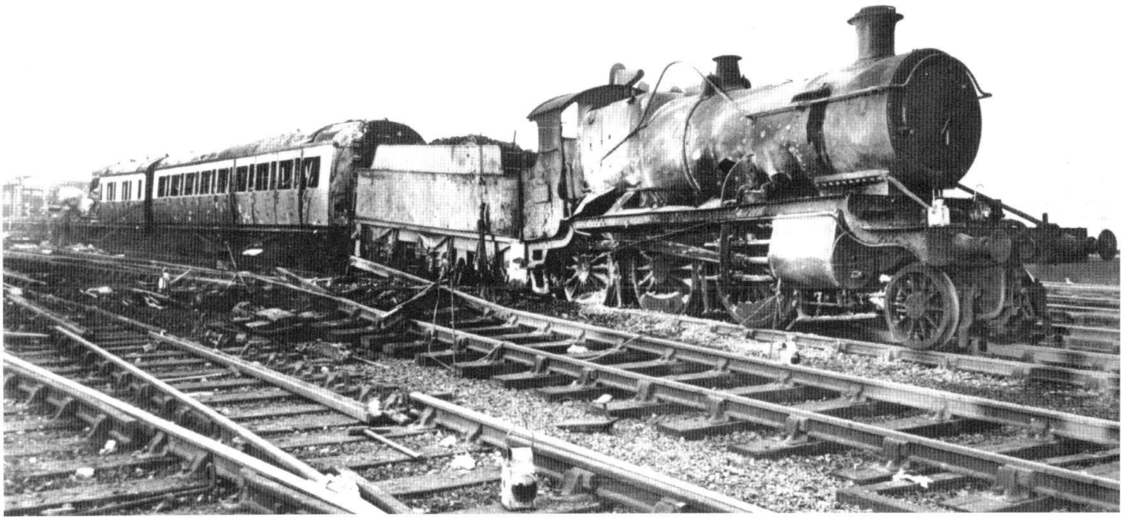

43XX class 2-6-0 No. 4358 at Bristol East. It was working the 7.10 p.m. to Salisbury, 6 October 1940, when a bomb exploded beside it, killing the driver. Another bomb struck the second coach. (*Author's Collection*)

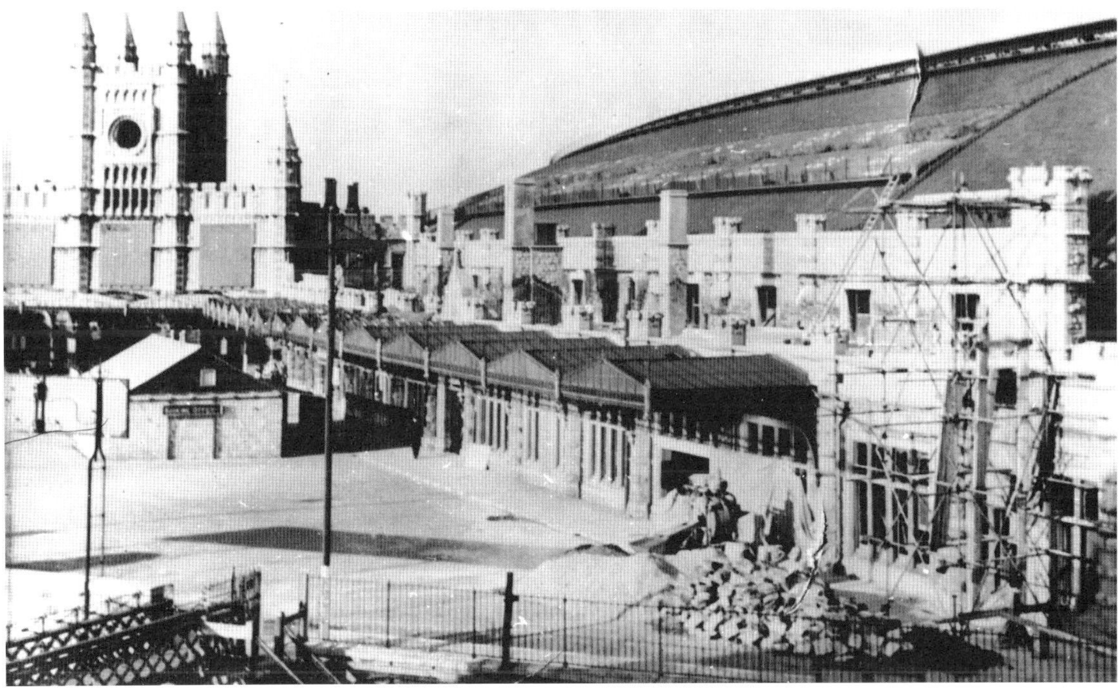

The frontage of Temple Meads following bomb damage – the spire is missing from the tower, as is the clock. The shed, centre left, is the temporary booking office. The footbridge, lower left, leads to offices in the former Bristol & Exeter building. (*Author's Collection*)

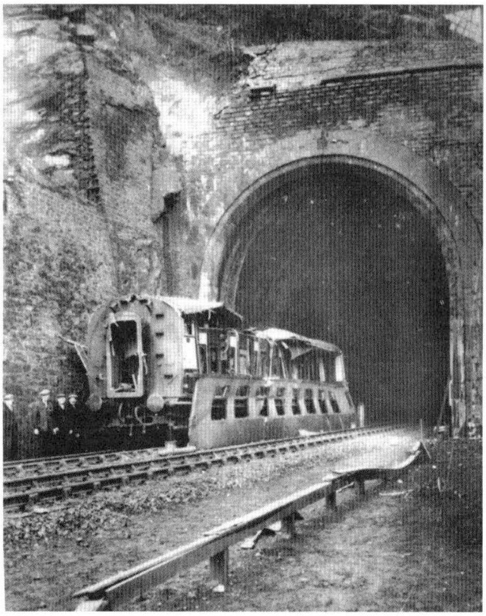

A bomb struck the east end of Bristol No. 2 Tunnel on 6 December 1940 and ricocheted into a coach of the 4.52 p.m. Salisbury to Temple Meads. (*Author's Collection*)

The line between Twerton Tunnel and Bath was struck by bombs in no fewer than nine places during the three Baedeker raids on Bath on 25/6 April 1942. At Twerton 100 ft of the 30-ft-high viaduct wall on the Up side was demolished. Sir Robert McAlpine & Sons Ltd temporarily supported the Down line on longitudinal timbers and it was reopened at 10.30 a.m. on 28 April. Restoration of the Up line was more difficult. In order to cater for traffic in both directions, a crossover was inserted between the Up and Down tracks either side of the breach in order that, for a short distance, Up traffic could work over the Down line. Meanwhile, a temporary bridge to carry the Up line was constructed by driving in timber piles with a 15-ton crane specially adapted with pile-driving leaders and steam hammer. To ease matters, some trains were diverted over the Bristol–Radstock–Frome line. On 15 May 1942, three weeks after the raid, the Up line was restored to traffic. During the same raids, Westmoreland Road goods depot received damage to the weighbridge office, cement stores, Customs & Excise Office and the loco depot, necessitating their rebuilding. At the passenger station a 50-kg bomb destroyed 60 ft of the east end of the Down platform and canopy, and for a few hours blocked all four tracks.

During the Second World War, when Paddington to Bristol expresses often had sixteen coaches, trains had to draw up twice at Bath, thus wasting time and fuel. In the blackout a sailor, towards the rear of a long train from Portsmouth Harbour which exceeded the platform length, stepped out on the stone bridge parapet thinking it was the platform and, taking a further stride, fell into the river and was dragged down by the weight of his kit. Fortunately, this mishap did not have a fatal ending but, taking heed of the warning, a fence was erected on the parapet to prevent a repetition.

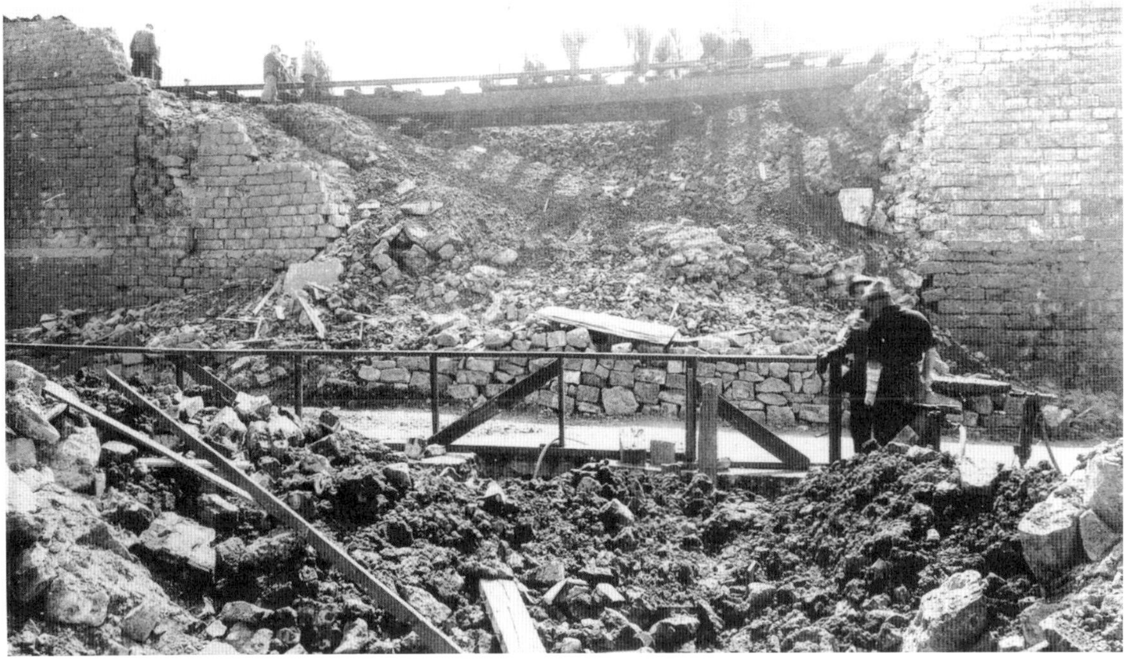

Twerton Viaduct, 27 April 1942, showing the effects of bombing. The Up line has been destroyed and the Down line is suspended. (*Author's Collection*)

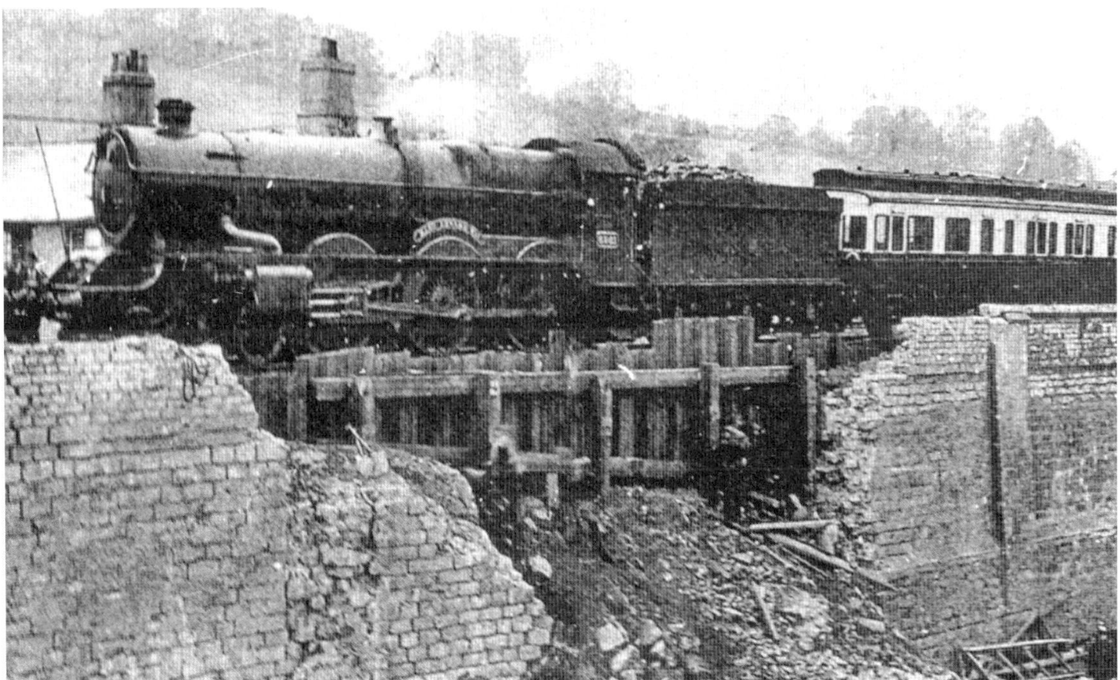

4-6-0 *King Edward VII* with an inspection car crosses the portion of the viaduct where temporary repairs have allowed single-line working. (*Author's Collection*)

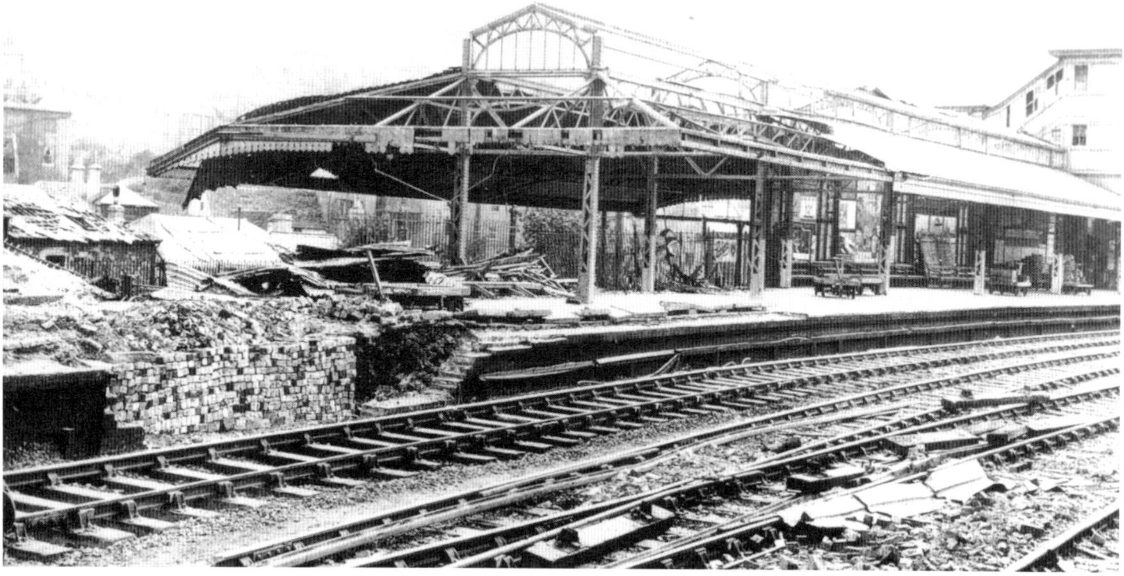

The east end of the Down platform at Bath on 27 April 1942, having received a direct hit. The signal box can be seen on the far right. (*Author's Collection*)

Because the war had interrupted the normal 'learn by experience' training of signal linesmen, from November 1946 the cellar under Platform 9 at Temple Meads – the main Up platform – was used as a technical school for a three-month intensive course in the installation and upkeep of electric and mechanical signalling apparatus, points, track circuits and telephones.

As a wartime economy, Castle and King class engines were turned out in plain green livery without lining, while other locomotives were painted black. Coaches were all-over chocolate instead of chocolate and cream. Paddington to Temple Meads trains were not usually in excess of sixteen coaches. Kings could have handled twenty or more, but the limiting factor was the lengths of platforms at Chippenham and Bath, both of which could only accommodate eight coaches.

To replace the 100 Dean Goods 0-6-0s requisitioned by the War Department, forty class 2F and 3F 0-6-0s were loaned by the LMS. Several of the LMS engines were allocated to the Bristol Division and on 14 October 1944 the author can remember seeing one with an empty coaching stock train in the Down refuge siding at Twerton Tunnel.

By Government order, Swindon was required to build LMS class 8F 2-8-0s, LMS Nos 8400–79 being turned out between June 1943 and July 1945, all on loan to the GWR. Twelve of these were allocated to the Bristol Division and were frequently seen between Bristol and Bath. They were equipped with the GWR's automatic train control – passing over a ramp at Caution would open a small capacity cylinder of the vacuum-operated steam brake valve and the steam brake would thus be applied immediately.

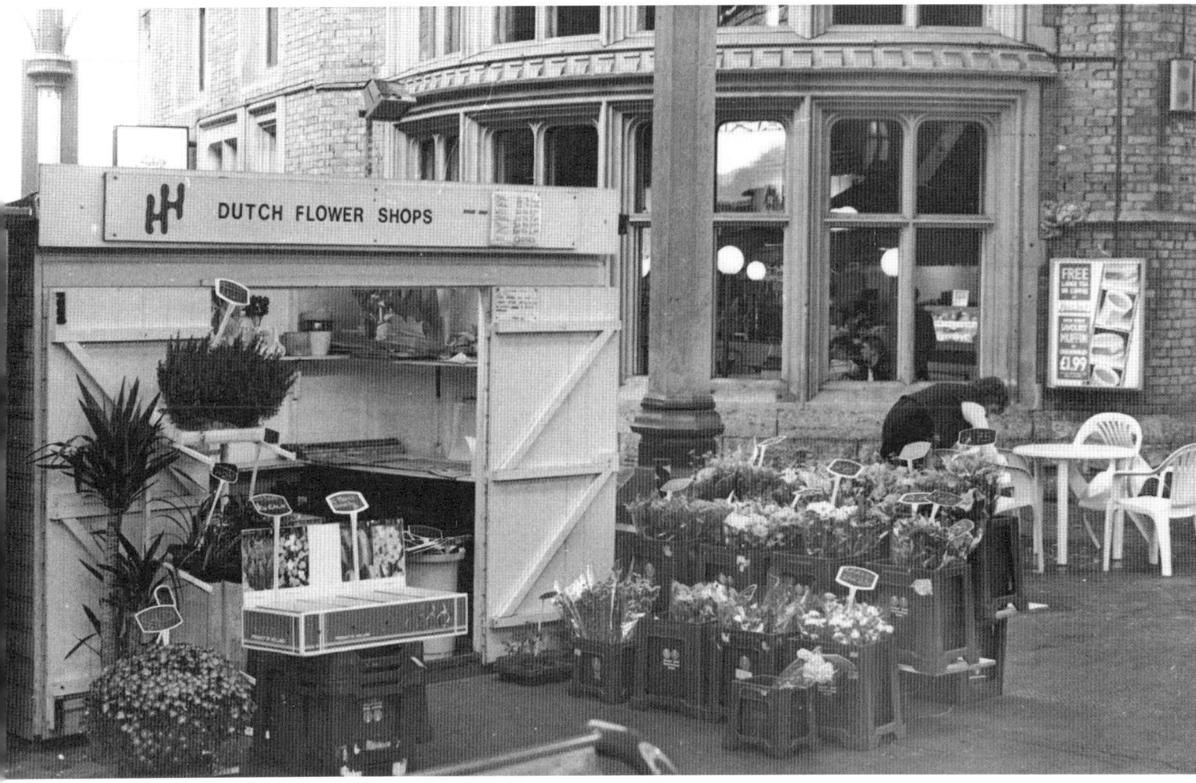

Above: A stall on Temple Meads Platform 3, 4 September 1986, conceals the building's architectural features. (*Author*)

Right: On 31 August 1990, to celebrate the 150th anniversary of the opening of the railway between Bristol and Bath, the mayor of Bath steps from the cab of HST No. 43019. The mayor of Bristol, who travelled in the cab with him, is already on the platform. (*Author*)

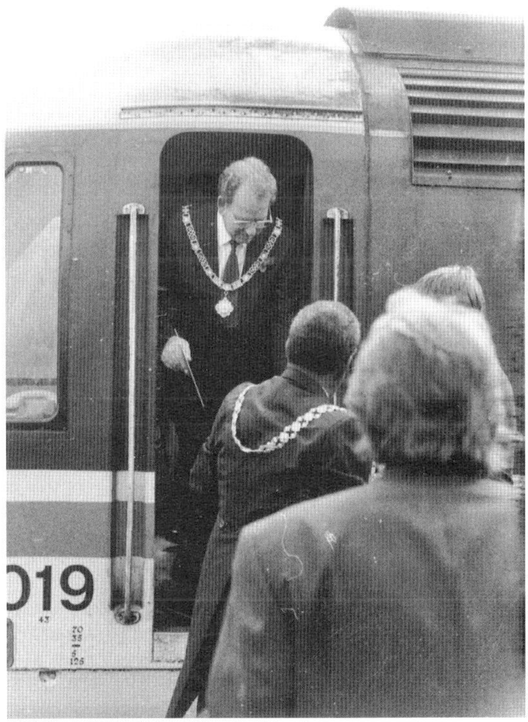

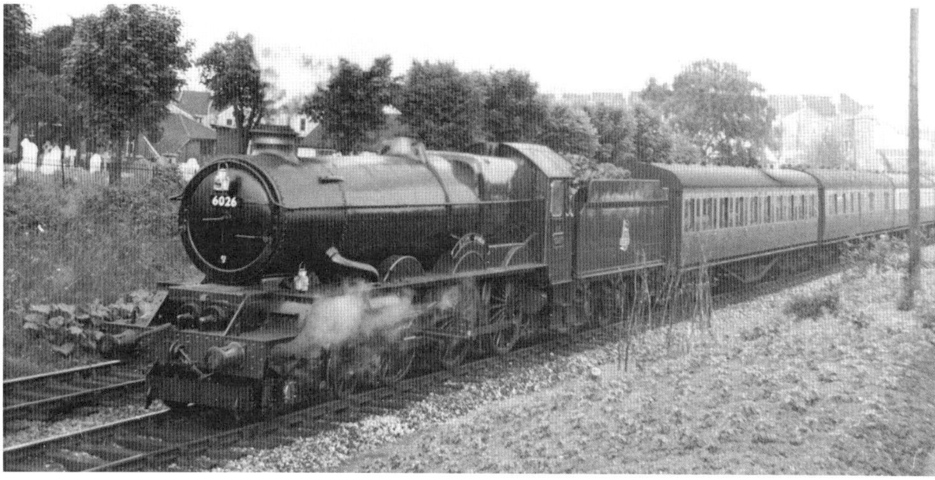

4-6-0 No. 6026 *King John* passes railwaymen's lineside allotments, Oldfield Park, 9 June 1952. (*R. E. Toop*)

With the entry of the United States of America into the war, 175 S160 class 2-8-0s, built by the American Loco Company, Baldwin Loco Works and the Lima Loco Works for the US Army and temporarily allocated to the GWR, arrived between January 1943 and February 1944. These engines were to become a common sight working heavy goods and mineral trains over the line between Bristol and Bath. Trains of dead USA 2-8-0s could be seen on the Up line during 1944, usually hauled by a GWR or USA 2-8-0 *en route* to Swindon after landing at Avonmouth. An American engineer rode on the dead engines to ensure that the bearings were not running hot and, to this end, the locomotives were stopped periodically. Although twenty-four USA Army 0-6-0Ts worked on the GWR for a few months in the summer of 1944, the author saw but one, No. 1975, and that was being hauled dead on the Down line.

Ambulance trains for the United States Army were fitted with the Westinghouse brake to enable them to be used on the Continent. In Britain they were hauled by LNER class B12/3 4-6-0s, which were equipped with this brake and were light enough to travel over most lines in the country. Hospital trains ferried the wounded to the large hospitals that the US Army had built around Bristol and used Platform 14 at Temple Meads, where the occupants could be loaded directly into ambulances. In the summer of 1944, following D-Day, these trains could be spotted quite regularly. Another sight was that of prisoner-of-war trains. Signalmen were instructed to keep these trains moving in order to reduce opportunities for the prisoners to escape, but traffic conditions did not always permit this advice to be heeded.

War conditions caused late running on occasions, a prime example being *The York*, carrying parcels, fish and a few passengers from York, which sometimes arrived at Bristol at 3.00 p.m. instead of about 7.00 a.m.

Chapter Eight

The Line in the Latter Half of the Twentieth Century and to the Present Day

Economies brought about by declining receipts from freight and local passenger traffic due to the development of road transport caused closure of facilities. Bristol East Depot closed on 7 August 1967; passenger traffic at St Anne's Park and Saltford ended on 5 January 1970. Keynsham was threatened with closure, but remained open to passengers and proved useful as road congestion and parking in Bath and Bristol became more and more severe. Keynsham station lost some traffic when the Brislington bus-served park-and-ride scheme opened on 25 October 1993. Keynsham closed to goods on 29 November 1965, while Saltford ceased accepting traffic on 1 September 1959. Dieselisation arrived in earnest on 6 April 1959 when stopping trains on the Swindon to Weston-super-Mare and Bristol to Westbury and Weymouth lines were worked by class 116 Derby-built suburban three-car units, while during that year Swindon-built Warship class diesel-hydraulics appeared on expresses.

Multiple Aspect Signalling (MAS) was installed at Temple Meads in 1970 at a cost of about £4 million to control 114 route miles from Cogload Junction to Bradford Junction, Corsham, Badminton, Charfield, Pilning and Avonmouth. Seventy signal boxes were closed and the cost of 343 staff saved. The associated track rationalisation at Temple Meads enabled the speed limit approaching the station to be raised from 10 to 25 mph. MAS started in the area on 16 August 1970 and Bath Goods, the last manual signal box between Swindon and Bristol, closed on 22 August 1970. At Temple Meads the initial through programming of locomotives and then the almost abolition of locomotives on passenger services (and their replacement with HSTs or DMUs) have almost entirely obviated engine changes at Temple Meads, both modifications reducing the number of movements required. The average time a train spends at a platform has been dramatically reduced from eighteen minutes in 1938 to, today, about six minutes for HSTs and also about six minutes for South Wales to Portsmouth Harbour trains on which the driver has to change cabs. Filton Abbey Wood station opened on 19 March 1996, serving a new Government office complex to which some of the officials from the Ministry of Defence at Bath were transferred. Train services were increased to cope with the new traffic, but complaints of overcrowding were received. A rail-served park-and-ride station was planned at Newton St Loe, immediately west of Twerton Tunnel, but funds could not be found for its implementation. Some Saltford residents are pressing for their station to be reopened and the former goods yard used for car parking.

An interesting development took place in 1991 when sidings at Keynsham were used for testing an inductive loop warning system. A transmitter on a locomotive sent a signal to a receiver on the track, which in turn sent a signal to a portable buzzer alerting workers on the ground. In 2009 it was announced that the Bristol–Bath–Paddington line was to be electrified.

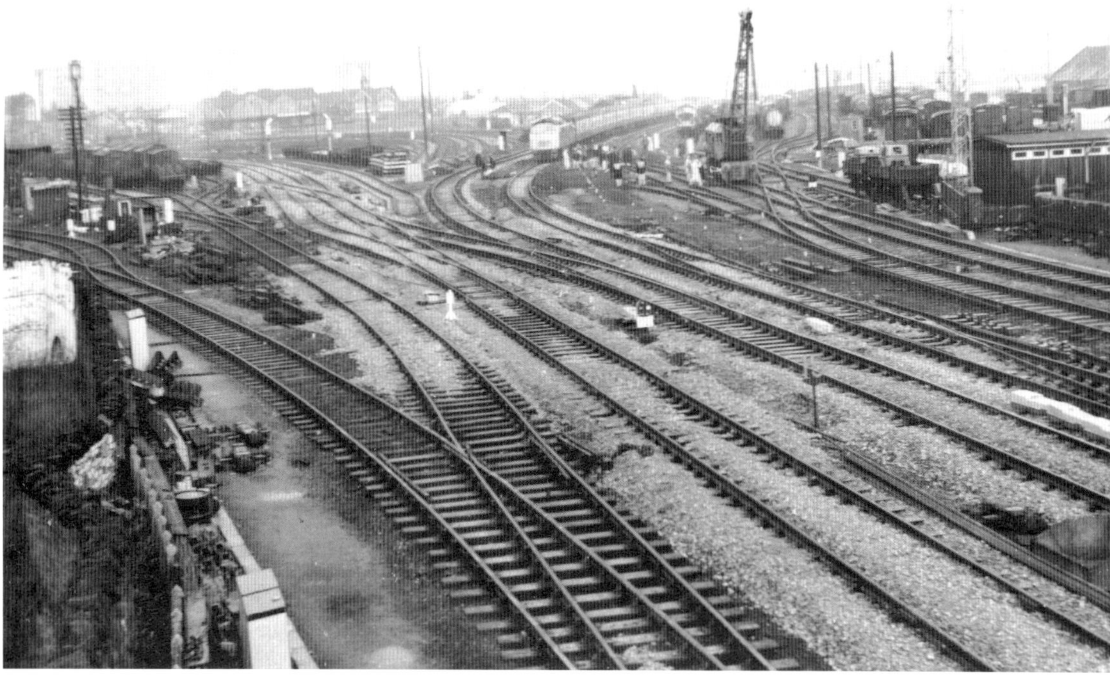

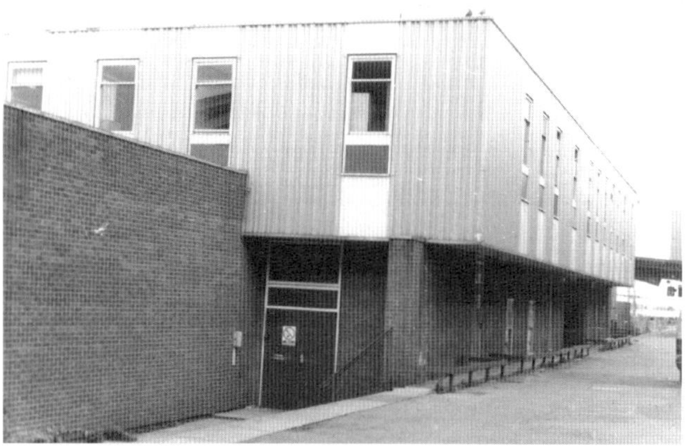

Above: View from Bristol East signal box to East Junction, showing track rationalisation taking place in 1970. A Down express approaches hauled by a Western class diesel-hydraulic. (*G. R. Dent*)

Left: The unattractively designed MAS box at Temple Meads, 31 October 1995. (*Author*)

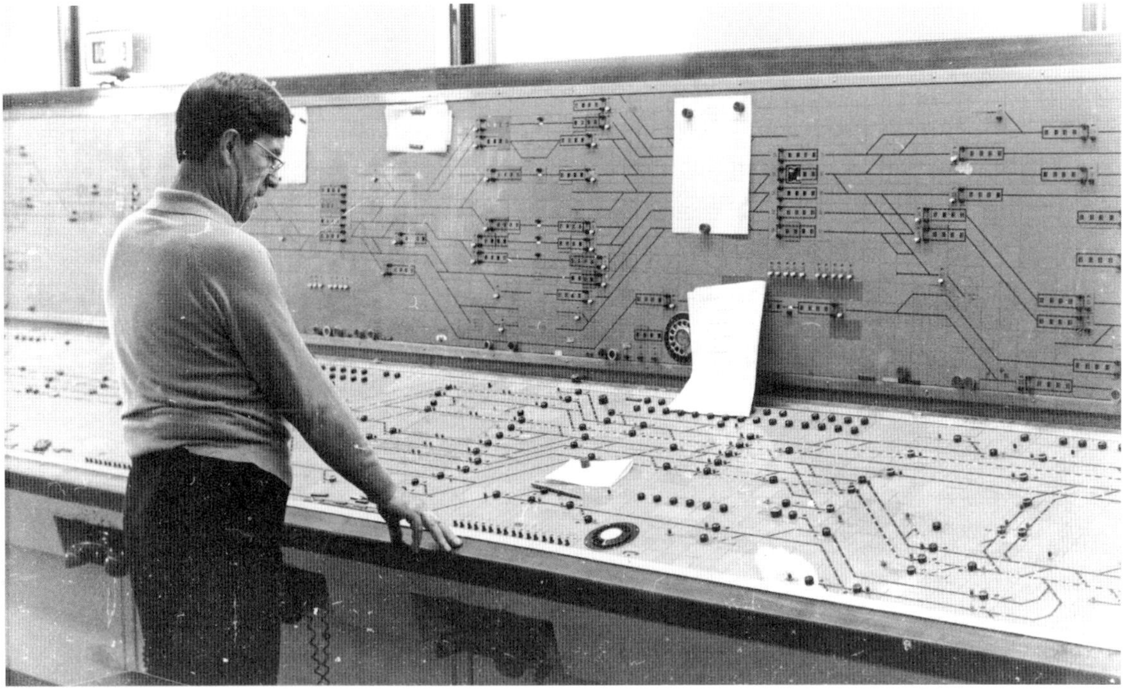

Main panel in the MAS box, Temple Meads, 29 July 1980. (*Author*)

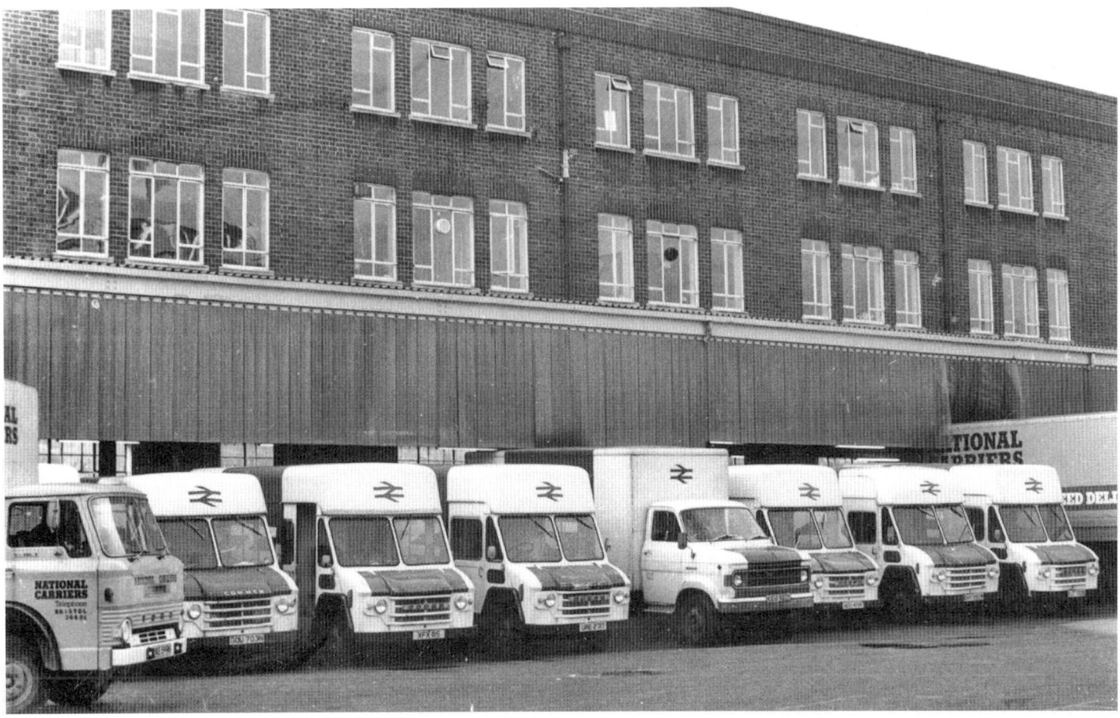

A line of vans outside the parcel depot, Temple Meads, 30 May 1980. The plastic fingers suspended from the canopy keep out draughts. (*Author*)

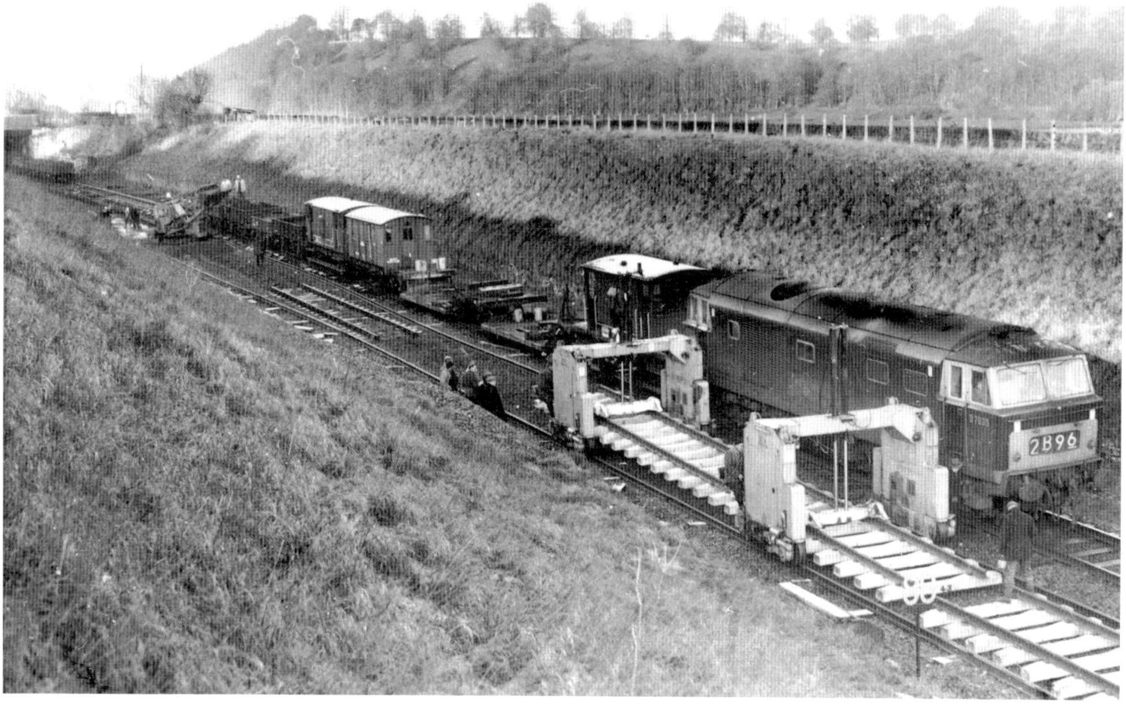

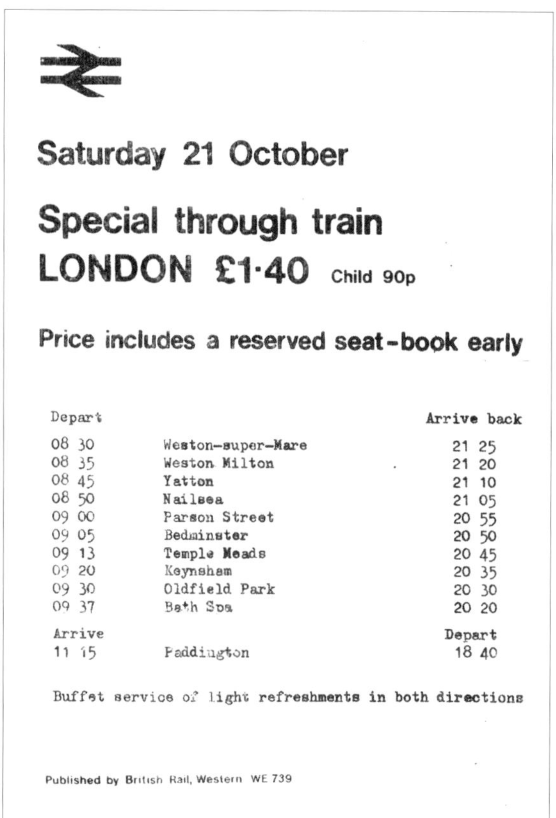

Saturday 21 October

Special through train
LONDON £1·40 Child 90p

Price includes a reserved seat-book early

Depart		Arrive back
08 30	Weston-super-Mare	21 25
08 35	Weston Milton	21 20
08 45	Yatton	21 10
08 50	Nailsea	21 05
09 00	Parson Street	20 55
09 05	Bedminster	20 50
09 13	Temple Meads	20 45
09 20	Keynsham	20 35
09 30	Oldfield Park	20 30
09 37	Bath Spa	20 20
Arrive		Depart
11 15	Paddington	18 40

Buffet service of light refreshments in both directions

Published by British Rail, Western WE 739

Above: Diesel-hydraulic Hymek class D7039 with a permanent way train near Twerton Tunnel, 1 January 1967. On the right, track is being relaid and left, spent ballast is being removed by elevator from the ground into a wagon. (*Author*)

Left: Handbill advertising a special through train from Weston-super-Mare and intermediate stations to Paddington, 21 October 1972.

Chapter Nine

Passenger Train Services

In 1840 the first service between Bristol and Bath offered ten trains daily, the fastest taking twenty-five minutes for the 11¾ miles, including a stop at Keynsham. With the opening of Saltford and Twerton stations in December, an additional train was added in each direction, but third-class passengers were not carried until the opening of the line from London on 30 June 1841, when the number of trains between Bristol and Bath was increased to fifteen. Most, whether stopping or nonstop, were allowed thirty minutes Down and twenty-eight Up, though mail trains were scheduled twenty-five minutes. On Sundays seven trains ran each way. A note in the early timetables stated that London time is kept at all stations on the railway, which is about eleven minutes before Bristol and Bath time, and fourteen minutes before Bridgwater time'. Because of the inconvenience of local time being different from railway time, Greenwich time was adopted at Bristol on 14 September 1852. By July 1854, sixteen trains ran each way and five on Sundays: expresses took seventeen minutes, first- and second-class stopping trains thirty minutes, and all-class stopping trains forty-five minutes. One curiosity in 1864 was a through service from Bristol and Bath to Victoria, the coach being slipped from an Up express at West London Junction and then taken on via Kensington. It was only shown in the timetable for five months as people found it quicker to travel to Paddington and then catch a hansom cab.

Early in 1876 a third-class coach on the Paddington to Penzance night train had just one lamp illuminating seven compartments. A letter writer to the *Bath Chronicle* refused to travel in it and used second class without any 'remonstrance on the part of officials'. The GWR was using recently acquired ex-Bristol & Exeter Railway coaches. The writer continued: 'It consisted simply of horizontal and vertical boards; so narrow was it that to find room for one's knees was a mathematical problem of some difficulty.'

Some first-class passengers solved the lighting problem by purchasing candlesticks, often electroplated, with hooks to attach them to vertical seat cushions. When the oval front of a lamp was raised, it formed a downward reflector. Of necessity, third-class passengers on wooden seats had to use a different form. These had rubber suckers to stick to windows. Both types could be purchased at station bookstalls.

In broad-gauge days, a very portly old lady with a huge, wide-mouthed basket met trains at Bath to supply passengers with oranges, apples, sweets and the like.

During the 1880s, eleven expresses ran each way between Bristol, Bath and Paddington. The most popular Up train was the 6.25 a.m. from Penzance, 3.00 p.m. off Bristol, because, unlike the Flying Dutchman, which preceded it, and the Zulu, which followed it, the 3.00 p.m. carried third-class passengers from Bristol in the reasonable time of three hours. In June 1882 the GWR abolished the practice of charging express fares and all trains, except for two expresses each way, carried third-class passengers. Although the Severn Tunnel opened in 1886, it was not until early 1887 that Paddington to South Wales trains were diverted via Bath and Bristol instead of around by Gloucester.

In 1887 a new broad-gauge express Paddington to Plymouth and return was put on to celebrate Queen Victoria's Jubilee; appropriately named the 'Jubilee', the service was broad-minded enough actually to carry passengers of all three classes. That year all passenger trains, with one exception, were worked to Bristol by London engines, the exception being the Up Dutchman, which was headed by a Bristol engine. Express trains of the period consisted of about six coaches, each weighing around 25 tons. Although carried on eight wheels they were not bogies, as the inside axles were rigid and the outer axles had side play. As the 3.00 p.m. Up was so popular, it comprised nine to eleven coaches, the 8-ft single piloted by another 4-2-2 or 2-4-0. Built in 1888, 2-4-0 engines Nos 14 and 16 were specially designed for the 3.00 p.m., and returned on the 5.30 a.m. newspaper train.

The January to April 1902 timetable showed thirty-six Down trains (sixteen being expresses from Paddington) and thirty-six Up trains (thirteen expresses to Paddington). Twelve trains ran each way on Sundays. Nonstop Down trains were allowed twenty-two minutes Bath to Bristol and stopping trains thirty-five minutes, while in the Up direction the figures were seventeen minutes and thirty minutes. By 1909 no less than fifty trains ran each way daily between the two cities.

TRAINS AND JOURNEY TIMES, BATH TO BRISTOL

Year	Direction	No. of trains daily	Express timing (mins)	Stopping train timing (mins)
1910	Down	42	18	35
	Up	47	16	30

1938	Down	58	16	24
	Up	59	15	24
1960	Down	61	16	24
	Up	59	15	25
2012	Down	80	11	20
	Up	75	11	17

The Keynsham service was improved in May 1985 when the number of trains calling rose from seventeen to twenty-four, but the opening of Brislington park-and-ride reduced the number of passengers using Keynsham station by a third to average 300 daily. The train service was therefore reduced from 24 September 1995.

The Paddington to Temple Meads HST service was launched on 4 October 1976 and by the 1980s long-distance commuting was common as people realised that they could travel daily to London by HST from Bristol and Bath in less time and in more comfort than was required for shorter journeys on Network South East's system. From 30 May 1994 an imaginative service was introduced running from Carmarthen to Bristol, Bath and Waterloo; apart from giving a connection with Eurostar trains, it offered direct access to stations *en route* to Waterloo. Another innovation was a train from Waterloo to Manchester Piccadilly via Bath and Bristol. On 30 March 1998 class 165 165110 was used for route clearance tests and from 21 June 1998 a Bicester–Oxford–Bath and Bristol service was inaugurated, which from the start enjoyed good passenger loadings. Nevertheless, this service was withdrawn in the summer of 2003.

The GWR was an early entrant in the excursion race and ran a trip from Bristol to Paddington at £1 1*s* 0*d* (half the normal fare) on 29 September 1842. It proved highly popular and the train of 700 to 800 passengers had to be double-headed. The first excursion from London to Bath, Bristol, Taunton and Exeter left Paddington at 7.00 a.m. on 2 September 1844 with almost 500 passengers. More joined at stations *en route* and by the time the train reached Bath there were about 1,000 on board, 150 of whom left here. A special excursion train left Bath at 6.30 a.m. on 10 July 1851 with visitors to the Great Exhibition; the twenty coaches held a total of more than 1,000 passengers. The entrance charge to the exhibition was 1*s* and this, plus the fare and lodging, placed it beyond the reach of those earning low wages. The return fare of 8*s* 8*d* enabled visitors to stay in the capital for four days, but because the ticket cost about half the price of an ordinary return, luggage was restricted to a carpet bag. Another excursion the following month carried 1,400 passengers in twenty-eight coaches. At least seven excursion trains were run in September, some being day returns at 5*s* second class, or 9*s* first and allowing no luggage. One excursion proved so popular that, according to the *Bath Chronicle*, 'open goods trucks had to be coupled on to provide sufficient accommodation' – these were probably old third-class open vehicles similar to open wagons. Despite the extra provision, there was still insufficient room for some ticket holders, who had to travel on a later express.

On 1 February 1855 the world's first exclusive postal train ran from Paddington to Bristol, pulled by a Fire Fly class 2-2-2. The service did not carry passengers until June 1869, when one first-class carriage was attached. In December 1877 two six-wheel sleeping cars commenced running over the line *en route* from Paddington to Penzance. Each had two sleeping compartments, one for seven men and the other for four ladies. These arrangements were disliked and in 1881 these compartments were replaced by six two-berth compartments, which offered more privacy.

Over the years, quite a number of named trains have run over the line. The first was the Flying Dutchman, named after a racehorse that won both the Derby and the St Leger in 1849. Perhaps not surprisingly, the name was transferred to the fastest train in the world, which ran from Paddington to Bristol in only 2½ hours, conveying, until 1890, only first- and second-class passengers. It made its last broad-gauge run on 20 May 1892 and ran as an undistinguished standard-gauge train until 1911. The Zulu was the unofficial name for the 3.00 p.m. Paddington to Plymouth, introduced in 1879 during the Zulu war; its length rarely exceeded five coaches. The nickname faded out in about 1914.

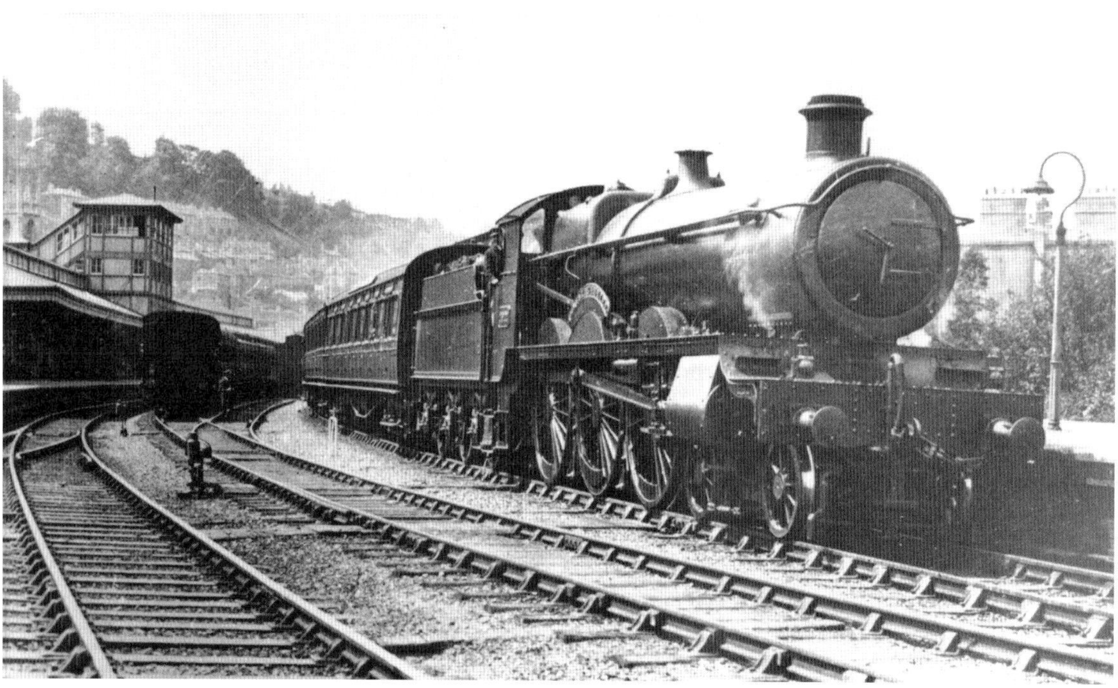

4-6-0 No. 2922 *Saint Gabriel* at Bath heading the first Cardiff to Brighton express, July 1922. The signal box can be seen above the platform canopy. (*Author's Collection*)

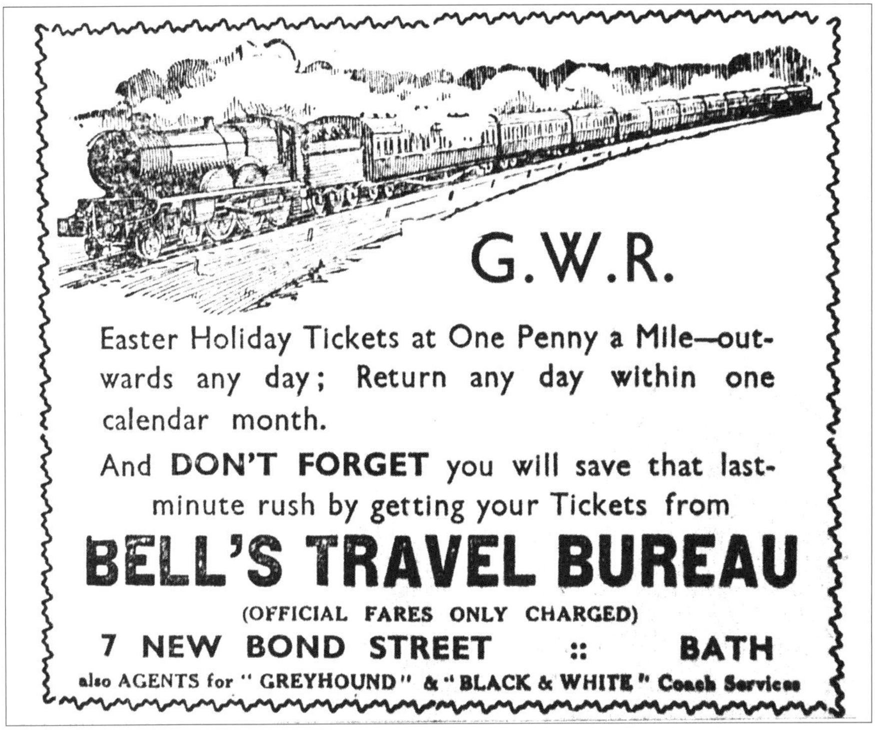

An advertisement in the *Bath & Wilts Chronicle & Herald*, 26 March 1934.

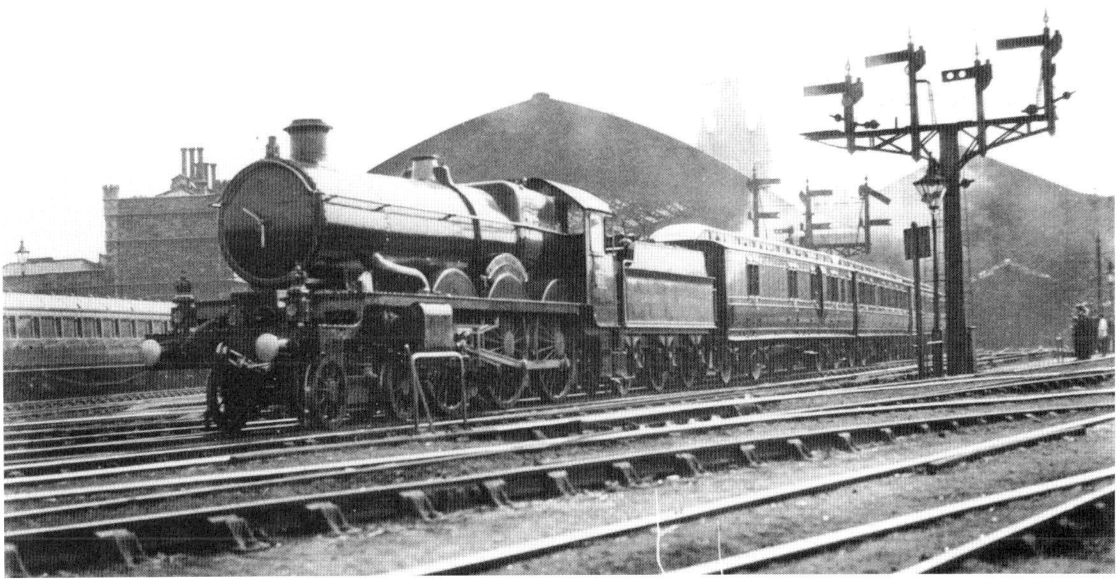

4-6-0 No. 4082 *Windsor Castle* leaves Brunel's Temple Meads terminus with the Royal train. (*M. J. Tozer*)

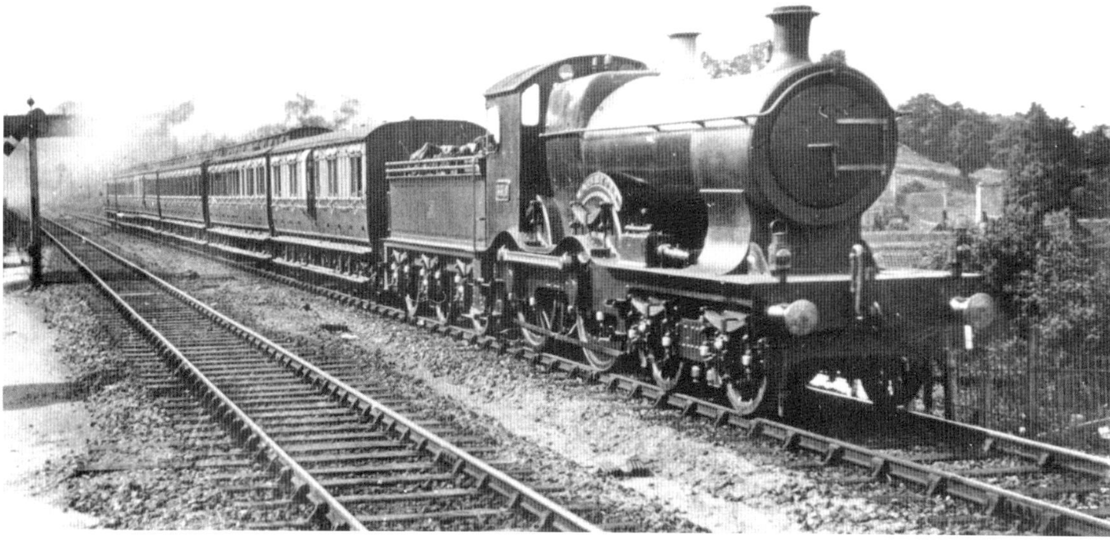

Badminton class 4-4-0 No. 3310 *Waterford* passes Saltford with an Up express *c.* 1908. (*Author's Collection*)

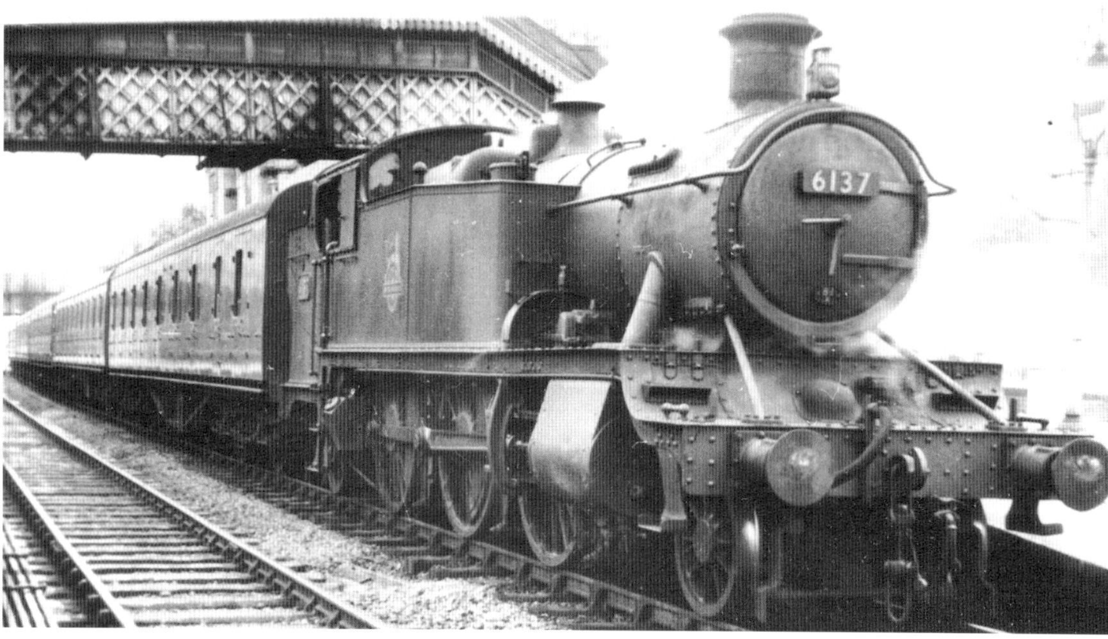

61XX class 2-6-2T No. 6137, newly transferred to Bath road shed but still carrying the 81A Old Oak Common shed plate, stands at Keynsham on 1 July 1955, with the 6.58 a.m. North Filton Platform to Westbury, a train carrying Fry's workers. (*Russell Leitch*)

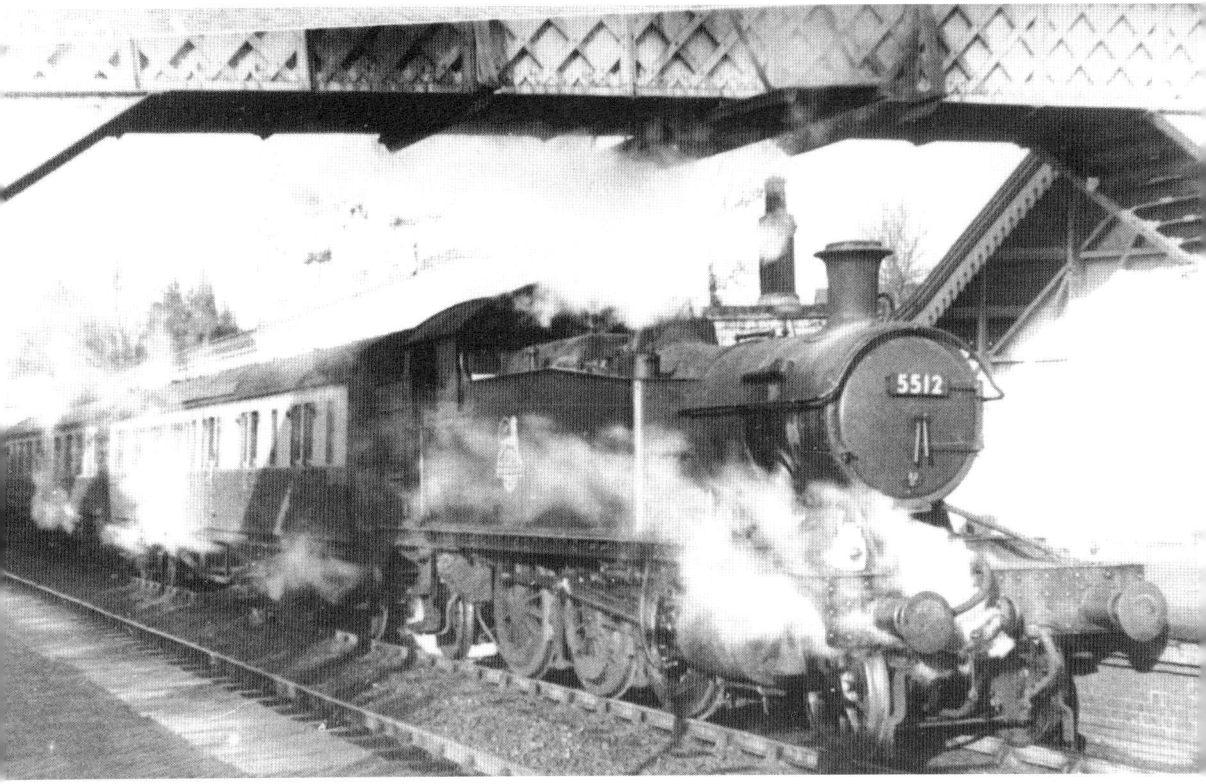

Above: 4575 class 2-6-2T No. 5512 at Keynsham 18 January 1953 with the 11.20 a.m. Temple Meads to Portsmouth express which started at Keynsham during the relaying of Keynsham water troughs. (*M. J. Tozer Collection*)

Right: A 1954 BR poster advertising Bath.

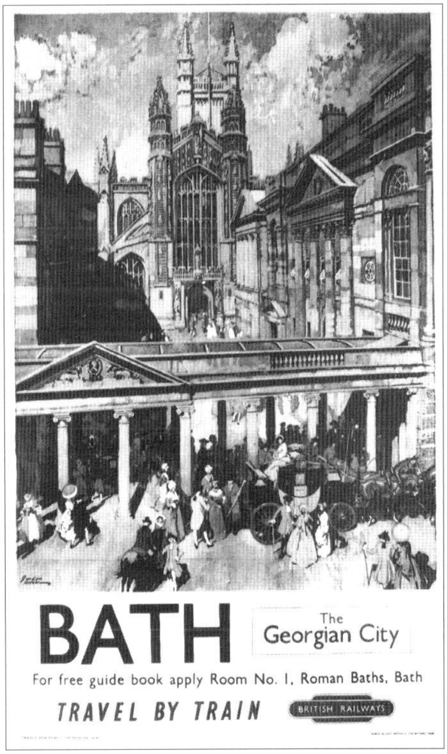

The broad-gauge Cornishman, introduced in 1890, carried third-class passengers at a time when many important expresses were restricted to holders of first- and second-class tickets. When the GWR purchased the refreshment rooms at Swindon and the compulsory stop there could be abolished from 1 October 1895, the Cornishman made the first nonstop run from Paddington to Bristol, passing through Bath without calling. On 1 July 1903 its Paddington to Temple Meads time was cut to two hours for the first time, 4-4-0 No. 3433 *City of Bath* hauling it on that occasion. A few days later, on 14 July, the same engine ran Paddington–Bath–Plymouth, making a record-breaking nonstop run. The Cornishman was withdrawn on 1 July 1904 when the Cornish Riviera Limited was introduced, running nonstop to Plymouth via Bath and Bristol on a regular basis.

The named train particularly associated with Bristol was The Bristolian, inaugurated on 9 September 1935 to mark the GWR's centenary It ran nonstop from Paddington to Temple Meads via Bath in one hour forty-five minutes, fifteen minutes faster than the previous best and requiring an average speed of 67 mph. It did not travel via Bath on its Up run and went via Filton and Badminton. The seven-coach train was drawn by a King for the first few months, but subsequently normally headed by a Castle. Withdrawn during the Second World War, its name was restored in 1951 but on a slower schedule than pre-war, and the service did not return to the one-hour forty-five-minute timing until 1954. In the summer of 1959, when hauled by a diesel-hydraulic Warship, the schedule was reduced to one hour forty minutes, requiring an average speed of 71 mph. From 1961 its loading was increased to ten to twelve coaches and a call at Bath Spa introduced. The name was soon dropped.

One of the named trains put on in 1951, the Festival of Britain year, was The Merchant Venturer, the first named train for many years actually to stop at Bath. Consisting of the new BR standard Mk I coaches, it left Paddington at 11.15 a.m., arrived at Bath Spa at 1.01 p.m., Temple Meads at 1.22 p.m. and terrnmated at Weston-super-Mare at 1.56 p.m. In the Up direction, it was even more sluggish and really a semi-fast, rather than a real express. It left Weston at 4.35 p.m, calling at Yatton, Nailsea and Backwell. It arrived at Temple Meads at 5.12 p.m., departed at 5.27 and arrived at Bath at 5.44 p.m. before calling at Chippenham, Swindon and slipping a coach at Reading General at 7.21 p.m. It finally arrived at Paddington at 8.00 p.m. Its average speed was a pedestrian 40 mph. The name was dropped in the 1965 timetable reorganisation, revived in 1984 and dropped again two years later.

The Bristol Pullman, inaugurated on 3 October 1960, was hailed as a great innovation and was considered unusual for several reasons. Firstly, Pullman cars were rare on the GWR or WR. They had appeared in July 1929 on the Torquay Pullman but did not prove a success and were withdrawn in 1930. Secondly, instead of being hauled by a traditional locomotive, the Bristol Pullman had a power unit at each end of the train and was, in fact, a precursor of today's

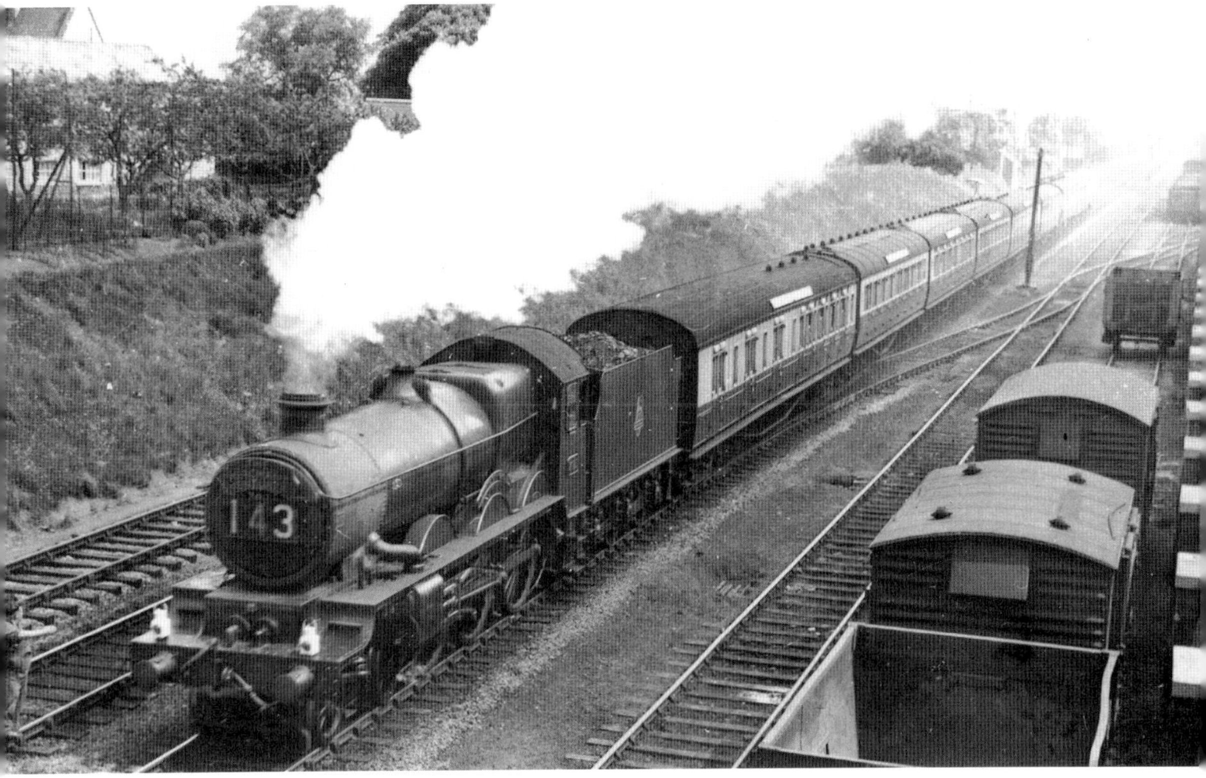

4-6-0 No. 7025 *Sudeley Castle* with the Down Merchant Venturer passes the goods sidings at Bath, May 1953. (*Revd Alan Newman*)

HSTs. Thirdly, the train's livery was blue and white – a startling change from the standard maroon of ordinary coaching stock or the brown and white of traditional Pullmans – in fact, it was not unlike the standard livery that BR adopted in 1965. Each power car had a North British/MAN 12 cylinder 1,000-bhp diesel engine, giving a maximum speed of 90 mph. The transmission was electric. The Bristol Pullman made two trips daily from Temple Meads to Paddington and back, not all via Bath. From October 1960 it called at Bath Spa four times daily and was scheduled fifteen minutes on its morning (and thirteen minutes for the midday) run Temple Meads to Bath, seventeen minutes for the Down midday, and sixteen minutes for the evening run. Between Bristol and Bath a supplementary charge of 2*s* first and 1*s* second was payable in addition to the usual first- or second-class fare. The riding quality of the Bristol Pullman was not above criticism. Its Swiss-designed Schlierer bogie was splendid with continental-length coaches but it failed to give the British shorter bodies a good ride. When the Bristol Pullman was unavailable, a set of ordinary Pullman cars was used, locomotive-hauled. The Bristol Pullman ceased running on 4 May 1973, by which time ordinary Mk IID coaches had air conditioning, rode more comfortably than the Bristol Pullman cars and did not charge a Pullman supplement.

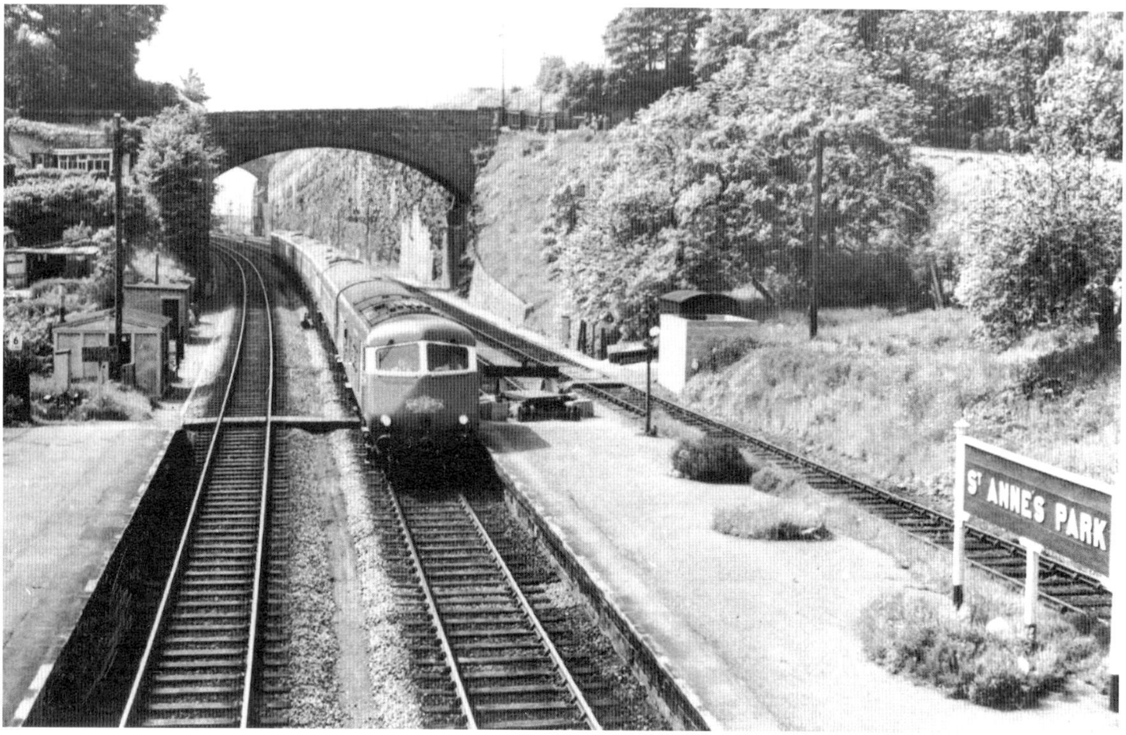

An Up Bristol Pullman approaches St Anne's Park, 29 May 1963. (*Author's Collection*)

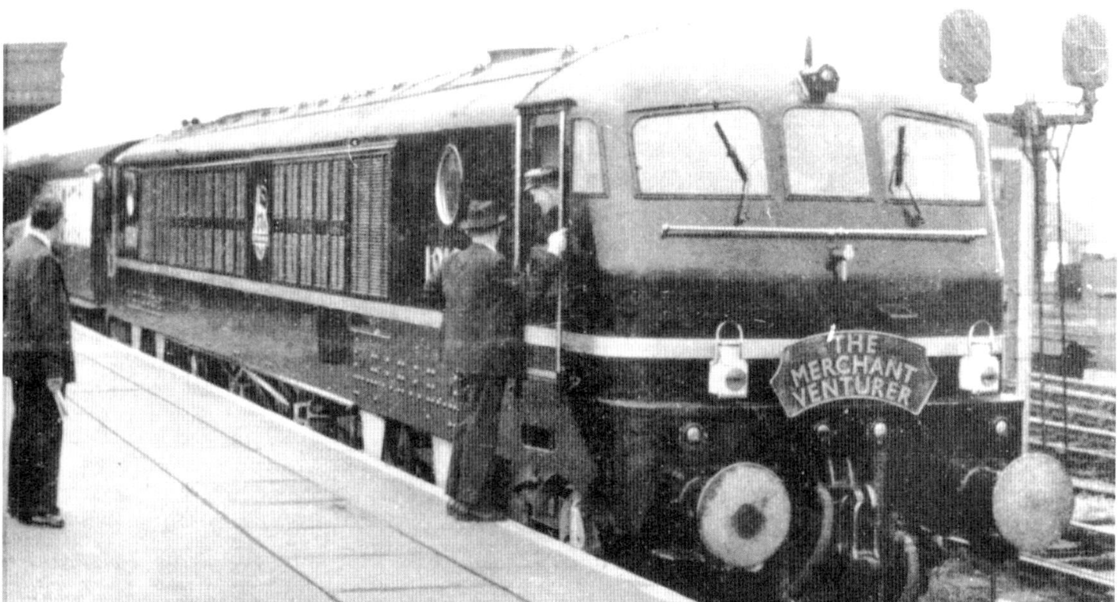

Gas turbine No. 18100 at Temple Meads *c.* 1952 having arrived with the Down Merchant Venturer. (*Author's Collection*)

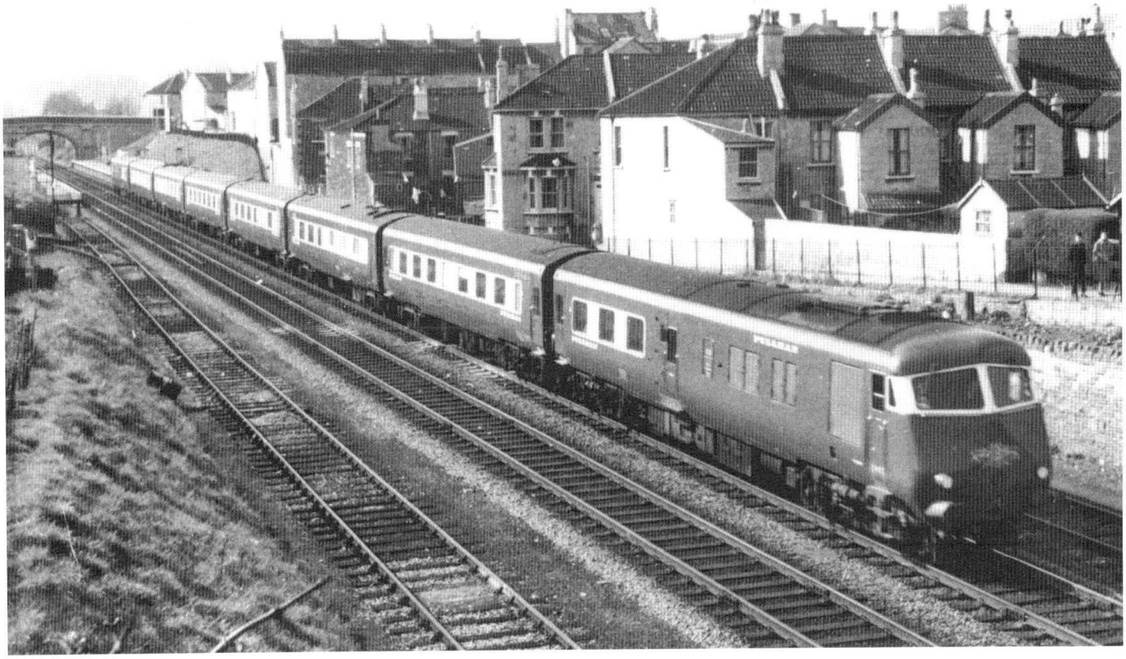

The Up Bristol Pullman in its original livery, passes Oldfield Park. (*R. J. Cannon*)

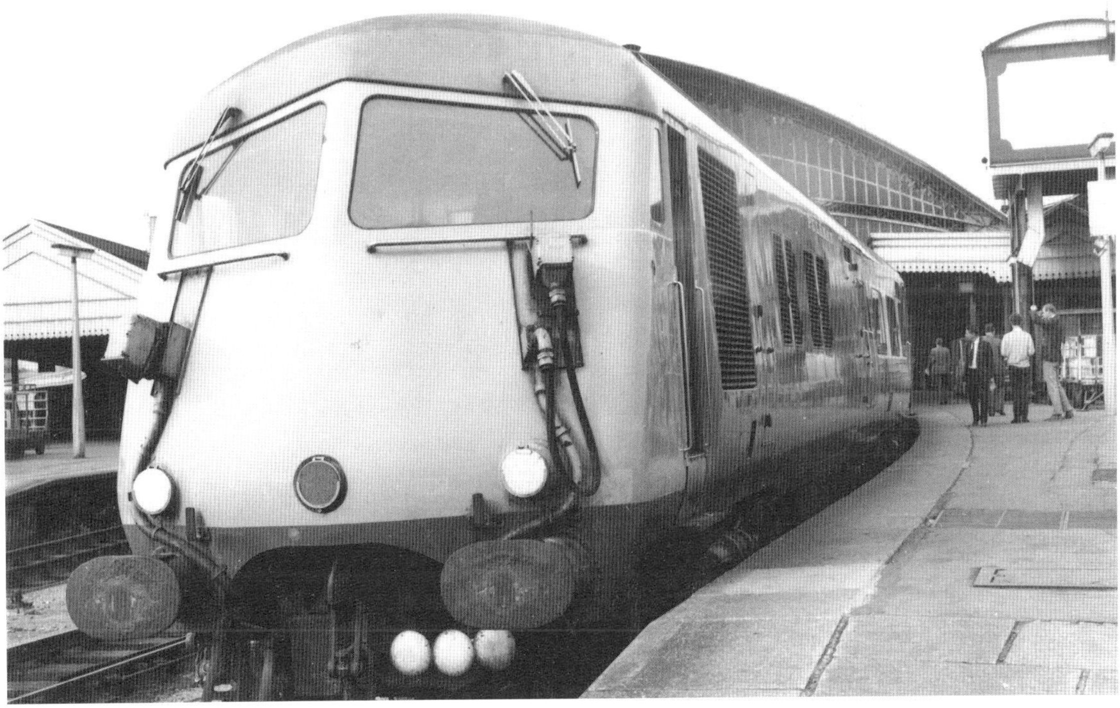

The Up Bristol Pullman at Temple Meads, 5 June 1968, with a yellow front. (*Author*)

THE BRISTOL PULLMAN

MONDAYS TO FRIDAYS

BRISTOL TO LONDON

Bristol (Temple Meads)	dep.	8.15 a.m.	3.15 p.m.
Bath Spa	,,	8.32 a.m.	3.32 p.m.
Chippenham	,,	—	3.49 p.m.
London (Paddington)	arr.	10.10 a.m.	5.15 p.m.

LONDON TO BRISTOL

London (Paddington)	dep.	12.45 p.m.	5.45 p.m.
Chippenham	arr.	2. 9 p.m.	—
Bath Spa	,,	2.25 p.m.	7.20 p.m.
Bristol (Temple Meads)	,,	2.45 p.m.	7.40 p.m.

FARES

Between		First Class (Ordinary)		Second Class (Ordinary)		Supplementary Charges (Single Journeys)	
		Single	Return	Single	Return	1st	2nd
		s. d.	s. d.	s. d.	s. d.	s. d.	s. d.
Bristol (Temple Meads)	**Bath Spa**	4 3	8 6	2 9	5 6	2 0	1 0
	Chippenham	8 6	17 0	5 9	11 6	2 6	1 0
	Paddington	41 0	82 0	27 6	55 0	10 0	5 0
Bath Spa	**Chippenham**	4 6	9 0	3 0	6 0	2 0	1 0
	Paddington	37 0	74 0	25 0	50 0	10 0	5 0
Chippenham	**Paddington**	33 0	66 0	22 0	44 0	10 0	5 0

NOTES APPLICABLE TO ALL PULLMAN DIESEL SERVICES.

1. Meals and refreshments served at every seat to the traditional high Pullman standards.
2. Limited accommodation, all seats reservable. Seats can be reserved in advance at stations and usual agencies for journeys from and to all calling points. Subsequent reservations may be effected with the Pullman Car Conductor on the train if accommodation is available.
3. Full supplementary charges payable for children.
4. Holders of Ordinary and Business Travel Season Tickets may travel by these trains on payment of the appropriate supplementary charge.
5. The fares and charges shown are liable to alteration.
6. Dogs, motor/scooters, perambulators, etc., are not conveyed on these services.

From the 'Bristol Pullman' advertising leaflet, 1961.

At various times slip coaches ran into Bath after being detached from Down trains. In about 1925 two coaches were slipped at Bath at 1.00 p.m. from the 11.15 a.m. Paddington to Weston-super-Mare. After arriving, two shunting horses drew them to one of the two centre roads before they were taken onwards to Bristol. Withdrawn during the Second World War, the first post-war slip arrived at Bath on 6 May 1946, the lip portion of the 9.05 a.m. Paddington to Temple Meads usually having at least three coaches. They were useful for Admiralty personnel travelling to visit offices relocated at Bath during the war. As a speed restriction of 30 mph was in force round the curve on which the station is situated, the point of detachment from the main train was fairly critical. It was slipped from the main train just before reaching the Up advanced starter, situated 340 yd from the centre of the platform.

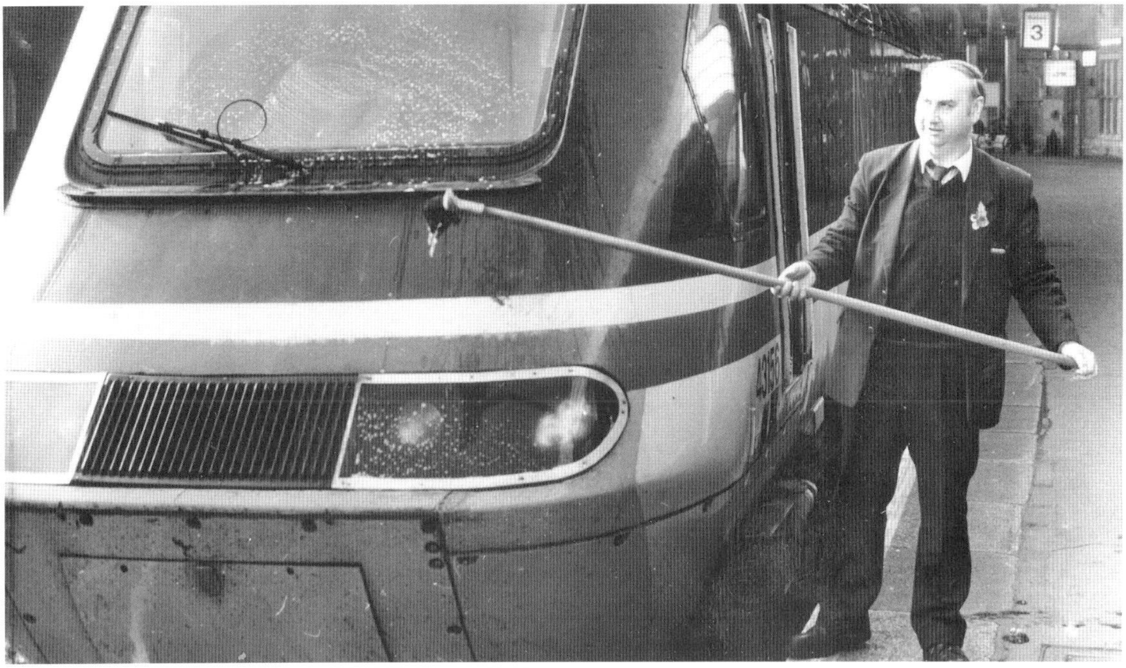

Driver David Chambers cleans the windscreen of HST No. 43156 at Temple Meads, 31 October 1995. (*Author*)

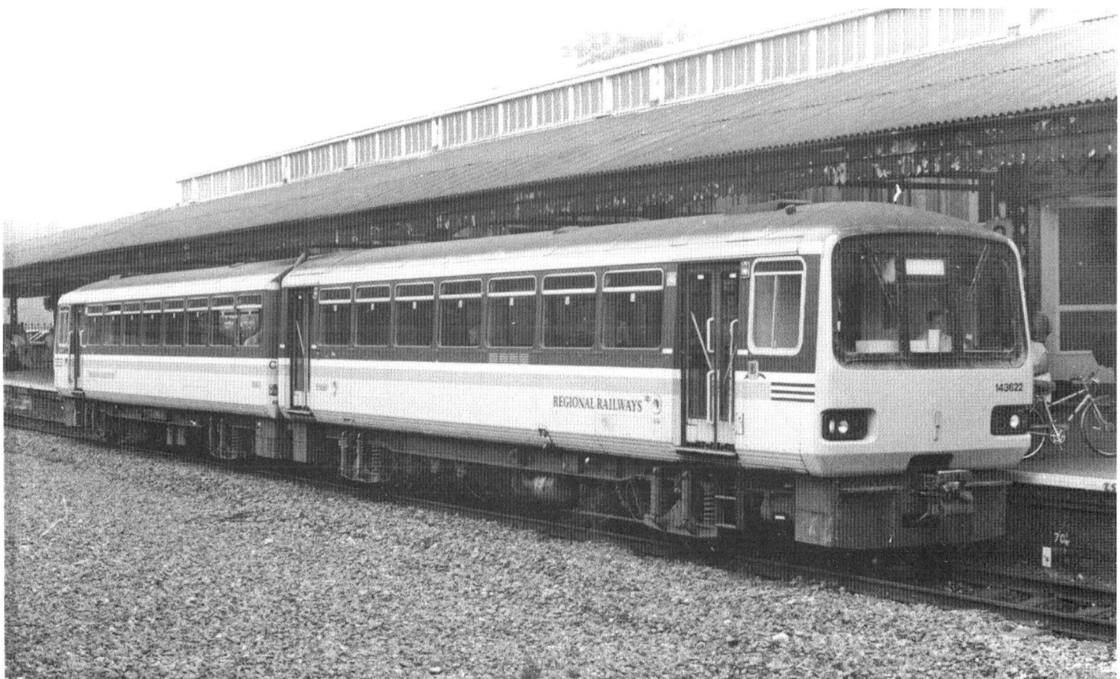

Regional Railways Pacer 143 622 at Bath with the 07.37 Llanelli to Westbury, 15 August 1996. (*Author*)

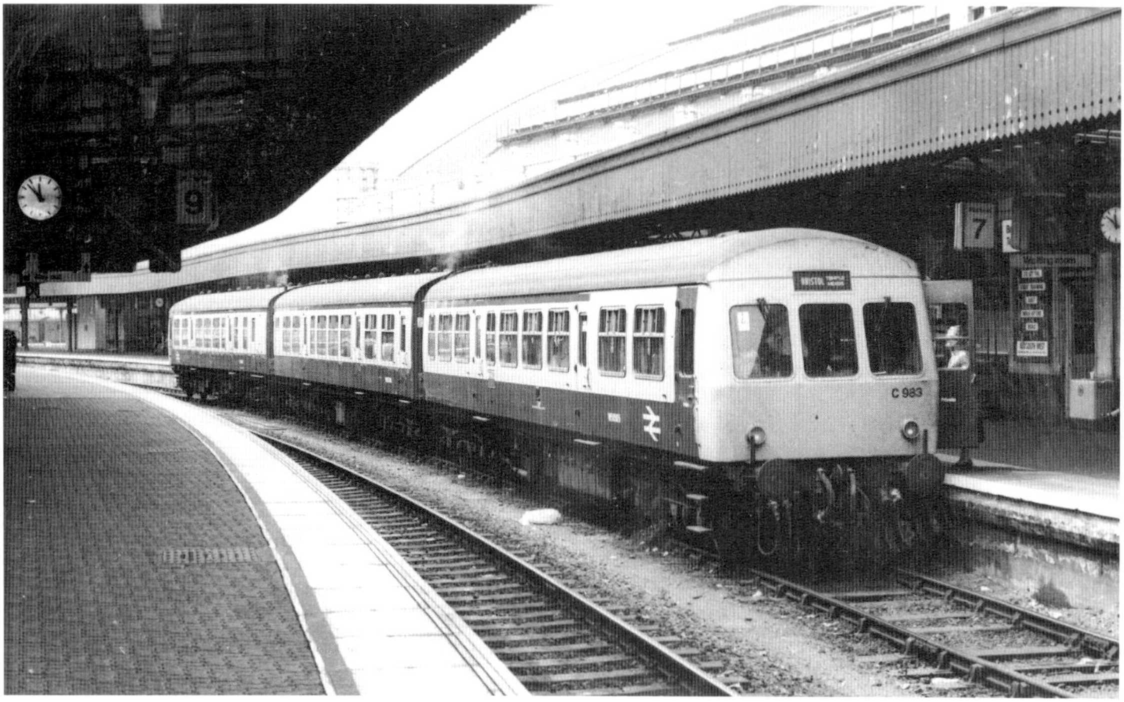

Three-car DMU C983, power cars W51505 and E53617, leaving Temple Meads with the 12.06 Temple Meads to Weymouth, 16 June 1988. (*Author*)

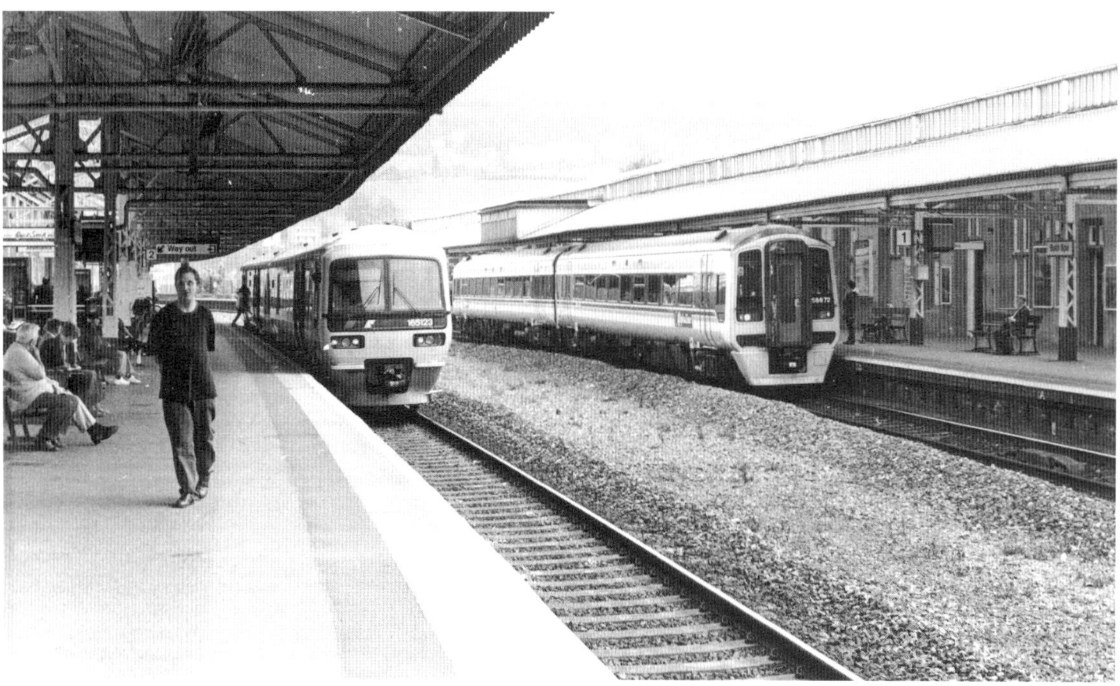

Left, at Bath Spa, 19 May 1999, Turbo 165 123 works the 12.28 Temple Meads to Oxford, while right, DMU 158 872 forms the 10.24 Portsmouth Harbour to Cardiff. (*Author*)

In the 1930s, mostly on Sundays in May and June, the Holiday Haunts Express ran from Bath, Bristol and Weston-super-Mare to such places as Penzance, Minehead, Weymouth, Paignton and Newquay, calling at intermediate stations *en route*. Fares ranged between 5*s* and 10*s* and sufficient time was allowed at the destination for passengers to book rooms for a holiday stay later in the year. In the first decade of the twentieth century people could often not afford a holiday, so long day trips were offered instead. In 1909 one such trip ran from Bath to Ireland, leaving at 6.32 p.m. on Friday and returning the following day. Fares to Wexford were 8*s* 3*d*, to Dublin 12*s* 0*d*, to Waterford 10*s* 0*d* and to Cork and Killarney 12*s* 6*d* with eleven hours being enjoyed at the latter location. Until the 1960s or '70s, the railway was very competitive. For example, in 1951 people despairing of waiting in a queue for a Bristol to Bath bus resorted to Temple Meads and were amazed when the booking clerk handed them a cheap day return and 8*s* 6*d* change from a 10*s* note. In 1963 the day return fare from Bath Spa to Temple Meads was 3*s* compared with a bus return of 3*s* 6*d*, while Oldfield Park to Temple Meads was 2*s* 9*d* and a passenger had the option of returning to Bath Spa.

A unique event occurred on 7 February 1940. When the Royal West Country tour was planned, it was not possible for Queen Elizabeth to begin the tour with King George VI, but it was arranged that on 7 February a private special would convey her from Paddington to Bristol so that she could join her husband on the Royal train, which was travelling via Westbury from Yeovil. By careful planning and locomotive performance, it was possible for the Royal train to run for the last quarter of a mile into Temple Meads simultaneously and parallel with that carrying the Queen, both trains coming to a stop at the same moment with the two Royal saloons opposite each other, the Queen at Platform 5 and the King at Platform 3.

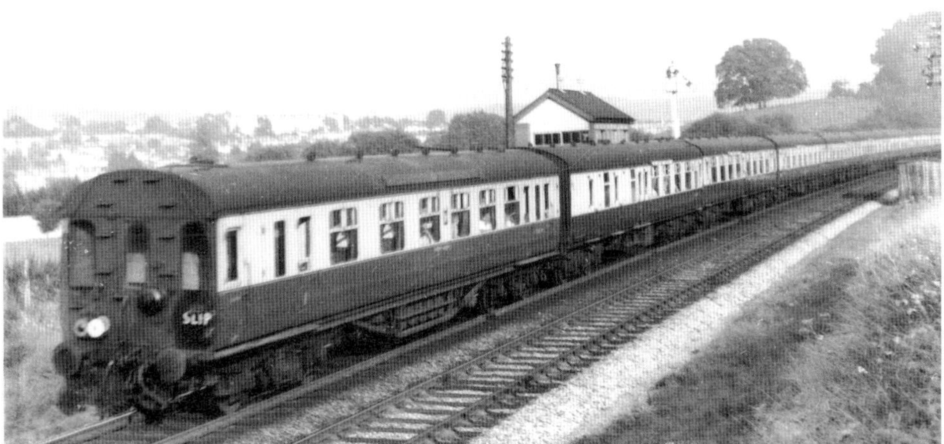

The slip coach for Reading on the rear of the Up Merchant Venturer passes Twerton Tunnel signal box, 11 September 1958. Note the special tail lamp. (*Author*)

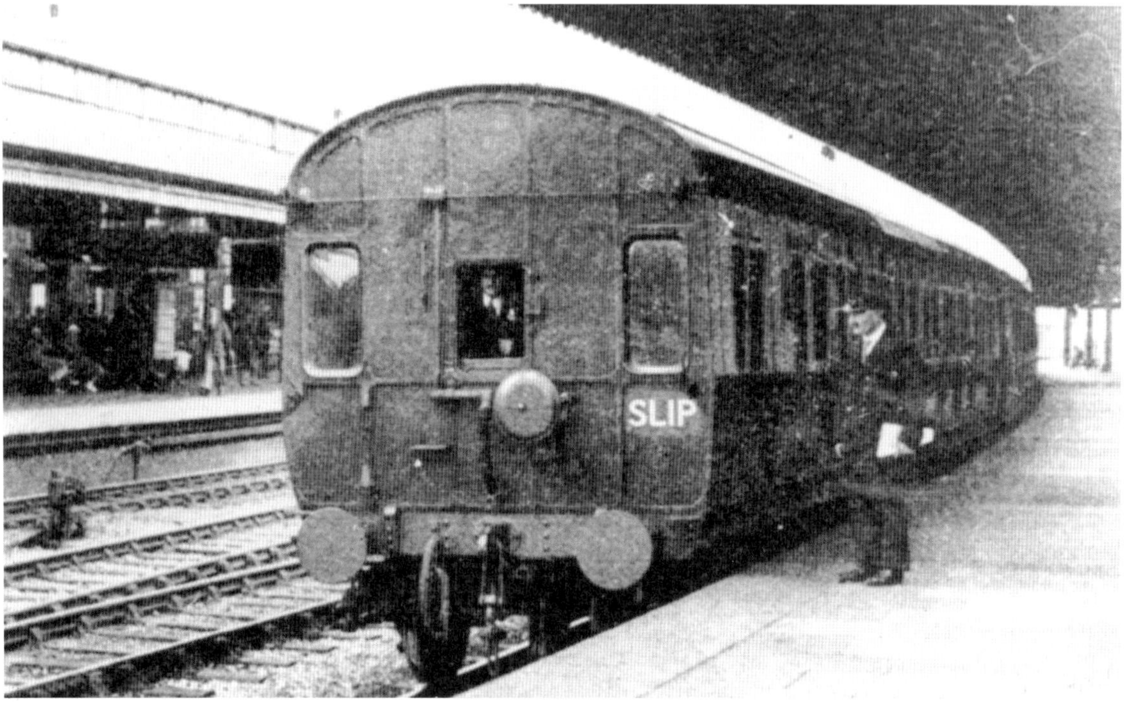

A coach slipped from a Down train, arrives at Bath *c.* 1935. The guard in the centre window stands at the controls. Notice the warning gong. (*Author's Collection*)

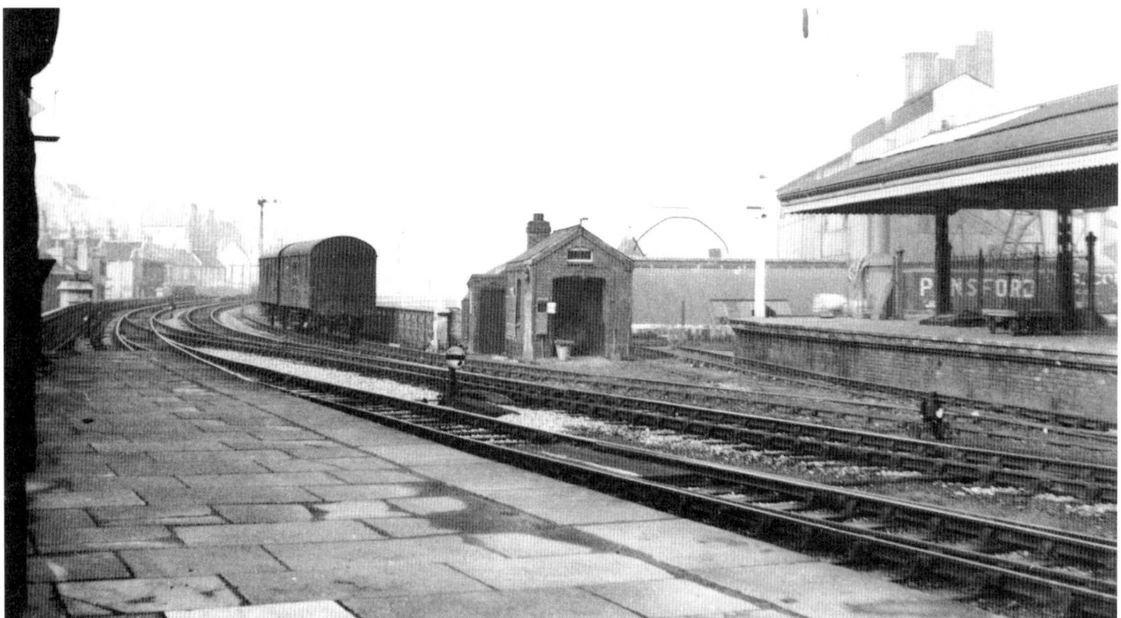

Bath, view west, Easter 1937. A brick-built stable for shunting horses lies in the centre and a Pensford colliery wagon stands at right angles to the siding, having been turned ready for discharge. (*M. J. Tozer Collection*)

Chapter Ten

Serving Industry

Goods traffic at Bristol was very important. As it would have been very expensive to have had the Temple Meads goods shed and tracks at the height of the passenger station, the goods yard was at ground level. The goods shed was sited at right angles to the passenger station, so wagons were swung through 90 degrees on a turntable before running to one of two hydraulically powered lifts. Each lift raised one wagon as it lowered another, thus providing an approximate counterbalance. It took thirty seconds to raise or lower a wagon through the 12 ft.

Brunel's goods shed was an excellent practical design and measured 326 ft by 138 ft. Its roof had a central span of 60 ft, plus two side spans of 40 ft each, and was supported by columns set at 35-ft centres. The combination of solid timbers and light metal ties made the roof both functional and attractive in appearance. With a capacity of 209 wagons, stock was moved on shed level by horses and hydraulic capstans, Brunel himself commenting that 'We have several small capstan heads in different parts of the station, which are always in motion running round and a porter takes a turn round one of these with a rope which is hooked on to any carriage he wishes to move'.

The shed was very busy because it not only dealt with GWR traffic, but also handled that of the B&ER until the latter opened its own depot at Pylle Hill on 1 May 1850. The GWR shed was used until 1858 by the MR as well, standard-gauge rails having to be laid in 1854 when the MR converted its Bristol to Gloucester line. The depot proved inadequate for the increasing traffic and Rowland Brotherhood, the Chippenham contractor, remodelled it between 1874 and 1876 to create more room. He filled in the dock that he had constructed thirty-five years earlier to give barge access, replacing it with a wharf equipped with steam and hydraulic cranes alongside the Floating Harbour. The goods yard was raised 3 ft 6 in, a new shed built with six platforms averaging 445 ft in length and accommodating 200 wagons, with space for an additional 232 in the open yard. Delays caused by using the lifts were intolerable, so a ramp on a gradient of 1:60 was built enabling locomotives to work to and from the depot, the gradient creating a natural hump yard. Inwards and outwards traffic was uneven: Platform 1 was used for unloading and the other five for loading, though until 9.00 a.m. No. 2 was used for goods from London. When emptied, wagons from these two inwards roads were shunted by capstan and horses without interfering with unloading operations, or shunting at the other end of the yard.

It was a busy depot and on one day in 1908 over 450 wagons left during a period of only six to seven hours. That year it had a clerical staff of almost 1,000 to deal with the accounts, correspondence and invoicing of goods traffic in the Bristol area. As all goods trains and light engines to and from the main line had to work over a short section of single line in order to reach the depot, sometimes it was difficult to keep to the timetable. By 1914, about 1,700 wagons used the depot daily, this figure including those for Redcliffe sidings, which was a detached part of Temple Meads used for accommodating mineral, flour and grain traffic. Temple Meads itself was confined to handling general goods, except for consignments of galvanised iron that were loaded at the wharf. In 1914, nineteen trains conveying a total of about 600 wagons left Temple Meads between 6.00 p.m. and 6.00 a.m.

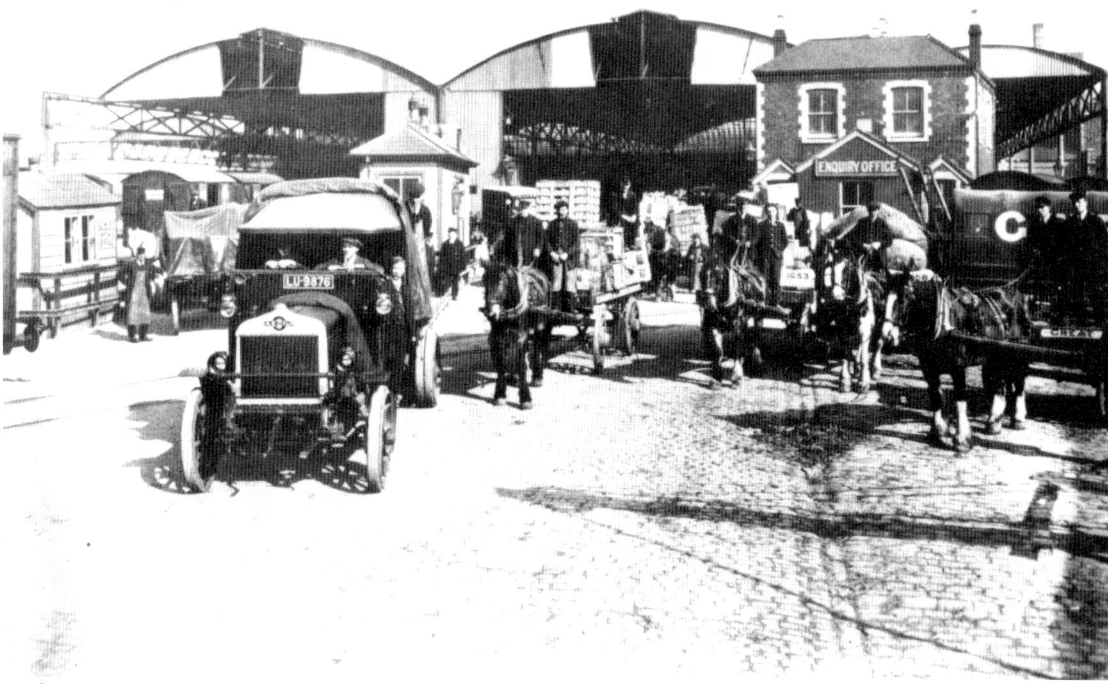

Above: Temple Meads goods depot *c.* 1920. (*M. J. Tozer Collection*)

Opposite top: The entrance to Temple Meads goods yard *c.* 1912, down a gradient of 1:50. Notice the barge dock on the right. (*Author's Collection*)

Opposite middle: Temple Meads goods yard, 18 April 1970, in the National Carriers era. Notice the unusually narrow Temple Meads goods signal box. (*Derrick Payne*)

Opposite bottom: The interior of Temple Meads goods depot *c.* 1971. (*W. F. Grainger*)

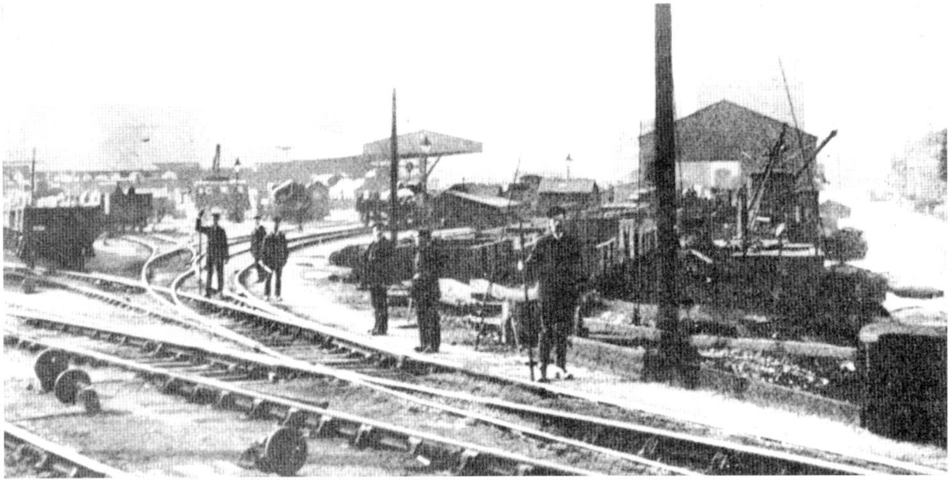

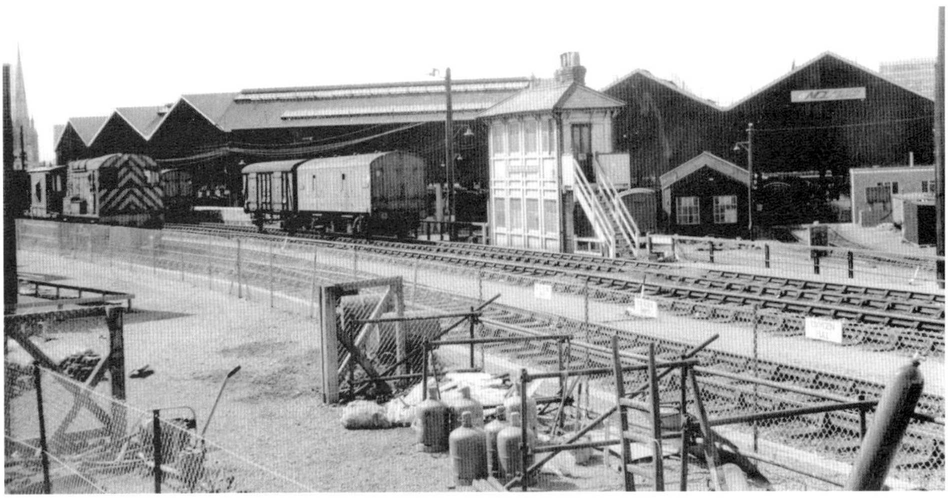

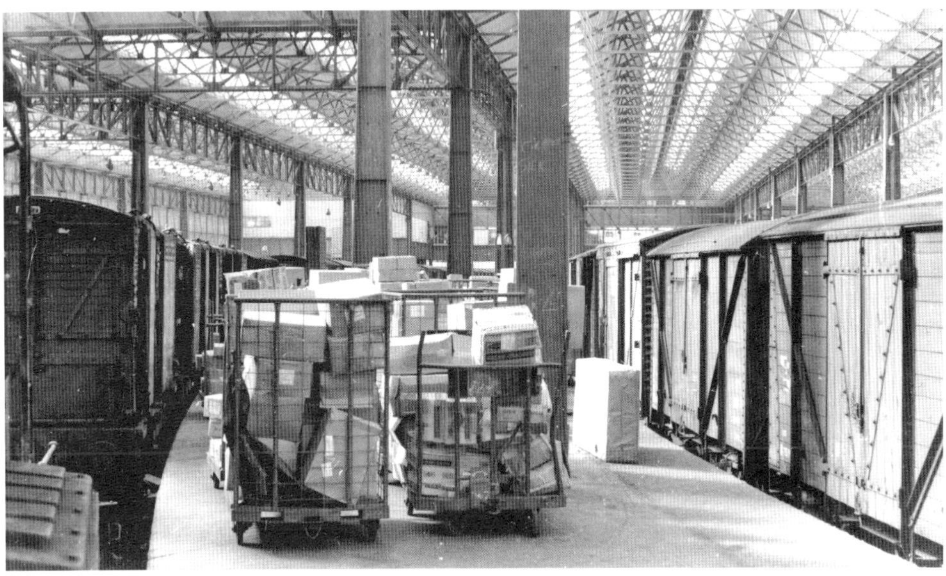

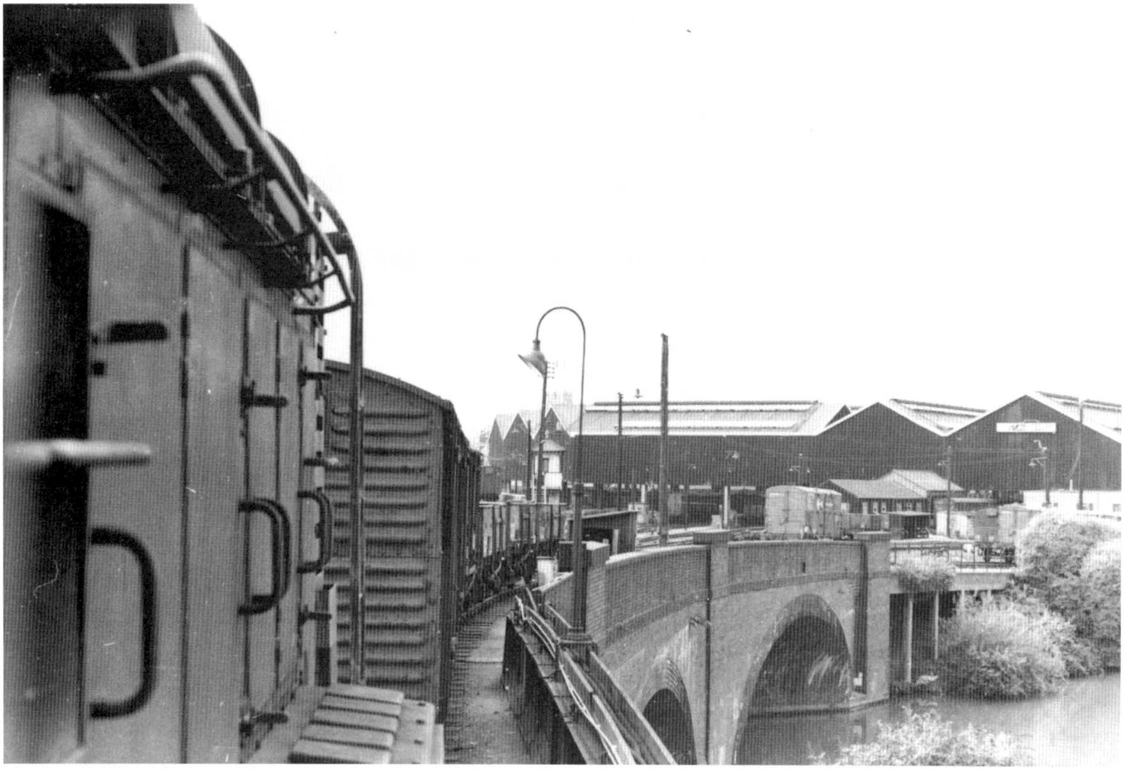

Temple Meads goods depot seen from the cab of a 08 class diesel electric shunter. (*W. F. Grainger*)

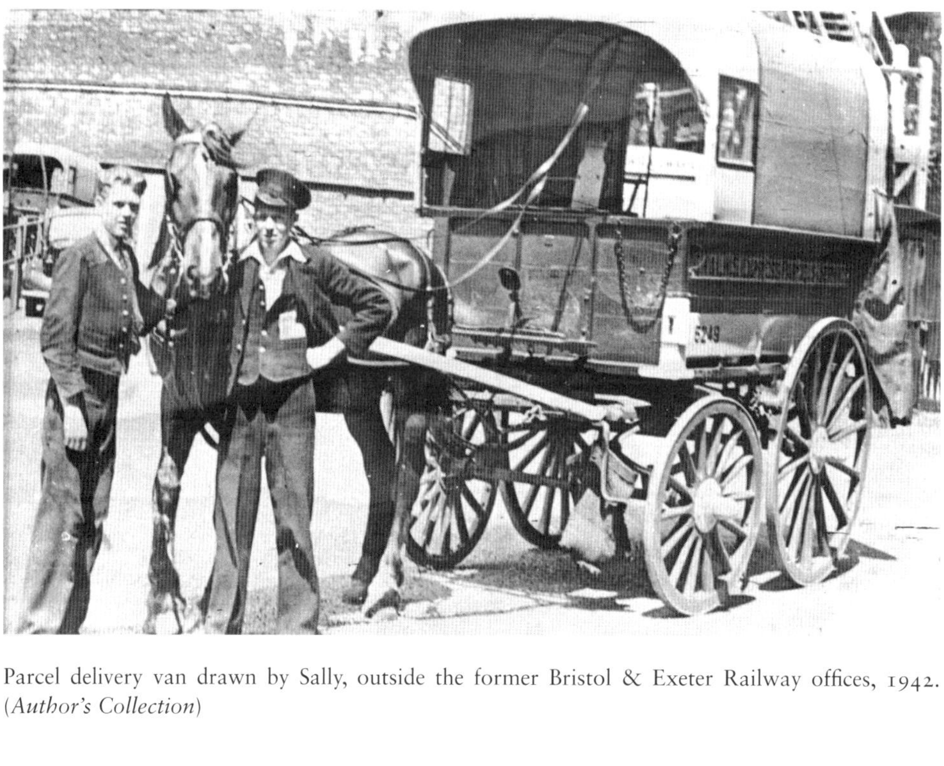

Parcel delivery van drawn by Sally, outside the former Bristol & Exeter Railway offices, 1942. (*Author's Collection*)

Once again the depot proved inadequate and in 1924 a larger depot was built, dilapidated property being acquired to give more space. Built at a cost of £556,450, the new depot covered an area of over 5 acres and at the time was the largest covered area in Britain. Fifteen platforms were under one roof. Each pair of platforms – 30 ft wide and 575 ft in length – was connected to those adjacent by means of tip-up balance bridges to facilitate the passage of trolleys. Unlike the old shed, each track had a platform. The new shed accommodated 408 wagons, while a further 308 could stand in the yard.

The latest technology was employed: electric points, electric capstans to move wagons, electric runways to convey documents between office and shed. Goods were moved by electrically powered platform trucks and an electric telepher carried up to a ton of goods to any part of the shed. Electric lifts gave access to the 390 ft by 100 ft cellars and overhead warehouse. Adequate cellarage was vital to satisfy the increasing demand for the storage of bacon, butter, cheese, lard and other perishables. A dock was dedicated to cars, furniture vans and other vehicles transported by rail. In 1934 the depot dealt with over four million parcels and one and a half million tons of goods. Immediately north of the goods depot, two tracks served a tobacco warehouse. In 1953 BR withdrew horses from Bristol streets and confined them to work within the goods yard, where they were finally rendered redundant in 1962. The depot, latterly used by National Carriers Ltd, was demolished in 1982.

Kingsland Road sidings, on the south side of the South Wales Junction triangle, was a busy depot with twenty-seven roads and, in addition to other traffic including livestock, approximately sixty wagons of coal were unloaded by grab daily for a nearby gasworks.

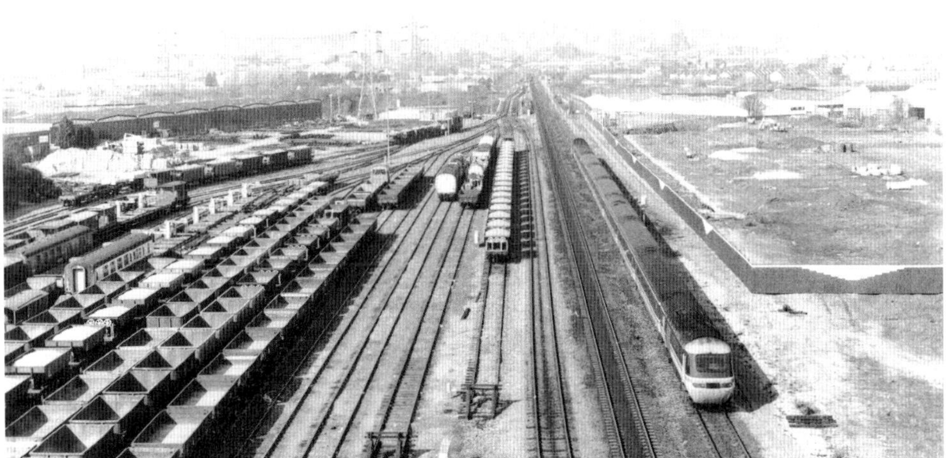

The 10.20 Temple Meads to Paddington HST passes the site of the former Bristol East Depot, 17 March 1990. The engineer's siding is on the left, with the permanent way yard beyond. The site of the Up yard is ripe for development. (*Author*)

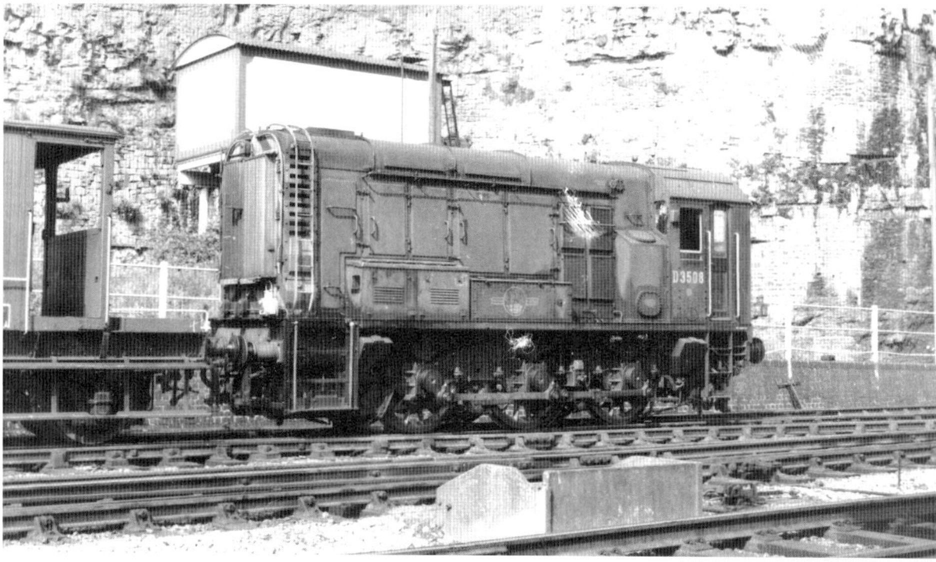

08 class diesel-electric shunter D3508 at Bristol East Depot July 1966. The shunting hump can be seen on the far side of D3508, while to its right is the large spanner used for tightening chair screws. (*W. F. Grainger*)

Bristol East Depot opened in 1890 to deal with the extra traffic brought to the area as a result of the opening of the Severn Tunnel four years previously. East Depot was Bristol's largest yard and had eighteen roads on the Up side and seventeen on the Down. A hump was inserted into the throat of the Up yard on 7 October 1923, creating a gravitational yard and saving 163 shunting engine hours weekly. An average of 1,300 wagons passed over the hump daily. The hump sidings held 468 wagons and its three reception sidings 131.

Up yard siding no.	Purpose	No. of wagons siding will hold
1	Wagons for transfer to Down yard	37
2	Spare vehicles and wagons for Clifton and Avonmouth Line	36
3	Newbury and beyond	35
4	Melksham, Holt Junction, and stations to Newbury (exclusive)	35
5	Reading, Acton, Old Oak Common and Paddington	37
6	Swindon and stations to Didcot (exclusive)	34

7	Chippenham and Calne	33
8	Stations to Corsham	33
9	Oxford, Banbury and LNER	33
10	Weymouth, Portland and Easton	32
11	Stations Witham to Dorchester (inclusive)	31
12	Southern Railway via Salisbury	31
13	Westbury and stations to Salisbury	31
14	Bradford-on-Avon and Trowbridge	30

A Klaxon horn allowed communication between the shunter at the ground frame and the engine driver, the code being:

1 Go ahead
2 Come back (i.e. to hump back toward the sidings)
3 Stop
6 Obstruction – Danger

In addition to numerous transfer trips from one yard to another at East Depot, the Up yard dealt with forty-one trains daily and during the first month of operation, an average of 1,300 wagons passed over the hump each day. Diminishing traffic caused the depot to be closed for marshalling purposes on 7 August 1967, but the Down yard was retained for use by the Civil Engineer for storing wagons, ballast and track panels. In the autumn of 1998 Tarmac Quarry Products made the experiment of moving stone from its Stancombe Quarry, Flax Bourton, to Bristol East Depot sidings by road then using train onwards to its Hayes Depot. Proving a success, from September 1999 a regular weekly departure was made. This traffic soon ceased and ESW opened a new freight terminal on 4 April 2005; this also failed to develop.

From 23 July 1924 until about 1964, a branch from a junction close to the shunting hump served John Lysaght Limited's steelworks on both sides of the river. The company had its own Hawthorn, Leslie & Co. 0-4-0ST. Normally only one locomotive was in use, but Lysaght's owned three at various times. Latterly, a Thomas Hill 4wDH was used. On 1 July 1924 an adjacent line led to the United Alkali Company's works, later taken over by ICI. This private siding agreement terminated on 5 August 1967. The gradient into Lysaght's sidings was 1:37, falling from the GWR yard, so A class engines shunting the sidings were restricted to twelve wagons of class 1 traffic; C class engines were limited to fifteen. Except when in use, the hand point in the hump line leading to Messrs Lysaght and United Alkali Company's sidings had to be set for the Up hump yard and the lever secured by chain and padlock, the key being kept in the hump yard ground frame.

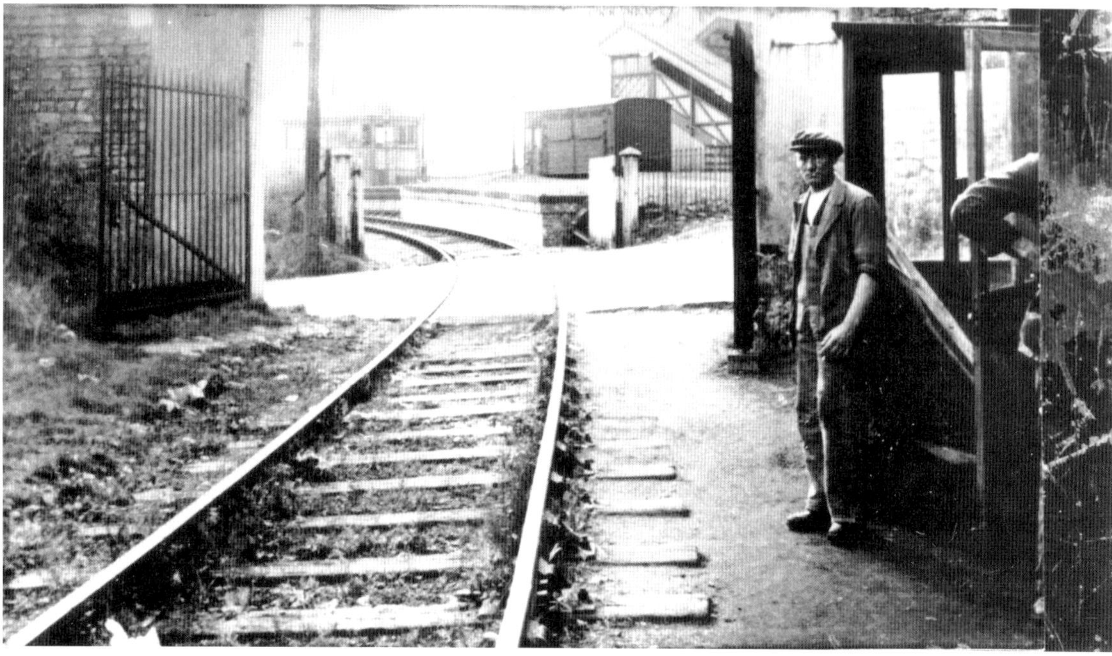

A 1936 view east from Messrs Fry's property across Station Road level crossing to Keynsham West signal box. A horse box stands in the dock siding. The notice on the right-hand side of the gate reads 'Beware of Motor Traffic'. (*Author's Collection*)

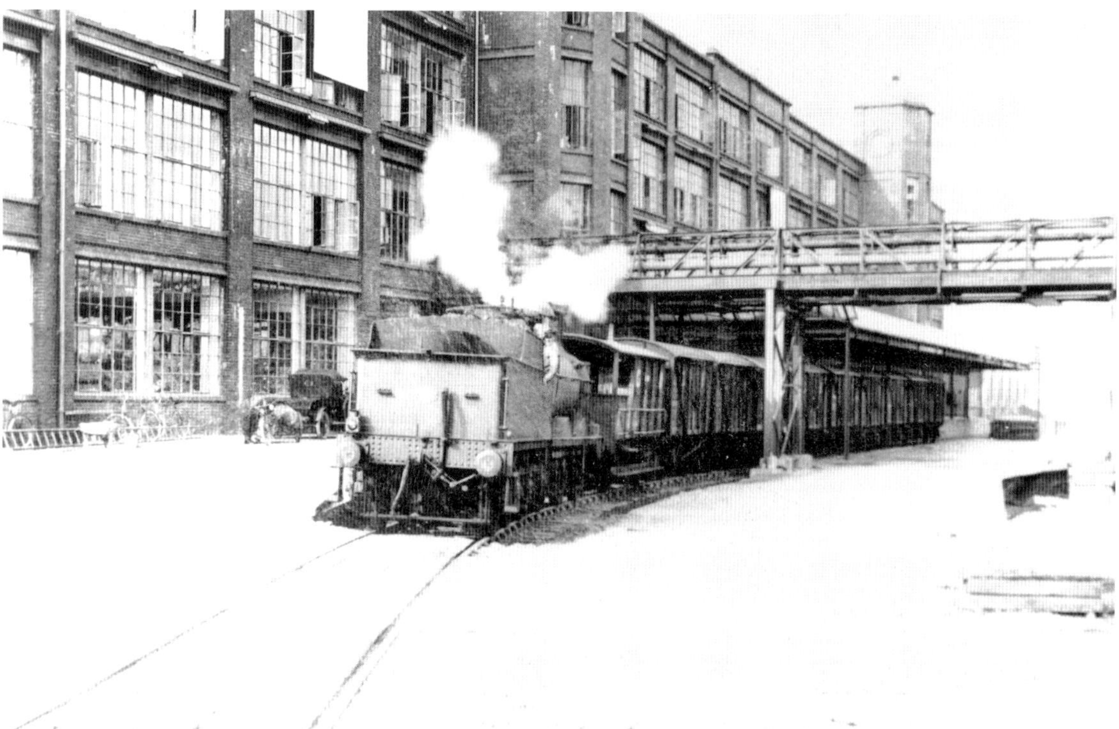

A GWR 0-6-0 in Fry's siding *c.* 1930. (*M. J. Tozer Collection*)

The principal private siding at Keynsham was that belonging to J. S. Fry & Sons, chocolate manufacturers. In January 1922 work started on laying the 2½ miles of track and initially was used to bring construction material for the factory, the first trading use of the siding taking place on 17 January 1925. As Station Hill level crossing between the GWR main line and Fry's factory was ungated, locomotives were prohibited from propelling wagons over this crossing even though a Fry's employee stood on either side of the track. As the siding faced Bath, this meant that the engine of a train leaving the factory had to run round its train in the loops at Keynsham East signal box before proceeding to Bristol East Depot. Inwards traffic comprised sacks of cocoa beans, sugar and wagons of coal, while outwards came chocolate products in TEVANS labelled 'Return to J.S. Fry & Sons siding, Keynsham & Somerdale, GWR'. The vans that had brought the ingredients were used for the despatch of the finished product, a fair proportion of which was consigned to Fry's distribution depots in various parts of the kingdom. TEVANS were MICAS converted for tea and cocoa use by Messrs Lyon and Fry. Conversion started in 1933.

The sidings within the factory grounds were worked by a four-wheeled vertical-boiler Sentinel locomotive, works No. 7492, built in 1928. It only ventured on to GWR metals to collect from, or deliver, a van to the loading dock. In January 1964 it was sold to the Grove Iron & Steel Merchants, Bristol, and resold for preservation at Bacton, Suffolk. It is presently being restored at Bitton by the Avon Valley Railway. Its replacement in 1956 was Hudswell Clarke 0-4-0DM, works No. D1009, named *Somerdale*. From 30 May 1933 Fry's owned a three-coach show train, consisting of adapted GWR coaching stock, which toured the country each year for publicity purposes. In three years it covered 16,000 miles, received over 130,000 visitors and collected £6,200 in return for samples, this money being given to charities in towns which the train visited.

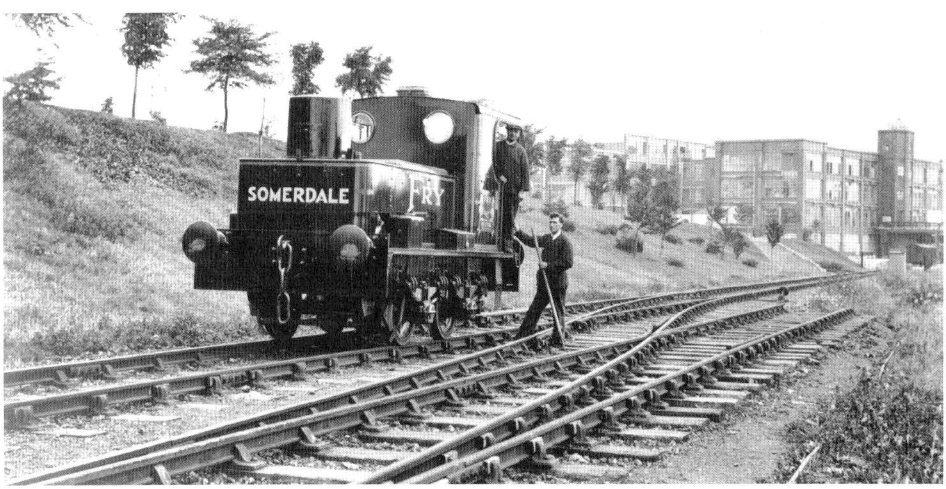

Fry's Sentinel shunter *Somerdale*. (*M. J. Tozer Collection*)

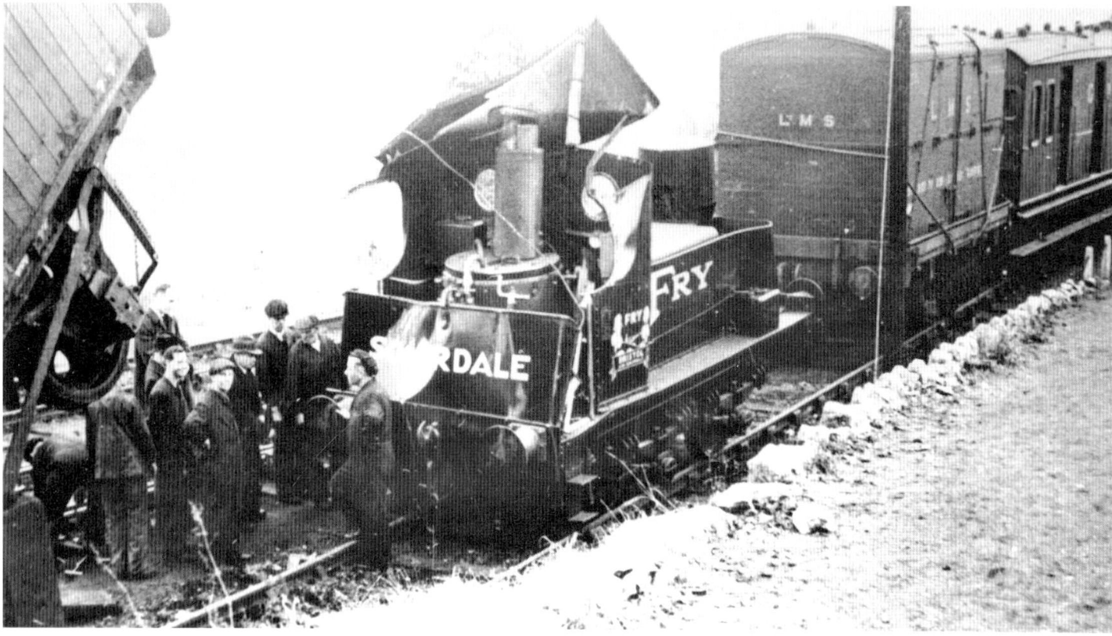

Fry's shunter *Somerdale* following a shunting mishap in November 1940, exposing the vertical boiler in the cab. A GWR tool and mess van is beyond the wagon with the LMS container. (*M. J. Tozer Collection*)

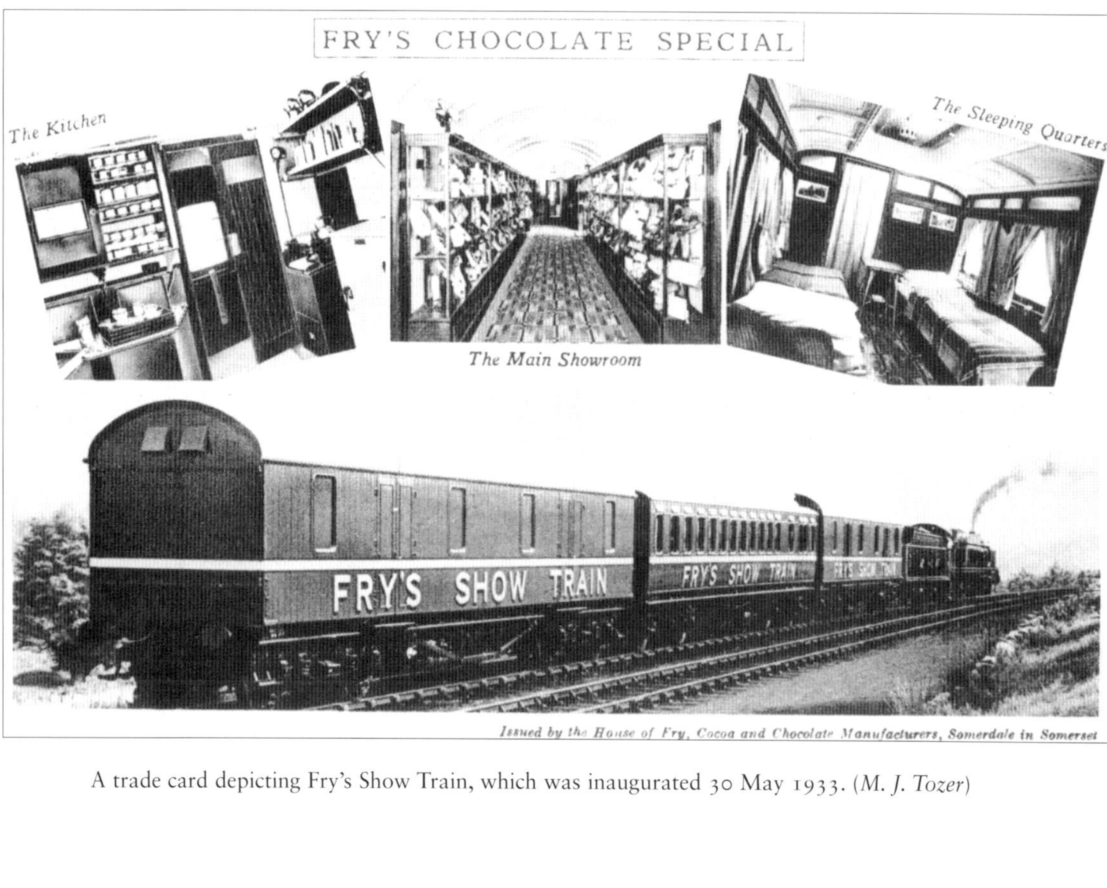

A trade card depicting Fry's Show Train, which was inaugurated 30 May 1933. (*M. J. Tozer*)

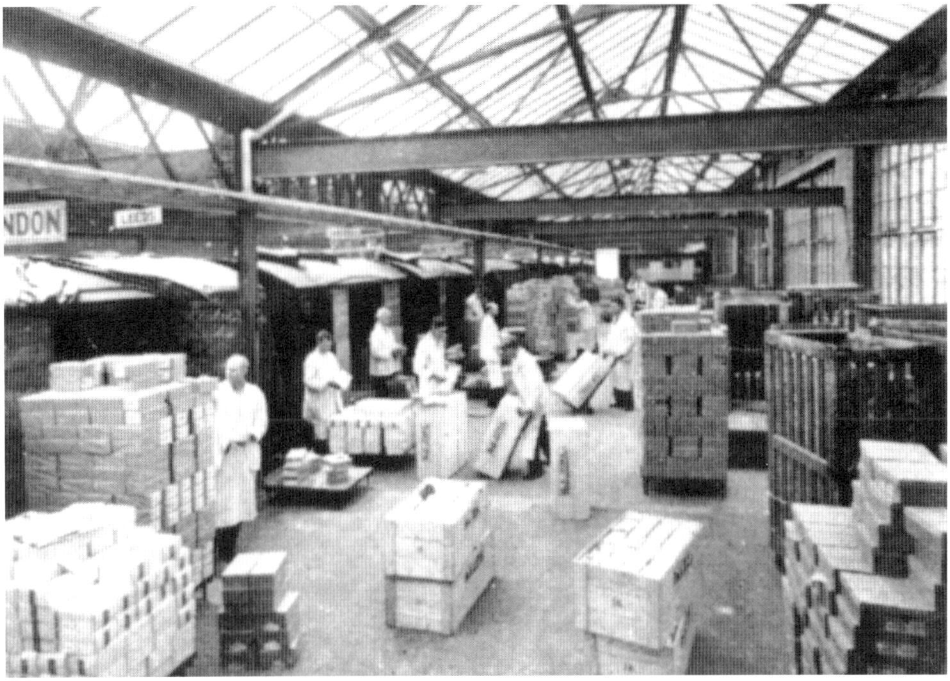

Above: Messrs Fry's loading bay *c.* 1930. The labels above the vans read 'London', 'Leeds' and 'Southampton'. (*Author's Collection*)

Right: Somerdale, a 0-4-0 diesel-mechanical shunter, Hudswell Clarke D1009 at Fry's works. (*W. F. Grainger*)

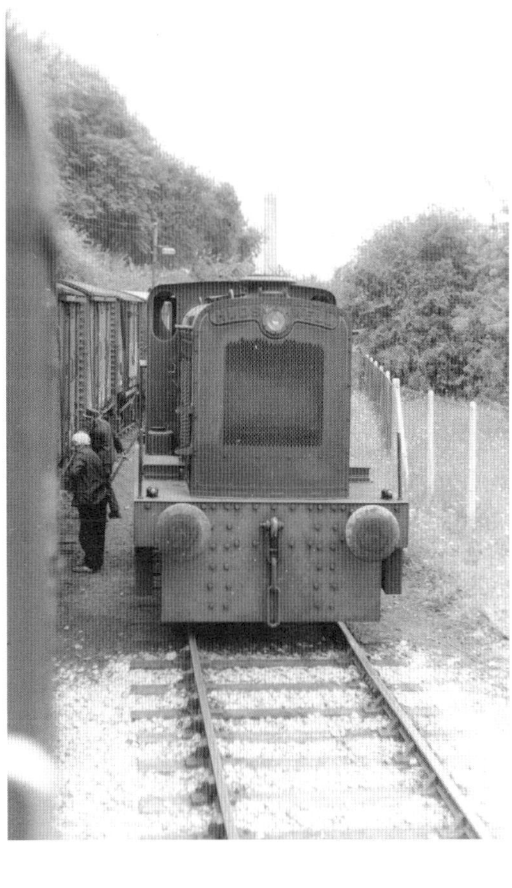

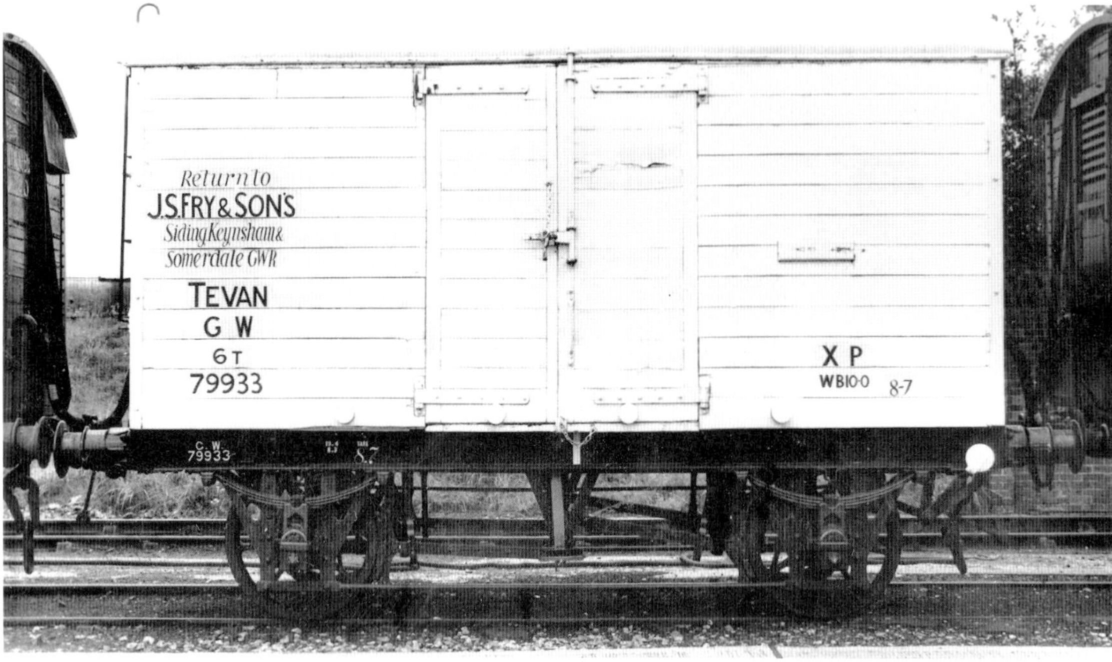

A 'TEVAN' used by Messrs Fry and preserved at the Didcot Railway Centre, photographed on 19 August 1992. (*Author*)

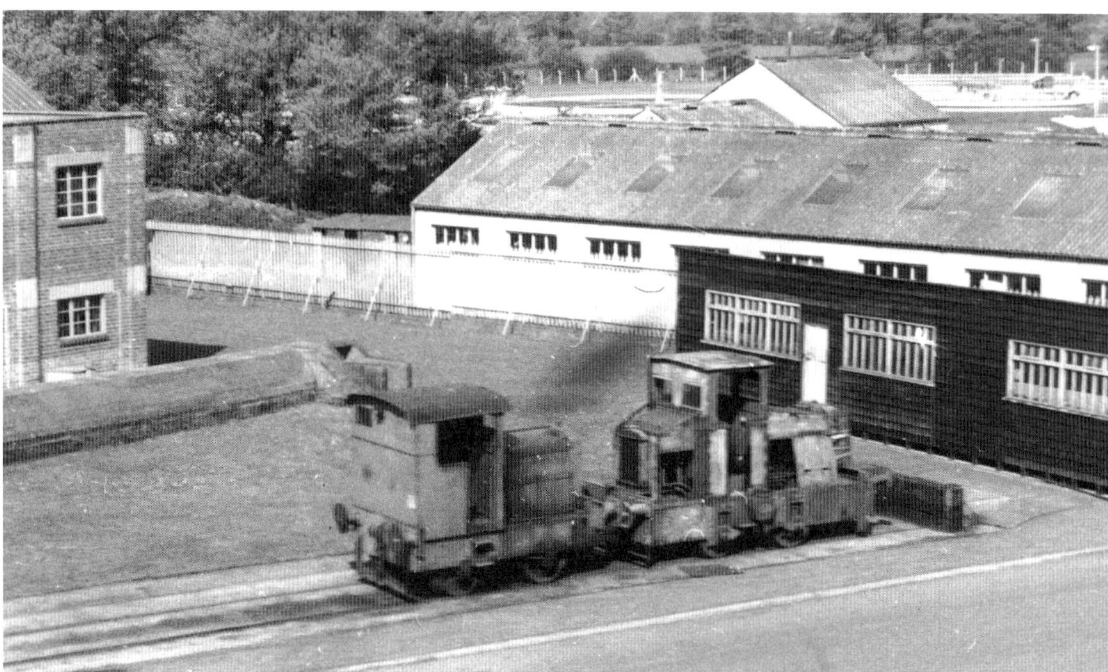

Messrs E. S. & A. Robinson's locomotive stud at Keynsham, 30 April 1966. Right, the four-wheeled petrol-mechanical Avonside Works No. 2013 of 1930, and left, Ruston Hornsby No. 235519 of 1945. The view was taken from a passing train. (*Revd Alan Newman*)

The longest regular commercial users of Keynsham goods depot, apart from coal merchants, were Polysulphin, manufacturers of industrial soaps, and Gould Thomas, manufacturer of vegetable dyes, Glauber salt and ammonium chloride. East of the goods shed was a siding opened in May 1929 on the Up side serving Paper Sacks Ltd. The firm moved in 1930, but two years later Messrs E. S. & A. Robinson opened a paper mill on the same site. The siding was used by wagons of pulp and coal, and for despatch of the finished product. Rail traffic ceased in October 1969. At first, the siding was worked by an Avonside 4wPM, works No. 2013, of 1930, sold for scrap in about 1968. It had two gears and its four-cylinder paraffin engine was started on petrol. It shunted wagons of 'duff', or coal dust from Eastern United's pit in the Forest of Dean. From 1945 it was assisted by a new 4wDM Ruston Hornsby, works No. 235519, which was moved on 26 January 1974 to the Avon Valley Railway at Bitton for preservation.

On the Down side, almost opposite where the two Up loops joined the main line, a siding served the Square Grip Reinforcement Co. (London) Ltd between 1955 and 1966, and steel bars arrived on bogie bolsters. The siding was worked from a ground frame released by Annett's key from an adjacent key release instrument and unlocked by the signalman in the East box. The siding was shunted by BR locomotives, as was Tate & Lyle's siding 90 yd to the east, which was open for fourteen years (1952–66) but little used. Its ground frame was similarly electrically interlocked and released by Annett's key. Two sidings were provided: one for the reception of loaded vehicles and the other for outwards traffic. Only four-wheeled vehicles with a wheelbase not exceeding 19½ ft were permitted to work into the sidings, all screw couplings had to be loosened to the fullest extent, and instanter couplings placed in the long position. The severe curvature and gradient meant that a raft of at least five additional wagons had to be used to propel inwards wagons, which were required to be placed at least 35 yd inside the entrance gate. This was because wheel stops were located 35 yd from the gate and when wagons were berthed, the shunter was required to see that the stops were padlocked across the rails and the keys returned to the Keynsham East signalman.

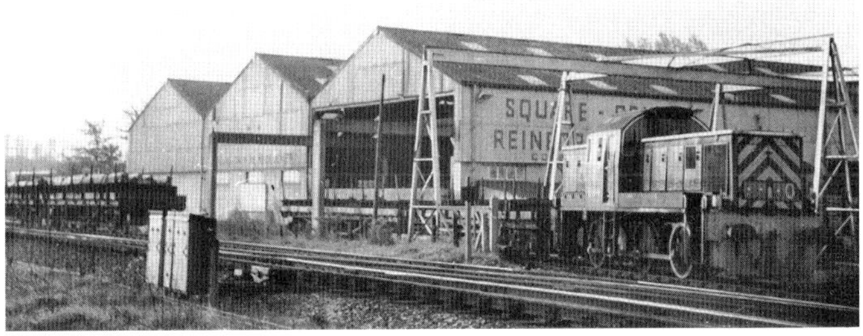

Diesel-hydraulic 0-6-0 D9525 removing empty wagons from the Square Grip Reinforcement Company's siding, Keynsham, 2 May 1966. Loaded wagons to be placed in the siding stand on the main line. (*Russell Leitch*)

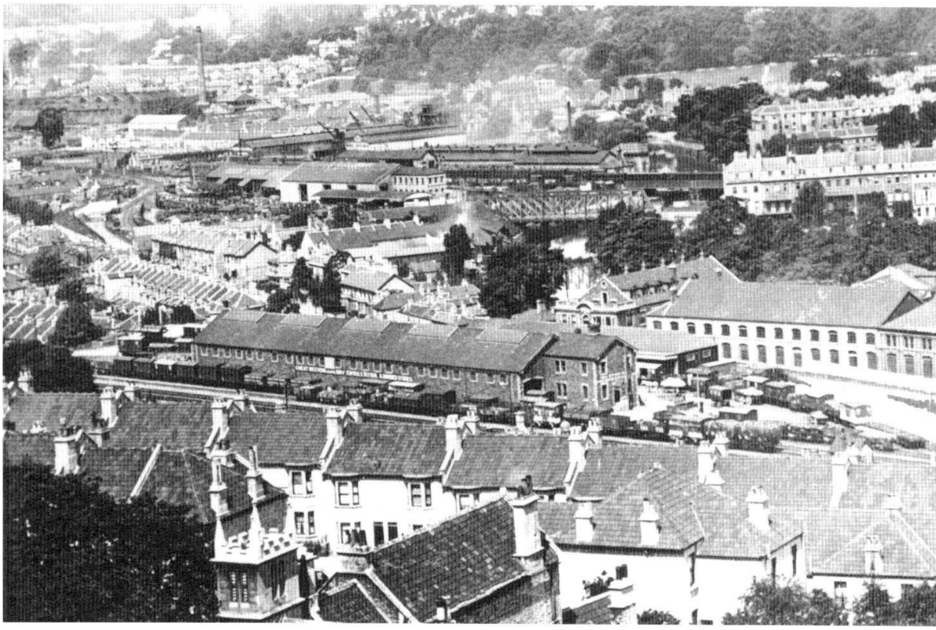

The GWR Bath goods depot from Beechen Cliff *c.* 1905. The Midland Railway goods depot can be seen in the distance. (*Author's Collection*)

Following the opening of the Severn Tunnel, the Bristol to Bath line became important for carrying coal from South Wales pits to Southampton, Portsmouth and to Great Western loco depots to the east of Bristol. Other significant traffic which developed with the growth of Avonmouth included bananas, animal feeding stuffs and oil. Steamers from Cork and Waterford moored alongside the Canon's Marsh branch at Bristol and lairage, cattle pens and sidings were provided, a proportion of these trains using the Bath line. The 'Paddy Mail', as the 2.25 p.m. Paddington to Temple Meads was known, called at all stations and arrived at Temple Meads at 10.00 p.m. with a load comprising anything from two to twenty-two vans. It could be hauled by any class of tender engine, even a King. Its return working, known as the Cocoa, was inaugurated in 1905 and was the first GWR vacuum-brake-fitted goods train. Around 1914, it was often headed by 4-6-2 No. 111 *The Great Bear*, which drew seventy wagons from Bristol East Depot to Acton in three hours five minutes. In later years, the train was usually worked by a 47XX class 2-8-0.

Chapter Eleven

Locomotives and Locomotive Sheds

The first trial trip between Bristol and Bath was in the form of a relay. Fire Fly class 2-2-2 *Arrow*, built by Stothert, Slaughter & Co., Bristol, was used for the Bristol to Keynsham leg, while Sun class 2-2-2 *Meridian*, built by R. & W. Hawthorn & Co., Newcastle, took the party on to Bath. The Sun class was a version of the Fire Fly class with 6-ft instead of 7-ft diameter driving wheels. Fire Fly class *Fire Ball* hauled the first train from Bristol to Bath and *Arrow* the first from Bath. Other Fire Fly class engines ready for the opening were *Dart*, *Lynx* and *Spit Fire*, while *Stag* joined the stud at the end of September 1840. *Antelope*, a Sun class built by Sharp, Roberts & Co. in May 1841, experienced teething problems as one of its boiler tubes burst near Twerton station on 12 June 1841. The engine of the next train pushed it to Bath before returning to Twerton to collect its own train. On 1 May 1844, to mark the opening to Exeter, Fire Fly class *Actaeon*, with six coaches, ran the 388-mile return journey Paddington to Exeter via Bath and Bristol.

In 1846 an enlarged Fire Fly, the 2-2-2 *Great Western*, appeared and ran Paddington to Exeter in three hours twenty-eight minutes compared with the five hours taken by a Fire Fly. This was hardly surprising as the *Great Western*'s heating area, grate area and working pressure were roughly double. Its only drawback was that there was too much weight on the leading axle, but this problem was cured by the frames being lengthened and the wheel arrangement converted to a 4-2-2. In 1847 similar, though slightly larger, 4-2-2 engines were built, forming the Iron Duke class – so called because the first engine ran its trial trip on the Duke of Wellington's birthday, 29 April. In size and power they were the largest engines in the country and introduced such typical broad-gauge features as a domeless boiler, firebox with raised casing, Gooch-designed safety valve cover, and cylinders enclosed in the smokebox casing. Their tenders had a hooded rear-facing seat to accommodate the travelling porter, whose task it was to keep a lookout and make sure nothing was amiss.

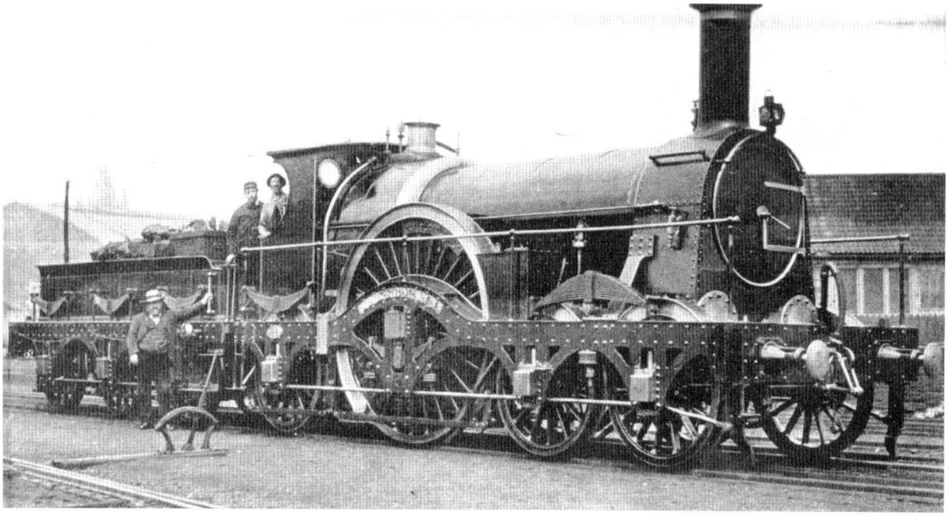

Rover class 4-2-2 *Inkermann* outside Temple Meads *c.* 1890. This is a modernised version of the Iron Duke class, a cab being a great comfort to its crew. (*Author's Collection*)

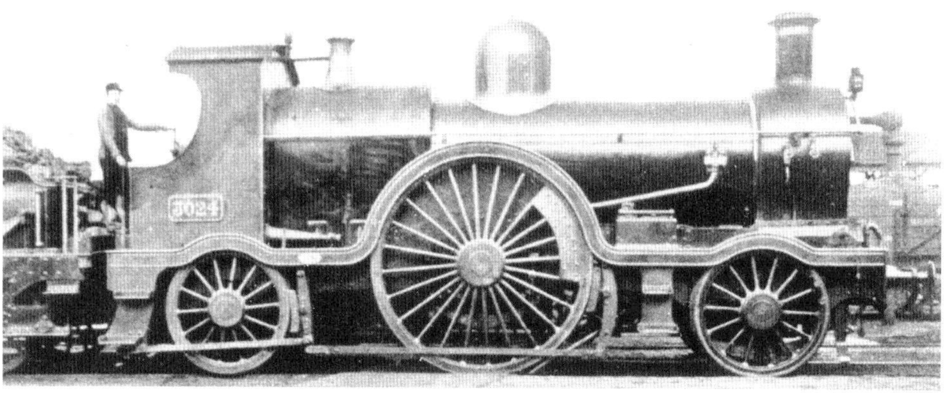

Achilles class 2-2-2 No. 3024 with 7-ft 8½-in driving wheels. Built in July 1891 as a broad gauge convertible, it was altered to standard gauge in August 1892, reconstructed as a 4-2-2 in December 1894, named *Storm King* and finally withdrawn in February 1909. (*Author's Collection*)

These engines worked the principal expresses Paddington to Bristol and burned about 35 lb of coke per mile. From 1871 engines of this class were replaced by new engines of the same design, but with weather-boards to give their crew a certain amount of shelter. Locomotives of the class turned out in 1873 had iron-roofed cabs to offer even more protection, but they rattled severely and in 1876 wooden roof cabs became standard.

When the Bristol to Bath line opened to goods on 30 June 1841, this traffic would probably have been handled by Leo class 2-4-0s. To give better adhesion, this class was converted to saddle tanks and some worked to Salisbury and Weymouth in this form. Premier class 0-6-0s appeared in 1846 and were the basic design for subsequent goods engines. All GWR broad-gauge locomotives were named but not numbered and two of the Caesar class 0-6-0s had very strange names for goods engines – *Coquette* and *Flirt*. One of the Swindon class engines of the same wheel arrangement was named *Bristol* and another *Bath*. The Waverley class had the only broad-gauge 4-4-0 tender engines and, although not generally fast, these engines were fine for working the slower and heavier passenger trains. As their rigid wheelbase was rather long, they were really only suited for the relatively straight road between Paddington and Bristol. The Victoria class 2-4-0s were similar engines. Hawthorn class 2-4-0s, designed by Joseph Armstrong, appeared in 1865 and were used on Bristol to Weymouth and Salisbury trains.

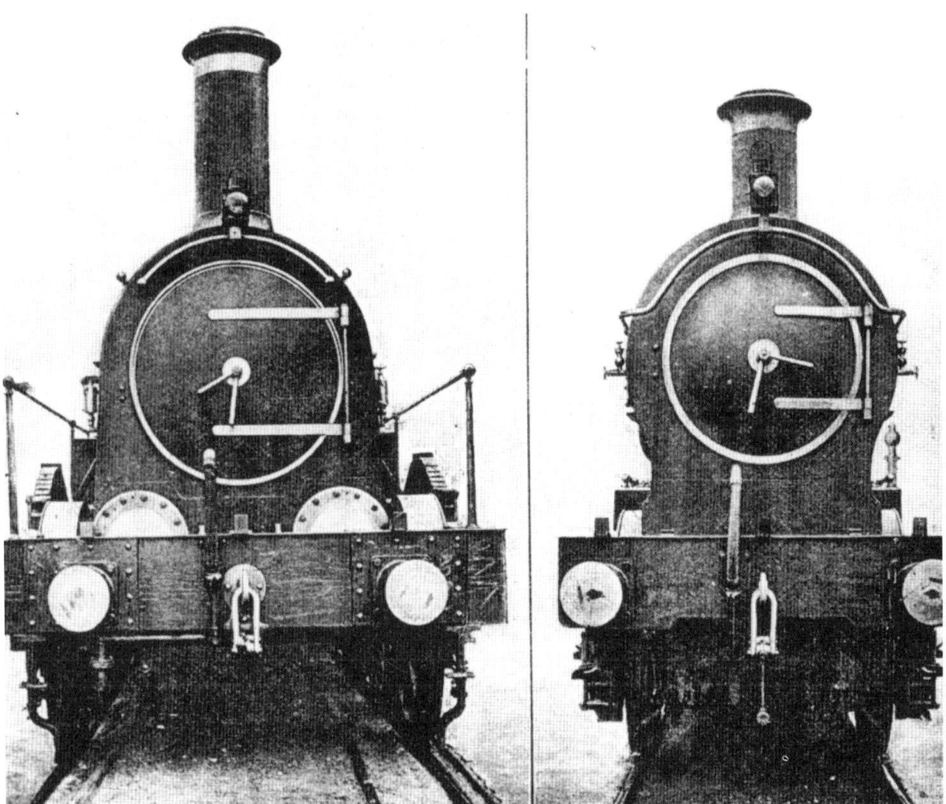

The broad- and standard-gauge engines named *Rover*, 1892. Notice that the boiler is higher on the standard-gauge locomotive in order to clear the driving wheels, thus giving a higher centre of gravity. Left is the 4-2-2 Iron Duke class renewal built in 1871 and withdrawn in May 1892. Right is Achilles class No. 3019 as a 2-2-2. It became a 4-2-2 in 1894 and was withdrawn in 1908. (*Author's Collection*)

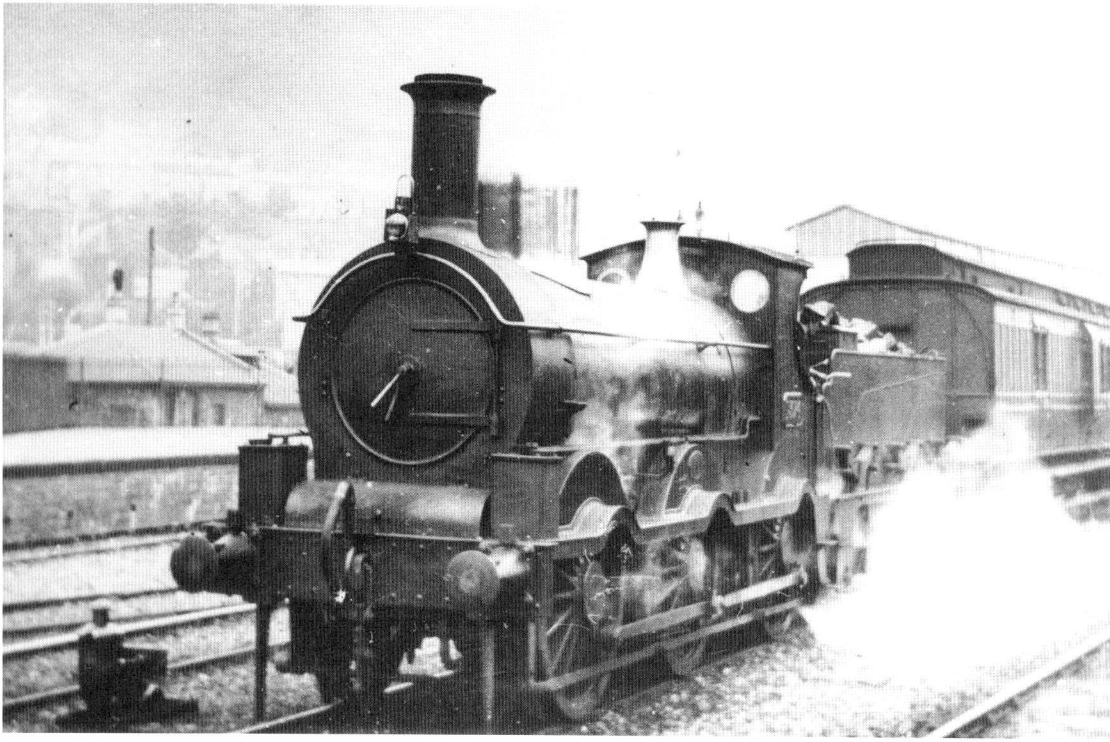

0-6-0 No. 1374 on the middle road at Bath *c.* 1905. Built in 1875 for the Bristol & Exeter Railway's standard-gauge trains, it was withdrawn in 1909. (*P. Q. Treloar Collection*)

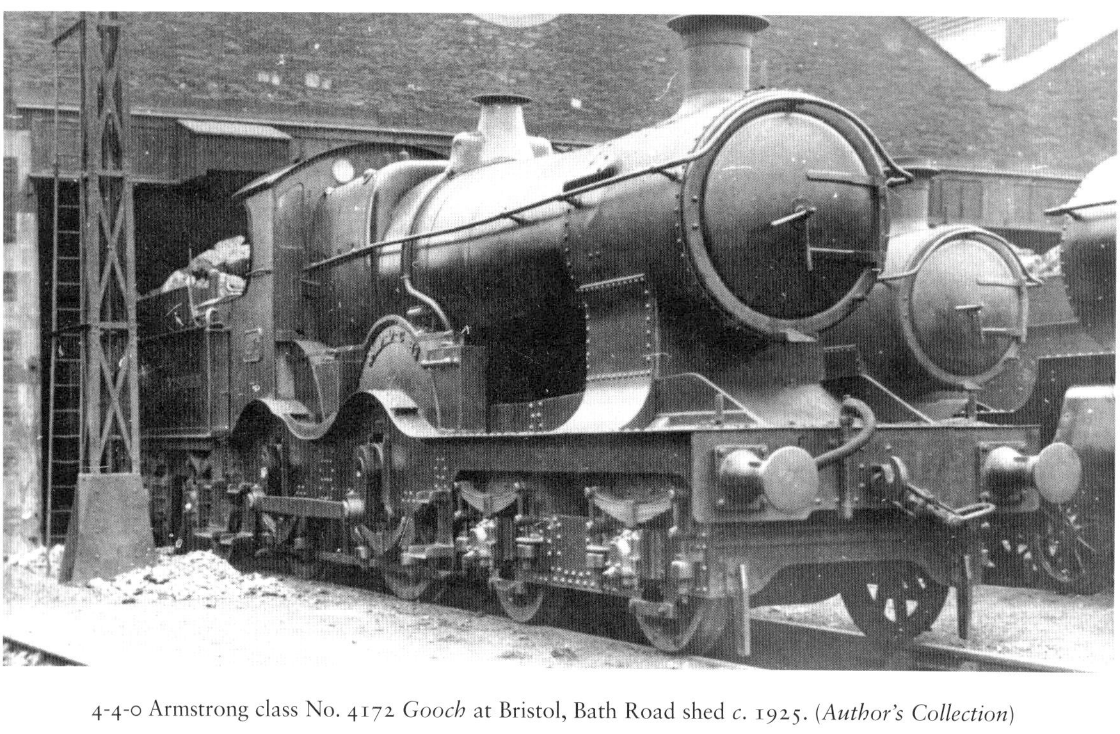

4-4-0 Armstrong class No. 4172 *Gooch* at Bristol, Bath Road shed *c.* 1925. (*Author's Collection*)

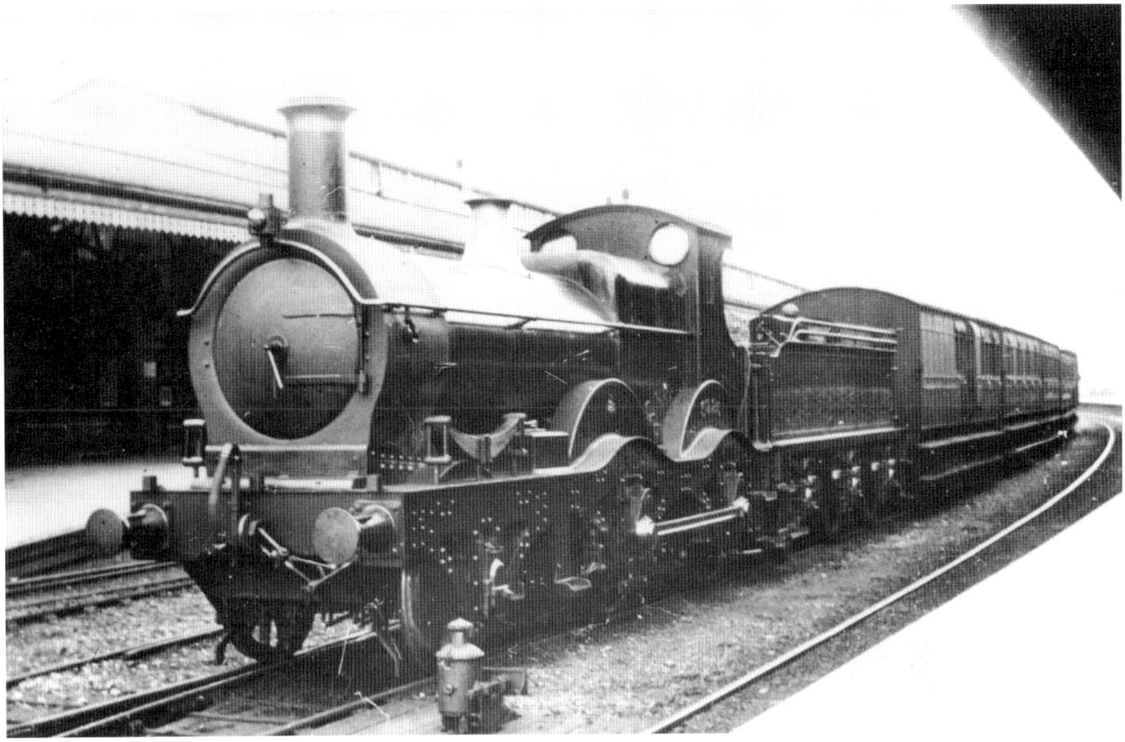

Barnum class 2-4-0 No. 3225 on a middle road at Bath with a Down stopping train. (*Author's Collection*)

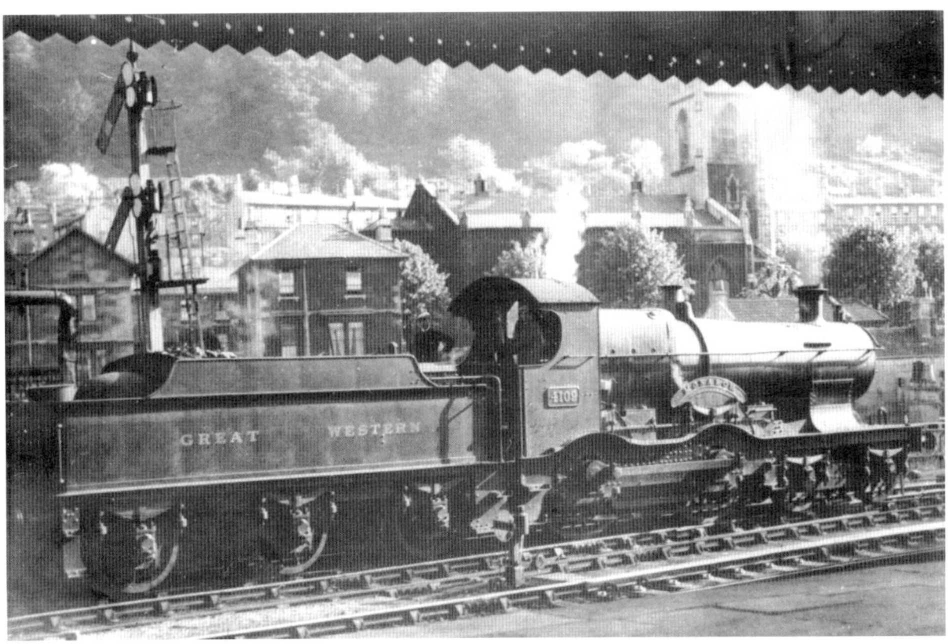

Badminton class 4-4-0 No. 4109 *Monarch* at Bath 21 May 1929 with a Down stopping train. (*Author's Collection*)

Apart from Iron Duke renewals, from 1876 onwards, as the end of the broad gauge was in sight, all new engines required for the broad gauge were standard-gauge engines with broad gauge axles. Armstrong's 0-6-0STs of the 1076 class, which appeared in 1876, were the first GWR convertibles and used as mixed traffic engines, some of those on passenger duty being altered to 0-4-2STs to allow freer runming. Because of the shortage of broad-gauge goods engines in 1884–88, twenty of Armstrong's Standard Goods 0-6-0s, built in 1876, were converted from standard to broad gauge and then, in 1892, back to standard gauge. When running on the broad gauge they drew old broad-gauge tenders and, as their standard-gauge width cabs remained, they had an odd appearance. Another group of convertible engines were 2-4-0s for express duty. No. 8 was an experimental four-cylinder compound 2-4-0. No. 14 and No. 16 were large 2-4-0s designed by Dean especially for working the heavy 3.00 p.m. express from Bristol to Swindon. Although convertible, these three engines were never actually converted but 'renewed' as 4-4-0s. The final development of the 2-2-2 arrangement was the 3021 class convertibles for use on express passenger trains.

Early broad-gauge livery varied, but was approximately: boiler and firebox lagged with wood strips painted green and bound with brass bands; the top of the haycock firebox, safety valve cover, brass; smokebox and chimney, black; wheels, dark green; buffer beams, vermillion; and buffers of leather. In 1881 outside frames were painted dark Indian red and in 1886 inside frames were vermillion inside and black outside. Wheel splashers and sandboxes were Indian red.

Practically all classes of standard-gauge GWR engines worked over the line at one time or another. Towards the end of the nineteenth century, express passenger trains were hauled by engines of the 2-4-0, 2-2-2 and 4-2-2 wheel arrangement, goods trains by 0-6-0s and stopping passengers by 2-4-0Ts or 0-4-2Ts. Sir Daniel class 2-2-2s worked the 9.35 a.m. express Bristol to Paddington and two trains Bristol to Swindon, but then as heavier loads demanded four-coupled machines and Sir Daniels were virtually the same as Dean's Standard Goods apart from wheel arrangement, they were converted to 0-6-0s. Their curved frames were retained, giving them a distinctly odd appearance as they had originally been above 7-ft diameter driving wheels. In the 1890s No. 9, a 2-2-2, worked slow trains Bristol to Swindon; considered a strong engine, it was easily recognisable because its valve gear was, unusually, placed outside the frames.

In 1894 Dean's Armstrong class 4-4-0s appeared and worked the heavier expresses rather than the Achilles class 4-2-2s. In 1892 Badminton class 4-4-0s supplanted the 4-2-2s, which encountered adhesion problems with the increasingly heavier trains. The Atbara 4-4-0s of 1900 had similar duties to the Badmintons and from 1912 to 1922 worked Cardiff to Salisbury trains. From 1901 the speedy City class 4-4-0s monopolised the Paddington to Penzance expresses. The 4-4-0 County class appeared on West of England expresses in 1904. Although otherwise similar in dimensions to the City class, their cylinder stroke was 4 in longer and the cylinders placed outside, rather than inside. Although satisfactory from the power point of view, their large outside cylinders and short wheelbase caused them to roll badly and earned them the nickname 'Churchward's Rough Riders'. They were soon superseded on main line expresses by 4-6-0s and all were withdrawn by 1932.

Two-cylinder 4-6-0 No. 100 (later No. 2900) *William Dean* appeared in 1902 and it, along with the rest of the Saint class, took over West of England expresses from the 4-4-0s. No. 171 (later 2971) *Albion* appeared in 1903 with an Atlantic wheel arrangement in order to give better comparison with No. 102 *La France*. This four-cylinder de Glehn compound 4-4-2, purchased in 1903, was followed by the larger No. 103 *President*, and No. 104 *Alliance* in 1905, and initially worked through Bath on West of England expresses. Churchward built a 'simple' engine with the de Glehn cylinder arrangement and produced a masterpiece that was the basis of all subsequent large GWR passenger engines. No. 40 (later No. 4000) *North Star* appeared as a 4-4-2 in 1906 for comparison with the French Atlantics, but was converted to a 4-6-0 in 1909. The Star class immediately became the principal express engines. In around 1907 No. 4001 *Dog Star*, with a 320-ton train, ran from Bristol to Bath in fourteen minutes fifty-two seconds, an average speed of 47 mph.

A super Star, Pacific No. 111 *The Great Bear*, appeared in 1908 but was simply for prestige as its wheels and mechanical parts were standard with the Stars, the difference being a larger boiler and firebox. Its weight restricted it to the Paddington to Bristol road and it tended to work an express passenger in one direction and return with a vacuum-fitted goods train. On one occasion it became derailed when entering the Up bay platform at Bath. In 1924 it was rebuilt as a Castle. The Castle class 4-6-0s had appeared in 1923 and were followed by the Kings in 1927. Both were used on Paddington to Bristol expresses, Kings hauling the heavier trains. Stars, and to a certain extent Saints at times, still appeared on expresses and gave a good account of themselves.

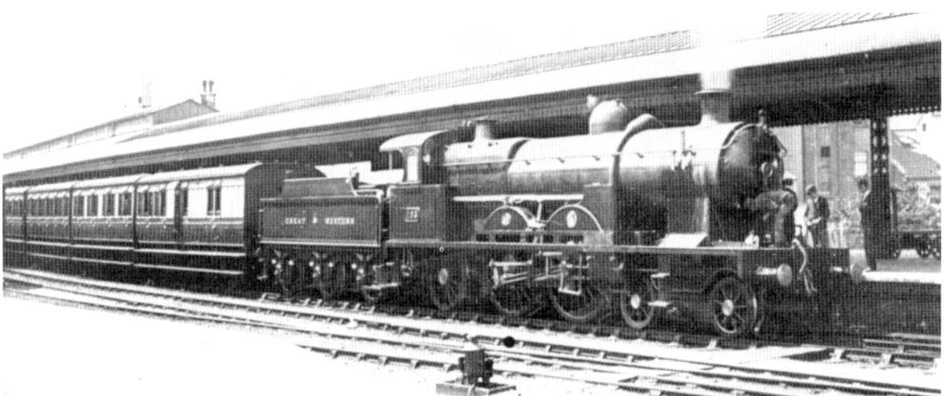

De Glehn compound 4-4-2 No. 103, later named *President*, built Belfort 1905, with an Up stopping train at Bath between 1905 and 1907. It was withdrawn in 1927. (*Author's Collection*)

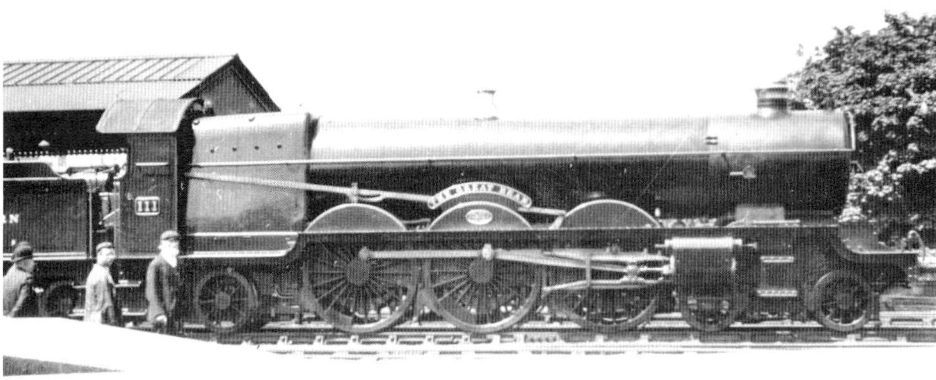

Pacific No. 111 *The Great Bear* at Bath with an Up stopping train *c.* 1920. Its weight and length confined it to working Paddington to Bristol. In 1924 it was reconstructed as a member of the Castle class. (*Author's Collection*)

With the craze for streamlining in the 1930s, No. 5005 *Manorbier Castle* had suitable, or perhaps unsuitable, appertenances added in March 1935, as did No. 6014 *King Henry VII*. As a very young boy, the author remembers seeing it from the upper deck of an open-top tram, leaving Bath with a Down express; he was not very impressed by its appearance. The 4-6-0 County class appeared from 1945 and, new from the works, often came through Bath on a running-in turn.

In 1907 the 5.30 a.m. newspaper and mail train from Paddington was worked to Temple Meads by a County tank, the 4-4-2T, arriving at 8.28 a.m. It returned on the 9.35 a.m. Weston-super-Mare express from Bristol, which arrived at Paddington at 12.20 p.m. The water pick-up apparatus on this class was designed to raise water whether running chimney or bunker first.

Although in the latter days of steam stopping trains were generally worked by tank engines, this had not always been so. In 1923 the 0-6-0 used on the 1.40 p.m. Bath to Temple Meads and 5.15 p.m. Temple Meads to Trowbridge was replaced by a 2-4-0 Barnum. At the end of the twenties, Barnums and 0-6-0s were replaced by the 45XX class 2-6-2Ts. Until about 1900, goods trains on the line were mainly handled by 0-6-0s, either tender or tank, but that year the Aberdare class 2-6-0s, really a goods version of the Bulldog and Atbara classes, appeared and initially were employed on heavy coal trains between Aberdare and Swindon. Just as the Atbaras and Cities were soon outclassed by Saints, so the Aberdares were eclipsed by 2-8-0s, the first of which, No. 97 (later No. 2800), a heavy freight design, appeared in 1903. They were the first engines of that wheel arrangement in Britain and the class was so successful that it continued to be built for the next thirty-nine years. Their larger mixed traffic sisters, the 47XX class, handled fast fitted freights of up to seventy vehicles. Freight trains on the line were also headed by the mixed traffic 43XX 2-6-0s and Hall and Grange class 4-6-0s, those shedded at St Philip's Marsh often working goods trains Mondays to Fridays and passenger trains on summer Saturdays. From 1934 some of the surplus 2-8-0Ts were converted to 2-8-2Ts and a few were used on coal trains from South Wales through Bristol to Salisbury. The enlarged bunker of 6 tons capacity held not far short of the 7 tons of a 28XX tender engine, while the water capacity was 2,500 galls and 3,500 galls respectively. A unique engine, the 0-4-4T No. 1490, which was the Bath shunter in the early years of the twentieth century, the bogie wheels being of Mansell's carriage type, had the distinction of being the first GWR locomotive to have pannier tanks. It was designed for use over the Metropolitan Railway, but proved too heavy. It also ran unsteadily at speed on other passenger duties, and was therefore relegated to shunting. It had a very short life; built in 1897, it was withdrawn in 1907. Another rare engine was one of the ex-London, Brighton & South Coast Railway Terriers that had come to the GWR via the Weston, Clevedon & Portishead Light Railway. The GWR loaned it to Messrs Fry, Keynsham, for month or so during the Second World War.

In June 1946 No. 5953 *Garth Hall* was converted to oil burning and renumbered 3950. She appeared at Bath on running-in trials. Ten others of the class were converted, as were five Castles and twenty of the 28XX class. The intention had been to convert further locomotives, but the scheme had to be abandoned owing to the post-war shortage of foreign currency. By 1950 all the engines had been converted back to burning coal.

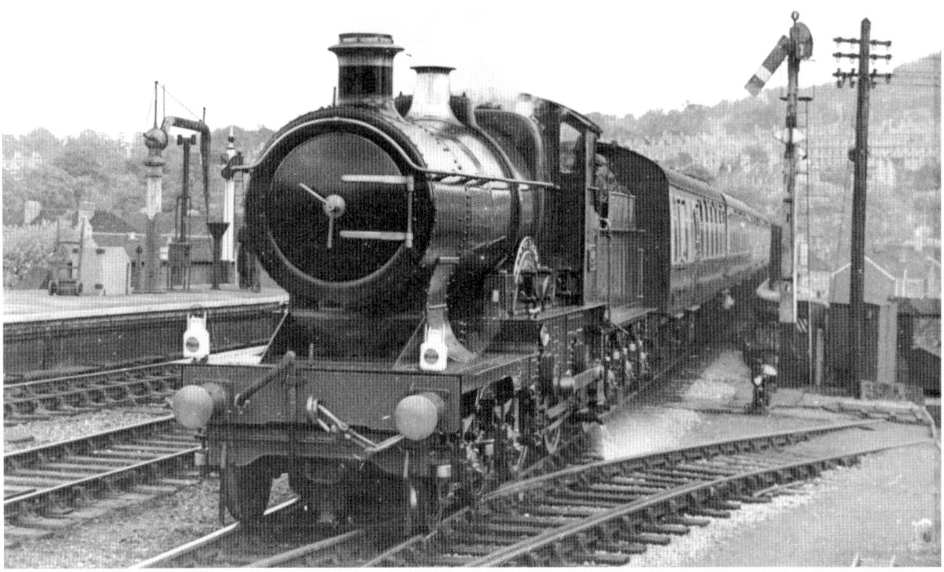

4-4-0 No. 3440 *City of Truro* enters Bath with a Paddington to Devon excursion, 19 May 1957. (*R. E. Toop*)

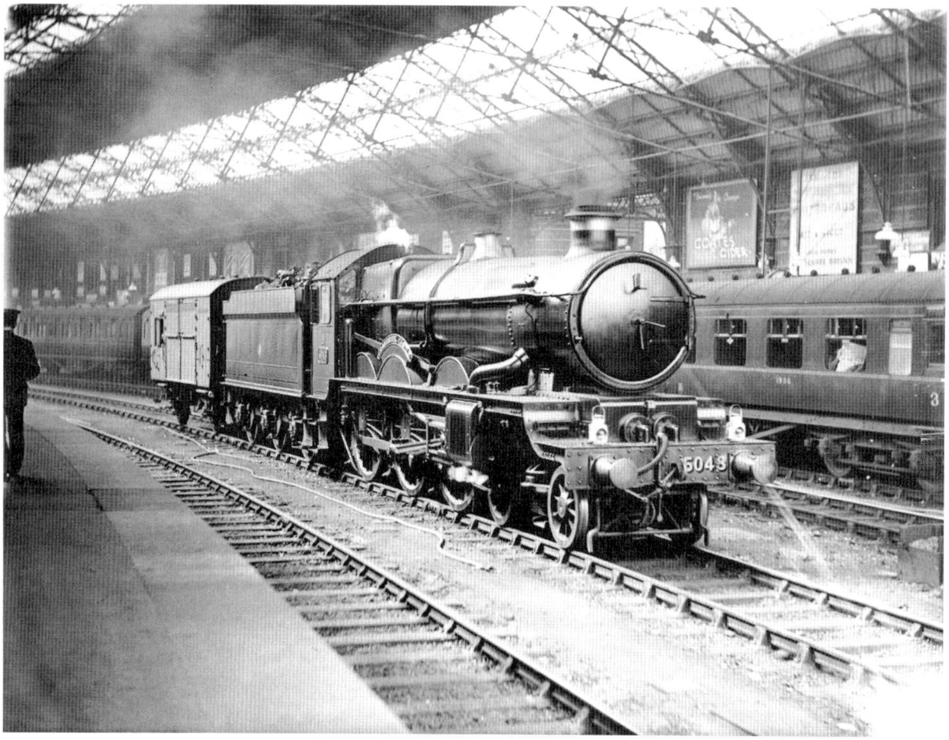

4-6-0 No. 5043 *Cranbrook Castle* at Temple Meads with a horse box, 1936. (*E. J. M. Hayward Collection*)

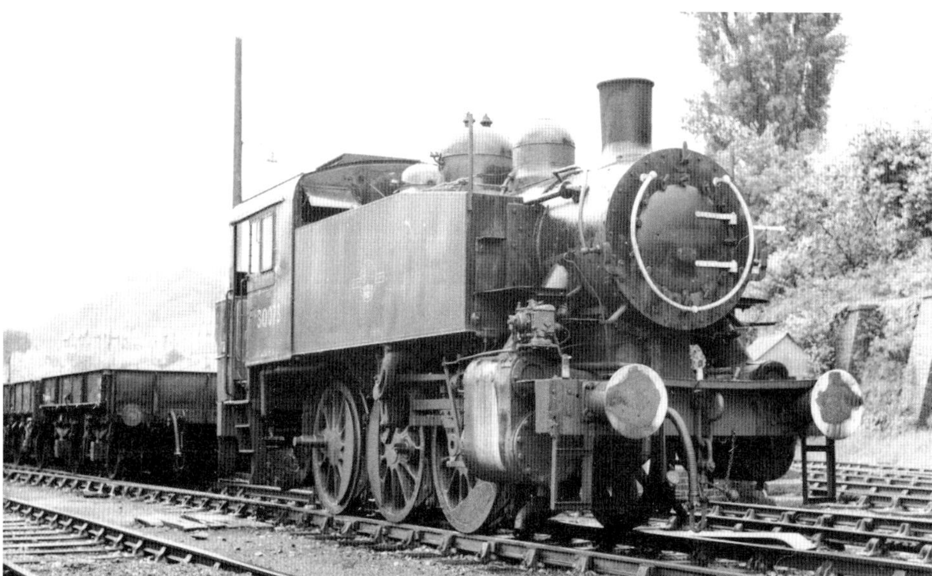

US-built 0-6-0T No. 30073 at Westmoreland Road goods yard, Bath, 24 May 1967, *en route* to the scrapyard. Only one of these engines was recorded working over the line during the Second World War. (*Revd Alan Newman*)

The first GWR steam rail motors entered service between Chalford and Stonehouse on 12 October 1903 and proved successful, a total of ninety-nine appearing before February 1908. Bath and Bristol sheds supplied rail motors to work some of the trains between the two cities, while a Yatton car travelled as far afield as Swindon, calling at stations between Bristol and Bath. However, the rail motors did not prove an unqualified success. As firing could only be done with the regulator closed and as there was no down gradient between Bristol and Bath, a fireman could only fire when steam was shut off at the approach to a station, or when actually stopped. Another weakness was the loss of steam not only through strained steam delivery pipes adjacent to the steam chest, but also through leaking tubes. Although the cars had a good turn of speed when running alone, jerking was felt when hauling a trailer. A curiosity was that the headlamp was supplied by the Locomotive Department and the tail lamp by the Carriage Department. In 1910 the first three trains between Keynsham and Bristol were steam rail motors.

Several 'foreign' engines have appeared on the line. In about 1903 Great Central Railway 4-4-2 No. 192 worked over the line with a train from Manchester to Plymouth via Leicester, Oxford and Temple Meads, a trip of 374 miles each way. In 1904 and 1905 GCR No. 267 repeated this feat. In August 1911 the Territorials returned to Bath from their summer camp in London & South Western Railway coaches headed by A12 class 0-4-2 No. 647. In 1917 South Eastern & Chatham Railway tank engines appeared regularly at Bristol, working local services. 0-4-4T Nos 58, 138, 350 and 359 arrived at Bath Road shed in February 1917 and No. 76 and No. 406 in April the same year. In 1919 a Glasgow & South Western Railway 0-6-0 built in 1899 on loan to the GWR was said to be not fit for main line work. The GWR redesigned the firebars to allow more air through and successfully put it to work on Bristol to London goods trains.

In the autumn of 1926 the LMS borrowed No. 5000 *Launceston Castle* for trials between Euston and Carlisle. In exchange, although for ordinary revenue-earning runs and not for trials, 4-4-0 class 4P Compound No. 1047 was stationed at Bristol Bath Road shed for three weeks. For the first week she worked the 9.15 a.m. Temple Meads to Paddington and the 1.15 p.m. Paddington to Temple Meads with a two-hour timing. On one of these runs, after slipping a coach at Bath, she reached Bristol with a load of six coaches in twelve minutes forty seconds, giving an average speed Bath to Bristol of 54½ mph. The second week she worked the 5.15 p.m. Bristol to Paddington, again with a two-hour timing, returning with the 10.10 p.m. West of England Postal. The third week, she ran to Birrmingham via Stratford-upon-Avon. During the Second World War, LNER B12/3 class 4-6-0s appeared on ambulance trains.

In the 1930s D15, L12 and T9 class 4-4-0s worked a Salisbury to Bristol train and a return working every evening, while for a period U class 2-6-0s, including the now-preserved No. 31625, worked regularly on weekdays, returning on the

8.45 p.m. Bristol to Eastleigh. Bulleid Pacifics occasionally appeared heading football specials from the Southern Region to Bristol. West Country No. 34047 *Callington* and No. 34048 *Crediton* worked these trains on 20 March 1954 when the class probably made its first appearance on the line, while on 8 January 1955 no less than four passed *en route* from Portsmouth to Stapleton Road: No. 34093 *Saunton*, No. 34020 *Seaton*, No. 34054 *Lord Beaverbrook* and No. 34051 *Winston Churchill*. Then, in early December 1960, a landslip occurred on the Somerset & Dorset line at Midford and on 5 December a Light Pacific worked the Pines Express throughout from Bournemouth West to Birmingham New Street over a diversion via Westbury, Bath and Bristol. On 6 December it worked to Gloucester and from 8 December until the slip was repaired, the Pacific from the Up Pines Express was removed at Bristol, turned at St Philip's Marsh depot and returned the same day on the Down Pines. In the week ending 9 July 1966, No. 34100 *Appledore* worked an ammunition train between Bath and Bristol and No. 34093 *Saunton* a mineral train, thus marking the first appearance of steam engines on this line for some time.

The first BR standard class to appear on the line was the class 7 Britannia, the author seeing No. 70017 *Arrow* on a running-in turn on 10 August 1951. Those initially allocated to the WR had names of broad-gauge locomotives. In the mid-fifties Castles and Kings were fitted with four-row superheaters and double chimneys, which made the excellent engines even more economical. In 1955 the WR's heavy freight stud was strengthened by the transfer of some Stanier class 8F 2-8-0s; they were chiefly based at Banbury and Bristol St Philip's Marsh, the author seeing the first on 24 October 1955.

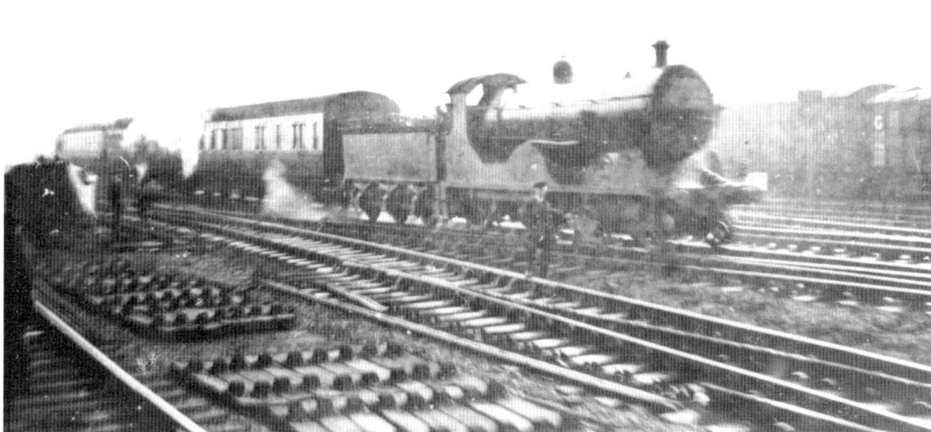

Southern Railway D15 class 4-4-0 No. 471 leaves Bristol with a train to Portsmouth Harbour *c.* 1934. (*S. Miles Davey*)

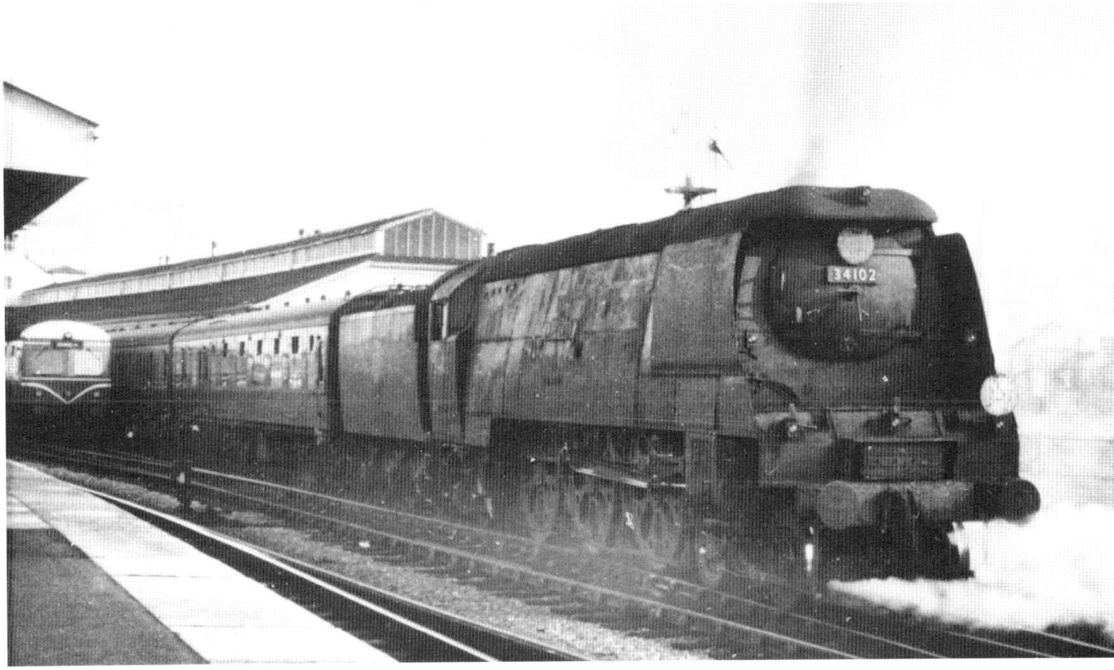

The Up Pines Express calls at Bath Spa, 5 December 1960, headed by West Country class 4-6-2 No. 34102 *Lapford*. (*Author's Collection*)

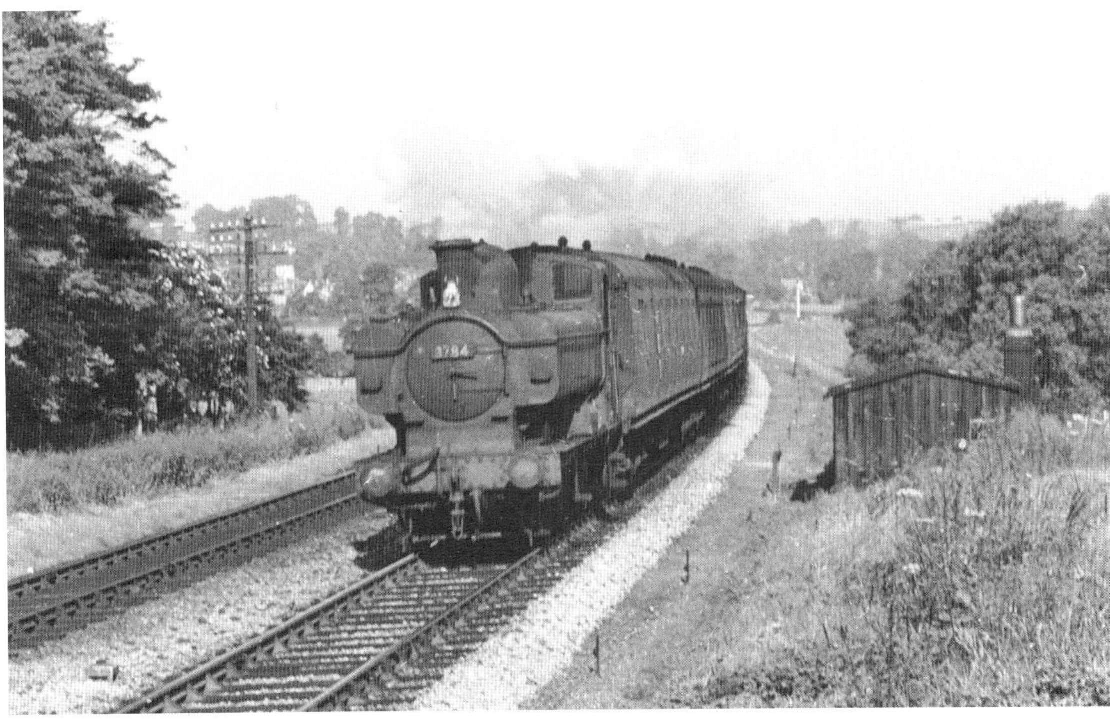

57XX class 0-6-0PT No. 3784 approaches Cross Post Bridge with the 7.53 a.m. Temple Meads to Bath stopping train, 25 June 1955. (*Author*)

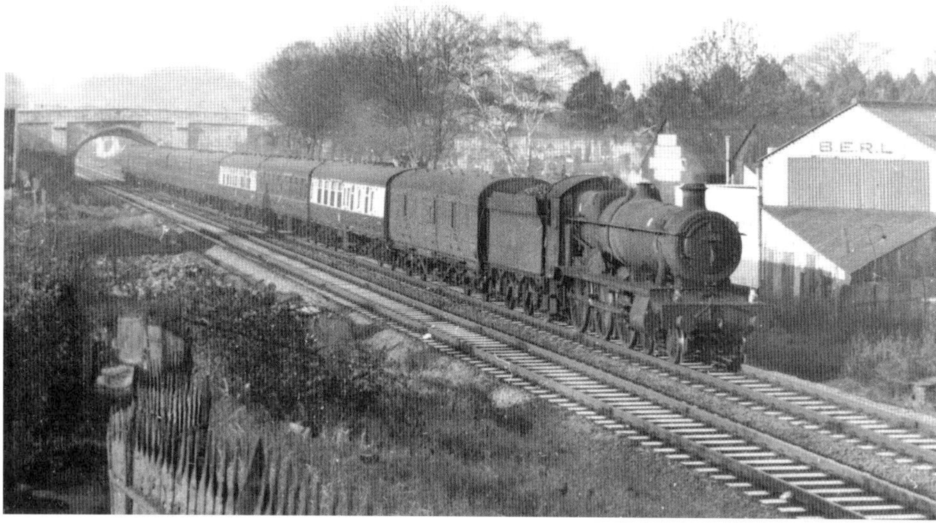

4-6-0 No. 6950 *Kingsthorpe Hall* heads a Cardiff to Portsmouth Harbour train approaching Oldfield Park, 24 December 1962. (*R. E. Toop*)

Running-in turns for passenger engines were the 7.35 a.m. Swindon to Temple Meads; 10.05 a.m. Temple Meads to Bath, which then waited in the bay platform or on a middle road before working the 11.23 a.m. Bath to Swindon; 5.00 p.m. Swindon to Temple Meads; and 8.25 p.m. Temple Meads to Swindon. Locomotive enthusiasts made an effort to see one of these trains, knowing it would be worked by a new or ex-works engine. No. 3440 *City of Truro* appeared on 25 March 1957.

Sometimes things did go awry and it would be down to the footplate men's imagination to get them out of trouble. One crew took a light engine from Bristol to Swindon and correctly carried a white light on the front and a red light on the back of the tender. Returning tender-first to Bristol with a goods train, the fireman forgot to change the lights and travelled with a red headlight. The engine was not stopped until Bristol East Depot Down yard signal box. As the signalman began to quote rules, the driver, thinking quickly, asserted 'It's a new rule – just come out – that trains carrying live ammo have to carry a red headlight'.

In June 1947 the GWR's General Manager, Sir James Milne, and his Chief Mechanical Engineer, Frederick W. Hawksworth, attended the International Railway Congress at Lucerne and visited Brown Boveri's works at Baden. Impressed by a gas-turbine locomotive built in 1941, and believing its characteristics were ideal for the gradients of Devon and Cornwall, they ordered a 2,500-hp A1A-A1A machine with a maximum tractive effort of 31,500 lb. It was not delivered until 3 February 1950 and received the number 18000. The author first saw it at Bath on 28 February 1950. After teething troubles, in the summer of 1950 it regularly worked trains from Paddington to Plymouth and Paddington to Bristol. By November 1958 it was working the 2.25 a.m. Paddington to Bristol newspaper train, returning on the 7.54 a.m. Temple Meads to Paddington express, going Down on the 1.15 p.m. Paddington to Temple Meads two-hour schedule express and returning with the 4.15 p.m. to Paddington. Nicknamed 'Kerosene Castle', it was efficient when working at full power up gradients, but displayed greatly reduced efficiency on less than full power, which was how it worked for most of the time.

A similar machine, but with motors driving all three axles on both bogies, was ordered from Metropolitan-Vickers Electrical Company Ltd. No. 18100 was delivered to Swindon on 16 December 1951 and taken into stock in April 1952, the month when the author noted it at Bath for the first time. Its maximum tractive effort of 60,000 lb made it the most powerful engine in the country. Eventually, both locomotives were modified to deliver maximum efficiency at 75 per cent of full load, but showed no better overall thermal efficiency than steam traction, were mechanically unreliable, and more expensive to purchase. They consumed almost as much fuel idling, or running under reduced power, as under full load. No. 18000 was withdrawn in December 1960 and No. 18100 in January 1958, the latter being modified as a 25-kV AC electric locomotive for crew training and catenary testing.

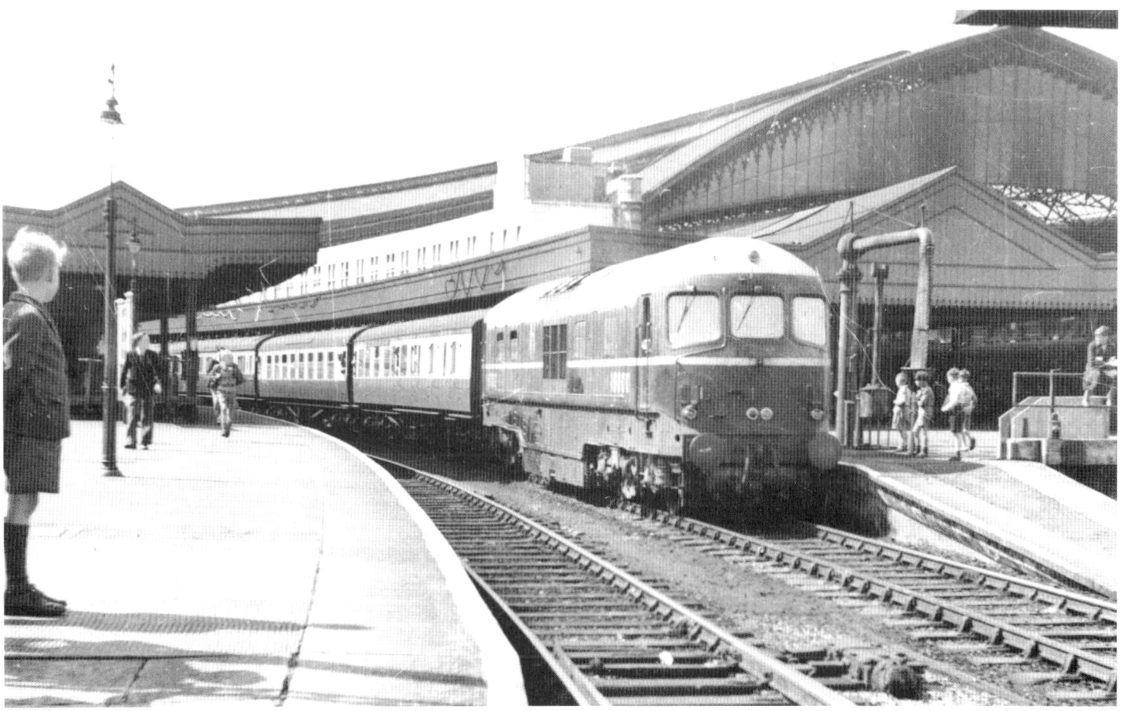

Gas turbine No. 18000 at Temple Meads with an express to Paddington. (*M. E. J. Deane*)

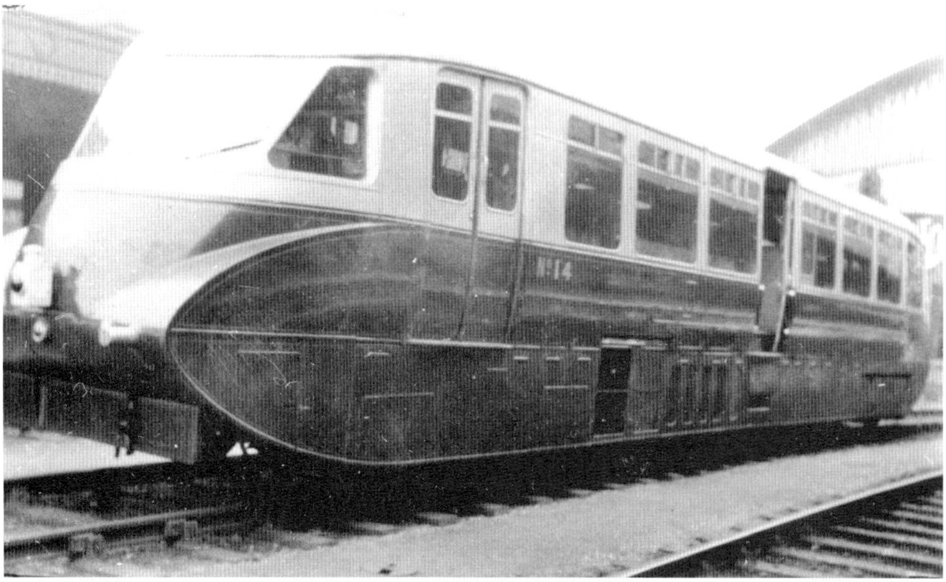

Diesel railcar No. 14 at Temple Meads *c.* 1938. It was new in 1936. (*Author's Collection*)

On 23 January 1936, sixty-three-seat diesel railcar No. 10, constructed by AEC, Southall, at a cost of about £5,000, made a trial run between Bristol and Weymouth. Proving a success, from 17 February 1936 Nos 10, 11 and 12 (with lavatory accommodation) regularly worked the 8.00 a.m. Temple Meads to Weymouth and the 10.55 a.m. return, while in the mid-1940s the service was generally operated by twin units Nos 35 and 36, or 37 and 38, with an intermediate trailer. In 1950, following its return to Bristol, it ran to Wells and then Portishead, thus covering a distance of 245½ miles daily. On the occasions when one of the twin cars was unavailable, a double-ended car was used to complete the set. To improve performance, early in 1956 the centre coach was removed from between Nos 35 and 36. Both these cars were destroyed by fire at St Anne's Park while working the 9.08 p.m. Bath to Temple Meads stopping train on 10 April 1956. Railcars in the area were maintained by AEC service mechanics in a dedicated building attached to St Philip's Marsh depot.

On 18 August 1958 driver training began with two BR Gloucester Carriage & Wagon Company single-unit railcars and driving-end trailers, and by 3 September the Bristol allocation of Derby Suburban three-car sets began to arrive and were used for the training trips. From 6 April 1959 stopping trains Swindon to Weston-super-Mare and Temple Meads to Westbury and Weymouth were DMU operated. 'D-Day' was set for 19 June 1959, when full diesel services started and many three-car sets were remarshalled into two- or four-car groupings. When Sprinters began in May 1988, the 12-in gap between the body and platform edge caused problems for small children and less able adults on curves at Bath and Temple Meads platforms, while the limited cycle accommodation was also criticised.

In the mid-fifties, with the realisation that diesel was the power of the future, the WR appreciated that high-speed engines and hydraulic transmission offered higher continuous tractive effort at low speed than could normally be obtained with electric traction. This advantage would prove particularly apparent on the Paddington to Plymouth route, where high-speed running to Exeter was followed by steep adverse gradients. Moreover, diesel-hydraulic locomotives were lighter, weighing about 40 tons less than a comparable diesel-electric, which meant less weight to move and fewer wheels to support it. The British Transport Commission was unhappy about such innovative thinking and instead of a four-axle locomotive weighing 78 tons, the machinery was placed inside a more conventional six-axle machine weighing 117 tons. D600 *Active* made a demonstration run Paddington–Bath–Bristol on 17 February 1958, reaching 94 mph down Dauntsey Bank and having no difficulty keeping the timings. This class mostly worked trains from Paddington to Torbay and Plymouth, but appeared on The Bristolian in August 1959. As with so many compromises, this class of diesel-hydraulic was not a success.

The WR still hankered after a lightweight diesel-hydraulic and in 1956 Swindon was allowed to build three. Each locomotive had a pair of Maybach 1400 rpm 1035 hp engines with Mekydro transmission. The next twenty-nine of the series were fitted with 1530 rpm 1135 hp engines and one with a British Paxman Ventura. The following thirty-three had MAN-type engines and Voith transmission. The last four were equipped with Maybach engines and Mekydro transmission. The introduction of the Warship class enabled The Bristolian to be accelerated from one hour forty-five minutes to one hour forty minutes in the summer timetable of 1959. Unfortunately, as the Warship mileage increased, so did their oscillation and they had to be restricted to a maximum of 80 mph.

Type 3 diesel-hydraulic (later class 35) Hymek appeared on Salisbury to Bristol trains in the summer of 1961 and were designed to replace the mixed traffic Hall and Grange classes. They were powered by a Maybach 1740 hp engine with Mekydro transmission.

The Western class diesel-hydraulic (class 52) had two 1500 rpm 1380 hp Maybach engines and Voith transmission. They weighed 108 tons and first appeared in experimental liveries: desert sand, maroon, and Brunswick green. The following year, Type 4 (class 47) medium-speed diesel engines with electric transmission offered 2750 hp for a weight of only 114 tons and their introduction marked the beginning of the end for diesel-hydraulic locomotives. The last of the Warships was withdrawn in 1972, the Hymeks in 1975 and the Westerns in 1977. In 1962 Brush, builders of the class 47s, built a prototype 2800 lip diesel-electric D0280, *Falcon*. Equipped with two 1500 rpm engines similar to those propelling the Western class diesel-hydraulics, *Falcon* weighed 115 tons. Between 1968 and 1969 it could often be seen heading a Bristol express and, in the author's experience, could always be relied on to arrive on time. *Falcon* was withdrawn in 1975.

In 1962 a consortium consisting of Associated Electrical Industries Ltd, Birmingham Railway Carriage & Wagon Co. and Sulzer loaned BR a prototype 2750 hp Co-Co D0260, *Lion*, which ran test trains over the line and also occasionally worked the 11.15 a.m. Paddington to Bristol. It had a striking livery of white with gold lining. Although no subsequent engines of this design were produced, its diesel engine was adopted as the class 47 power unit.

SR class 205 DEMUs appeared at Bath on Portsmouth to Bristol trains. To obtain a certain degree of standardisation with its electric stock, the SR opted for DEMU, rather than the DMUs adopted by other regions. The single English Electric 500 hp engine and generator demanded floor rather than under-floor mounting. The design proved particularly reliable. class 31/4s took over these workings in 1977; class 33s in 1980; class 155 in 1988; and class 158 in 1992.

In 1965 English Electric class 37 1750 hp diesel-electrics were used in pairs on some trains, heading The Bristolian on 22 May 1965, and their success persuaded the BRB to allow the WR in 1966 to re-gear D6875-95 for 100 mph running. From 18 April 1966 they hauled one of two specially prepared train sets: one of XP64 coaches with folding doors, pressure heating and ventilation carried on Swindon-designed B4 bogies, and the other comprising Mk I coaches on Commonwealth cast-steel bogies. When Paddington to Bristol expresses were equipped with Mk IID air-conditioned, electrically heated coaches in the summer of 1973, it meant exclusive haulage by the 2750 hp class 47 Brush/Sulzer machines as the Westerns were not equipped to provide electric power for the coaches' auxiliaries.

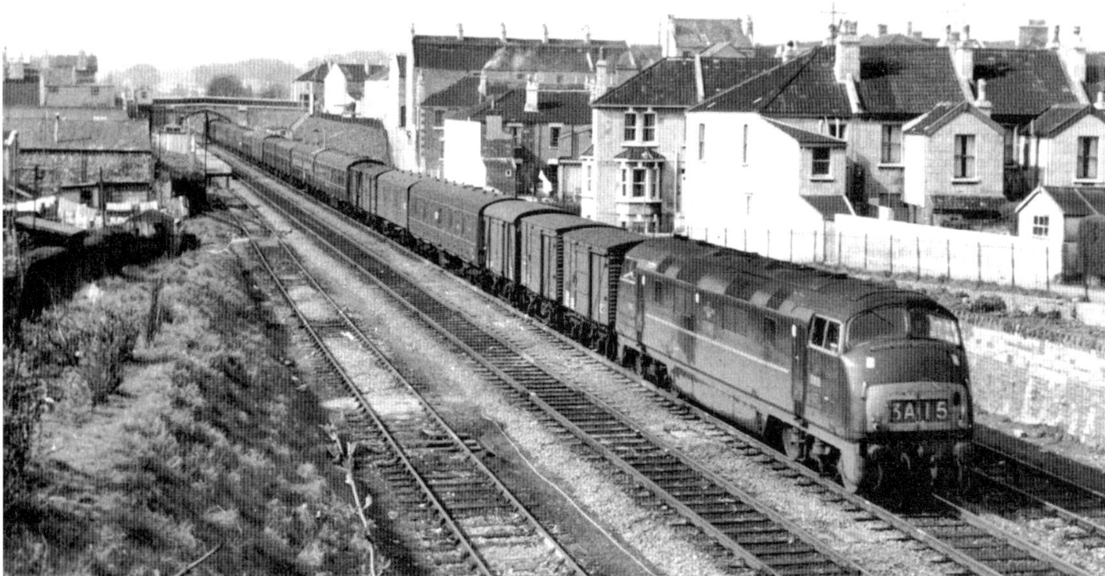

A Warship class diesel-hydraulic passes Oldfield Park with an Up van train. (*R. J. Cannon*)

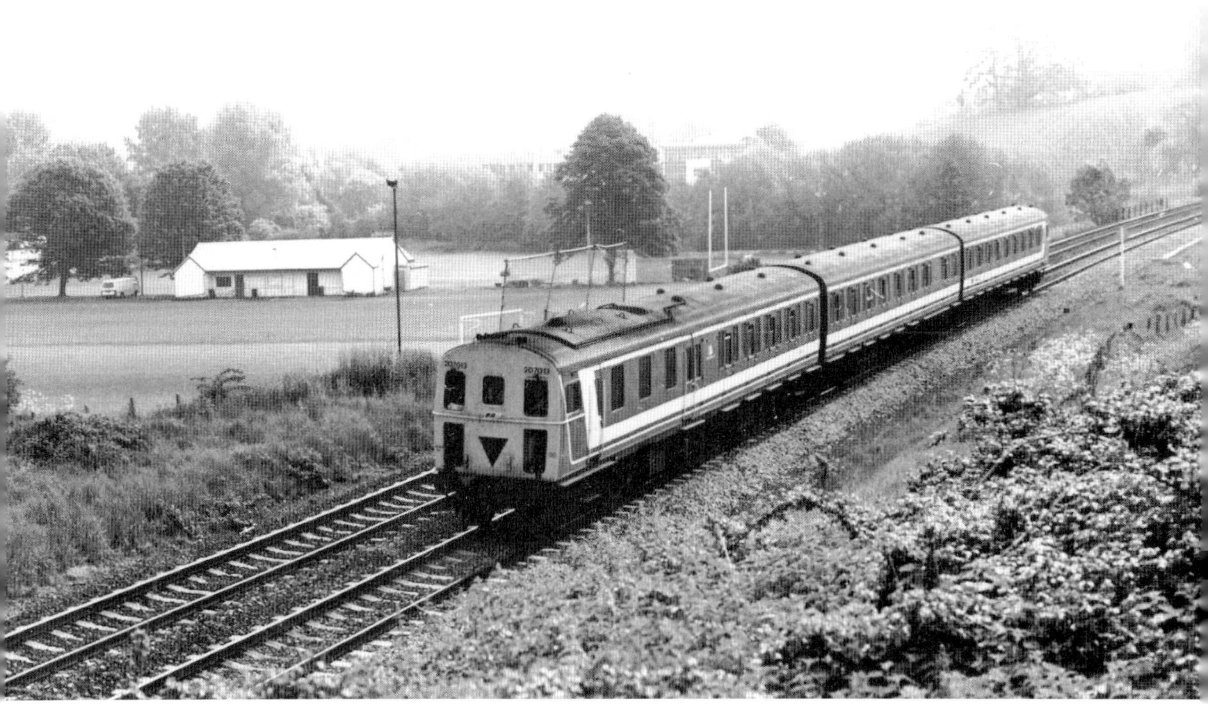

Southern Region DEMU 207 013 west of Twerton Tunnel, 25 May 1991, with the 08.35 Southampton to Temple Meads. (*Author*)

Class 50s made redundant by the LMR's West Coast electrification superseded class 47s and Westerns on Bristol to Paddington trains on 6 May 1974. Then, following trial runs between Bristol and London on 16–19 December 1974, HST No. 252001 appeared on some trains in 1975, a regular service starting in the spring of 1977. HSTs proved a great success and, within a few months, patronage rose by nearly 18 per cent. As insufficient HSTs were available to operate a full Paddington to Penzance service, between May 1980 and May 1981 locomotive and coach working was reintroduced for some Paddington to Bristol trains which stopped only at Reading and Bath. Twelve sets of these eight air-braked coaches were available and, as they were lirmited to 100 mph, they were allowed a slightly more generous schedule than HSTs.

Today locomotives are rarely seen on regular passenger trains: Bristol to Paddington expresses are HSTs; Weymouth trains class 150; those to Portsmouth and Brighton class 158 and to Waterloo class 159.

Engine Sheds

The first GWR engine shed at Bristol was a stone-built three-road affair situated at Barton Hill, near the later South Wales Junction. In about 1872 a standard-gauge four-road shed was built on an adjacent site. Both sheds closed in 1877 when the depot was converted into a carriage shed. Engines were transferred to the former B&ER shed and works west of Temple Meads, the GWR having absorbed that company in 1876. The building that formerly housed the works was converted into a standard-gauge shed, while the B&ER shed was retained for broad-gauge engines, though as the broad-gauge stud decreased, it became used for mixed gauge and finally standard gauge only in 1892.

The hotch-potch of buildings was replaced under the 1929 Railway Development Scheme by a new ten-road, brick-built shed, situated approximately on the site of the B&ER locomotive works. Set beside it was a three-road repair shop, steel-framed with brick walls, a coal stage surmounted by a 135,000-gallon water tank separating the two buildings. Water came from Fox's Wood pumping station. On the cast side of the complex was the gasworks, supplying fuel for lighting the adjacent GWR property. It was also piped to Dr Day's, Marsh Pond and Malago Vale sidings for gassing coaches. Rail tank wagons were sent to stations in the area to replenish coach gas tanks.

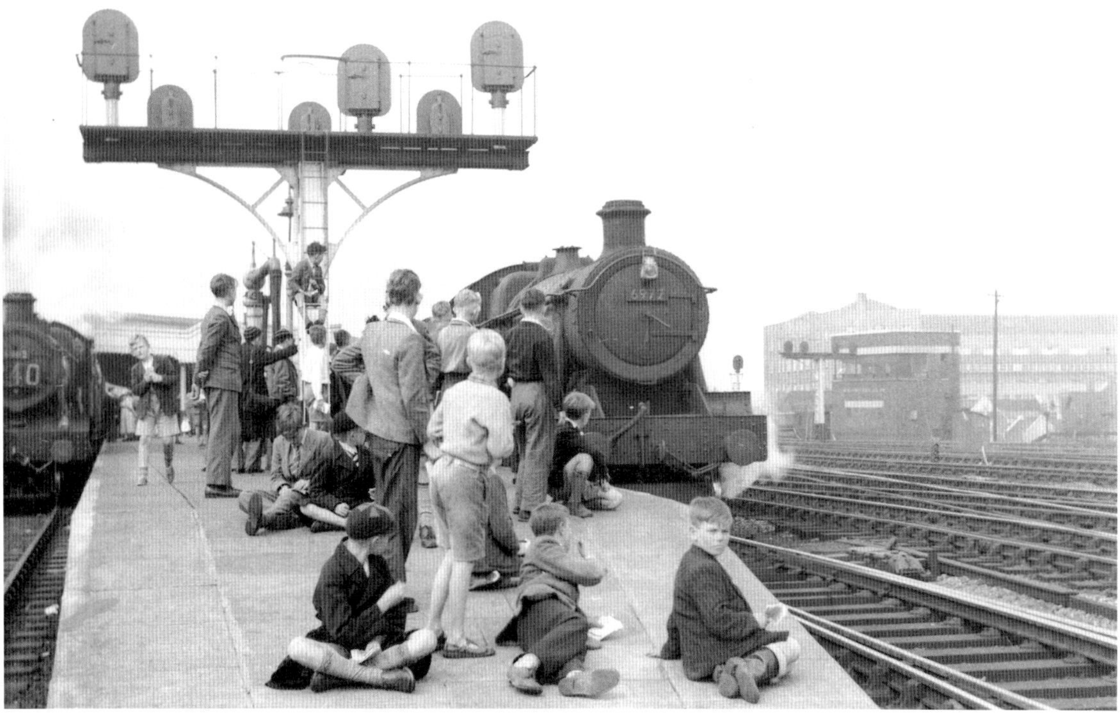

In the 1950s Temple Meads was a highly popular station for locomotive spotters. 4-6-0 No. 5982 *Harrington Hall*, left, and No. 6972 *Beningbrough Hall*, right, 5 September 1953. (*R. E. Toop*)

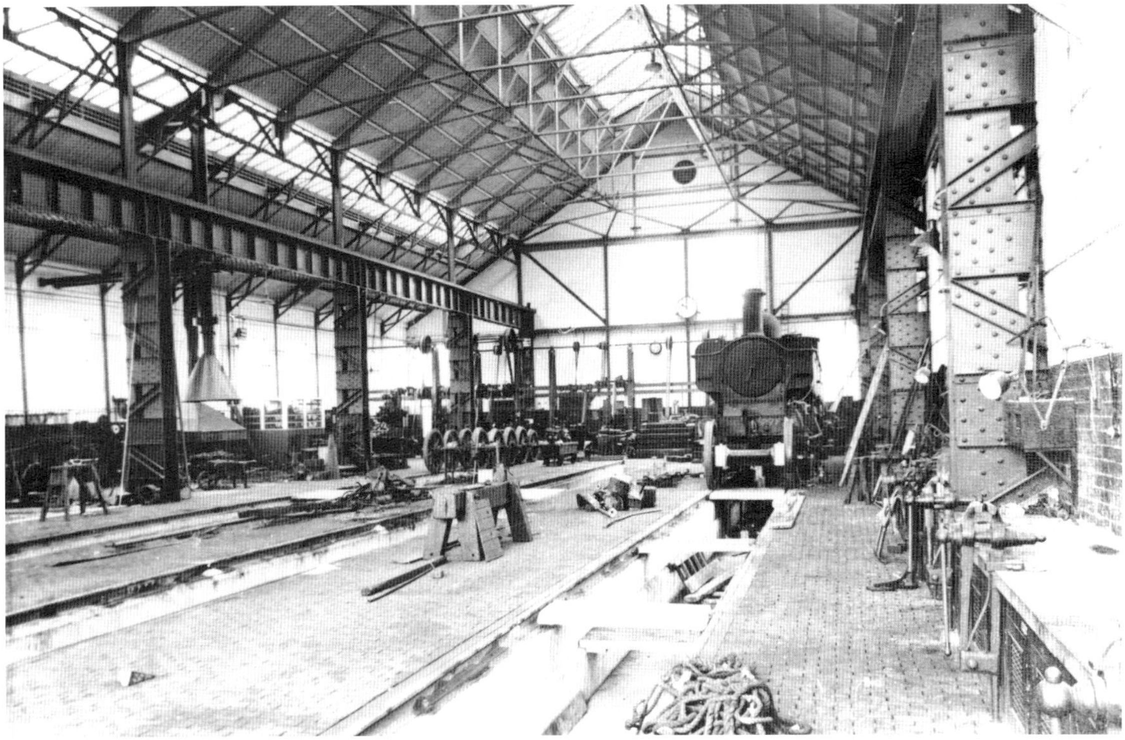

Bristol, Bath Road running shed in 1934 with a 0-6-0PT undergoing attention. (*Author's Collection*)

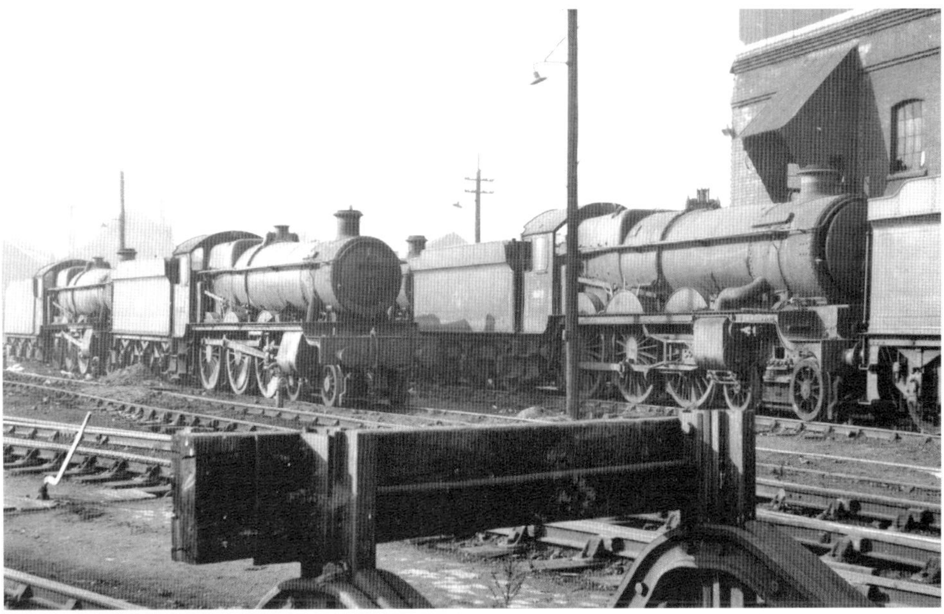

4-6-0 locomotives beside Bristol, Bath Road coaling bank, 6 February 1964, right to left: No. 5050 *Earl of St Germans*; No. 6981 *Marbury Hall*; and No. 4983 *Albert Hall*, though later it was proved to be No. 4965 *Rood Aston Hall.* (*Revd Alan Newman*)

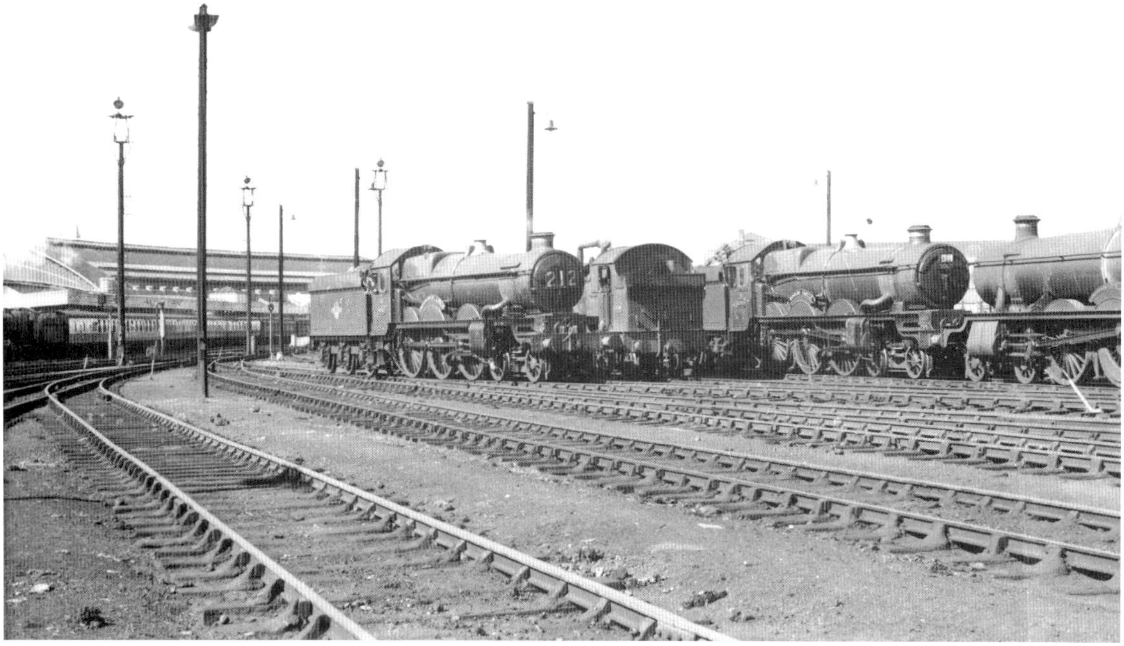

Members of the Castle class at Temple Meads: No. 7033 *Hartlebury Castle*, left, and No. 5008 *Raglan Castle*, right. (*R. J. Cannon*)

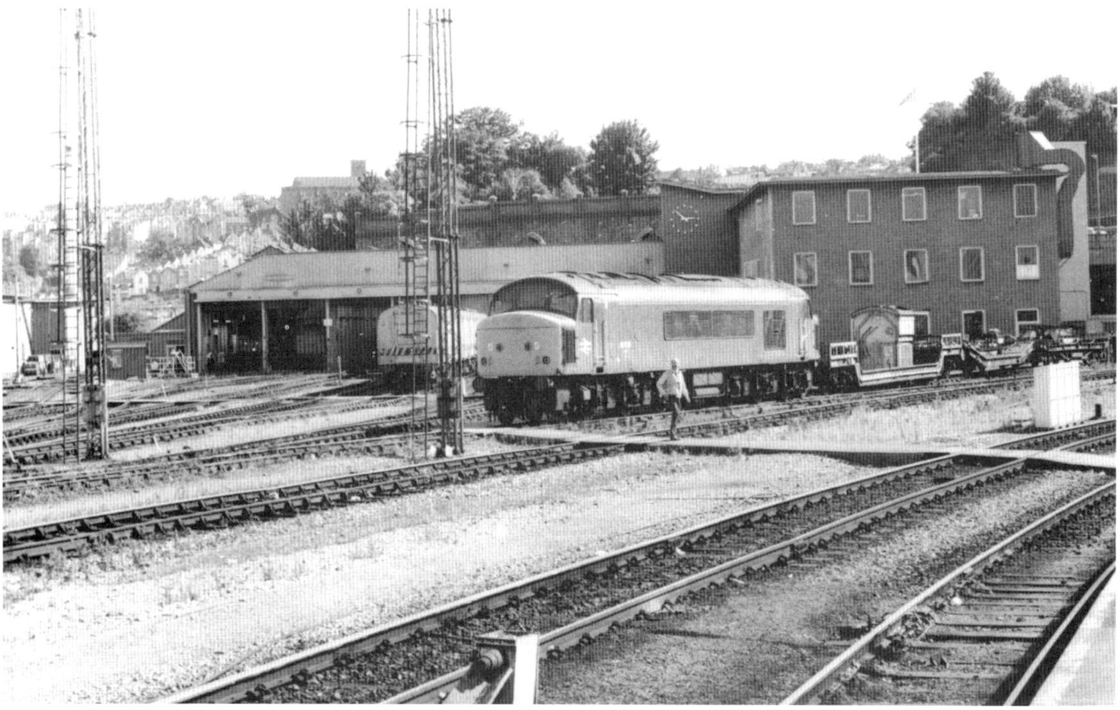

Bath Road diesel depot, 4 September 1986: 45 076 heads a goods train. (*Author*)

Bath Road shed (BL in the GWR code until 1934, then BRD; 82A in BR code) closed to steam on 12 September 1960. At a cost exceeding £700,000 it was rebuilt and opened on 18 June 1962 as a diesel depot, six roads servicing about 140 engines. With the reduction in locomotive-hauled trains, the shed became redundant and closed on 23 September 1995; the building was demolished in 2003.

St Philip's Marsh depot opened on 9 July 1910 and primarily supplied goods engines, leaving Bath Road to concentrate on those for passenger duty. Twenty-eight roads radiated from each of the two turntables. A manually operated turntable used for the larger engines was situated in the roundhouse furthest from the Avoiding Line, while the electric turntable for smaller engines was in the other half of the building. The brick-walled depot stood on concrete piles as it was on 'made' ground. Adjacent was a two-road repair shop, which later had a steel-framed corrugated iron extension for the maintenance of GWR diesel railcars. GWR cleaners simply wiped the bodywork with cleaning oil. Below the 145,000-gall water tank was a two-road coal stage. The depot (GWR code BL until 1934, subsequently SPM until the BR era when it became 82B) closed on 13 June 1964, the shed later being demolished and a wholesale fruit and vegetable market erected. The four-road Marsh Junction DMU depot opened on 23 February 1959 (Code BJ May 1973 to December 1976 and PM subsequently), closed as a DMU depot on 18 May 1970 and was then used for the maintenance of the Chief Civil Engineer's plant. In September 1975 a 700-yd-long, three-road, purpose-built HST depot opened. After servicing, HSTs are stabled at Victoria Sidings on the site of St Philip's Marsh goods yard.

Meanwhile, the former GWR locomotive sheds at Barton Hill had long been wagon shops. When a Dutch barn-like maintenance shed was added in 1975, the wall of the old broad-gauge locomotive turntable pit was unearthed. The shed now has walls of steel cladding. Res (later EWS and LNWR) developed Barton Hill into a depot for maintaining its locomotives as well as rolling stock.

The original locomotive shed at Bath was adjacent to the passenger platform. Sun class 2-2-2 *Sun* and Fire Fly class *Fire King* were stabled there in early days and 4-4-0ST Bogie class *Homer* in the 1850s. In November 1880 a single-road shed, probably mixed gauge, was opened at the Westmoreland Road goods yard. It was not immediately recognisable as a shed as its brick walls were partly concealed by the cast-iron columns supporting the tank which formed the roof: a passing glance suggested that it was just a water tank. On 24 January 1914 rail motors No. 7 and No. 42 were allocated to the shed, and on 28 January 1923 rail motor No. 95 and 0-6-0PT 1813 class No. 1837. Bath shed had at least one rail motor from July 1908 until November 1925, operating services to Chippenham, Bristol, and Limpley Stoke to Hallatrow. For the longer distance duties, sacks of coal were stacked round the vertical boiler. Following the demise of the rail motor, a 45XX class 2-6-2T was allocated to Bath. Bath shed was a sub-shed to Bath Road, Bristol, with two sets of men employed on the Bath shunter – early and late turn. In addition to shunting the yard, half a dozen wagons were taken to the electricity works adjacent to the passenger station and also the engine moved any slip coach arriving at the

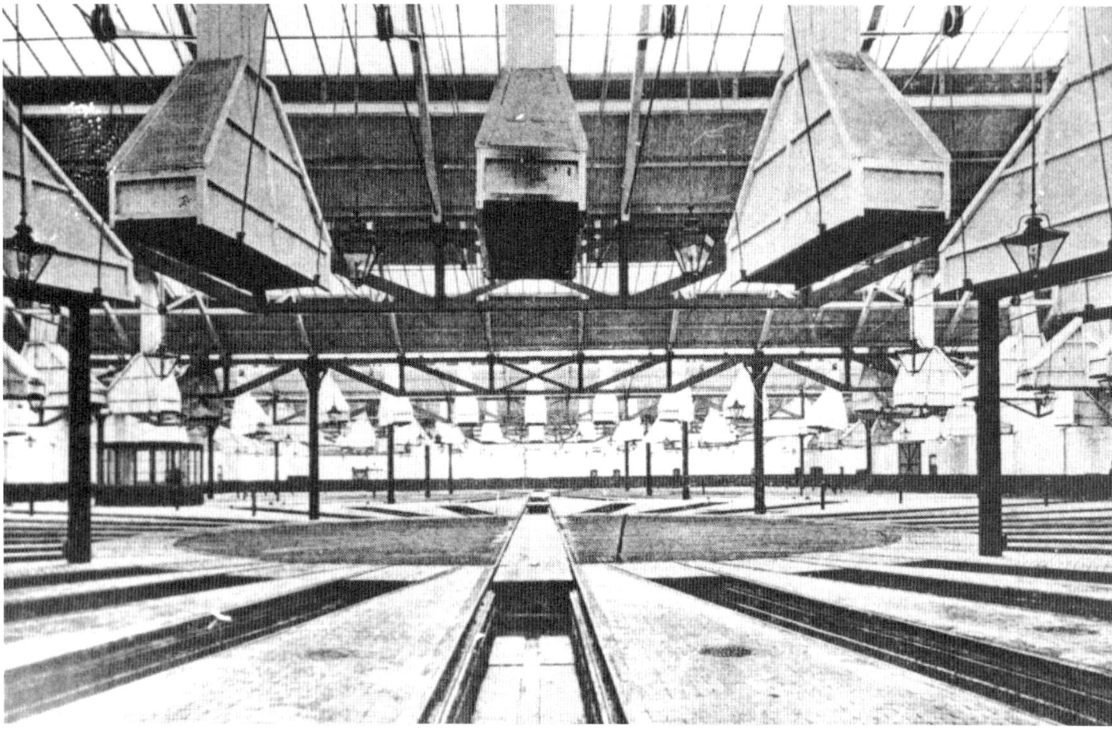

The interior of St Philip's Marsh shed, 1910. (*Author's Collection*)

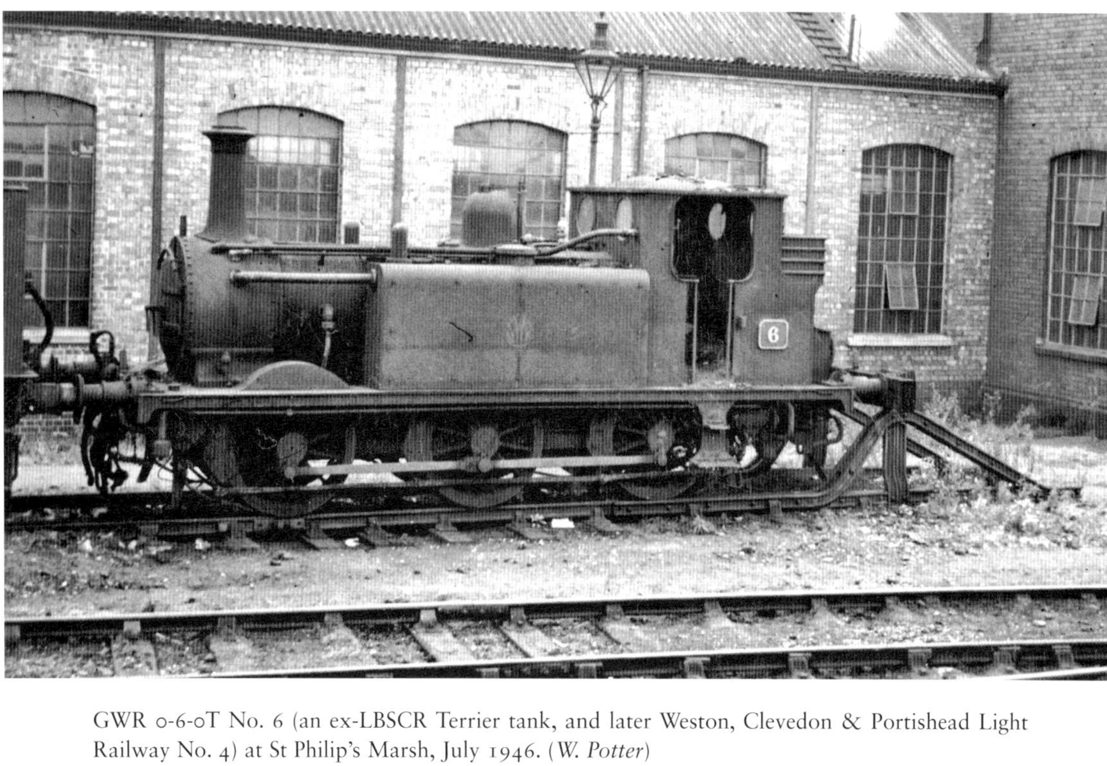

GWR 0-6-0T No. 6 (an ex-LBSCR Terrier tank, and later Weston, Clevedon & Portishead Light Railway No. 4) at St Philip's Marsh, July 1946. (*W. Potter*)

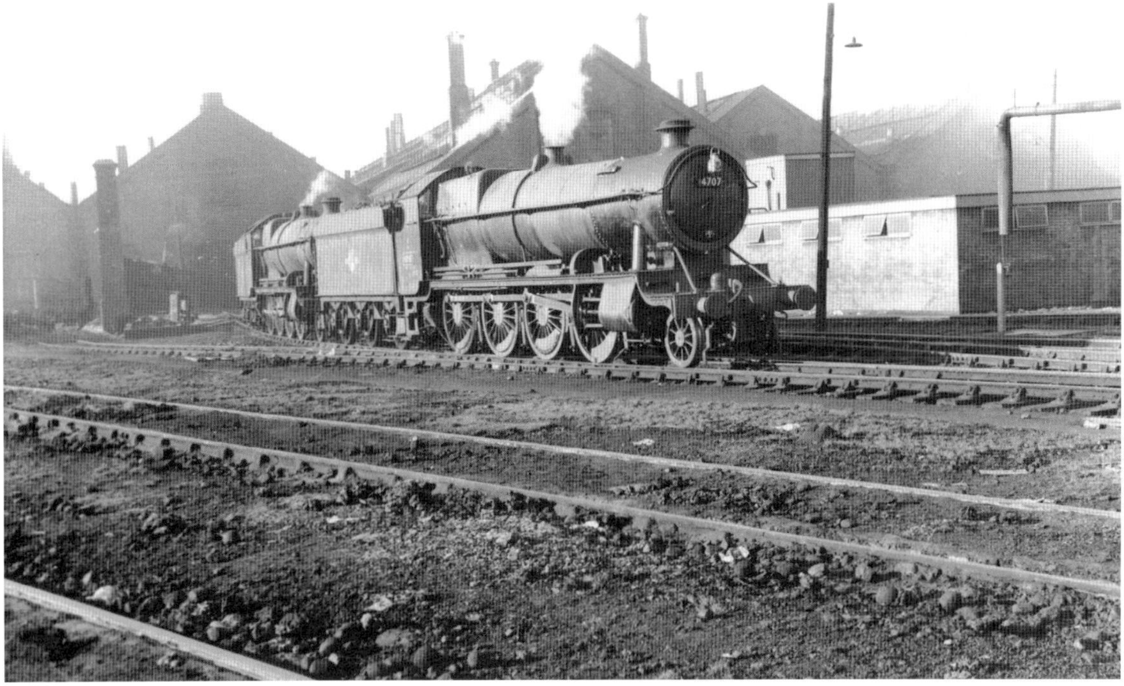

47XX class 2-8-0 No. 4703 at St Philip's Marsh, 2 December 1961. (*Michael Jenkins*)

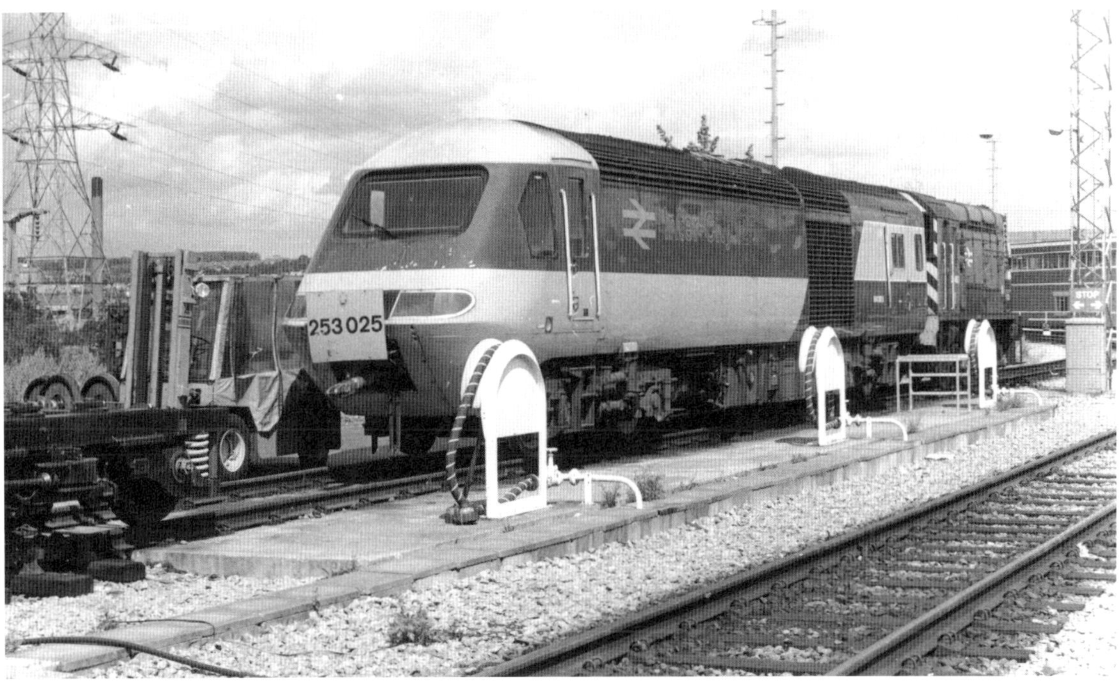

St Philip's Marsh diesel depot, 31 July 1980: 08 483, an air-braked buckeye coupled HST shunter has propelled HST power car 253 025 from Bath Road depot. (*Author*)

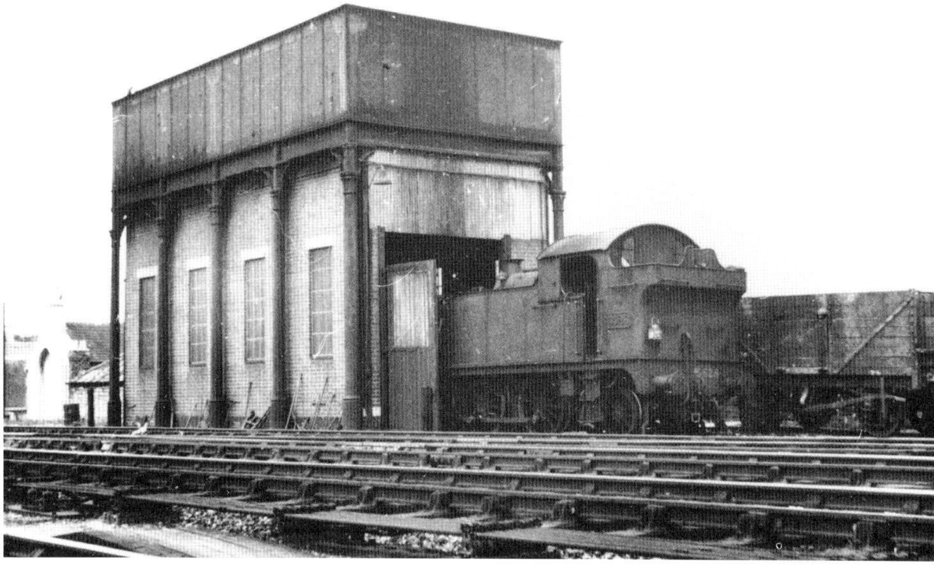

4575 class 2-6-2T No. 5528 outside Bath locomotive shed, 1 September 1949. A water tank forms the roof. (*Author's Collection*)

passenger station. When 0-6-0PT No. 4603 left the shed on 13 May 1961, it was replaced by a diesel shunter. The shed finally closed on 5 February 1966.

Passenger Engines In Steam At Bristol 13–27 July 1850

2-2-2 Fire Fly class
Arrow, *Elk*, *Cerberus*, *Centaur*, *Erebus*, *Hector*, *Mars*, *Venus*

2-2-2 Prince class
Prince, *Queen*

Bath Road and St Philip's Marsh Allocation 1914

0-6-0 Standard Goods
238, 504, 674, 792, 886, 1112, 1196, 1205, 1209

0-6-0ST 1076 class
1271, 1589, 1601

2-4-0T Metro
459, 624, 632, 979, 1456

0-6-0ST 1854 class
1712 PT, 1719 PT, 1761 ST, 1794 PT, 1864 PT, 1877 PT, 1889 PT, 1893 ST, 1899 PT

0-4-2T 517 class
519, 528, 537, 539, 553, 599, 837, 846

2-4-0 806 class
823

0-6-0ST 653 class
1746

0-6-0ST/PT 850 class
989PT, 1224ST, 1916PT, 1919PT, 1928PT, 1946ST, 1952ST, 1954PT, 1964ST, 1978ST, 1995PT, 1996PT, 1998PT, 2012PT, 2015ST, 2017ST

0-6-0ST 1813 class
1852

0-6-0-ST/PT 2021 class
2031ST, 2035ST, 2044ST, 2059ST, 2102PT, 2115PT, 2127ST, 2130PT, 2158ST

2-4-0 3201 class
3201

2-4-0 3226 class
3231

2-4-0T 2201 class
2201

4-4-0 Duke class
3254 *Boscawen*, 3268 *River Tamar*

0-6-0 Dean Goods
2304, 2308, 2320, 2382, 2383, 2389, 2392, 2395, 2396, 2411, 2415, 2421, 2422, 2423, 2435, 2440, 2461, 2470, 2481, 2485, 2520, 2526, 2533, 2543, 2547, 2551, 2557, 2565, 2580

4-4-0 Atbara class
3387 *Roberts*, 4136 *Terrible*, 4144 *Colombo*, 4145 *Dunedin*

4-4-0 3521 class
3533

0-6-0 2361 class
2369, 2370, 2376, 2378

2-6-0 Aberdare class
2622, 2648

4-4-0 City class
3708 *Killarney*, 3715 *City of Hereford*, 3717 *City of Truro*

0-6-0 ST/PT class
2729ST, 2761PT, 2776ST, 2786ST, 2793PT

4-4-0 County class
3802 *County Clare*, 3807 *County Kilkenny*, 3815 *County of Hants*, 3824 *County of Cornwall*, 3832 *County of Wilts*, 3833 *County of Dorset*

2-8-0 28XX class
2809, 2821, 2828, 2854

4-4-0 Badminton class
4114 *Shelburne*

4-4-0 Flower class
4153 *Camellia*, 4160 *Carnation*, 4164 *Mignonette*, 4166 *Polyanthus*

4-6-0 Saint class
2900 *William Dean*, 2922 *Saint Gabriel*, 2930 *Saint Vincent*, 2946 *Langford Court*, 2971 *Albion*, 2973 *Robins Bolitho*, 2974 *Lord Barrymore*, 2976 *Winterstoke*, 2982 *Lalla Rook*, 2983 *Red Gauntlet*, 2985 *Peveril of the Peak*, 2986 *Robin Hood*, 2987 *Bride of Lammermoor*, 2990 *Waverley*

2-6-0 43XX class
4323, 4324, 4334, 4339

2-6-2T 3150 class
3159, 3168

Total: 150

Bristol Bath Road Shed Allocation 31 December 1947

0-4-2T 14XX class
1430

4-6-0 Hall class
3950 (5955) *Garth Hall*, 4942 *Maindy Hall*, 5949 *Trematon Hall*, 6958 *Oxburgh Hall*

4-6-0 Modified Hall
6971 *Athelhampton Hall*, 6972 *Beningbrough Hall*

4-6-0 County class
1002 *County of Berks*, 1005 *County of Devon*, 1007 *County of Brecknock*, 1011 *County of Chester*, 1013 *County of Dorset*, 1014 *County of Glamorgan*, 1028 *County of Warwick*

4-6-0 Star class
4019 *Knight Templar*, 4020 *Knight Commander*, 4030, 4033 *Queen Victoria*, 4034 *Queen Adelaide*, 4035 *Queen Charlotte*, 4041 *Prince of Wales*, 4042 *Prince Albert*, 4043 *Prince Henry*, 4047 *Princess Louise*

0-6-0PT 2021 class
2072

0-6-0 Dean Goods class
2444, 2462

4-6-0 Castle class
4080 *Powderham Castle*, 4084 *Aberystwyth Castle*, 4089 *Donnington Castle*, 4093 *Dunster Castle*, 4096 *Highclere Castle*, 5019 *Treago Castle*, 5024 *Carew Castle*, 5025 *Chirk Castle*, 5048 *Earl of Devon*, 5074 *Hampden*, 5076 *Gladiator*, 5082 *Swordfish*, 5083 *Bath Abbey*, 5084 *Reading Abbey*, 5091 *Cleeve Abbey*

4-6-0 Saint class
2929 *Saint Stephen*, 2931 *Arlington Court*, 2939 *Croome Court*, 2942 *Fawley Court*

2-6-2T 45XX class
4535, 4536, 4539

2-6-0 43XX class
5325, 5327, 5543

2-6-2T 4575 class
4577, 4580, 4595, 5511, 5512, 5514, 5523, 5527, 5528, 5535, 5536, 5539, 5546, 5547, 5548, 5553, 5555, 5558, 5559, 5561, 5564, 5572

0-4-2T 58XX class
5803, 5809, 5813

4-6-0 Manor class
7809 *Childrey Manor*, 7812 *Erlestoke Manor*, 7814 *Fringford Manor*

2-6-2T 5101 class
4142, 4143, 4151, 4152, 4155, 5169

Total: 86

Bristol St Philip's Marsh Shed Allocation 31 December 1947

0-6-0T ex-LBSCR Terrier class
5 *Portishead*, 6

0-6-0PT 1501 class
1538

2-8-0T 42XX class
5241

0-6-0PT 2021 class
2031, 2064, 2070, 2135

2-6-0 43XX class
5351, 5358, 5374

0-6-0 2251 class
2220, 2225, 2251, 2253, 2265, 2269, 2293, 3215

0-6-0PT 57XX class
5784, 7711, 7718, 7719, 7726, 7728, 7729, 7779, 7782, 7783, 7790, 7793, 7795, 8702, 8703, 8713, 8714, 8722, 8730, 8737, 8741, 8746, 8747

0-6-0 Dean Goods class
2322, 2340, 2426, 2534, 2578

0-6-0PT 655 class
2702, 2709

0-6-2T 56XX class
6601, 6656, 6670, 6671

0-6-0PT 2721 class
2786

4-6-0 Grange class
6830 *Buckenhill Grange*, 6836 *Estevarney Grange*, 6842 *Nunhold Grange*, 6846 *Ruckley Grange*, 6850 *Cleeve Grange*, 6852 *Headbourne Grange*, 6861 *Crynant Grange*, 6863 *Dolhywel Grange*, 6867 *Peterston Grange*, 6876 *Kingsland Grange*

2-8-0 28XX class
2844, 2846, 2859, 4804 (2839), 4810 (2853)

2-8-0 ROD class
3013, 3017, 3022, 3034, 3041, 3046

2-8-2T 72XX class
7208, 7215, 7234, 7237

4-6-0 Manor class
7801 *Anthony Manor*, 7804 *Baydon Manor*

0-6-0PT 8750 class
3604, 3614, 3623, 3643, 3676, 3720, 3746, 3759, 3763, 3764, 3765, 3773, 3784, 3795, 4603, 4607, 4612, 4619, 4624, 4626, 4647, 4655, 8766, 8790, 8793, 8795, 9604, 9605, 9606, 9620, 9626, 9629, 9732, 9764

2-6-2T 81XX class
8105

4-6-0 Hall class
3900 (4968) *Shotton Hall*, 3951 (5976) *Ashwicke Hall*, 4965 *Rood Ashton Hall*, 4969 *Shrugborough Hall*, 4986 *Aston Hall*, 4990 *Clifton Hall*, 5964 *Wolseley Hall*, 5984 *Linden Hall*, 6909 *Frewin Hall*, 6912 *Helmster Hall*, 6922 *Burton Hall*, 6944 *Fledborough Hall*, 6954 *Lotherton Hall*

2-8-0 WD class
70801, 70836, 70876, 77116, 77142, 77200, 77247, 77289, 77326, 77508, 79261, 79301, 79309

Total: 142

Bristol St Philip's Marsh Allocation October 2011

Class 08/0 0-6-0
08633, 08822

Sprinter class 150/1
150 101, 150 102, 150 108, 150 120, 150 121, 150 122, 150 123, 150 126, 150 127, 150 128, 150 129, 150 130, 150 131

Class 150/2
150 201, 150 219, 150 221, 150 232, 150 233, 150 234, 150 238, 150 239, 150 243, 150 244, 150 246, 150 247, 150 248, 150 249, 150 261, 150 263, 150 265, 150 266

Class 158/0
158 763, 158 766, 158 767, 158 769, 158 798, 158 950, 158 951, 158 952, 158 953, 158 954, 158 955, 158 956, 158 957, 158 958, 158 959

Total: 48

'Foreign' Locomotives Allocated to St Philip's Marsh Shed

LMS class '2F' 0-6-0
On loan during period October 1939 to October 1945
3039, 3047, 3071, 3078, 3085, 3090, 3094, 3103, 3473, 3492, 3517, 3536, 3543, 3603, 3739

LMS class 8F 2-8-0
Built at Swindon, on loan during period 1943 to 1947
8400, 8401, 8402, 8403, 8410, 8411, 8412, 8415, 8421, 8424, 8441, 8448

War Department 2-8-0
On loan during period 1944 to 1945
7261, 7385, 7399, 7453, 7455, 7456

LNER 04 class 2-8-0
On loan during period November 1940 to July 1942
5391, 6209, 6245, 6594, 6629

War Department 2-8-0
On loan during post-war period
70801, 70836, 70876, 77116, 77142, 77200, 77247, 77289, 77326, 77508, 79261, 79301, 79309

United States Army S180 class 2-8-0
On loan during period 1943 to 1944
1632, 1681, 1682, 1683, 1687, 1749, 1757, 1913, 2122, 2164, 2167, 2408, 2433, 2450

Total: 65

'Foreign' Locomotives Allocated to Bath Road Shed

SR I3 class 4-4-2T
On loan during 1943
2089, 2091

Total: 2

Chapter Twelve

Accidents, Mishaps and Noteworthy Events

As in most areas of life, the railways saw their fair share of the criminal fraternity. However, new as the system was, the speed at which the railway and its staff responded to a crisis could still surprise the perpetrators of any misdemeanours. In the inaugural week, a passenger from Bath, on arrival at Temple Meads, discovered that he had been robbed of £120 – a considerable sum in those days and amounting to more than two years' wages for an agricultural labourer. The passenger told the railway authorities that he believed the thief had boarded a Bath train, which had already left. The gentleman was strapped to an engine (safety belts are by no means a new invention) that sped 'wrong line' to Bath at an average speed of 60 mph and overtook the train on which the thief was travelling *en route*. As soon as the special arrived, the railway police were informed and the thief was arrested as he stepped from the train.

Temple Meads station narrowly avoided being burnt to the ground on 28 April 1841. Between the passenger station and the river, timber was stacked for the construction of the Bristol & Exeter Railway. At about 8.00 p.m. the accidental ignition of a tank of creosote set the pile ablaze. The 'varying colours of the flames and the immense volumes of fiery smoke poured from the principal stack' attracted crowds of sightseers as the burning mass occupied at least 2 acres. Brunel directed that the three sides of the stack not facing the river be removed to stop the fire spreading and that the trees should be cut down in Pipe Lane, which was almost immediately north of the passenger station. These precautions had the desired effect and saved the nearby saw-mills of Mr Kidd and the numerous courts and alleys in the densely populated district of Temple Back. Fortunately, the wind was blowing from the direction of the station, so the terminus was not threatened. A party of seamen from the brig HMS *Savage*, lying in King Road between Avonmouth and Portishead, gave help. After destroying £5,000 worth of timber, the fire eventually died down at 2.00 a.m. As it was insured, B&ER shareholders did not have to bear the loss, The total value of the timber was £30,000, but eight trow loads had already been sent down the line and, only twenty-four hours earlier, more timber had been placed in tanks of sulphate of copper, which was used as a preservative, and, on this occasion, it worked in more ways than one.

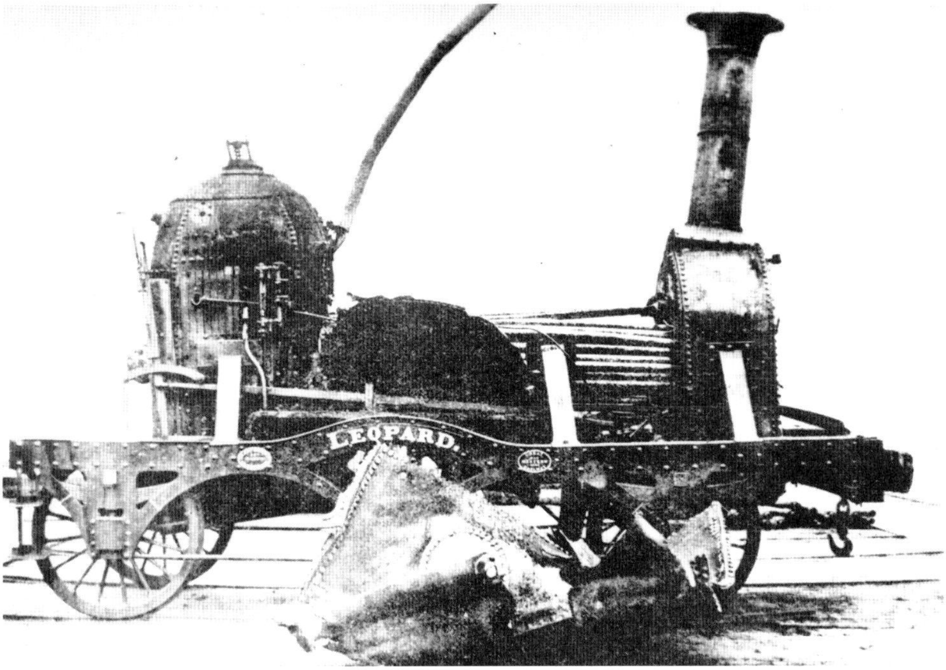

Fire Fly class 2-2-2 *Leopard*, built in 1840 and shown here in 1857. Its boiler exploded at Bristol in 1857 and the engine was rebuilt in 1859. It was not withdrawn until 1879, being the last of its class to survive. (*Author's Collection*)

Three months later Temple Meads station had another lucky escape from fire. On 17 July a smell of gas was detected in the offices. A workman from Messrs Jefferies & Price rather unwisely searched for the leakage with a lighted candle, with the result that the accumulated gas exploded, injuring him so severely that he needed to be conveyed to the infirmary. His stunned colleague soon recovered and the lad with them was completely unhurt.

Mercifully, the busy line between Bristol and Bath has never had a very serious accident involving a passenger train. The first of any consequence occurred on 18 July 1845. Just west of Saltford Tunnel the tyre worked its way off a driving wheel of an engine hauling an Up timber train. The last wagon was consequently derailed and turned onto the Down line. The locomotive of the 2.00 p.m. passenger train Paddington to Bristol struck the wagon, throwing the fireman from the footplate and dislocating his shoulder. Because of the inherent stability of the broad gauge, the coaches stayed on the track; the passengers were all unharmed and collected in a special sent from Bristol. As the blockage meant that all traffic had to use the Up line for twenty-four hours, to avoid the possibility of trains colliding head-on, a pilot engine was used between Keynsham and Cross Post Bridge, no train being allowed to proceed without it. The express engine only suffered minor damage, although the *Bath Chronicle* commented, 'Some of its external works and ornamental appendages were much injured.'

Fox's Wood was the locality of a collision on 10 August 1851. A twenty-six-coach train carrying passengers returning from the Great Exhibition left Bath at 3.00 a.m. Two minutes after its departure, a tank engine arrived, returning to Bristol after having assisted a goods train through Box Tunnel. Block signalling was still a thing of the future and, obeying the rule book, the engine was detained for twenty minutes and left at 3.23 a.m.

Meanwhile, the excursion had made good progress to Twerton where it 'exhibited unmistakable signs of distress'. The driver coaxed it through Keynsham but, believing that the feed pumps had failed and being afraid of a boiler explosion, he drew to a halt outside the eastern portal of Bristol No. 3 Tunnel, quite unaware of the presence of the tank engine behind. Just before it stopped, the tank engine struck the rear coach – fortunately a strong second-class vehicle with an iron frame – at about 16 mph, 'throwing those in the hinder carriages with great violence from their seats against each other and filling them with the utmost consternation and alarm'. Immediately after the news reached Bath station, John Barrett, surgeon, was sent for, and on arrival found his colleague, Mr Kiddell, assisting at the scene. Casualties were relatively light – one passenger received a fractured kneecap and several others suffered various contusions. The train was eventually propelled into Bristol by the very engine that had caused the damage. The tank engine's crew was taken into custody and pleaded guilty – it was believed they were asleep. Charged before magistrates at the Lamb Inn, Keynsham, Driver Thomas Coltman was fined £5, or one month's imprisonment with hard labour, and Fireman John Wright £3, or twenty-one days' hard labour. Their respective wages were 5*s* 6*d* and 3*s* a day.

The environs of Keynsham were the scene of a collision on 6 June 1865. A double-headed Down express had stopped because just west of Saltford Tunnel, one of the drivers had felt a shock and believed his engine to be damaged. As the time interval system was in operation, the guard, as required by the rule book, walked back to protect his train and, when recalled by the engine whistle, left a fusee – this was a device like a Roman candle firework which, when struck smartly, would burn for ten minutes. The light of the fusee could be seen for a considerable distance and acted as a caution signal to indicate that a train had left within ten minutes. The express was just about to proceed when it was struck by the Down Mail. Three men in the end compartment of the last coach had a lucky escape. Its doors were locked according to regulations, but fortunately one man had a carriage key and, seeing the approaching train, they were able to make their escape before the Mail engine struck. About fifteen passengers in other compartments were injured.

Stunned by the collision, the Mail train guard was slow at protecting his train and had only walked back about 150 yd when a Down empty carriage train passed and struck the rear of the Mail. Both of the latter trains had been kept at Bath for the regulatory ten minutes, but as there were no signals at night between Bath and Bristol, there was no means of maintaining the time intervals.

The coach roofs of the period were fitted with outside luggage racks and one rather gruesome detail recorded by a contemporary paper was that, on arrival at Bristol, a dead Shetland pony was found lying on the roof of a first-class coach of the express, where it had been thrown by the force of the collision.

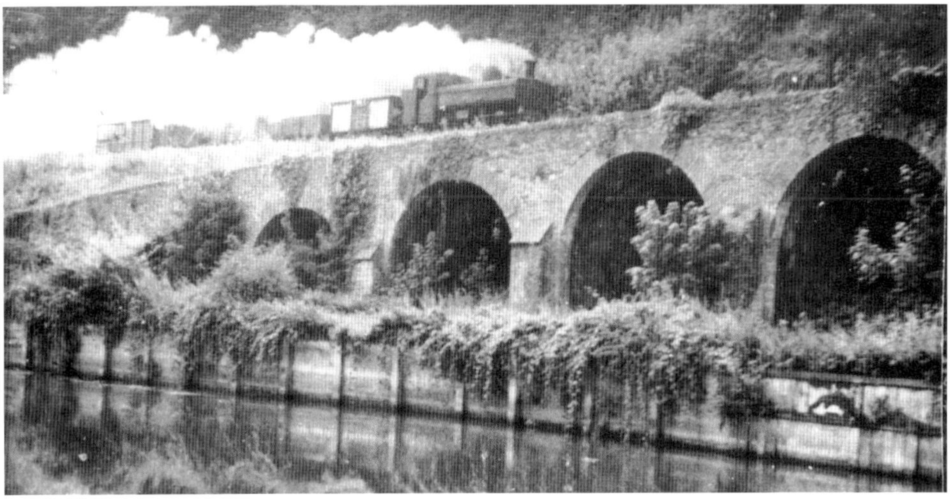

A 0-6-0PT heading the Keynsham to East Depot transfer goods, 31 August 1963. It is above the Avon between Bristol No. 3 and No. 2 tunnels. Had John Chiddy not moved the stone, the express would have plunged off the shelf here. (*Russell Leach*)

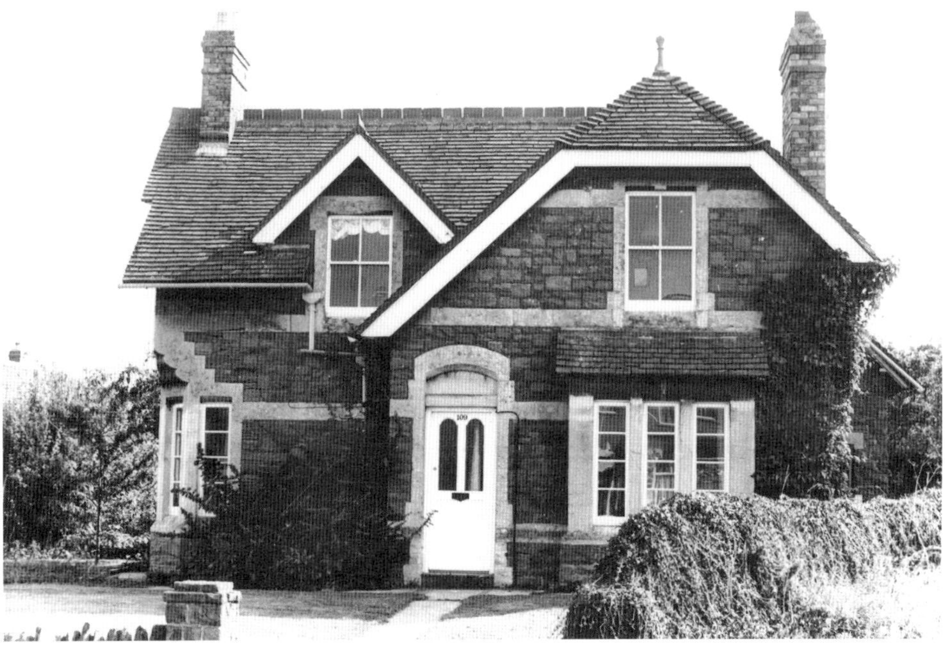

Memorial Cottage erected at Hanham for the family of John Chiddy. This view was taken 11 September 1990. (*Author*)

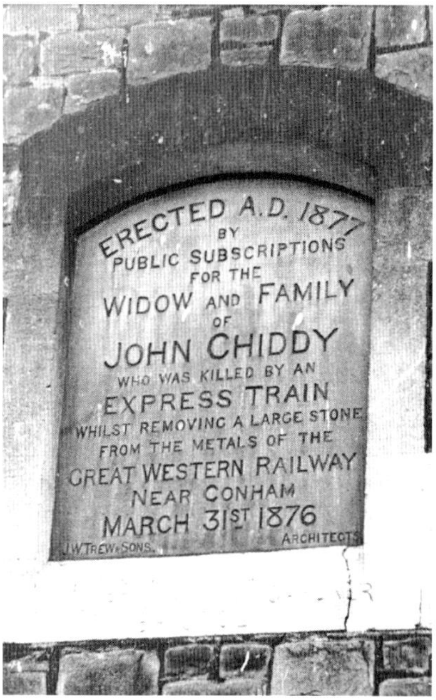

The plaque on Memorial Cottage, Hanham, 11 September 1990. (*Author*)

John Chiddy was foreman of Birchwood Quarry, situated near the eastern mouth of Bristol No. 2 Tunnel. Just before 2.00 p.m. on 31 March 1876 an Up stopping passenger train dislodged a large stone from the quarry's stack beside the line and fouled the Down track. Knowing that the approach of the Down Flying Dutchman was imminent, John Chiddy tried to shift the obstruction. This he succeeded in doing but at the cost of his own life, for the engine struck him before he could stand clear. In due course, the train, which had been travelling at 50 mph, stopped and a collection was made. At the point where John had saved it, the Flying Dutchman had been on a ledge high above the Avon and, had it become derailed, it would most certainly have plunged into the river with considerable loss of life. How much did those thankful passengers give? £3 17*s* 0*d* – precious little compensation for a wife and seven children who had lost their father, not to mention their breadwinner. Lord Elcho was so incensed that he took up the case in Parliament and said that if a man risked his life to save others, he should do so 'with the consciousness that his family would not be dependent on charity or the workhouse'. The Chancellor of the Exchequer explained that he had no funds to help such people. However, the press publicity resulted in an account being opened in Bath and another in Bristol, the Bank of England contributing £10 when informed that two of its officials were on the train with a large quantity of gold. The total of £400 purchased a ½ acre of land on which the six-bedroomed Memorial Cottage was built in what is now Memorial Road on the Hanham bank of the Avon. On the north side of the house a plaque carries the inscription: 'Erected AD 1877 by public subscription for the widow and family of John Chiddy who was killed by an express train

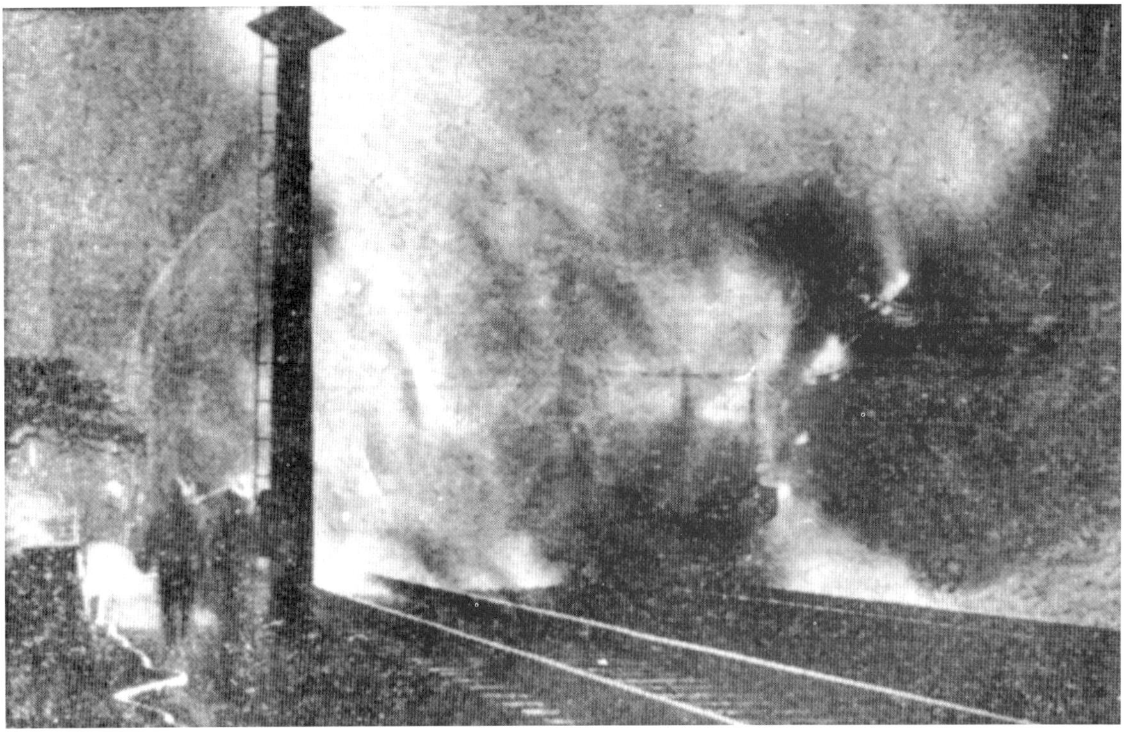

The 9.05 p.m. diesel railcar ablaze at St Anne's Park, 10 April 1956. (*Author's Collection*)

whilst removing a large stone from the metals of the Great Western Railway near Conham, March 31st 1876.'

Although not actually railway property, Widcombe toll footbridge was closely associated with the GWR as it offered a convenient short cut from the foot of Lyncombe Hill to Bath station. It was 100 ft long and 9 ft wide, designed on the bowstring principle and erected in 1862. At 10.47 a.m. on 6 June 1877, 900 excursionists arrived by train from the Salisbury and Weymouth lines *en route* for the 100th Bath & West of England Agricultural Show, which, on this occasion, was being held beside the Wells Road on the site now occupied by Poets' Avenues. A notice near the station exit announced in large red and blue letters on a sheet of canvas several feet in length: 'The nearest way to the show field over this bridge. Toll one halfpenny'. A crowd of 200 to 300 from the train overwhelmed the toll keeper on the further bank and their weight caused the bridge to collapse with a loss of ten lives, nine killed outright and one dying later. More than fifty people were injured. The proprietors were successfully prosecuted for manslaughter. The replacement footbridge, still standing, was designed by T. E. M. Marsh, formerly resident engineer at Bath when the Bristol to Bath section of railway was being constructed. Plaques at each end of the bridge credit the design to him.

A pickpocket was apprehended at Bath station in 1874: 'He [the platform inspector] followed him and saw him push against a lady and with his left hand working at the folds of another lady's dress. He carried partly on his left arm and wrist a mackintosh. Whilst the inspector stood watching him, he happened to turn round and seeing that he was observed, he hurriedly left the platform and hastened downstairs.' The thief stole 7*s* 10*d* and received three months' imprisonment with hard labour.

The *Bath Chronicle* reported that on 5 January 1889:

> As the Flying Dutchman express, which leaves Bristol at 12.09 and is due at Bath at 12.23, was running through Number 3 Tunnel, near Keynsham, on Saturday ... a large stone became detached from the roof and fell onto the six-foot way. The Dutchman was apparently the first train to pass through after the fall. The footboard of the leading coach came into violent collision with the obstruction, which it seems to have slightly moved, for the other coaches did not receive so much damage. No stop was made, but the passengers were naturally much alarmed by the occurrence.

The damaged coaches were shunted off at Bath and services cancelled until the tunnel was cleared.

By the east portal of Saltford Tunnel is a deep and steep cutting. On 27 February 1900, after excessive rain, 3,000 tons of earth and stone slipped and covered the Down line for 40 yd immediately east of the tunnel. Before it could be warned, the 4.40 p.m. from Salisbury, which had left Bath at 6.02 p.m., plunged into the landslide, derailing the engine and first four coaches and throwing them over to the Up line. It was fortunate that the derailed Down train was running late and had passed an Up train before reaching the slip, otherwise the Up train would have crashed into it. Since the line was impassable, passengers had to walk round the slip before joining another train on the far side of the tunnel. Because of the cutting's steep slope, working to clear the obstruction was fraught with difficulty. One hundred men had ropes attached to their waists, with the other ends fastened to strong stakes driven into the field above. When darkness fell, they worked by the light of naphtha flares. On two occasions, trucks being filled with the fallen earth were buried by more slides, and stout chains used in an attempt to draw the wagons clear snapped under the strain of the locomotives hauling them. The Up line was eventually opened the following noon. In order to facilitate single-line working, pending the re-opening of the Down line, an electric staff system was introduced between Saltford and Keynsham, a temporary facing crossover laid at Saltford and worked from a ground frame, its two levers locked by Annett's key from Saltford station signal box.

The author witnessed what was almost a derailment at Twerton Tunnel signal box in September 1944:

> I was standing about 15 ft above rail level on the footpath between Gypsy Lane overbridge and the signal box. As an Up stopping train, consisting of 45XX class

> 2-6-2T and a 'B' set, passed at about 55 mph, there was a loud bang and the engine rocked violently, which I attributed to the locomotive passing over the points to the Up refuge siding at speed. I entered the engine number in my notebook and looked back at the train, expecting to see the last coach entering the tunnel. I was amazed to find that it was drawing rapidly to a halt. It stopped. The guard jumped down and came back towards the signal box, as did the fireman. They spoke with the signalman and as they came to the part of the track at the foot of the embankment where I was standing, they stooped down, picked up pieces of metal and threw them on the side of the cutting. I heard one man exclaim: 'Look, it's cut the b..... sleeper in half.' Apparently, as the engine passed over the points, a driving wheel spring broke. The signalman, who had an almost head-on view, told me later that the engine rocked so much that he believed it was coming off the rails. If it had, it would have landed literally at, or on, my feet.

On 10 April 1956 diesel railcars W35W and W36W were working the 9.05 p.m. Bath to Temple Meads and as they threaded Fox's Wood Tunnel the driver noticed an ominous red glow on the wall. He continued until clear of the tunnel and stopped immediately outside. Fortunately there were no passengers on board.

Both cars were burnt out and, of the original total of thirty-eight cars, five had now been destroyed by fire. W35W and W36W were never repaired and officially condemned on 20 April 1957. Each had cost £6,537 when new in 1941.

On 11 January 1967 the 11.45 Paddington to Bristol express, headed by Western class diesel-hydraulic D1067 *Western Druid*, was held at a signal between No. 3 and No. 2 Tunnels. Its rear coach was struck by sister engine D1071 *Western Renown*, hauling the 12.45 p.m. Paddington to Swansea, which had been diverted via Bath because of a freight train derailment at Westerleigh East Junction. Thirteen passengers received minor injuries. Warship class D864 *Zambesi*, passing light on the Up line, was slightly damaged when it scraped against the Bristol train's last coach. As the line was now blocked and the Westerleigh problem cleared, long-distance trains were diverted via Badminton and local passengers served by a special shuttle bus service between Bath and Bristol, a maximum of twelve vehicles being used. The line was cleared seven hours later.

Appendices

Appendix 1: Weekly Paid Staff 1898

Bath: 2 inspectors: £1 15*s* 0*d*; 1 cab inspector £1 5*s* 0*d*; 1 passenger guard £1 7*s* 0*d;* 8 ticket collectors £1 3*s* 0*d*; 2 policemen £1 1*s* 0*d*; 1 district reliefman £1 7*s* 0*d*; 8 signalmen £1 7*s* 0*d*; 1 parcels porter; £1 3*s* 0*d*; 6 luggage stowers £1 0*s* 0*d*; 1 cloakroom porter £1 4*s* 0*d*; 3 porters 19*s* 0*d*.

Twerton: stationmaster £1 7*s* 0*d*; 2 signalmen £1 4*s* 0*d*; porter 15*s* 0*d*.

Saltford: stationmaster £1 7*s* 0*d*; 2 signalmen £1 4*s* 0*d*; 1 porter 15*s* 0*d*.

Keynsham: 3 signalmen £1 4*s* 0*d*;1 ticket collector £1 3*s* 0*d*; 3 lad porters 19*s* 0*d*.

St Anne's Park: stationmaster £1 10*s* 0*d*; ticket collector £1 3*s* 0*d*; 2 porters 15*s* 0*d*; 1 lad porter 12*s* 0*d*; 3 signalmen £1 4*s* 0*d*.

Appendix 2: Extracts from the Author's Diary

18.5.46 See No. 5099 *Compton Castle*, a post-war addition to the class.
24.1.47 See No. 100A1 *Lloyds* fitted for oil-burning.
See a WD 2-8-0, they had recently started being used on goods trains.
11.9.47 Up noon express from Bristol double-headed. (For a few weeks it was fairly frequently after this date. Generally double-heading rare.)
11.10.47 See No. 5972 *Olton Hall* with new Hawksworth welded tender.
12.2.48 No. 4084 *Aberystwyth Castle* in GWR livery but 'British Railways' in GWR-style lettering on the tender.
24.6.48 No. 6001 *King Edward VII* painted blue.
21.8.48 See train in experimental 'plum and spilt milk' livery.
24.8.48 See an Austerity 2-10-0 No. 73774 with a dynamometer car – the 1948 Trials.
1.9.48 Ex-LMS No. 48189 with dynamometer car on an Up goods.

2.9.48 A class 8F with dynamometer car on the Down line.
5.6.49 Corridor coaches for the first time in the new standard BR colours.
6.7.49 See non-corridor coaches for first time in new BR livery.
28.2.50 See gas-turbine No. 18000 for first time. Has dynamometer car and 5 coaches.
19.12.51 See taper-boilered Pannier tank at Bath for first time.
17.2.52 See diesel shunter No. 15100 going Down with brake van.
15.8.54 Class 2MT 2-6-0 No. 46526 on Down permanent way train.
30.6.55 See class 2MT 2-6-2T No. 41202. First time this class seen on line.
8.10.55 See a Star – the last one I shall see?
9.4.56 See a double chimney King for first time.
6.5.56 An 0-4-2T on the Down line running light. The first time I have seen an engine of this class on the line.
17.6.56 See for first time a 94XX class 0-6-0PT hauling a Down stopping train.
21.6.56 See for first time a BR Standard coach painted 'tea and cream' livery.
22.6.56 No. 3215 with 'GWR' on the tender – 8½ years after Nationalisation.
27.8.56 See on Down line the first BR DMU set.
1.9.56 2251 class 0-6-0 with Down passenger – not seen this class on passenger duty on the line before.
4.10.56 See an SR, four-wheeled Utility van painted green. (They have all been red for some years.)
10.10.56 See a train of six articulated compartment WR coaches.
19.5.57 4-4-0 No. 3440 *City of Truro* on 10.25 a.m. excursion to Dartmouth.
10.5.58 See BR Standard class 3MT 2-6-2T on Down stopping train for first time.
10.6.60 See the blue Bristol Pullman for the first time.
1.7.60 D0226 passed through Bath on down cattle train.
2.3.62 Warship and seven Pullman coaches replace Up Blue Pullman.
19.8.62 See for first time an Up loose-coupled goods train hauled by a diesel.
5.6.65 See the new blue and white liveried Pullman coaches for first rime.
14.5.66 See a maroon coach as trailer behind a three-car DMU.
1.11.69 Several two-car DMUs around this week – usually three-car hitherto.
30.5.70 9.45 a.m. Paddington to Bristol hauled by a maroon-painted Warship. Both maroon engines and Warships rare at this period.
9.10.71 No. 6000 King George V on Bulmer's special train. First steam engine seen on line since 1966.
30.5.78 See refurbished three-car DMU for first time.
23.5.81 At 5. 10 a.m. see a very long goods train on Down line – about 100 four-wheeled wagons. Probably hauled by a class 37.
2.12.87 See class 59 at Bath for first time.

Appendix 3: Speeds of Trains Between Mileposts 109 and 109¼

Mileposts 109 and 109¼ are situated just east of Twerton Tunnel signal box.

Fastest Up express:	5957	4 coaches + bogie van	67 mph
Fastest Down express:	Castle	7 coaches, Down Bristolian	53 mph
Fastest Up stopping:	7916	4 coaches	60 mph
Fastest Down stopping:	4-6-0	3 coaches	50 mph
Fastest Up parcels:	2-6 0	10 vans	31 mph
Fastest Down parcels:	1000	9 vans	48 mph
Fastest Up freight:	0-6-0ST	3 wagons	33 mph
Fastest Down freight:	4-6-0	32 wagons	32 mph

The following compares the average speed and length of trains in 1948 and 1955:

Up express:	1948	12 coaches	47 mph
	1955	8 coaches	50 mph
Down express:	1948	9 coaches	36 mph
	1955	7 coaches	40 mph
Up stopping:	1948	5 coaches	39 mph
	1955	3 coaches	38 mph
Down stopping:	1948	7 coaches	30 rnph
	1955	4 coaches	33 mph
Up freight:	1948	33 wagons	23 mph
	1955	34 wagons	24 mph
Down freight:	1948	44 wagons	23 mph
	1955	45 wagons	23 mph

Appendix 4: Observations at Twerton Tunnel

4 July 1955

Loco	Time	Train
3812	6.07	Up freight, 30 wagons
6966	6.07	Down freight, 30 wagons
6814	6.14	Up stopping, 3 coaches
1010	6.24	Down stopping, 5 coaches + van
5019	6.34	Up express, 6 coaches + van
2826	6.35	Down freight, 54 wagons
4082	6.42	Down express, 10 coaches
5535	6.48	Up stopping, 2 coaches
2203	6.49	Down freight, 41 wagons
4084	7.05	Down express, 11 coaches
2250	7.08	Up fitted freight, 20 vans
7023	7.15	Down express 10 coaches + van
6954 7300	7.19	Down light engines
4917	7.33	Up stopping, 5 coaches, 2 vans, 2 gas cylinder wagons
5396	7.38	Up express, 10 coaches
7905	7.44	Up express, 7 coaches + 2 vans
5548	7.45	Down stopping, 3 coaches

30 July 1963

Loco	Time	Train
3864	18.06	Up freight, 32 wagons
D7003	18.12	Down express, 6 coaches, 2 vans
W50737	18.18	Up DMU 3 car
W51098 W51070	18.29	Down 3 car DMU + van
D812	18.33	Up express, 8 coaches and van
D860	18.42	Down express, 10 coaches
9623	18.42	Up light engine and van
7250	18.50	Down, 8 bogie rail wagons + brake van
4904	18.51	Up freight, 35 wagons
9623	19.00	Down freight, 34 wagons

14 September 1974

Loco	Time	Train
47446	08.55	Up express
47229	09.08	Up express, 8 coaches
1588	09.19	Up express, 6 coaches
31193	09.31	Down parcels, 7 vans
W51094	09.43	Up 2 3 car DMUs
47424	09.50	Up express, 10 coaches
50014	09.54	Down express, 10 coaches

46007	09.54	Up express
D1049	10.00	Up parcels
1103	10.05	Down Hampshire 3 car DEMU
31273	10.06	Up passenger, 3 coaches
W51576	10.10	Down 3 car DMU
W51322 etc.	10.23	Up 2 3 car DMUs
50013	10.29	Up express, 10 coaches
50001	10.31	Down express, 10 coaches
D1069	10.41	Up light engine
47245	10.53	Up express, 10 coaches
47511	11.26	Up express, 9 coaches
47320	11.31	Down ECS, 11 coaches
46017	11.40	Down passenger, 4 coaches, 2 vans
50014	11.41	Up express, 10 coaches
47438	11.46	Down express, 10 coaches
D1069	11.50	Down freight, 47 wagons
1103 1127	12.00	Up 2 Hampshire 3 car DEMUs
W51510 W51587	12.07	Down 3 car DMU

26 August 1981

Loco	Time	Train
253014	09.03	Up HST
33030	09.24	6 coaches Up
31210	09.29	Down parcels, 10 vans
253010	09.36	Down HST
253033	09.40	Up HST
33112	09.42	Down, 6 coaches
47069	09.48	Up, 10 coaches
W50329	09.50	Down 3 car DMU
47539	09.56	Up, 10 coaches
31301	10.02	Up freight, 5 wagons
253010	10.17	Up HST
33059	10.28	Up, 6 coaches
33032	10.34	Down, 6 coaches
253033	10.44	Down HST
W51071	10.47	Up 2 3 car DMUs
50040	10.58	Up light engine
31165	11.04	Up light engine
253032	11.24	Up HST
33014	11.29	Up, 6 coaches
253011	11.32	Down HST

253038	11.39	Down HST
33019	11.49	Down, 6 coaches
37382	11.54	Down, 6 vans

15 May 2000

Loco	Time	Train
-	08.54	Up HST, 10 cars
158820	08.57	Up, 2 cars
150278	09.00	Down, 2 cars
150261	09.01	Up, 2 cars
165118	09.07	Up, 2 cars
43135	09.13	Down HST, 10 cars
153370/353	09.15	Up 2 single cars
150261	09.19	Down 2 cars
-	09.24	Up HST 10 cars
158863	09.31	Up 2 cars
165136	09.31	Down 2 cars
158831	09.35	Down 2 cars
153353/370	09.38	Down 2 single cars
150278	09.45	Up 2 cars
-	09.50	Down HST 10 cars
-	09.53	Up HST 10 cars

165136	10.07	Up 2 cars
-	10.10	Down HST 10 cars
150244	10.18	Down 2 cars
-	10.23	Up HST 10 cars
158821	10.32	Up 2 cars
-	10.36	Down HST 10 cars
158824	10.41	Down 2 cars
150243	10.45	Down 2 cars
153302	10.47	Up single car
-	10.53	Up HST 10 cars
165002	10.59	Down 2 cars
153305	11.10	Down single car
-	11.21	Down HST 10 cars
-	11.25	Up HST 10 cars
150267	11.31	Up 2 cars
158832	11.33	Down 2 cars
156002	11.38	Up 2 cars
158823	11.44	Up 2 cars
165119	11.51	Down 2 cars
-	11.57	Down HST 10 cars
-	12.01	Up HST 10 cars

Appendix 5: Van Lad at Bath
Mervyn Halbrook

My father worked on the GWR as a platelayer. When I reached fourteen, and the time came for me to leave school, I thought I could do worse than work on the railway. My father had a word with the Freshford stationmaster, Mr Crossman. This resulted in my being called to Bristol for a medical. Passing it successfully, I was told to report at Bath station on 7 August 1944.

I started as a van lad under Charlie Hooper, a short chap with bushy moustache. Parcels were brought down from the platforms to the back of the station near the river. They had to be sorted in order of delivery and sheets made out requiring the signature of the consignee. The parcels for delivery towards the end of the round were stacked in the van first and put right at the front, those to be delivered first being placed at the back. We managed to get all the parcels into one load. Delivery was made in the morning and collection in the afternoon, though we delivered more parcels than we collected. Shops rang the station if there was something to collect. To help me get up and down between road level and the van floor, a rope was suspended from the back of the roof.

While I was busy sorting parcels at the rear of the station, Charlie collected the horse from its stable at Westmoreland goods yard and backed it between the shafts of the van, which was kept overnight on the river side of the station. The horse had a nosebag filled with oats and chaff to provide sustenance while on the delivery round. A water container was tied carefully inside the van so that it did not tip over and wet the parcels. We had a bowl for the horse to drink from.

We delivered to lots of shops because most of their goods arrived by rail. We particularly enjoyed making a daily delivery to Lyons's in Union Street as the supervisor always gave us a jam roll each. We kept north of the river, only crossing it to deliver to the shops in Argyle Street. Our route varied according to deliveries, but tended to be Dorchester Street, Southgate Street, Stall Street, Westgate Street, the Sawclose, High Street, Broad Street, George Street, the Paragon and Walcot Street. The horse was used to traffic and I never experienced one bolting.

My hours were 7.30 a.m. to 4.30 p.m. Mondays to Fridays and I was paid 48*s* a week. I wore a uniform consisting of trousers, waistcoat, jacket and cap; the driver wore the same with the addition of a leather apron.

Having proved my worth on the horse van, I progressed to one of the four motor vans which served Lansdown and Weston; Bathampton, Batheaston, St Catherine's and Bathford; Odd Down, Twerton, and Claverton Down, Combe Down and South Stoke. One of the more gruesome deliveries was that of blood boxes to the Royal United Hospital, a special delivery having to be made as soon as one arrived.

Later on I became a signalman in the area and was at Westbury Panel Box when I retired.

Appendix 6: Working for British Rail in the Sixties
Alan E. Canterbury

When I was thinking of leaving school at the age of fifteen there were plenty of jobs a young lad could do and many of these were working on the railway. As my mother had worked for the LMS on the Clifton Down line during the war and my maternal grandfather had worked for GWR, you could say it was in my blood.

The jobs an unskilled youth of fifteen could do on the railway at that time were numerous – engine cleaner, booking boy in a signal box, lad porter, van guard and so on; jobs that sadly no longer exist today but jobs that gave you a start in life. It was possible to start in one of these humble positions and become stationmaster or shed master, many did.

I chose van boy or van guard as my start on BR(W) – as it was known in the early sixties but it was very much GWR. Even my pay tally, No. 130, was GWR. The van drivers were known as carters and the van guard was supposed to protect the goods on the van while the carter delivered, but in practice the boy did most of the deliveries.

There were two classes of road delivery: Goods and Passenger. Passenger was normally small packages, urgent goods, club book parcels and the like, plus PLA – Passenger's Luggage in Advance. These items were sent all over the UK by passenger train or overnight by express parcel trains. A parcel could be picked up by van in Kingswood at 4.00 p.m., taken to Temple Meads and be delivered next morning in Newcastle or London. The system was good.

I went all over Bristol delivering parcels but mostly worked the Horfield, Bishopston, Victoria Street and Clifton areas of Bristol. In Clifton at the end of each school term, we had three or four vans to pick up the trunks from the colleges, plus tuck boxes. We used to deliver fish to the zoo for the sea lions and penguins.

The vans we used were varied, and included Morris Commercials, pre-war Thornycrofts and one van that we all called the 'flying flea'. It was a small Morris and we boys used to get behind the van and four of us could lift it off the ground and when the driver put it into gear to drive off, nothing would happen, the wheels were off the ground and they just went round and round. The driver would get out and we would run for it, laughing our heads off.

We clocked on at the end of Platform 9 near the entrance to Collett House and the day started there. You went down the stairs by the old goods lift (you were not allowed in the lift), then along to your bay and sorted what looked like a mountain of parcels in delivery order, last off, first on, while the driver or 'carter' went to get his van. The vans were garaged under Temple Meads in the arches that formed the vaults under the platforms. This was like a holy of holies to us boys as we weren't supposed to go in them for safety reasons and one of the arches contained the secure store where tobacco was kept. The goods lifts at the eastern end of the main station came down into this labyrinth.

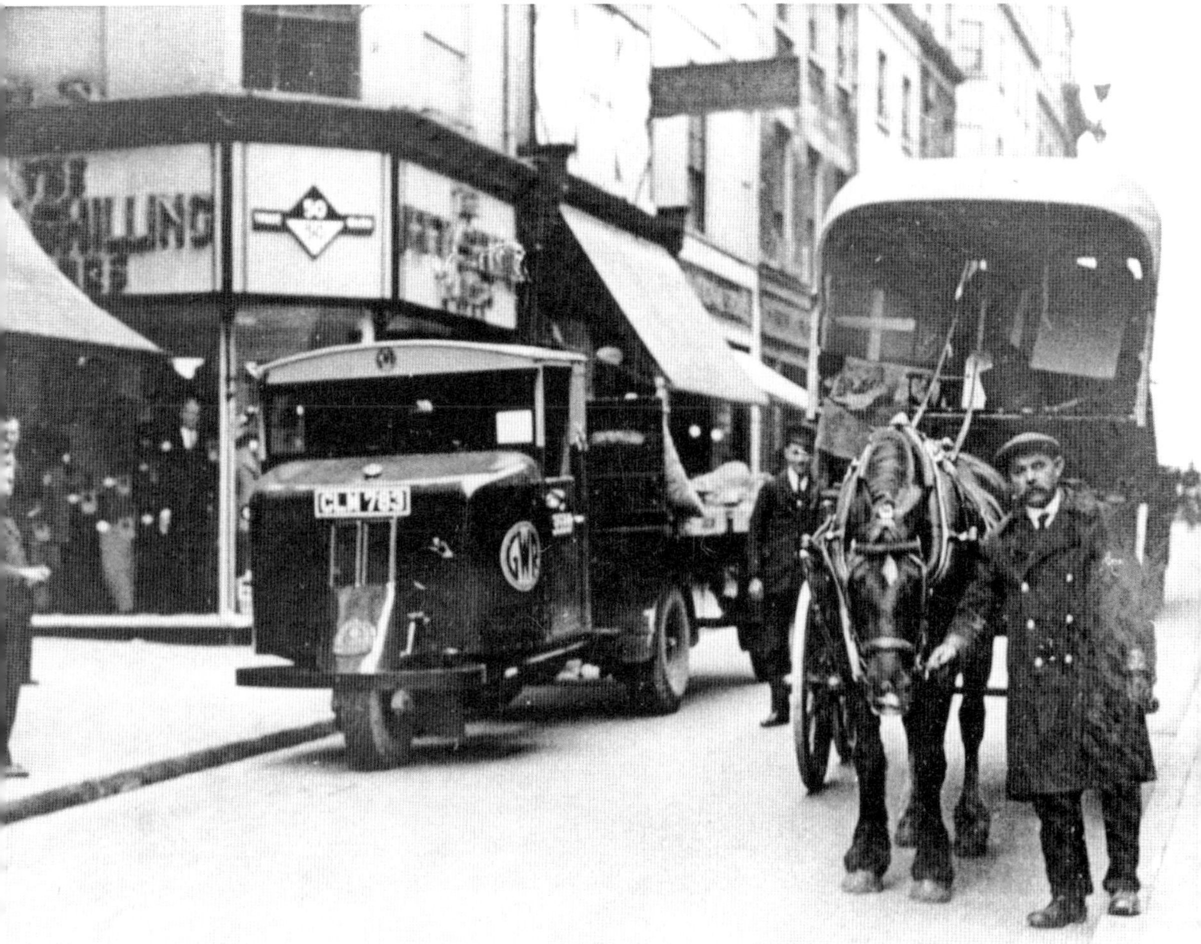

GWR Scammell mechanical horse and trailer, with Charlie Hooper and his horse-drawn van delivering parcels in Westgate Street, Bath, *c.* 1947. (*Author's Collection*)

When the driver arrived with the van, we would load up. If it was a busy round, there might be two boys, in which case the junior boy sat in the back on the parcels, and the senior boy in front with the driver. Mornings were spent delivering and in the afternoons we did pick-ups and call-backs. The work was not unlike what many parcel firms still do, but sadly today it all goes overnight by road and not rail.

As time went on I got to hear of a job as lad porter at Kingswood Receiving Office. This was a town office where tickets could be bought in advance, parcels could be left, in other words a 'station with no trains'. There was a goods carter and passenger carter who called in and at one time there were stables and it was run as a station. But in its later days we collected parcels and PLA and sold a few tickets in advance.

I will never forget when the coal and wood for our heating was delivered. The coal came from Swindon on a BR (ex-GWR) lorry and the wood was a dozen or so old sleepers that I was expected to chop up for the fire in the office. Lighting was still gas.

Well, our good life at Kingswood Receiving Office came to an end one winter when all the pipes burst and water came down through the office. When I got in that morning there was ice all down the front of the building. It was not decided for some weeks what should be done. I went to work each day and kept the place warm and cleaned it up, but we never opened to the public again.

I moved from there to Temple Meads and helped out in the main booking office and Temple Gate plus the subway. At that time there were four public entrances and exits to the main station, one of these being the subway entrance from Cattle Market Road. It was the first attempt at park-and-ride in a way, as people could park in the old cattle market then enter through the subway to get the train. The booking office was of the passimeter type more often seen on the London Underground with entry on one side and exit on the other and a pedal to operate the gates. If you had long legs you could sit on the stool and stretch across, almost doing the splits, to open both gates. GPO staff were a nuisance, using the entrance as a shortcut instead of using the post office entrance, especially at night when they would go to the Tavern for their meal break.

Evenings were long and Sundays quiet – just the popping of the gas light. Water for boiling in a kettle on a gas ring was brought down on a trolley in containers the same as those that supplied crossings and signal~boxes that had no mains water. If only I had kept that container labelled 'Bristol T. M. Subway' when the booking office closed. When I required physical relief I had to phone the main booking office for 1976–85 a relief to come down.

When the subway booking office closed in the early sixties for the final time, I left British Rail for pastures new with a brief return in the 1980s, but that is another story.

Appendix 7: Traffic Dealt with 1903 to 1933

TRAFFIC DEALT WITH AT STATIONS.

BRISTOL DIVISION.
(Steventon to Highbridge.)

Station.	Year.	Staff. Supervisory and Wages (all Grades).	Staff. Paybill Expenses.	Total Receipts.	Passenger Train Traffic. Tickets issued.	Passenger Train Traffic. Season Tickets.	Receipts. Passengers (including Season Tickets, etc.)	Receipts. Parcels.	Receipts. Miscellaneous.	Receipts. Total.
		No.	£	£	No.	No.	£	£	£	£
Bath Passenger.	1903	76	4,621	84,160	405,577	*	66,584	10,861	6,715	84,160
	1913	76	6,059	86,371	402,301	*	70,246	10,905	5,220	86,371
	1923	84	13,788	153,872	470,378	5,103	131,628	15,453	6,791	153,872
	1924	82	13,588	158,049	404,893	4,512	136,359	15,056	6,634	158,049
	1925	77	13,238	157,412	528,938	5,599	135,072	15,310	7,030	157,412
	1926	77	13,157	146,852	473,742	8,536	125,147	14,865	6,840	146,852
	1927	79	13,556	153,566	485,874	9,719	129,786	15,798	7,982	153,566
	1928	† 79	†13,626	147,125	460,066	9,151	122,864	16,598	7,663	147,125
	1929	† 81	†13,566	133,847	387,867	7,362	110,342	15,711	7,794	133,847
	1930	† 80	†13,635	126,680	355,887	6,738	103,807	14,870	8,003	126,680
	1931	† 79	†12,952	114,661	304,022	6,049	92,537	14,448	7,676	114,661
	1932	† 76	†12,406	105,874	288,719	5,787	85,016	13,927	6,931	105,874
	1933	† 76	†12,347	103,250	274,976	5,610	82,996	13,604	6,650	103,250
Bath Goods..	1903	*	*	43,362						
	1913	64	4,690	53,433						
	1923	65	10,474	82,857						
	1924	61	10,259	80,450						
	1925	61	10,210	79,690						
	1926	61	9,775	75,320						
	1927	61	10,828	86,166						
	1928	60	9,832	80,936						
	1929	60	9,720	78,455						
	1930	60	9,923	75,268						
	1931	60	9,689	70,859						
	1932	57	8,866	57,448						
	1933	54	8,748	58,516						
Oldfield Park Halt.				Opened	February, 1929.					
	1929	Included		4,789	55,761	1,265	4,746	43	—	4,789
	1930	with		5,356	63,502	1,951	5,300	56	—	5,356
	1931	Bath.		4,873	57,152	1,720	4,811	62	—	4,873
	1932			5,251	56,539	1,852	5,199	52	—	5,251
	1933			5,260	54,866	2,045	5,205	55	—	5,260
Saltford.. .. (‡)	1903	5	355	1,529	26,331	*	1,351	81	97	1,529
	1913	5	357	3,142	31,030	*	1,664	72	215	1,951
	1923	7	1,184	3,399	35,228	753	2,359	74	327	2,760
	1924	7	1,300	3,262	35,379	669	2,348	70	179	2,597
	1925	7	1,192	3,240	33,458	789	2,310	69	206	2,585
	1926	7	1,077	3,410	32,910	1,125	2,041	79	122	2,242
	1927	7	1,113	2,995	34,299	1,656	2,133	86	125	2,344
	1928	7	1,092	2,670	29,257	1,965	1,916	87	99	2,102
	1929	7	1,104	2,400	24,249	1,730	1,660	93	86	1,839
	1930	7	1,100	2,274	24,043	1,727	1,555	73	68	1,696
	1931	5	1,024	2,533	23,670	1,469	1,505	56	23	1,584
	1932	5	719	2,134	23,438	1,327	1,326	44	6	1,376
	1933	5	725	1,763	24,870	1,330	1,361	45	4	1,410

Station.	Year.	Goods Train Traffic. Forwarded. Coal and Coke "Charged."	Forwarded. Other Minerals.	Forwarded. General Merchandise.	Received. Coal and Coke "Charged."	Received. Other Minerals.	Received. General Merchandise.	Coal and Coke "Not Charged" (Forwarded and Received).	Total Goods Tonnage.	Total Receipts (excluding "Not Charged" Coal and Coke).	Livestock (Forwarded and Received).	Total Carted Tonnage (included in Total Goods Tonnage).
		Tons.	Tons.	Tons.	Tons.	Tons.	Tons.	Tons.	Tons.	£	Wagons.	Tons.
Bath Goods..	1903	814	3,207	19,341	12,344	33,083	31,118	6,605	106,602	43,362	1,046	21,318
	1913	867	40	26,259	18,772	10,353	53,265	12,720	122,276	53,433	1,247	28,446
	1923		1,799	17,247	16,904	6,557	46,550	6,278	95,335	82,857	942	22,962
	1924	20	1,373	19,129	16,246	7,259	48,590	6,304	98,981	80,450	884	23,671
	1925	41	1,027	19,003	15,567	7,160	45,085	9,832	98,805	79,690	904	23,977
	1926	152	1,452	17,131	10,428	7,779	43,157	11,084	91,183	75,320	820	22,886
	1927	35	2,473	18,808	11,745	9,003	46,814	14,783	103,681	86,166	848	24,863
	1928	15	3,055	18,249	9,093	7,998	43,975	18,544	101,829	80,936	744	22,819
	1929	59	3,255	15,680	12,452	6,811	39,082	21,830	99,779	78,455	714	23,618
	1930	14	2,088	14,593	9,726	4,520	40,900	25,912	97,653	75,268	705	23,503
	1931	7	1,285	12,672	8,518	5,223	39,759	25,025	92,489	70,859	456	22,698
	1932	–	1,434	8,688	7,151	3,466	31,666	27,788	80,193	57,448	447	19,760
	1933	248	2,488	10,226	8,643	4,415	33,896	30,740	90,656	58,516	319	20,354
Saltford.. .. (‡)	1903			Opened	for Goods	Traffic	31st	December,	1909.			
	1913	—	27	270	278	1,300	1,800	371	4,055	1,191	—	186
	1923	15	180	216	305	165	314	421	1,616	639	—	154
	1924	7	245	204	183	329	258	691	1,917	665	—	135
	1925	—	279	201	282	150	318	795	2,025	655	—	138
	1926	7	501	203	150	211	450	385	1,907	1,168	—	149
	1927	6	237	121	534	34	214	838	1,984	651	—	134
	1928	—	52	90	336	356	261	921	2,016	568	—	80
	1929	20	79	48	251	97	227	1,266	1,988	561	—	68
	1930	—	58	14	410	—	331	499	1,212	578	—	26
	1931	—	13	17	867	6	427	513	1,843	949	—	17
	1932	—	4	6	425	22	741	236	1,434	758	—	13
	1933	—	2	35	358	—	329	368	1,092	353	—	39

* Not available. † Including Telegraph Staff and Expenses from 1928.
‡ Controlled by Keynsham and Somerdale from December, 1931.

24 25

TRAFFIC DEALT WITH AT STATIONS.

BRISTOL DIVISION.
(Steventon to Highbridge.)

Station.	Year.	Staff. Supervisory and Wages (all Grades).	Staff. Paybill Expenses.	Total Receipts.	Passenger Train Traffic. Tickets issued.	Season Tickets.	Receipts. Passengers (including Season Tickets, etc.)	Receipts. Parcels.	Receipts. Miscellaneous	Receipts. Total.
		No.	£	£	No.	No.	£	£	£	£
Steventon to Keynsham and Somerdale.	High bridge (contd.).									
	1903	10	679	7,524	72,735	*	3,579	312	367	4,258
	1913	14	1,044	10,353	98,536	*	4,502	267	297	5,066
	1923	19	3,352	18,776	110,886	1,362	5,796	629	325	6,750
	1924	19	3,242	16,868	102,853	1,173	5,406	455	272	6,138
	1925	10	3,435	20,140	102,046	1,420	5,184	542	173	5,899
	1926	20	3,102	23,616	88,863	2,088	4,680	560	219	5,459
	1927	20	3,334	30,263	100,035	2,521	4,812	694	166	5,672
	1928	20	3,297	35,734	94,218	2,255	4,826	924	469	6,219
	1929	22	3,402	47,394	89,108	2,044	4,510	870	181	5,561
	1930	24	3,833	61,486	87,511	2,707	4,268	1,440	159	5,867
	1931	24	3,704	58,957	82,699	2,349	3,701	1,578	351	5,630
	1932	24	3,672	53,490	78,964	2,310	3,578	1,480	365	5,432
	1933	24	3,883	52,624	87,456	2,526	4,167	1,166	363	5,696
St. Anne's Park.	1903	9	532	883	21,586	*	858	25	—	883
	1913	5	354	1,383	34,542	*	1,358	25	—	1,383
	1923	5	742	2,357	26,445	308	2,269	81	7	2,357
	1924	5	758	2,715	31,172	330	2,599	113	3	2,715
	1925	5	831	2,812	38,628	479	2,597	215	—	2,812
	1926	5	852	2,362	30,427	660	2,238	120	4	2,362
	1927	5	847	2,724	30,112	2,126	2,637	83	4	2,724
	1928	5	825	3,164	48,105	2,530	3,085	79	—	3,164
	1929	5	843	3,784	60,538	3,092	3,718	66	—	3,784
	1930	5	871	3,743	72,893	3,628	3,678	65	—	3,743
	1931	5	819	3,154	59,457	2,566	3,083	71	—	3,154
	1932	5	736	3,017	53,548	2,112	2,949	68	—	3,017
	1933	5	806	3,015	50,305	2,274	2,942	73	—	3,015

Station.	Year.	Goods Train Traffic. Forwarded. Coal and Coke "Charged."	Forwarded. Other Minerals.	Forwarded. General Merchandise.	Received. Coal and Coke "Charged."	Received. Other Minerals.	Received. General Merchandise.	Coal and Coke "Not Charged" (Forwarded and Received).	Total Goods Tonnage.	Total Receipts (excluding "Not Charged" Coal and Coke).	Livestock (Forwarded and Received).	Total Carted Tonnage (included in Total Goods Tonnage).
		Tons.	Tons.	Tons.	Tons.	Tons.	Tons.	Tons.	Tons.	£	Wagons.	Tons.
Steventon to Keynsham and Somerdale.	1903	1,576	2,025	1,107	1,629	3,077	982	2,029	12,425	3,266	72	1,207
	1913	6	1,909	2,762	2,530	2,906	2,440	2,521	15,074	5,287	453	1,956
	1923	16	818	2,649	3,117	2,631	4,511	3,385	17,127	12,026	341	2,716
	1924	28	1,626	2,905	2,789	1,047	2,929	4,445	15,769	10,735	859	2,559
	1925	8	2,762	4,831	2,939	1,271	2,732	5,802	20,345	14,241	412	3,627
	1926	72	2,772	4,813	2,988	6,297	4,480	4,102	25,524	18,157	443	3,918
	1927	42	3,334	6,067	2,339	2,519	9,204	6,804	30,309	24,591	477	4,373
	1928	19	3,498	10,342	1,996	2,180	8,855	7,117	34,007	29,515	493	8,791
	1929	—	2,263	18 628	1,377	621	17,464	8,645	48,998	41,833	479	9.624
	1930	11	2,755	24,074	1,848	1,649	18,083	9,208	57,718	55,619	371	15,843
	1931	—	1,724	20,696	2,479	2,836	22,750	9,642	60,136	53,327	294	15,061
	1932	7	1,264	20,458	1,571	2,399	23,065	10,578	59,342	48,058	181	17,131
	1933	—	1,059	19,742	2,100	3,240	26,320	14,539	67,000	46,928	135	17,276
St. Anne's Park.	1903–1933	No Goods Traffic dealt with.										

26

TRAFFIC DEALT WITH AT STATIONS.

27

BRISTOL DIVISION.
(Steventon to Highbridge.

STATION.	YEAR.	STAFF: Supervisory and Wages (all Grades).	STAFF: Paybill Expenses.	TOTAL RECEIPTS.	PASSENGER TRAIN TRAFFIC: Tickets issued.	Season Tickets.	Receipts: Passengers (including Season Tickets, etc.)	Receipts: Parcels.	Receipts: Miscellaneous	Receipts: Total.
		No.	£	£	No.	No.	£	£	£	£
Steventon to	High	bridge	(contd.)							
Bristol (Lawrence Hill) Goods. (§)	1903	*	*	24 414						
	1913	64	4,652	48,231						
	1923	78	12,712	85,127						
	1924	87	13,543	82,919						
	1925	87	13,937	83,128						
	1926	89	13,886	80,287						
	1927	89	14,102	83,164						
	1928	90	13,705	80,286						
	1929	89	13,545	82,156						
	1930	89	13,350	75,888						
	1931	87	13,070	74,901						
	1932	‖	‖	60,307						
	1933	‖	‖	59,914						
Bristol (Temple Meads) Passenger. (‡)	1903	434	27,234	242,705	1,047,925	*	175,873	38,370	28,462	242,705
	1913	318	28,085	260,174	1,119,898	*	201,595	38,457	20 122	260,174
	1923	389	60,638	484,511	1 215,840	7,425	373,329	84,676	26,506	484,511
	1924	348	59,891	497,591	1,211,076	7,536	390,244	79,872	27,475	497,591
	1925	310	56,134	479,784	1,211,676	8,413	370,484	80,798	28,502	479 784
	1926	300	52,506	446,908	1,087,574	8,763	333,405	83,363	30,140	446,908
	1927	333	61,065	451,018	1,106,613	9,505	338,496	85,054	27,468	451,018
	1928	†330	†61,789	451,225	1,100,184	9,547	334,837	87,208	29,180	451,225
	1929	†337	†61,745	442,121	1,071,039	7,762	323,819	90,484	27,818	442,121
	1930	†339	†64,164	431,277	1,022,635	7,979	315,821	89,404	26,052	431,277
	1931	†338	†61,831	403,911	916,558	6,774	293,811	85,987	24,113	403,911
	1932	†340	†60,410	381,344	844,269	5,934	277,067	79,418	24,859	381,344
	1933	†336	†61,937	387,871	856,778	6,076	270,882	91,926	25,063	387,871
Bristol (Temple Meads) Goods.	1903	*	*	688,163						
	1913	969	70,877	736,257						
	1923	948	161,672	1,154,785						
	1924	990	165,950	1,102,667						
	1925	990	172,190	1,120,094						
	1926	996	166,798	1,101,749						
	1927	994	177,904	1,163,844						
	1928	994	182,616	1,153,540						
	1929	994	183,674	1,127,758						
	1930	1,035	186,109	1,060,706						
	1931	1,037	187,270	1,002,945						
	1932	1,097	187,566	890,493						
	1933	1,065	183,935	890,691						

STATION.	YEAR.	GOODS TRAIN TRAFFIC: Forwarded: Coal and Coke "Charged."	Forwarded: Other Minerals.	Forwarded: General Merchandise.	Received: Coal and Coke "Charged."	Received: Other Minerals.	Received: General Merchandise.	Coal and Coke "Not Charged" (Forwarded and Received).	Total Goods Tonnage.	Total Receipts (excluding "Not Charged" Coal and Coke).	Livestock (Forwarded and Received).	Total Carted Tonnage (included in Total Goods Tonnage).
		Tons.	Tons.	Tons.	Tons.	Tons.	Tons.	Tons.	Tons.	£	Wagons.	Tons.
Bristol (Lawrence Hill) Goods. (§)	1903	43	1,297	15,357	30,551	4,270	13,281	14,284	79,083	24,414	—	11,619
	1913	105	3,242	26,775	26,130	4,035	24,968	32 347	117,602	48,231	—	29,036
	1923	95	2,836	25,835	12,982	4,666	30,493	33,716	110,623	85,127	—	32,508
	1924	210	1,968	29,001	20,169	2,824	31,744	35,378	121,204	82,919	—	35,592
	1925	147	2,065	29,073	14,366	3,675	31,464	42,419	123,209	83,128	—	36,482
	1926	204	2,611	27,069	9,024	3,199	29,990	28,441	100,838	80,287	—	35,493
	1927	140	3,969	28,058	8,629	3,900	29,366	38,096	112,158	83,164	—	35,247
	1928	208	3,237	27,055	8,245	2,752	30,054	33,927	105,478	80,286	—	34,427
	1929	97	3,654	27,237	8,019	3,455	31,972	36,329	110 763	82,156	—	36,842
	1930	60	2,655	26,295	6,758	3,008	30,994	41,916	111,686	75,888	—	33,866
	1931	5	2,783	26,662	7,560	2,807	30,348	45,884	116,049	74,901	—	33,911
	1932	23	3,222	23,395	5,166	1,470	22,245	42,188	97,709	60,307	—	27,336
	1933	22	3,362	22,608	4,284	1,425	21,282	41,966	94,949	59,914	—	27,077
Bristol (Temple Meads) Goods.	1903	45,649	207,639	875,275	111,716	241,364	221,585	72,811	1,776,030	688,163	14,170	371,873
	1913	34,904	70,956	893,993	81,741	36,815	375,765	90,104	1,584,458	736,257	10,811	446,358
	1923	19,854	41,837	654,136	74,367	57,579	411,318	144,031	1,403,622	1,154,785	7,200	398,217
	1924	4,402	45,473	667,360	92,716	73,762	407,809	164,074	1,455,656	1,102,667	7,701	417,218
	1925	5,013	38,986	683,502	82,257	77,017	427,347	184,493	1,498,615	1,120,094	5,508	426,914
	1926	26,514	43,473	654,899	58,159	78,232	415,191	159,834	1,436,302	1,101,749	4,746	403,452
	1927	7,487	51,837	659,535	100,244	68,219	419,972	185,312	1,492,606	1,163,844	3,600	415,582
	1928	6,945	48,281	656,679	88,801	61,751	418,535	178,332	1,459,324	1,153,540	3,749	453,364
	1929	5,726	51 430	637,117	104,205	63,944	449,377	187,173	1,498,972	1,127,758	4,341	440,733
	1930	4,918	40,846	579,374	100,290	71,819	454,747	176,947	1,428,945	1,060,706	3,761	410,087
	1931	4,100	46,651	538,323	98,199	111,031	443,007	170,325	1,411,636	1,002,945	3,041	387,587
	1932	3,484	40,279	479,208	74,128	82,282	409,270	170,086	1,259,637	890,493	2,427	369,809
	1933	4,070	32,486	492,524	69,159	70,120	416,414	174,421	1,259,194	890,691	2,027	406,057

Bibliography

Ahrons, E. L., *Locomotives & Train Working in the Latter Part of the Nineteenth Century*, vols 2 & 4, Cambridge, Heffer, 1952

Allen, C. J., *Titled Trains of the Western*, London, Ian Allan, 1974

Biddle, G., Nock, O. S., *The Railway Heritage of Britain*, London, Michael Joseph,1983

Bourne, J. C., *The History & Description of the Great Western Railway*, London, David Bogue, 1846

Bradshaw's Railway Guide (various dates)

Channon, G., *Bristol & the Promotion of the Great Western Railway*, Bristol, Historical Association, 1985

Churton, E., *The Rail Road Book of England*, London, 1851

Clark, R. H. & Potts, C. R., *An Historical Survey of Selected Great Western Railway Stations*,Vol 1 to 4, Oxford, OPC, 1976–85

Clinker, C. R., *Register of Closed Passenger Stations & Goods Depots*, Weston-super-Mare, Avon-Anglia, 1988

Coleman, T., *The Railway Navvies*, Harmondsworth, Penguin, 1968

Cooke, R. A., *Track Layout Diagrams of the GWR & BR WR*, Section 19A & Section 21, Harwell, Author, 1992, 1987

Hateley, R., *Industrial Locomotives of South West England*, Greenford, Industrial Railway Society, 1977

Leitch, R., *The Railways of Keynsham*, Long Stratton, Railway Correspondence & Travel Society, 1977

Lyons, E., *An Historical Survey of Great Western Engine Sheds 1947*, Oxford, OPC, 1974

Lyons, E., Mountford, E., *An Historical Survey of Great Western Sheds 1837–1947*, Oxford, 1979

MacDermot, E. T., Clinker, C. R. & Nock, O. S., *History of the Great Western Railway*, London, Ian Allan, 1964 and 1967

Maggs, C. G., *Bristol Railway Panorama*, Bath, Millstream, 1990

Maggs, C. G., *Rail Centres: Bristol*, London, Ian Allan, 1989

Maggs, C. G., *Bristol & Bath Railways: The Age of Steam*, Newbury, Countryside Books, 2011
Measom, G., *The Official Guide to the Great Western Railway*, London, Griffin, Bohn, 1861
Oakley, M., *Somerset Railway Stations*, Wimborne, The Dovecot Press, 2002
Oakley, M., *Somerset Stations Then and Now*, Wimborne, The Dovecot Press, 2011
Oakley, M., *Bristol Railway Stations 1840–2005*, Bristol, Redcliffe Press, 2005
Railway Correspondence & Travel Society, *Locomotives of the Great Western Railway*, Vols 1 to 14, Long Stratton, RCTS, 1952 to 1993
Russell, J., *The Roman Villa at Newton St Loe*, Bristol, Bristol & Avon Archaeology, Volume 9, 1992
Searle, M. V., *Down the Line to Bristol*, London, Baton Transport, 1986
Sekon, G. A., *A History of the Great Western Railway*, London, Digby, Long, 1895
Williams, F. S., *Our Iron Roads*, 1883

Newspapers and Journals

Bath & Cheltenham Gazette
Bath Chronicle
Bath Herald
Bristol Journal
Bristol Standard
Engineering
Great Western Railway Journal
Railway Magazine

Index

Pages in italics indicate illustrations.

Avon, River 5, 6, 12, 14, 16, 18, 19, 21, 23, 29, 30, 31, 32, 33, 35, 37, 41, 78, 81
Bath 5, 6, 9, 12, 13, 14, 15, 18, 20, 23, 28, 29, 30–36, 39, 40–49, 51, 97–101, *102*, *103*, 104, *105–109*, 111–113, *118*, 120, 124, *126*, *127*, 129, 133–135, *136*, 139–141, 144, *145*, *146*, 147, *148*, *166*, *167*, *169*, *170*, *171*, 173, *175*, *188*, 197, 202, 204, 213, 215
Bristol 5–7, 9, 12–15, 23, 28, 32–36, 42–49, 115, 116, *118*, *119*, 129, 130, 133, 140, 141, 149, 150, *166*, 173, *175*, 197, 214–216
Brotherhood, Messrs 51, 149
Brunel, I. K. 10, 11, 15, 16, 20, 23, 24, 35, 36, 52, 63, 105, 149
Brunton, William 9, 14, 52
Chadwick, W. 29
Chiddy, John 200, 201
Coaches
Railway 40, 42, 44, 46, 48, 49, *50*, 134, 140, 141, 144, *148*, 173
Stage 12, 13, 46, 47
Cross Post Bridge 23, 24, 37, *38*, 82, 175
Culverhouse, P. E. 60
East Depot 19, 65, 71, *153*, *154*, 155, 176, 200
Fox, Francis 55
Fox's Wood 37, 70 72, 73, 75, 199
Frere, G. E. 16, 37, 82
Gibbs, George 11
Guppy, Richard & Thomas 10
Johnathan, John 49
Kennet & Avon Canal 5, 13
Keynsham 16, 18, 32, 37, 40, 43, 44, 45, 73, 74, 75, *76*, 77, 83, 115, 129, 130, 133, 135, *138*, *139*, *156–159*, *160*, *161*, 163, 199, 200, 204
Locomotives 32, 33, *34*, 35–37, *38*, 39–44, 47, *84*, 85, 86, *92*, *93*, 94, *95*, *96*, 103, *120*, *123*, *125*, *128*, 129, 134, *136*, *138*, *139*, 140, *141*, *154*, 156, 162–181, *198*, 204, 205
Locomotive depot 37, 71, *166*, 171, 174, 182–196
Marsh, T. E. M. 16, 82
McAdam, J. L. 9
McIntosh, D. 20, 82
Newton St Loe 23–25, 78, 82, 115, 130
Oldfield Park 91, 92, *94–96*, 112, 128, *143*, 147, *176*, *180*
Ranger, W. 16, 18, 21
Roman villa 82, *83*
St Anne's Park *67–69*, 129, *142*, *204*, 204
Saltford 9, 16, 18, 23, 28, 45, 47, 77, *78–80*, 81, *82*, 116, 122, 129, 133, *138*, 204
Saunders, Charles Alexander 11, 14, 20
Signalling 42, 63, *64*, *65*, *67*, 71, 77, 83, *84*, 89, 97, *108*, 113, 114, *116*, 122, 126, 129, *130*, *131*, 136, *147*, *151*, 161, 203
Temple Meads 10, 21, 23, 27, 32, *33*, 35, *37*, *38*, 39, 40, 44, 49, 52, *53*, 54, 55, *56–62*, 63, 64, *117–120*, 121, *122*, *123*, *127*, 128, 129, *131*, 135, *137*, *142*, *143*, *145*, *146*, 147, 149, *150–152*, 162, *164*, 170, *172*, *177*, *178*, *182*, *184*, 197, 198, 215, 216
Townsend, W. H. 11, 16
Twerton 13, 16, 27, 42, 47, 48, *84–89*, 92, 93, 124, *125*, 133, 163, 199, 204, 213
Tummy, W. T. 89

Tunnels
Bristol No. 1 18–21, 37, 41, 65, *66*
Bristol No. 2 18, 21, 22, 24, 37, 41, 43, *67*, *69*, *70*, 71, 72, 122, *124*, 201, 204
Bristol No. 3 18, 21–24, 27, 28, 32, 37, 41, 45, 73, 202–204
Saltford 21, 77, 198, 199, 202, 203
Twerton 16, 21, 28, 83, *84–86*, 115, *116*, 122, 130, 133, 181, 208, 212
Water Troughs *70*, 71, *73*, 139
Watt, J. 9
Westmoreland Road goods depot 92, 97, *98*, 112, 115, 124, *162*, *172*, 213
World War 1 116
World War 2 117, 120–126
Wyatt, Sir Matthew Digby 54, 55, 59, 60, 61, 63

ALSO AVAILABLE FROM AMBERLEY PUBLISHING

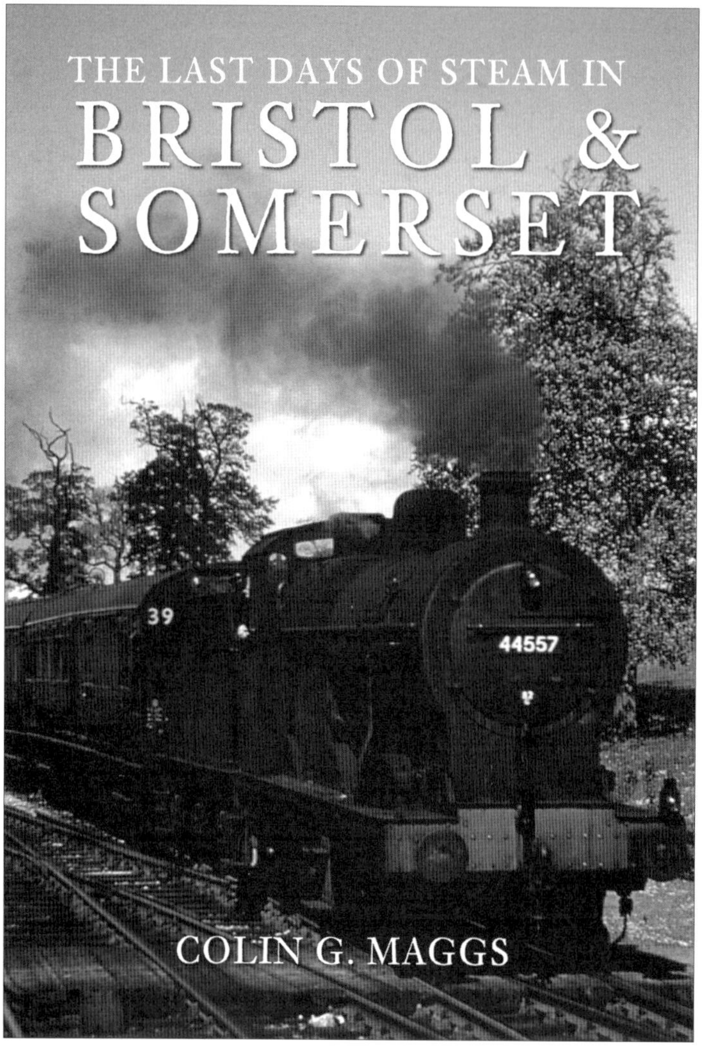

The Last Days of Steam in Bristol & Somerset
Colin G. Maggs

A fascinating collection of photographs of the last steam locomotives to run on Bristol and Somerset's railways.

978 1 84868 340 2
192 pages, 200 b&w images

Available from all good bookshops or order direct from our website www.amberleybooks.com